The Norman Conquest of the North

THE NORMAN CONQUEST
OF THE NORTH

The Region and Its Transformation,
1000–1135

BY WILLIAM E. KAPELLE

THE UNIVERSITY OF NORTH CAROLINA PRESS
CHAPEL HILL

Library of Congress Cataloging in Publication Data

Kapelle, William E
    The Norman Conquest of the north.

    Bibliography: p.
    Includes index.
    1. Great Britain—History—Anglo-Saxon period,
499–1066. 2. Great Britain—History—Norman
period, 1066–1154. 3. Peasantry—England—
History. I. Title.
DA154.7.K36   942.02   79-10200
ISBN 0-8078-1371-0

CONTENTS

TABLES

Maps

The Norman Conquest of the North

1. The Danes of York

and the

House of Bamburgh

The Norman Conquest of the North has never been adequately explained even though the resistance of the northerners was one of the most dramatic episodes of the Conquest. The reasons for this neglect are uncertain. It may be merely a side effect of the conviction that the South was the more important part of England. Alternatively, northern history threatens to complicate our picture of the Conquest. A close study of the northern resistance to William the Conqueror inevitably discloses that he made at least two blunders in dealing with the North and that he rescued himself from the results of these mistakes by committing genocide. Emphasis on these events fits poorly into the current appraisal of the Norman impact on England. The behavior of the northerners in the face of the Conquest may also reveal a distressing exception to the precocious unity of Anglo-Saxon England. The idea of backwoods northerners being so impertinent as not to appreciate the splendid unity offered them by the West Saxon kings with their shires, fyrd, and Danegeld is undoubtedly as unpalatable to some historians as the picture of William the Bastard making mistakes is to others. In any case, in most accounts of the Norman Conquest, the men from beyond the Humber come on stage long enough to revolt a few times out of conservatism; the establishment of Norman rule in the North immediately follows their failure.

This view is false. It is a creation of the prominence we give to the Norman Conquest. The behavior of the Northumbrians and

Political Divisions of the North in 1000

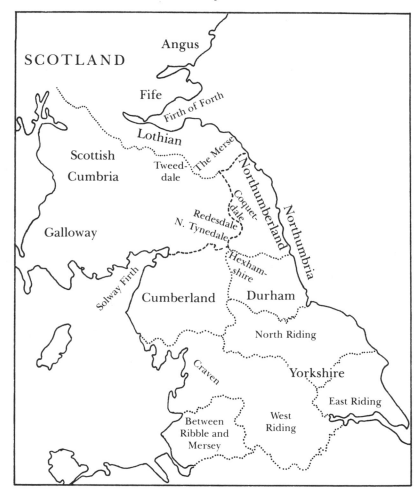

the Yorkshire men during the reign of William the Conqueror is inexplicable if it is separated from their pre-Conquest history— William's victory at Hastings did not wipe out the past. In the 1060s and 1070s, the men of the North acted as much in response to past realities as in reaction to the coming of the Normans. This chapter will begin the difficult task of determining the political experience and traditional concerns of the nobilities of Northumberland and

Yorkshire. I will discuss the more important aspects of northern geopolitics and reconstruct the history of the North from the second period of Danish invasions to the reign of Edward the Confessor. Such an early beginning is necessary because the history of the North has never been properly understood and the insights of earlier northern scholars have been largely ignored in the court-centered political narratives that dominate our picture of the Conquest.[1] The basic question to be answered is whether there was a political side in Anglo-Saxon times to the cultural regionalism of the North or, stated more traditionally, whether northern separatism was a serious political force in the eleventh century.

The first necessity is to define the extent of the North. To the unwary, this may seem a straightforward task. In the eleventh century, the North consisted, more or less, of the present counties of Yorkshire, Durham, and Northumberland on the east and Lancashire with the southern parts of Cumberland and Westmorland on the west. Except for one brief period, the northern parts of the latter two counties were included in the kingdom of Strathclyde or Cumbria.[2] Such a definition is reasonably accurate in a political sense, but it contributes little to a real understanding of the region. It is necessary to perambulate different bounds to adequately define the North. In few parts of Anglo-Saxon England did the shape of the land structure the opportunities for human endeavor, whether peaceful or warlike, with less subtlety. Northern landforms hindered internal communications, limited agricultural possibilities, and left what good land there was open to invasion. Indeed, the North had imposing natural defenses in only one direction: toward the South. The Humber has been said to mark a line of very ancient division among the Anglo-Saxons;[3] indeed, prior to the Danish invasions, the power of the *Bretwalda* did not usually cross the Humber unless this position was occupied by the Northumbrian king.[4] The Humber was important as a dividing line probably because for most purposes the North was nearly a separate island during this period. The Humber comes far inland before turning north toward York, and its function as a barrier to land travel was taken over west of the turn by the swamps along the lower Ouse. West of the mountains, the peat moss bogs along the Mersey formed an effective barrier between Lancashire and Cheshire.[5] The only good land routes to the Midlands were between the Ouse swamps and the Pennine foothills on the east and through the Manchester

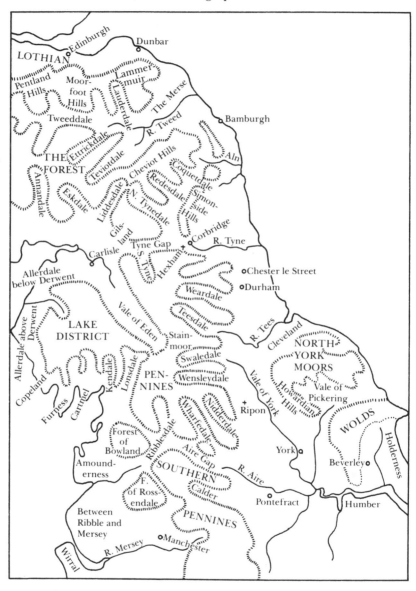

area on the west, but both these passages are crossed by transverse rivers and were easily defended against an invading army. Moreover, these roads north were very bad in the early twelfth century, even for small groups of travelers, and, as a result, York's main connection with southern England was by ship, either up the Trent to Lincoln or down the east coast.[6]

The North was cut off from easy communications with the South and even more cut up internally. Beginning in the South, the Pennines run north between the Humber and the Mersey and continue all the way to the Tyne Gap. In Cumberland they are flanked by the Lake District, the highest and wildest area in northern England. The Tyne Gap runs from the head of the Solway Firth to the North Sea, but north of it rises another range of hills that merge into the Southern Highlands of Scotland. These highlands stretch from Galloway on the west all the way across southern Scotland and reach the North Sea between Lothian and Tweeddale.

Although these upland regions are not of awe-inspiring height and can be crossed by a number of routes, they effectively divided the North into three areas: the east coast plain, the west coast plain with the Vale of Eden, and the uplands. These mountains and hills functioned as a serious barrier to communications between the coastal plains and were agriculturally marginal. Except where pierced by river valleys such as the Vale of Eden or the Tweed-Teviot system, much of the uplands was useful only as summer pasture for the settlements in the valleys. Consequently, a big slice of the North running from top to bottom was lightly exploited, nearly empty land. Unfortunately, in the Middle Ages, the usual corollary of low settlement density, pastoralism, and poor communications was a "free zone," that is, an area that was normally beyond the control of local forces of law and order and became the refuge for the peasant's primeval enemy, the wolf, and his societal enemy, the outlaw. Such was certainly the case in the North of England.

Thus the North was a more complicated area than its outlines on a political map would indicate. It was cut off from the South and had a dangerous and unproductive free zone running up its middle. In terms of agricultural wealth, the most valuable parts of the North were the two coastal plains, especially the one on the east. The latter runs north through the Vale of York, eastern Durham, and Northumberland to Tweeddale. Above this rich area

Sketch Map of the Terrain of the North

(the Merse) it is broken by the Lammermuirs, the eastern end of the Southern Highlands, but reappears in Lothian and broadens into the Midland Valley of Scotland. West of the Pennines, a poorer, smaller plain reached from the Mersey bogs north through western Lancashire, around the Cumberland coast to the Vale of Eden, and finally west into Galloway south of the Southern Highlands.

The east coast plain, which was the most developed part of northern England, was a land of moderate rainfall, indifferent to good soils, and village agriculture, with the potential to carry a large peasant population. The western plain was smaller and wetter. Its inhabitants practiced mixed agriculture and usually lived in hamlets. Both these areas were dangerously open to invasion from the north and the sea. The Southern Highlands of Scotland could be crossed in the west either by Annandale or Nithsdale, routes that linked Clydesdale with the Galwegian plain and thence to Cumberland. In the east there were two routes between Lothian and Tweeddale: by Lauderdale or the coast road. Lothian had no natural frontiers except to the south. Finally, the long coasts of the North had traditionally stood open to seaborne invasion, preeminently by the Tyne and Humber, but also from the Irish Sea up the rivers and creeks of the West.

The North's geography, then, divided it into three natural regions and left the most important of these open to invasion. This emphasis on the negative aspects of northern geography is essential for an understanding of the history of the lands beyond the Humber. Most accounts of the Norman Conquest give one the vague impression that Anglo-Saxon England was an ancient kingdom. In fact, the power of the West Saxon kings had come late to the North. Northumbria had been an independent kingdom prior to the Danish invasions of the ninth century and had stretched from the Humber north along the eastern plain across the Lammermuirs into Lothian, probably all the way to the Firth of Forth. During their days of greatest power, the Northumbrian kings had also extended their rule over the Pennines into Cumberland, Lancashire, and the Galwegian coastal plain. In the ninth and tenth centuries, this kingdom collapsed. The Northumbrians were unable to withstand the attacks of the Danes, who conquered Yorkshire and probably much of the land between the Tyne and the Tees and set up their own kingdom. The Northumbrians living above the Tyne kept their independence, but were militarily weak after the loss of

Yorkshire. In the tenth century, their northern neighbors took advantage of their decline. From at least 900, the Strathclyde Britons (the Cumbrians) expanded south over the Southern Highlands and gained control of Cumberland and probably of Lancashire.[7] Sometime during the same century, probably around 973, the Scots took control of Lothian and perhaps Tweeddale, the northernmost provinces of the defunct kingdom. Meanwhile, the Danish kingdom of York had been replaced by a Norwegian kingdom, and the rump of Northumbria, the lands between the Tyne and the Tweed with the northern part of Durham, endured—perhaps because it was the most worthless part of the eastern plain.[8] In 954, the situation in the North finally stabilized when, after several abortive attempts, the king of Wessex annexed York and Northumbria (the land between the Tees and the Tweed).

This was only a little over a century before the Norman Conquest. To understand the post-Conquest history of the North, we must know to what extent the Anglo-Saxon kings succeeded after 954 in incorporating the North into their kingdom despite the distractions of the second wave of Danish invasions, the period of Danish kings, and the political crises of Edward the Confessor's reign. These disturbances probably retarded unification. Moreover, the kings may not have had the same success throughout the region. The North was not homogeneous either geographically or ethnically, although this fact is usually obscured by the habit of calling all the inhabitants of the east coast plain or any part of them "Northumbrians." This usage reflects the original meaning of "Northumbrians" and also southern English usage in the twelfth century. It also leads to unwarranted vagueness and false conclusions. I will follow later northern usage, in which "Northumbrians" refers to the people living between the Tweed and the Tees. If it is necessary to single out the people between the Tyne and the Tees, they will be called the "men of St. Cuthbert," the "men of Durham," and so forth. The inhabitants of Yorkshire will be called the "Yorkshire men." "Northerners" will refer to all the peoples between the Humber and the Tweed.

Yorkshire was a large, complex area that ran roughly from the Humber to the Tees, with a substantial extension south of the line of the Humber on the southwest. It also included the central Pennines and the northern part of Lancashire (the area above the Ribble). It is an easy enough task to point out the cultural pecu-

liarities of Yorkshire east of the Pennines. The dialect spoken by
the natives was unintelligible to men from southern England.[9] In
the Pennine foothills on the west, remnants of both the Northumbrian aristocracy and the traditional social structure of the North
survived the Danish invasions.[10] Most scholars would add that these
invasions and the subsequent Danish settlement had produced a
distinctive society in the eastern part of the shire. This point will be
discussed later. For the moment it can be safely said that a Danish
aristocracy had been created in Yorkshire and that the area was
part of the Danelaw. Miscellaneous examples of Danish influence
can be found, such as its distinctive body of customary law, its system of monetary reckoning, and the names of the agricultural
tenements of its peasants.[11] The relative freedom of many of the
Yorkshire peasants and the absence of the manor (in a southern
sense) in the county have also been ascribed to Danish influence;[12]
the attribution is doubtful, but the basic phenomenon is not.

The political position of Yorkshire within the kingdom was
also somewhat unusual. In particular, the king appears to have had
less power in this shire than south of the Humber. He had demesne
lands in Yorkshire, but they were small in comparison with those of
the earl, who also had the lordship of most of the small thegns.[13]
The earl's power thus limited the king's authority, but the king
retained important rights. The king had the power to appoint the
earls of the shire and the archbishop, and he exercised these pre-
rogatives. He also received the pleas of the crown and heriots of
important thegns. Even though his power to enact new laws was
supposedly limited by Edgar's grant of legal autonomy to the northern Danelaw in 962 in return for their loyalty, it is doubtful if later
kings felt bound by this provision. In conclusion, the king's power
in Yorkshire has been described as essentially that of an overlord,[14]
but this is an understatement. The Anglo-Saxon kings had important rights in the shire and tried to exercise them. What is uncertain
is how well they succeeded.[15]

Northumbria (Bernicia) was as exotic as Yorkshire in its own
way. The earldom stretched from the Tees to the Tweed between
the central hills and the North Sea. This area had been spared significant Danish settlement and had an Anglian population similar
to the one in Lothian across the Tweed,[16] and recent scholarship
has stressed the similarities between the somewhat archaic structure
of Northumbrian society and the cultures of the lowland Scots and

Welsh.[17] In Northumbria, the nobility does not seem to have been numerous, and the demands of lordship were not as extensive as in southern England. Manorial dues still retained something of a public character, and the peasants were indirectly exploited. In fact, Northumbria was so peculiar that it stood outside the recognized threefold division of English law.[18]

This last point raises a very important question: in what sense was Northumberland part of the kingdom? If it had been regarded as part of the kingdom in a normal sense, one would expect scholars to speak of a fourfold law system in Anglo-Saxon England. This point would be pedantic if other evidence did not point in the same direction. Either during or shortly after Earl Robert de Mowbray's rebellion in 1095, Rufus granted some charters to the St. Albans monks at Tynemouth. In one of these he confirmed all their possessions and customs *In nort de Tyne et in suth de Tyne et in Anglia* ("to the north and to the south of the Tyne and in England").[19] This phrase draws a clear distinction between England and the lands above the Tees (Northumbria). If the charter is a forgery, this usage would still be significant. If the phrase is a formula, it represents Anglo-Saxon conditions. In some sense there was a distinction between Northumbria and England.

This idea is strikingly confirmed by Domesday Book, which literally stops at the Tees; no part of Northumbria is described in its folios. This fact has never been adequately explained. Scholars have suggested that it was left out either because it was too devastated to be worth anything to the king or because the natives were hostile,[20] but neither of these explanations will do. Yorkshire was surveyed, yet it had been devastated very thoroughly. At the time of the survey, Northumberland had both a Norman earl and bishop who could have given adequate protection to the judges if such had been necessary. In fact, Domesday confirms in a negative sense the distinction drawn in Rufus's charter: England and Northumberland were different. The same idea is found in the *Dialogue of the Exchequer*: the counties that belonged to the king "of ancient right" paid their dues to the king by blanched farm, but those acquired "through some incidental cause" paid by tale. This second group comprised Sussex, Shropshire, Cumberland, and Northumberland.[21]

The difference between England and Northumbria might be explained by inferences drawn from the supposed purpose of

Domesday or similar logic based on the *Dialogue of the Exchequer*. Safer evidence is available that requires no long line of sequential reasoning. The difference amounted to the fact that north of the Tees the king was literally the overlord and had no direct powers. There is no evidence, for instance, that the king had any demesne lands in Northumberland prior to the suppression of the earldom. Before the reign of William the Conqueror, there were no royal mints or burghs in the area. It was unshired and, as mentioned earlier, stood outside the recognized bodies of law. No royal writs or charters survive that relate to Northumberland, and it is clear that the kings did not have the power to make them.[22] Finally, and this is the crucial point, the king lacked the power of appointment beyond the Tees until very late. No bishop of Durham was chosen by the king until Siward was earl; and, even after this, the choice seems to have lain more with the earl than with the king. Twelfth-century Durham tradition suggests that before Siward the bishop was elected by the clerks of the church.[23] With one possible exception, the earls of Northumberland were also not chosen by the king. From at least 954 they were all members of one family, the house of Bamburgh; and the family itself probably goes further back into the tenth century.[24] The house of Bamburgh to all intents and purposes ruled Northumberland; later evidence suggests that they paid no tribute to the king (see Chapter 4).

In Yorkshire royal power was somewhat stronger but still weak in comparison to the South. This situation undoubtedly went back to the submission of the North to King Eadred in 954; perhaps it was the price of Danish and Northumbrian submission. If so, the earls of Northumberland preserved more local autonomy than the Danes of York. The important fact, for the purpose of this discussion, is that royal weakness in the North persisted well into the eleventh century. Politically, the North had not been well integrated into the rest of the kingdom. It must have been difficult for the king to exercise control in York and nearly impossible for him to do so in Northumbria.

But was this weakness politically important? Was the regional identity of the North expressed politically? Did the Danish aristocracy of York want their own kingdom or did the house of Bamburgh resent the overlordship of the house of Wessex? If neither of these situations existed, royal weakness in the North meant only that the kings received less money from the area than they might have and there was no northern separatism. Indeed, there is no sign that the Northumbrian earls were unhappy with their position within the kingdom prior to 1016. Times had been hard in Northumberland before 954, when it was caught between the Vikings of York, the Scots, and the Cumbrians, and at that time the earls must have valued royal support.

The situation in Yorkshire was different. A few signs suggest that the inhabitants cherished memories of independence, but unfortunately, there is no explicit contemporary evidence on this question. A thirteenth-century chronicle says that the Yorkshire men did not like Athelstan being their king and taking tribute and that in 966 Edgar feared a separatist movement in the North. This chronicle is not, however, particularly trustworthy, and these statements, found nowhere else, are doubtful evidence. They are not, on the other hand, inconsistent with certain other facts known about Yorkshire after 954. All of the archbishops of the city after Wulfstan I, in the mid-tenth century, came from south of the Humber, most of them from the eastern Danelaw, and this should be understood as an attempt by the king to provide archbishops able to deal with the Danish inhabitants but unlikely to work for local independence. A number of these men also held a southern bishopric in plurality, and this may have been another way to ensure their loyalty, although the poverty of York could also have been a reason.[25]

This same lack of trust in natives is found in the selection of the earls of Yorkshire. Before 1016, two of the earls, Osulf and Uhtred, were members of the Bamburgh family; and two others, Oslac and Ælfhelm, were from south of the Humber. Only Thored may have been a local man,[26] but it is equally possible that he was Oslac's son. These appointments of archbishops and earls indicate that the kings feared giving the Yorkshire men local leadership, and there are signs that even outsiders could not necessarily be trusted beyond the Humber. In 975, Earl Oslac was banished from the kingdom. Around 992, Earl Thored disappeared without explanation, and in 1006, Earl Ælfhelm was killed at court and his sons blinded.[27] No reasons for any of these events are given in the *Anglo-Saxon Chronicle*, but the mortality rate is suspicious.

The impression that the men of York could not be trusted is strengthened by certain aspects of the second period of Danish invasions. In particular, the North and the Danish Five Boroughs just to the south were left almost untouched through thirty-six years of raids. Furthermore, on the one occasion when the Danes did trouble the North, the men of York behaved suspiciously. In 993, when the Danes sacked Bamburgh and, after entering the Humber, plundered Lindsey (the northern part of Lincolnshire) and the East Riding of Yorkshire, the northerners raised an army, but it would not fight the Danes. The *Anglo-Saxon Chronicle* says that this happened because the leaders of the army fled, and Florence of Worcester adds that they fled because they were descended from Danes.[28] Probably Florence was right. After 993 the Danes did not return to the North until 1013, and this twenty-year interval could not have been the result of chance. Swein, the Danish leader, must have thought that the inhabitants of the northern Danelaw were already sympathetic to his cause for otherwise he would have raided them. He might, of course, have been deceiving himself, but the event proved otherwise. When he sailed up the Humber and Trent to Gainsborough in 1013, the North immediately submitted to him. Uhtred of Northumbria led the way, and he was followed by the Danes of the Five Boroughs, those of Lindsey, and finally all Danes living north of Watling Street. Swein then moved south and only began to harry the countryside after he passed Watling Street. The men of York had not fought one battle to oppose him; and when he suddenly died in 1014, his body was brought north to York where it was felt that it could lie safe from desecration.[29]

It is difficult to be certain how to interpret these events. The submission of 1013 is not particularly significant because by then the kingdom was falling apart. Swein's sparing of the northern Danelaw means more, and it was presumably based on the same reading of the loyalties of the Danes of York as the one that had lain behind the refusal of the Anglo-Saxon kings to give them native archbishops and earls. Indeed, the Danish aristocracy probably was separatist, although they may have been merely unreliable against Danes. At least, there is no direct evidence that they actively aided the invaders.

The removals of Thored and Ælfhelm presumably indicate that their loyalty was suspect; in any case, the inactivity of the Danes of York was probably the result of King Ethelred's political support in the North. Earl Uhtred of Northumbria was loyal to the king until 1013, and it would seem that the king had raised him in power to stand as a counterweight to the Danish inhabitants of York. Uhtred was the son of Earl Waltheof of Northumbria of

whom little more is known than the bare fact of his existence and
that he was an old man by 1006. In that year Malcolm II, king of
Scots, invaded Northumbria and, after the usual harrying, besieged
the newly founded episcopal city of Durham. The situation clearly
was serious, for the Danes were raiding southern England at the
time and Ethelred could send no help.[30] Earl Waltheof stayed in
Bamburgh and did nothing, and Earl Ælfhelm of York also apparently took no action. Malcolm met no known opposition until
Waltheof's son Uhtred intervened. He had married the daughter
of Bishop Aldhun of Durham and held a number of estates that belonged to the church. Several other members of the upper Northumbrian nobility had held estates of Durham in the past, and these
leaseholds were probably intended to obtain protection for the
church. Certainly it worked this way in the case of Uhtred. Apparently relying on the traditional authority of his family, he called
together an army from Northumbria and (it is said) from Yorkshire
and defeated the Scots.[31]

    Uhtred achieved a great victory although it ultimately had
tragic consequences. The city was saved, and its walls were festooned
with the heads of the dead Scots, which had been washed and
groomed by local women in return for cows. Uhtred had proved
himself an able leader, and Ethelred allowed him to succeed his
father as earl even though the latter was still alive. The king also
made him earl of York, a position he had just made vacant by
killing Earl Ælfhelm.[32] The joining of both earldoms in the hands
of a member of the house of Bamburgh was an expedient that had
been resorted to only once before, in the years immediately after
the reconquest of York, and its revival in 1006 indicated that once
again the West Saxon king feared for his authority in the North.
Moreover, after receiving these honors, Uhtred dismissed his
first wife, the daughter of the bishop of Durham, and married
Sige, the daughter of a rich citizen of York, Styr, son of Ulf. This
incident is usually cited to show the loose marriage customs of the
northerners, but it has a second meaning. By this marriage Uhtred
was trying to gain local political support south of the Tees. This
is made quite clear by the fact that the bishop of Durham sent
Uhtred's former wife south also and married her to an important
Yorkshire thegn.[33] Bishop Aldhun and Uhtred were still working
together; their object was to assure Uhtred could rule Yorkshire.

    Apparently the new earl was strong enough to govern the

Danes of York successfully, although there are no details. *De Obsessione Dunelmi* does say that Uhtred was quite successful in war after becoming earl, but it does not name his enemies. It only tells a story, somewhat confused in details, about how Uhtred refused to desert Ethelred in favor of Swein, and this was apparently true for Ethelred gave Uhtred his own daughter, Ælfgifu, in marriage,[34] a sure sign that the king valued Uhtred's support. Little is known about Uhtred after this. In 1013, he submitted to Swein, but by then everyone was going over to the Danes. When Swein died in 1014, Uhtred did not support his son Cnut. He seems instead to have gone back to Ethelred's side, for the king's expedition into Lindsey in 1014 would have been very dangerous if Uhtred were hostile. Perhaps the earl participated in the expedition. He did campaign with Ethelred's son, Edmund Ironside, in 1016 in Cheshire and the surrounding shires. This was Uhtred's only known campaign in direct support of the royal house, and it is probably significant that it occurred the year after the two chief Danish thegns of the Seven Boroughs had been killed. Edmund had installed himself in their place, and this change probably freed Uhtred for operations to the south. Unfortunately, in the middle of this campaign Cnut moved north and invaded Yorkshire, and he was too strong for Uhtred to fight: Wessex had already submitted to him and Earl Eadric was his ally. Uhtred therefore agreed to submit, but he was assassinated when he went to meet Cnut, who then made a Norwegian, Eric of Hlathir, earl of Yorkshire.[35]

This is the end of the story as it is usually told. The sources for Cnut's reign in general are inadequate, and for the North they are almost nonexistent. One curious tale survives from these years; if properly understood, it throws a great deal of light both on Uhtred's role as earl of York and on Northumberland after 1016. This is, of course, the famous Northumbrian blood feud. Uhtred is said to have obtained his second wife, the daughter of Styr, son of Ulf, at a price: he had to kill Styr's enemy Thurbrand. Uhtred failed to do this, although he presumably tried. Thurbrand certainly came to hate Uhtred and killed him when the earl arrived to submit to Cnut in 1016. Eadulf Cudel, Uhtred's brother, then became earl of Northumberland and ruled for a short time. He was followed by Earl Ealdred, Uhtred's son by Bishop Aldhun's daughter. Ealdred avenged his father's death by killing Thurbrand, but he was later killed in a particularly underhanded fashion by

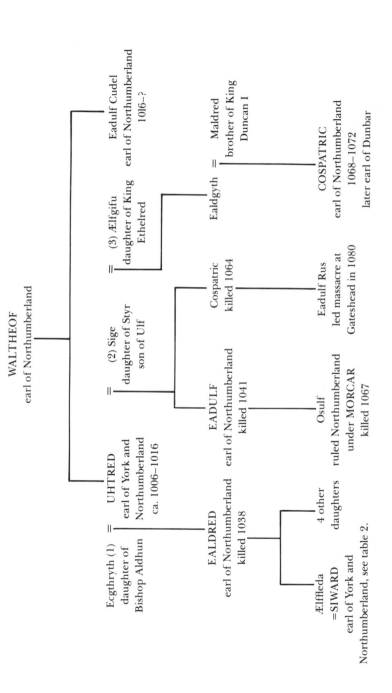

Table 1. *Genealogy of the Earls of Northumberland, part 1*

Thurbrand's son Carl. The two had made peace and promised
to go to Rome together, but when their departure was delayed
by a storm, Carl took Ealdred to his hall and, after entertaining
him, killed the Northumbrian earl in the woods. This crime was
not avenged by Ealdred's half-brother Eadulf, who became the
next earl of Northumberland, apparently because he was killed in
1041 by Siward. Justice waited until the 1070s when Siward's son
Waltheof, grandson of Earl Ealdred through his mother, had his
soldiers kill most of Carl's sons and grandsons, who were assembled
for a banquet near York.[36]

This tale is curious as it stands, and few historians have been
able to omit the story from their accounts of the North. Usually
they employ it to show the barbarity of the Northumbrians, but it
has a greater significance. The story was not written down until
around 1100, by which time its general meaning had been forgotten
and only the memory of the major events remained.[37] Its details,
however, suggest that the original events were not a straightforward
blood feud at all. Thurbrand in particular is a suspicious figure
because, in addition to being a rich and powerful Dane who lived
in York, he bore the title of "hold," in northern law the Danish
equivalent of a king's high-reeve, which raises the possibility that
he was the leader of the Danes of York. Thurbrand is also said to
have been the enemy of Styr, son of Ulf, a rich citizen of York.[38]
Although it has been generally assumed that their enmity stemmed
from some personal rivalry, such was not the case. A source, distinct
from the blood feud sources, records Styr's gift of some land to
Bishop Aldhun, and the details of this transaction clarify what was
actually happening. Styr made the grant when Ethelred was in
York. Part of the land had belonged to Styr, and he gave it to
Durham with the king's permission. The rest Styr purchased. In
the course of the transfer, Styr is described as an important supporter of Ethelred (*unius de melioribus suis*).[39] This discovery puts
the relationship between Uhtred and Styr in a different light. When
Uhtred married Styr's daughter, he was not simply trying to gain
political support in Yorkshire; rather, he was allying with Styr, another supporter of Ethelred, against Thurbrand, who probably
was the local Danish leader in York. Uhtred's promise to kill Thurbrand was part of this alliance. Moreover, Styr's gift of land to
Aldhun reinforces the idea that Aldhun was working with Uhtred.
The Northumbrian "blood feud" actually had its origin in Uhtred's

attempt to control the Danes of Yorkshire, who were sympathetic to Swein and Cnut.

The manner of Uhtred's death puts this interpretation beyond dispute. The fullest account of this event is in *De Obsessione Dunelmi*. It says that Uhtred was ambushed by Thurbrand as he was on his way to make peace with Cnut, and the details of the murder show that it was not an act of private vengeance. To carry out the deed, Thurbrand used some of Cnut's soldiers, whom he hid behind a curtain in the hall where Cnut and Uhtred were to meet. When Uhtred entered, the soldiers jumped out and killed him. The use of Cnut's soldiers implies his consent as does the fact that the killing was done literally under Cnut's nose with no ill effects for Thurbrand—despite the fact that Cnut had given Uhtred a safe-conduct.[40] Furthermore, *De Primo Saxonum Adventu* says the killing was done *per voluntatem Cnutonis regis* ("by the wish of King Cnut").[41] Cnut clearly was as responsible for the killing as Thurbrand. Finally, the idea that this was a feud is reduced to absurdity by the fact that Uhtred was not the only man killed that day: forty important Northumbrians who had come with him were also slaughtered.[42] The incident was, in fact, an attempt by the Danes of York and Cnut to destroy Ethelred's main political and military support in the North by annihilating the nobility of Northumberland. The implications are clear. The Anglo-Saxon kings had not mistrusted the Danes of York without reason—they could not be trusted in the face of a Danish invasion and were probably a center of plots and intrigues in peaceful times. In this sense, northern separatism existed by 1016. This reconstruction shows with equal clarity that until 1016 the earls of Northumberland were loyal to the kings despite the small power the kings had above the Tees. The Northumbrians were not separatist, and this is not surprising given the enemies they faced on all sides.

The next major problem is to determine what happened in the North between 1016 and 1041 and, in particular, whether the rule of a Danish king had any political impact on the nobles of York or Northumberland. The sources for Cnut's reign are limited, and the few pieces of evidence that survive are obscure and conflicting. It is not clear, for example, who ruled York for part of this period. In 1016, Cnut appointed one of his generals, Eric of Hlathir, earl; but Eric's last genuine signature as *dux* is found in 1023. For a ten-year interval between this date and 1033, when Earl Siward first witnessed a charter, it is not known who was earl of York.[43] In Northumberland, the names of the earls were remembered, but little else. After Uhtred's death, his brother Eadulf Cudel became earl. He lived only a short time and was followed in turn by Uhtred's sons Ealdred and Eadulf. These Northumbrian earls are said to have ruled in subordination to the earl of York,[44] but the few pieces of information out of these years that can be reconstructed cast doubt on this idea.

Eadulf Cudel, the first of these earls, is described as lazy and timid, but this is probably a monk's judgment of his character based on his only recorded act, the cession of Lothian. After he became earl, he is said to have given Lothian to the Scots because he feared that they would take revenge on him for Uhtred's victory over them (presumably in 1006). In return for Lothian, Eadulf received a "firm peace" with the Scots. These events, which are recorded only in *De Obsessione Dunelmi*, a northern tract from around 1100,[45] are in direct conflict with a second northern tradition on the loss of Lothian. The section on the Northumbrian earls in *De Primo Saxonum Adventu* asserts that King Edgar had given Lothian to King Kenneth of Scotland in 973.[46] Neither of these sources mentions an important event that probably occurred while Eadulf Cudel was earl. The narrative sources from Durham (which say nothing about the loss of Lothian) report that in 1018, Malcolm II again invaded the North and annihilated a Northumbrian army drawn from between the Tees and the Tweed at Carham, a ford over the Tweed. An associated source further obscures these events by asserting that Uhtred led the Northumbrians at Carham.[47] This was presumably a major Scottish victory, yet it seemingly had no consequences for the North. The chronicles from Durham report neither a siege nor the plundering of the countryside.

Scholars have assumed that the problem posed by these unconnected accounts is one of reconciliation, and the better discussions of these events have endeavored to fit them together without arbitrarily ignoring one or more of them. Because the accounts are contradictory, this is impossible, and historians have had to content themselves with dismissing what seemed to be the weakest element in the supposed series. This judgment has varied. The battle of Carham has been moved from 1018 to 1016 so that Uhtred could lead the Northumbrians to defeat, and his death has been stayed for two years to the same end. More self-confident scholars have denied that the battle took place, that it was important, or that Eadulf's cession ever occurred.[48] History has become remarkably pliable at this point; but the weak element is not the occurrence of a battle of Carham, its date, or the year of Uhtred's death. Rather, it is the statement in the *Historia Regum* that Uhtred led the army, a mistake that stemmed from the chronicler's ignorance. Once this is understood, the most plausible explanation is that suggested by Marjorie O. Anderson.[49] She assumed that Uhtred had recovered part of Lothian after defeating Malcolm in 1006 and that Eadulf Cudel ceded this land to the Scots. She also believed that Eadulf had gone over to the Scots and that this was the reason he gave up the land, but there is no evidence to support this suggestion. In fact, there is no need for such a hypothesis to explain Eadulf's absence from Carham. Symeon of Durham, who gives the earliest account of the battle, probably did not know the names of the Northumbrian earls before Siward and was, in any case, determined to minimize their activities in favor of St. Cuthbert who was the true defender of the Northumbrians.[50] These considerations suggest the less elaborate idea that it was Eadulf who lost the battle of Carham and, after the defeat, ceded Lothian to the Scots. Presumably, the land that he gave up was either some part of Lothian recovered by his brother or a section of the province (perhaps Tweeddale) which the Scots had not obtained in 973.

The theory that Earl Eadulf gave up some land to the Scots because they had beaten him badly is probably correct as far as it goes, but questions remain. Why should the earl have been particularly fearful after his defeat? He ought to have been able to expect royal help in this circumstance, but it is known that Cnut did not make a countermove in the North for at least nine years. Why did he delay? In any case, how could Eadulf give up land without the king's consent? Finally, why was there no contingent from Yorkshire at the battle of Carham? The men of Northumberland were foolish to fight the Scots alone if they could avoid it.

The immediate implication of these questions is that some important aspects of the northern political situation after 1016 are still hidden, and this impression is strengthened by the next known incident. After Eadulf Cudel's death, his nephew Ealdred became earl. He killed Thurbrand, his father's killer, and was killed in turn by Carl, Thurbrand's son, in 1038—the blood feud story again. The origins of this affair lay in the contest between Thurbrand and

Uhtred for control of Yorkshire, and the question now is whether these killings (the second and third) represent a blood feud or whether the original contest continued under Carl and Ealdred.

Again the details of the story combined with outside evidence show that the latter was the case. This is initially suggested by the fact that the slaughter should have ended with Ealdred's killing of Thurbrand. He had taken an eye for an eye and ought to have been content; the same should have been true of Carl. But this was emphatically not the case, for the level of murderous activity increased. Not only did Carl attempt to kill Ealdred, but Ealdred tried to kill Carl. They plotted against each other, harassed each other with tricks, and lay in ambush for each other,[51] apparently until Carl succeeded through the stratagem mentioned earlier. Eadulf, Ealdred's half brother, then became earl.

One might suggest that northerners took their feuds very seriously and that this explains both the continuation of the killings and the intensity of the attempts, but such an objection could not be sustained. For this incident to be regarded as normal in northern society, one would need to cite other examples of the same sort of thing, and other examples do not exist. Furthermore, it is clear that Carl's true identity had been forgotten by the time the story was written down. As mentioned earlier, there is a ten-year gap between Earl Eric, who last witnessed a charter in 1023, and Earl Siward. A certain *Karl minister*, however, began to witness in 1024, the very next year after Eric's disappearance, and continued to witness until 1045. This man was a northerner and undoubtedly identical with the Carl who fought with Ealdred. Presumably like his father, he was a hold and acted as the king's high-reeve (the Northumbrian equivalent of a hold) in Yorkshire. After 1033, when Siward became earl of Yorkshire, Carl remained in this position for he continued to witness—always in the company of Siward.[52] His omission from the Northumbrian earl lists is not significant because they do not deign to mention any earl of York between Oslac and Siward except Uhtred. If this identification is accepted, the feud between Ealdred and Carl becomes a conflict between the earl of Northumberland and the hold of York. Yet Cnut is unlikely to have tolerated such a disturbance.

Once charter evidence is brought into the discussion, the problem vanishes. Carl probably did defend Cnut's interests in the North between 1023 and 1033. More interesting, however, is the fact that Eadulf Cudel, Ealdred, and Eadulf do not seem to have occupied any official position. They do not witness royal charters as earls or in any other capacity.[53] It may be objected that not enough charters survive for this observation to be significant, but the earls of York as well as Carl witnessed a substantial number of charters during this period, and the immediate predecessors of Eadulf Cudel witnessed surviving charters. Earl Waltheof witnessed one, and Uhtred witnessed five despite the Danish invasions.[54] The only explanation for the failure of these three earls to witness is that they did not come to court, and this must mean they were in revolt. The plotting and ambushing between Carl and Ealdred was a minor war between Cnut's representative in the North and the earls of Northumberland. There was no northern blood feud.

This conclusion greatly clarifies the history of the North after 1016. By this date hostility probably already existed between the Northumbrians and the northern Danes, and the murders of Uhtred and the nobles of Northumberland plus the prospect of a Danish monarchy produced a revolt beyond the Tees. The term "revolt," however, must be used with caution. Uhtred's successors probably refused to make a formal submission to Cnut, and, given the tenuous bond between Northumberland and the king, the earls may not have viewed their action as a revolt. In the long run, of course, their policy was hopeless because Northumberland could not stand alone.

On the one hand, the earls faced the hostility of Carl. On the other, they had to withstand the Scots, who were all too ready to take advantage of the situation. When Malcolm II invaded in 1018, Eadulf Cudel had to fight him without support from the South and lost badly. Because of the revolt, Eadulf could expect no avenging expedition and had to give up Lothian. He may even have made some submission to Malcolm, although there is no proof.[55] The defeat at Carham also put the clerks of St. Cuthbert (of Durham) in a difficult position. Bishop Aldhun died after learning of the slaughter, and the clerks were unable to elect a successor for over two years. The traditional explanation is that none of them wished to become a monk, a requirement for being bishop of Durham.[56] In fact, they probably could not decide whether Carl or the earl of Northumberland was more dangerous. In the end they chose a man from outside their circle, an obscure priest named Edmund, who could take the blame for the false moves that appeared inevitable while the clerks rode out the storm.[57] The office of bishop was forced on him, and he was sent south to get Cnut's approval for his consecration,[58] thereby becoming the first bishop of Durham known to have sought royal approval.

Edmund proved to be a good bishop, but the clerks' fears had not been imaginary. After Eadulf Cudel's death, Ealdred and Carl fought for some years. Probably Carl made occasional forays into Northumberland, and Ealdred hid in the hills until he went home. This lasted until an unspecified date when the two became "sworn brothers,"[59] supposedly at the urging of friends. Swearing brotherhood was the northern equivalent of a peace treaty. The most likely explanation for this reconciliation was Cnut's northern expedition. This is a shadowy affair, but at some time between 1027 and 1031, the king came north and received the submission of Malcolm II and two northern subkings.[60] No one is likely to have been eager to fight Cnut at this time, and Ealdred probably also submitted to him and became Carl's sworn brother. While the king was in the North, he gave Edmund some land;[61] he would hardly have done so if Ealdred was still in revolt. For a period in the 1030s, Ealdred acknowledged Cnut's overlordship, but the submission of Northumbria ended in 1038 when Carl murdered the earl.

His brother Eadulf then became earl and went back into revolt. The immediate results were similar to those faced by Eadulf Cudel in 1018: the Scots took advantage of the weakness of the earl. Around 1040, King Duncan invaded the North, and this time the Northumbrians did not try to meet him in the field. The battle of Carham was not to be repeated. They probably retreated to their fortified places, churchyards, and into the hills. Duncan moved south and besieged Durham, but he was defeated by the Northumbrians, who had taken refuge in the city and fled, losing many men.[62] Eadulf probably had directed the defense of Durham, and after this success he was "exalted with pride" and ravaged the land of the Galwegians, who had undoubtedly taken part in Duncan's expedition.[63] Despite this victory, the earl must have been aware of the weakness of his position because he opened some sort of negotiations with Hardacnut, the English king, and went south to see him in 1041 under the king's safe-conduct. Unfortunately for Eadulf, however, Hardacnut's promise was no better than Cnut's had been for Uhtred. The king betrayed Eadulf, and he was killed by Siward, the earl of York.[64] Thus died the last earl of the house of Bamburgh through the male line—betrayed by a Dane and killed by a Dane in circumstances remarkably similar to those in which his brother and father had died.

The family itself was not extinct for one more son of Earl Uhtred still lived, Cospatric, and he may have proclaimed himself earl, although the northern earl lists say that he did not. They assert that upon the murder of Eadulf, Siward became earl of all of Northumbria from the Humber to the Tweed, thus adding Northumberland to Yorkshire.[65] A hitherto ignored source, however, shows that Siward's acquisition of the land between the Tees and Tweed was not that simple or immediate. The defiance of the Northumbrians continued for another year or two, probably under Cospatric's leadership. The murder of Eadulf was no more effective in reducing Northumberland than had been the murders of Uhtred and Ealdred. Finally in 1042 or 1043, Siward had to invade Northumberland and waste the countryside to gain control of the province.[66] He was successful, and Cospatric probably fled to Scotland.

The conclusions to be drawn from this reconstruction of northern history up to 1043 are startling. It is clearly a mistake to assume that the North was in any sense united by this date or to talk of some generalized northern "separatism." Separatism there certainly was, but its content varied between Yorkshire and Northumberland. Its seriousness depended upon who was king and who, if anybody, was invading the kingdom. Ultimately these political feelings probably were based on cultural differences and past political experience. The men from above the Tees certainly hated and feared the Danes and with good reason. The Yorkshire Danes had not been loyal to the West Saxon kings during the invasions of Swein and Cnut. They had been kept within the kingdom by Earl Uhtred. There was a Danish separatism that was important— at least when Danes were invading. Finally, at the beginning of Edward the Confessor's reign, Northumberland was a conquered province. The Northumbrians had gone into revolt when Uhtred was killed. Two more of their earls had been killed by Danes, and they had been brought back within the kingdom by conquest. Separatism above the Tees existed by 1043, and it is very doubtful if the accession of Edward did anything to quiet it. He may have been a member of the royal house of Wessex, but Siward was their earl. He undoubtedly loomed larger than the king, and he was a conquering Dane.

2. Earl Siward
and the Scots

Earl Siward was the last great earl of the North before the debacle of the 1060s, and there is consequently a strong temptation to picture him as a primitive monolith who represented the traditional order of government above the Humber. Siward, however, cannot be used as a general symbol for the old political arrangements of northern England. He was originally an outsider, and during the years of his power, he brought no real solution to the problems of the North. At best, he kept his earldom quiet, and in some ways he created new problems.

Siward was hardly an ideal earl from the English king's point of view. No direct evidence remains to indicate Edward the Confessor's opinion on northern problems in the 1040s. At the beginning of Edward's reign, the political and military situation in the North could not have appeared promising. The history of the region before 1042 reveals three basic problems. The most serious was that the Danes of York had not been loyal to Ethelred, and Edward probably could not expect any greater devotion from them should the kingdom be threatened by renewed Danish invasions. In Ethelred's days, these Danes had been kept in check only by the power of Uhtred, earl of Northumbria and York, but Edward could expect no such support because Northumbria was a conquered and hostile province in 1042. Thurbrand, Carl, and Siward had made it impossible for the king to balance Danes with Northumbrians and loyal elements within Yorkshire. Finally, the Scots were becoming a serious threat to the peace and prosperity of northern England. They had invaded three times since 1000, taking advantage on each occasion of English distraction caused by either the Danish invasions or the rebellion of the Northumbrian earls. The ultimate aim of these Scottish incursions was the annexation of Northumbrian lands, not an impossible hope given conditions in the North.

Siward was therefore something of an embarrassment to the king. He was a Danish parvenu similar to Earl Godwin of Wessex and had risen to power under Cnut and his sons. Siward had become earl of Yorkshire about 1033 and had added Northumberland to his earldom by conquest about 1042. When Edward became king in 1042, Siward, along with the other great earls, was a political reality with whom Edward had to deal. It was beyond the king's power to remove him, even if to do so seemed desirable, and on the level of high politics it probably did not. The fall of Siward would only have increased the power of the other earls, a most undesirable result. His remaining in power was also undesirable because there was only a partial correspondence between his self-interest and that of the king. He was both an ambitious new man and a Dane, and his major interest was to maintain his own position. He was undoubtedly popular in York because he was Danish and a holdover from Cnut's reign and perhaps found it easier to govern that shire than had most of his predecessors. Yet this aptness itself raised a question: how would Siward react if a Danish fleet sailed up the Humber? Such an occurrence was not impossible, and Siward would have had little reason to be loyal to Edward if it happened. A wise counselor could have pointed out to the king the wisdom of giving the Northumbrians an earl from their native house and thus reestablishing the traditional relationship with the province, but this was impossible. Siward could not be deprived of a major portion of his earldom. The only point at which there was any real correspondence between the king's interest and the earl's was on the Scottish problem. Siward was determined to keep the Scots out of his earldom and devoted a sustained effort to this end.

Given these factors, it should not be surprising that Siward made no significant contribution to solving the major internal political problems of the North. Probably they were beyond solution, and the situation had some advantages from the standpoint of court politics—provided there were no Viking attacks. Siward's unpopularity above the Tees meant that the earl was not as powerful as the extent of his lands suggested and that one of his main concerns was to keep Northumbria quiet. Thus his freedom of action was limited and he was unable to become deeply involved in southern politics. He was not, as has been suggested, uninterested in southern affairs.[1] Siward faced serious problems in the North and, as a result, was usually loyal to the king.

In terms of policy, the requirements for governing the North must have been clear. Siward had to keep watch on the Danes of York, make sure that the Northumbrian rebellion did not flare up again, and thwart Scottish raids. To accomplish these tasks, he needed to be rich enough to maintain a large band of professional warriors (housecarls),[2] and apparently the resources of the earl-dom were not sufficient because the king gave him extra lands in the South. Siward held Northamptonshire from (probably) the early 1040s, and he acquired the neighboring shire of Huntingdon in the early 1050s.[3] Although the grant of this Midland earldom may have been intended in part to ensure the earl's loyalty, the additional revenues these shires yielded allowed him successfully to dominate the North.

Fortified with a private army of perhaps as many as two to three hundred housecarls, Siward governed his earldom success-fully.[4] The nobility of Yorkshire were presumably receptive to his rule. In Northumbria he may have had more difficulties, but he made an attempt to appease local feelings by marrying Ælfleda, a daughter of Earl Ealdred.[5] The latter, who had been Uhtred's eldest son, had himself begotten only daughters, and since North-umbrian women could inherit land, it is nearly certain that by his marriage Siward acquired part of the lands of her family[6] and possibly also some legitimacy as earl in the eyes of the Northum-brians. The Northumbrian earls, however, may have followed the Scottish rule of succession by which brother succeeded brother,[7] in which case, Cospatric, Uhtred's youngest son, would have had a better claim to be earl than Siward.

Siward's attempts to reconcile the Northumbrians may have included conceding to Cospatric a subordinate position in the gov-ernment of the earldom, for evidence exists that Cospatric was important in local affairs, perhaps before 1056, and he may have worked in conjunction with Siward. This question will be discussed later; nevertheless, Siward clearly did attempt to ally himself with the native house of Bamburgh. By Ælfleda, who was evidently his second wife, he had a son whom he named Waltheof in honor of the boy's maternal great-grandfather. Some fifty years later there

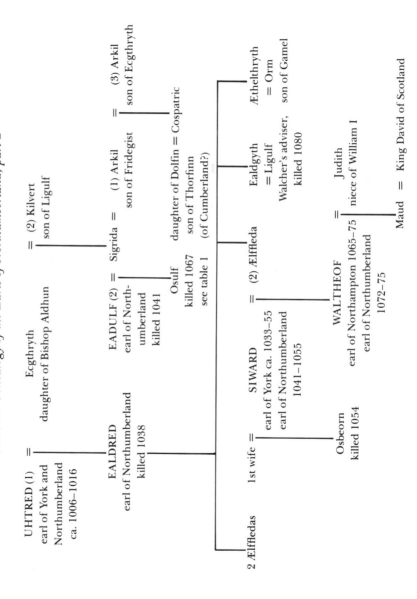

Table 2. Genealogy of the Earls of Northumberland, part 2

was a tradition at Durham that Siward had given to Waltheof, presumably as a child, the earldom of Northumbria with the boundaries it had had in Ealdred's day.[8] If the story is true, Siward may have intended that his eldest son, Osbeorn, should become earl of York, which Ealdred had not controlled, and this would amount to a tacit admission that it was proper for a Dane to rule York and a Northumbrian to rule Northumbria. The division never seems to have occurred, but Waltheof considered himself a member of the house of Bamburgh by the time he reached maturity.[9]

The success of Siward's attempts to identify himself with the Bamburgh family is difficult to establish. He faced only shadowy opposition in Northumbria, but this can be explained as easily on the basis of his military strength as on the basis of his marriage. From nine hundred years after the event, his marriage seems prudent; to Northumbrians at the time, it may have appeared the brash move of a parvenu bent on acquiring a local name.

The sensibilities of the Northumbrian nobles are unfortunately lost beyond recall. In another area, however, Siward's actions clearly struck the natives as being highhanded and aroused resentment. He offended the most powerful body of men in the North, the clerks of St. Cuthbert, and their feelings are part of the historical record. These clerks constituted a privileged corporation that tended to control the bishopric of Durham in most respects. They elected the bishop, who was usually one of their number, and carried out the more important functions of the cathedral church. Being also essentially secular canons who held property and married, they occupied a unique position in Northumbrian society that ensured their inordinate prestige. Some of these clerks were known descendants of the original porters of the holy body of St. Cuthbert.[10] This uncorrupted corpse was the most precious relic in the North and the most powerful talisman between the Humber and the Orkneys. During the original Danish invasions, these porters had cared for the body after the destruction of Lindisfarne and had trekked all over the North with it before finally reestablishing the bishopric at Chester-le-Street.[11] The clerks were thus not only rich and powerful; they were also a direct link with the North's pre-Viking past.

Siward offended these men in two ways. First, he appropriated some of their lands. Earlier in the century Bishop Aldhun had given Uhtred several of the church's villages when the latter had married his daughter. After becoming earl, Siward claimed these villages in the name of his wife, who was an offspring of Uhtred's marriage.[12] This action angered the clerks, but they could do little to oppose it. Other northern earls had taken church lands. The second and far more serious offense was that Siward and Edward threatened the ancient privileges of the clerks. Hitherto they had elected their bishop, who traditionally had been either one of their number or a northern cleric. In 1042, Bishop Edmund went south to visit King Hardacnut at Gloucester. The reason for the visit was not recorded although it was probably connected with Siward's recent conquest of Northumbria. The Durham church is unlikely to have come through the complicated politics of the years after 1018 uncompromised, and, no doubt, Edmund needed to explain some of his past actions. During the early eleventh century, however, it had become risky for important Northumbrians to go south, and this proved true again, for Edmund died while visiting the king.[13] The sources do not suggest any foul play, but certainly Bishop Edmund's death was exceedingly convenient for Hardacnut and Siward in that it opened the way to the establishment of royal control over the bishopric of Durham. The clerks may have gone through the usual election process to choose a new bishop, but the sources do not explicitly say so. Rather, they report that Eadred, the principal clerk, bought the bishopric from the king with the church's money, apparently an innovation.[14] The first step in the clerks' downfall had been Edmund's trip south in 1020–21 to seek Cnut's approval for his consecration. The second step came when the clerks were required to pay for the privilege of electing their bishop.

The end followed quickly—perhaps suspiciously soon. Eadred sickened after purchasing the bishopric and died within ten months.[15] This time the clerks did not select his successor. They may have lacked the money to buy the freedom to elect a second bishop after such a short interval. King Edward and Siward used the opportunity of Eadred's death to control the selection of his successor and to install Durham's first nonnorthern bishop. In 1020–21, Bishop Edmund had brought north some monks from Peterborough to instruct him in the monastic vows he had taken to become bishop, and Æthelric, the new bishop, was one of these monks. One source says explicitly that Edward appointed him bishop.[16] In a way it was a reasonable choice since Æthelric had lived at Durham for twenty years and was familiar with northern customs and men. But the method of his elevation was bound to arouse resentment.

His appointment was a frontal attack on the privileges and freedom of the clerks, and they viewed it as such. They despised him both for being an outsider and for gaining office against their will. Æthelric in turn made the situation worse by extending the attack on the clerks' powers. He directly reduced their administrative role by granting the most powerful position in the church government after his own to his brother Æthelwine, who had also been a monk at Peterborough and had come to Durham during Edmund's episcopate. Not surprisingly, these innovations were too much for the clerks to bear, and in 1045 or 1046 they rebelled against Æthelric and drove him out of Durham. This action did not, however, restore their freedom for long because the bishop sought out Siward and obtained his support against the clerks. The earl then forced them to take back the bishop, but the reconciliation was not accomplished through negotiations and compromise. The clerks yielded only through fear of Siward's power, and Æthelric remained their bishop until after Siward's death.[17] On the surface, the policy had been successful, but its wisdom is debatable. Siward could now count on the support of the bishop in governing Northumbria, and this must have been his aim. Yet the clerks were unreconciled to their loss of power and their domination by southern monks; and Siward, who was responsible for this situation, must have been very unpopular at Durham. Furthermore, he had left the clerks with their local prestige undiminished, a dangerous oversight because they were destined to use it to overturn his successor, who continued Siward's church policy.

While Siward lived, however, his control over both the church of Durham and the house of Bamburgh remained firm, and he was free to deal with the threat posed by the Scots to the North, which was probably his major concern. To understand the gravity of the situation he faced, it must be realized that the necessity of guarding the border against the Scots was not a traditional problem of northern government. The imperatives of the high medieval border were only now coming into being because the threat to Northumbria from the Scots had greatly increased during the early decades of the eleventh century as a result of a basic shift in northern power relationships that was one of the fundamental

steps in the formation of the Anglo-Scottish border. This power
shift has gone unnoticed in the interplay between the fragmentary
evidence on the kingdom of Strathclyde and conceptions of the
border based on how it worked in later times.

Siward was confronted with a novel problem. For perhaps
one hundred twenty years, the main threat to the North had lain in
the West. Throughout the tenth century, the lands between the
Humber and the Forth had had a dangerous western border that
had come into being early in the tenth century with the expansion
of the British kingdom of Strathclyde or Cumbria. This development has traditionally either been ignored or not dealt with as part
of the general history of northern Britain even though its general
outlines are fairly clear. Around the year 900, the Cumbrians, as
they called themselves, began to expand out of Clydesdale toward
the south. They crossed the Southern Highlands of Scotland and
took control of the Galwegian coastal plain on both sides of the
Solway Firth and the Vale of Eden. At its height, their kingdom
apparently reached from the head of Loch Lomond at least to the
Rere Cross of Stainmore in the North Riding of Yorkshire,[18] and
there is some evidence that it may have stretched as far south as the
Mersey.[19] Thus a western kingdom in northern Britain suddenly
appeared that comprised all of the west coast plain and a large
portion of the uplands. The established political powers on the east
coast plain, the Danes of York, the house of Bamburgh, and the
Scots, probably found the rise of Cumbria threatening since there
is no reason to believe that the Cumbrians were any better neighbors than their southern cousins the Welsh. In fact, the expansion
of the Cumbrians represented only the initial disintegration of society on the west coast plain, for during this same period Norwegian
Vikings from Ireland began to settle along the eastern shores of
the Irish Sea from Galloway as far south as the Wirral Peninsula below the Mersey.[20] The results of this invasion on the Cumbrians as
a people and on their kingdom are exceedingly obscure. The Norwegians had been subject to Irish influence before settling in Britain and ultimately merged with the native Britons to produce the
people known in the twelfth century as the Galwegians.[21] The kingdom of the Cumbrians apparently survived the influx of Vikings,
and the Cumbrians were able to maintain a line of kings of their
own who are intermittently recorded down to 1018. But the reality
of the power of the Cumbrian kings is in doubt. It is known that the

Norse, who had settled around the littoral of the Irish Sea, came up the Clyde and crossed the Scottish Midland valley to raid the Scots and used the Tyne Gap, the Vale of Eden–Stainmore route, and the Wirral Peninsula—all theoretically within Cumbria except perhaps the latter—as passages by which to plunder the Northumbrians, the Danes of York, and the English Midlands. Ultimately, Ragnall, grandson of Ivarr, was able to overwhelm the Danish kingdom of York with an army drawn from these Norse settlers and to reestablish his family there.[22]

These developments were significant because the incursions from the West became so serious that any ruler wishing to control the North's eastern plain had to dominate the invasion routes through Cumbria used by these marauders. Bishop Cutheard of Chester-le-Street, for example, created a marcher lordship that covered the mouths of Tynedale, Weardale, and Teesdale, and the Mercians and West Saxons sought to obtain the alliance or submission of the Cumbrian kings. Cumbrian cooperation was useful against the Irish Sea Vikings, although it is unclear whether this was because they had enough power partially to control the movement of the Vikings through their kingdom or whether it was simply desirable that they not come raiding through the hills in alliance with the Vikings. The direct relationship between security in the East, on the one hand, and control of the invasion routes from the West coupled with the submission of the Cumbrian kings, on the other, is clear in tenth-century Anglo-Saxon sources. When the Norwegian incursions first assumed serious proportions in the early tenth century, the powers of the North tried to meet the threat by banding together. Æthelflæd of Mercia allied with the Cumbrians and the Scots against these new Vikings, and even the Danes of York sought her protection. In addition to aiding these allies actively, Æthelflæd built fortresses at Chester, Eddisbury, and Runcorn to protect her northwestern frontier. After King Edward took direct control of Mercia in 918, he followed a similar policy. He built a number of boroughs in Cheshire and Derby, including the ones at Manchester, Bakewell, and Thelwell, fortresses that clearly seem designed to secure the invasion routes from the Irish Sea littoral into the Midlands and to dominate the southern routes east into Yorkshire, and he attempted to gain the same ends by diplomatic activity. After he had built Bakewell in 920, the king of the Strathclyde Welsh (the Cumbrians), the king of Scots, and the rulers of York and Bamburgh all came to him and "chose him as father and lord."[23] Presumably this meant that they would co-operate in maintaining the peace of the North and deny passage through their lands to the Irish Sea Vikings.

The same sequence of events was repeated under Athelstan during the 920s and 930s. After he took control of the Viking kingdom of York in 927, he moved immediately to secure the western borders of his new province by crossing the Pennines. Athelstan met the kings of the North at Eamont in the Vale of Eden, which apparently marked the eastern border of the Cumbrian kingdom, and there the kings of the Cumbrians, the Welsh, and the Scots plus the rulers of Bamburgh made peace with him.[24] This agreement did not last for long, however, and in 934, Athelstan invaded Scotland. Although the chronicles concentrate their attention on his war against Constantine, the Scottish king, it is clear that this expedition also included operations against the Cumbrians because in the same year Athelstan purchased Amounderness, a large section of Lancashire above the Ribble, from the Vikings and gave it to the archbishop of York.[25] Amounderness dominated the western end of the Aire Gap, the easiest passage between the Irish Sea and York, and control of this route was necessary for the defense of York. The ascendancy in the North which Athelstan won by the campaign of 934 and his victory at Brunanburh in 937 ended with his death, and his successor Edmund had to retrace Athelstan's steps. His attempt to do so provides perhaps the clearest example of the importance of pacifying the West. In 944, Edmund came north and drove out the Norwegian kings of York. The following year he crossed the Pennines into Cumbria, ravaged the countryside, and gave the kingdom of the Cumbrians to Malcolm, the king of Scots, on the condition that the latter be his ally.[26] This ambitious attempt to solve the problem of the North's western border unfortunately seems to have had no permanent results, for there is no evidence that Malcolm had more than nominal control over Cumbria, and the native line of Cumbrian kings was in power again within a generation.[27] Indeed, well before that, in 954, Eric Bloodaxe, the last Norwegian king of York, was killed in battle on the heights of Stainmore, the gateway to York from the head of the Vale of Eden. Although the account of this event does not disclose whether Eric was retreating or trying to regain his lost kingdom, neither possibility suggests that the Scots had much control over Cumbria.[28]

After 954, the power of the Vikings of the Irish Sea littoral began to decline. This was a slow process, however, that lasted into the twelfth century, and incidents still continued to occur that show that the North still faced danger along its western border. In 966, for instance, a Yorkshire noble ravaged Westmorland, undoubtedly in response to raids over Stainmore,[29] and six years later Kenneth II harried Cumbria all the way to its southern border.[30] The sequel shows that the mechanics of the western border had not changed. Kenneth's expedition presumably gave him some control over the northern end of the western frontier; probably as a result, King Edgar "granted" him Lothian a year later.[31] The continuing need to control the West in order to hold the eastern plain is confirmed by another incident that occurred in 973. During the summer, King Edgar brought his navy north to Chester, where he received the submissions of six northern kings including the Cumbrian monarch.[32] Even at this date, Edgar may have been on the border of Cumbria when he was in Chester. The Scottish chronicle that describes Kenneth's invasion of the year before says that he ravaged Cumbria all the way to the Dee, the river upon which Chester stands, and if this statement is correct, Cumbria still included Lancashire.[33] Finally, in the year 1000, King Ethelred harried Cumbria while his fleet wasted the Isle of Man. Given the threat from the Danes which Ethelred faced, this expedition is again proof that the western Vikings were still dangerous and had been raiding the North. It may also be significant that the earliest indication that the English held southern Lancashire comes from the will of Wulfric Spot, which dates from 1002–4, at most four years later than Ethelred's invasion of Cumbria.[34]

The existence of this dangerous western border was a crucial element in the relations between the Scots and the English during most of the tenth century because the Scots were themselves threatened by the Cumbrian kings and the western Vikings. In 962, King Indulf was killed by Vikings, and as late as 971, Cullen, Kenneth II's predecessor, was killed by the Cumbrians. Kenneth's invasion of their kingdom was apparently launched in revenge.[35] The corollary of this threat was that throughout most of the tenth century, Anglo-Scottish, or at least Northumbrian-Scottish, relations were usually good. The only exception was the later part of the reign of Constantine II (ca. 933–43) and perhaps the years immediately afterward. He invaded the North in 937 in alliance with the Vikings and Cumbrians, and he may have attacked the North on a second occasion. Yet his reputation as an enemy of the English is compromised by the fact that in 914 and 918 he had defended the Northumbrians against Ragnall, and his later cooperation with the Vikings was probably the result of his isolation and weakness.[36] The usual relationship was in fact one of friendship. The submissions of the Scottish kings to Edward, Athelstan, Edmund, and Edgar were essentially alliances against the extension of Viking power through Cumbria or against the Cumbrians themselves.[37] After Constantine's death there were no invasions of the North by the Scottish kings or any Anglo-Saxon expeditions into Scotland.

This situation changed radically after 1000 for between this date and the 1060s most of the elements that were to characterize the northern border during the high Middle Ages came into being. The first sign of this transformation took place in 1006, when Malcolm II invaded Northumbria and tried to take Durham. This was the first Scottish invasion of the North in over fifty years, and it probably came as a shock to the aging Waltheof.[38] Why Malcolm invaded is problematical, but the general political context that made his attack possible is clear. The Cumbrians and the western Vikings, while not without power, were no longer the overwhelming threat that they had been. Furthermore, both the Northumbrian earl and the Anglo-Saxon king were now completely distracted by the Danish invasions. Malcolm II thus had a freedom of action his predecessors had lacked, and he used it to try to take over Northumbria. After the invasion of 1006 failed, Malcolm did not give up the new policy, which is a clear indication that his invasion had been more than a whim. In 1018, he moved south again, this time presumably in alliance with the Cumbrian king, and won the battle of Carham. The results of this victory were grave in the long run because they produced a further shift in the power relationships in the North. The victory perhaps resulted in the advance of Malcolm's frontier in Lothian, as was suggested earlier, but its real importance lay in the West because Owen the Bald, king of Strathclyde (Cumbria), the last of his line, died in the battle. With his death, Malcolm was able to extend his rule over at least the eastern part of the Cumbrian kingdom, and it is likely that he installed his brother as ruler of the area.[39] This must have involved fighting and explains why Malcolm did not exploit his victory at Carham by further raids in Northumbria after 1018. The stakes in the West were ultimately higher because control of Cumbria would give Malcolm access to at least three important routes between west and east (from the upper Clyde down the Tweed, the Tyne Gap, and the Stainmore passage) and to a host of secondary routes that in effect turned the flank of the North of England. Scottish control of the West thus offered the hope of control of the East, and the first attempt at the fulfillment of this hope was not long delayed. Malcolm's grandson Duncan was the first king of Scots to utilize his position as king of the Cumbrians to attack Northumbria when he invaded and besieged Durham in 1040. The fact that he had led the Cumbrians over the border, in addition to his own Scots, is shown by Earl Eadulf's reprisal: he ravaged Cumbria after Duncan's defeat.[40]

This was the basic geopolitical problem that Siward faced. With the Scots in control of Cumbria, their king could lead an army over the Tweed in a frontal attack on the earldom while sending the Cumbrians east through the hills to raid and disrupt communications. Such tactics could place the Northumbrians in an extremely perilous position and could ultimately lead to Scottish control of Northumbria. Consequently, the possibility that Duncan's invasion of 1040, the first of this type, might be repeated had to be forestalled, and Siward applied his energies to the task. Apparently he followed a twofold policy of expansion in the West to close the major invasion routes combined with an attempt to put the Scottish king in a dependent position. No chronicler, of course, says that these were Siward's intentions, but his recorded actions indicate that they were. To a certain extent, his policy was opportunistic. As a result of circumstances he had had no hand in creating, Siward possessed the perfect means with which to interfere in Scottish affairs: he could make use of Malcolm Canmore, the son of King Duncan.

This possibility was the direct result of the succession crisis that marred the last years of Malcolm II and the short reign of his grandson Duncan. Malcolm II (1005–34) had been a very powerful king. He had invaded the North twice, and after 1018, his rule, which encompassed Lothian as far as the Tweed and Cumbria in

Table 3. The Kings of Scotland from 1005 to 1153
The order of Malcolm III's sons follows Duncan, Scotland, p. 124, n. 6

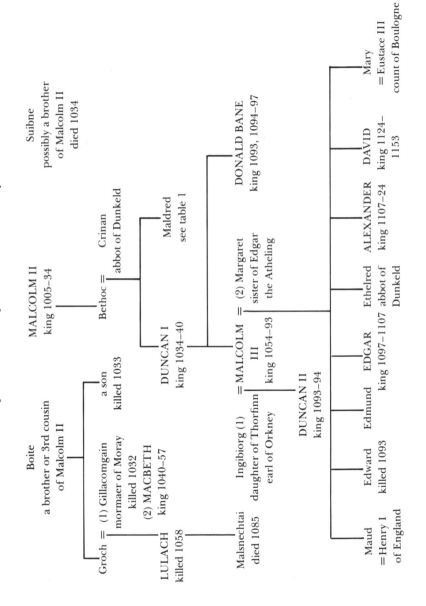

addition to Scotland, had stretched further south than that of any of his predecessors. During his later years, neither the earls of Bamburgh, who were usually in revolt against Cnut, nor the great Danish king himself made any serious attempt to push back his power.[41] Nevertheless, the last part of Malcolm's reign was filled with turmoil and battle, probably because he had no male heir. He did have a daughter, named Bethoc ("Birchtree"), who had married Crinan the thegn, the abbot of Dunkeld, and who had had two sons, Duncan and Maldred.[42] Malcolm may have wanted his grandson Duncan to succeed him, although this would have been a break with the customary rule of succession, under which either his brother or a representative of a collateral branch of the royal family would have become king before Duncan. It is probably more likely that Malcolm's potential successors by the traditional rule were encouraged by his lack of an heir to hasten his death. Since he had no son, he could be killed without fear of reprisal. There would be no one seeking vengeance and the throne ten or twenty years after the deed. But if this second hypothesis is correct, Malcolm's relatives gravely misjudged him; by the time of his death in 1034, nearly all of the possible claimants to the throne except his own grandsons had been exterminated.

The king had had either a brother or a third cousin named Boite, of whom nothing is known except that he had a son and a daughter and that he himself predeceased Malcolm. In 1032, the daughter's husband, Gillacomgain, the mormaer of Moray, was burned to death, probably by Malcolm or his agents, and a year later Malcolm himself killed Boite's son.[43] These two incidents neutralized the descendants of Boite. In 1034, Malcolm died after defeating an unnamed enemy. The circumstances of his death are very obscure, but an Irish chronicle records that Suibne, son of Kenneth, king of the Galwegians, also died in the same year. Given the events of 1032 and 1033 and the common patronymic of Malcolm II and Suibne, these deaths were not coincidence. Suibne, who was probably a brother of Malcolm II and who had ruled Cumbria for the king, must have died in battle against his brother in 1034.[44] In any case, Malcolm II's murderous efforts were quite successful. By 1034, only his own grandsons and Groch, Boite's daughter, were still alive, and Duncan, his eldest grandson, was therefore able to become king without opposition. He reigned until 1040 when, after his unsuccessful invasion of Northumbria, he was killed by Macbeth, the mormaer of Moray, who had married Groch.[45] Once he was in power, someone, probably Crinan, Duncan's father, sent the dead king's sons out of the country.[46]

Thus Malcolm fell into Siward's hands, and he may not have been alone. A late source says that at this time Siward received a number of other refugee Scottish nobles.[47] Duncan's younger brother Maldred certainly could not have felt secure in Scotland and probably came south; this is particularly likely because he had married a daughter of Earl Uhtred and would have been among relatives south of the Tweed.[48] In later years, Maldred's son, Cospatric, seems to have thought of himself as a Northumbrian, which would be understandable if he had been reared among his mother's people while his father was in exile. Even Crinan may have come south, although there is no direct evidence. The usefulness to Siward of Malcolm, Maldred, and whatever other Scots were in Northumbria was twofold. Ultimately, either Maldred or Malcolm could be used as an excuse for direct intervention in Scotland since they both had claims to the throne. Short of direct action, Siward could use their presence in Northumbria to control Macbeth simply by threatening to allow them to come over the border with a Northumbrian army if Macbeth caused trouble. The earl of Northumbria was thus in a comfortable position. Siward's ability to threaten Macbeth was perhaps the reason why the latter failed to imitate his two predecessors by launching a major invasion of the North. Macbeth only raided the North, and his relative restraint was certainly not caused by his insecurity within Scotland. Regardless of the validity of his claim to the throne, he feared no rivals when he made his pilgrimage to Rome,[49] and this security could have been possible only if he had reached some understanding with Siward.

In addition to the diplomatic leverage that Maldred and Malcolm supplied, there was another possibility in the situation. Malcolm must have been a boy in the early 1040s and consequently of little immediate use to Siward in the diplomatic game. Maldred was older, and his claim to the throne undoubtedly took precedence over his nephew's, but Malcolm had another importance.[50] Fordun says that Duncan had given Cumbria to Malcolm, and this statement may have some basis in fact, despite Fordun's general unreliability on Cumbrian affairs. Florence of Worcester refers to Malcolm as the son of the king of the Cumbrians, and this is a suspicious title to apply to Duncan.[51] He had been, of course, their king, but "king of Scots" or some equivalent would have been a more appropriate title. Florence's choice of this unlikely title to describe Malcolm's father probably reflects what seemed important about him to the English. If Duncan had been king of the Cumbrians, the English would have considered Malcolm his heir. This was significant because there is evidence that Siward had taken over Cumberland, the area south of the Solway. If Siward felt the necessity for a legal title to these lands, Malcolm could grant it as the "heir" to the Cumbrian kingdom. This may, in fact, have been Siward's price for supporting the cause of Malcolm and Maldred.

The evidence that Siward expanded into Cumberland comes from a unique charter that dates from between 1041 and 1065 and probably from between 1041 and 1055.[52] The charter was granted by Cospatric, the third son of Earl Uhtred, to Thorfinn mac Thore and concerns certain property rights, judicial privileges, and fiscal exemptions in Allerdale, roughly the northwestern section of the modern county of Cumberland. The address of the charter contains the most significant information. Cospatric greets the men "dwelling in all the lands that were Cumbrian,"[53] and this establishes that by the time of the grant the lands south of the Solway were no longer part of the kingdom of Cumbria. The nature of the charter is in accordance with a change in lordship; and indeed, such a change must have been the occasion for the making of the charter. Apparently it is a confirmation of rights already held by Thorfinn and probably held by his father Thore before him.[54] Cospatric confirms and perhaps extends Thorfinn's holdings. This is just the type of document one would expect to find relating to lands that had been transferred from one kingdom to another, for the local landholders would naturally want the new rulers to recognize the legitimacy of their tenures. It is also clear that the ultimate lord of this area was the English king. Although Cospatric was a great lord in Cumberland and confirms Thorfinn's possessions without mentioning anyone else's permission, the fact that Earl Siward had granted peace, that is, protection, to Thorfinn establishes that Siward had the general lordship of the area. Furthermore, Cospatric was geldfree, as were a number of other local landholders, and in the charter he extends the same privilege to Thorfinn and his retainers.[55] Such a concern with not paying geld is explicable only if the English king was the ultimate lord of Allerdale. This consideration negates any suggestion that these lands were held by Cospatric under the Scottish king.[56]

This charter has been interpreted as containing evidence that Anglo-Saxon control of Cumberland dated from before Siward's time because it mentions rights Thore and two other men had had "in the days of Eadred." "Eadred" has been identified with Earl "Ealdred," but this hypothesis is not justified on linguistic grounds.[57] Earl Ealdred had spent most of his time in rebellion against Cnut, and it is very unlikely that he had been able to wrest this land from the Scots. Siward was the first earl in the eleventh century who had the power to make such a transfer. Perhaps taking advantage of Earl Eadulf's ravaging of this area and of his control over Malcolm, Siward had pushed through the Tyne Gap and annexed Cumberland. The area was then linked ecclesiastically to England. Archbishop Kynsige of York (1051–60) is said to have ordained two bishops of "Glasgow" while at York, and the sphere of operations of these bishops must have been in Siward's newly won lands in the West.[58] By annexing Cumberland, Siward had in one stroke closed the two best invasion routes from the West, Stainmore and the Tyne Gap. This important rectification of the northern frontier meant increased protection for both Yorkshire and Durham. The acquisition of Cumberland also had a secondary advantage. The Cospatric who granted the charter seems to have been Earl Uhtred's youngest son.[59] Siward had apparently put him in charge of the area and thereby paid off, at least partially, old grievances.

These gains offset the Scottish annexation of the old kingdom of Cumbria and perhaps blunted the resentment of the house of Bamburgh. It is regrettable that the charter cannot be more closely dated than between 1041 and 1065.[60] It shows only that Siward had controlled Cumberland at some time and does not disclose when he took it over. As a result, the chronological position of Siward's westward expansion in the development of his Scottish policy cannot be determined. The general direction of his relations with Scotland is quite clear from the mid-1040s, however, and the charter may well come from these years. Control over the invasion routes from the West would seem to be a precondition for any active intervention inside Scotland, and Siward led his first army over the Tweed in 1045 or 1046. This expedition is not described

Political Divisions of the North in 1056

in detail in the chronicle that mentions it, but it seems to have been an exact parallel of the famous invasion of 1054 except that it failed. Siward had apparently decided to create his own king of Scotland, a policy that theoretically would ensure good relations with the northern kingdom and peace for the North. The account of the expedition, however, does not name Siward's candidate for the Scottish throne, although it was probably Maldred, Duncan's

younger brother. The sequence of events is also difficult to reconstruct. Siward apparently had the support of a party of Scots
led by Crinan, the father of Duncan and Maldred, but it is unclear whether Crinan invaded Scotland from Northumberland or
whether he was already in Scotland and rose in revolt against
Macbeth. Probably the latter was the case, and the revolt was to be
coordinated with Siward's invasion. Crinan met Macbeth in battle,
however, and was slain. Siward subsequently led an army into
Scotland and drove out Macbeth, according to the chronicle, which
probably means that Macbeth fled into Moray in the face of Siward's
advance. The earl then raised Maldred to the throne and returned
to Northumberland.[61] He may have thought that he had accomplished his aim, or he may have been unable to stay above the
Tweed. Successful invasions of Scotland normally required a supply
fleet because it was all but impossible for an English army to live
off the Scottish countryside for long, and there is no indication
that Siward had one on this occasion.[62] In any case, once he was
gone, Macbeth returned and recovered the kingdom.[63] The fate
of Siward's king is unrecorded.

This king, who was probably Maldred, presumably was
killed, because Siward waited some eight years before he invaded
again. If Malcolm had been born in about 1031, he would have
reached the age of twenty-three by 1054, a prime age to try for a
throne that had to be won through battle. Certainly relations with
Scotland did not improve during these years. Scottish border raids
on the North either began or continued after 1046.[64] The years
around 1050 must have been quiet, while Macbeth is said to have
gone to Rome, but this peace did not outlast his pilgrimage, for in
1052, Macbeth received the Normans who had been expelled from
England as a result of Earl Godwin's restoration and took them
into his own service.[65] Macbeth's employment of mercenaries who
could only be profitably used against Siward shows that the situation was becoming serious again, and the events of 1053 imply that
he was raiding the North. In that year Siward went to Scotland
and made some agreement with Macbeth; he may have conducted
a full-scale invasion, although the evidence for supposing so is not
very satisfactory. In any case, Macbeth soon broke the agreement
and continued to raid the North.[66]

Thus the stage was set for Siward's famous invasion of
Scotland. In 1054, the earl collected an army from the North which

was reinforced by a group of King Edward's housecarls and by a contingent from Cumberland led by Dolfin, Thorfinn's son, and obtained a fleet that could bring supplies to the army.[67] The object of the expedition was to put Duncan's son Malcolm on the Scottish throne; both Edward and Siward must have hoped that as king he would end the hostility that had characterized the northern border since 1006. To achieve this end, Siward moved north and defeated Macbeth on the Day of the Seven Sleepers (July 27). The encounter was apparently a pitched battle in which many Scots and all of Macbeth's Norman mercenaries were killed. Siward lost a number of his own and the king's housecarls. Even though Macbeth himself escaped to Moray, where he survived for three anticlimactic years, Siward's victory had been complete enough for Malcolm to become king. The oldest accounts say no more; in fact, they fail to mention that Malcolm replaced Macbeth. Florence of Worcester, however, says that King Edward had ordered Siward both to make the expedition and to establish Malcolm as king.[68] Both statements are undoubtedly true in a simple descriptive sense, but it is inaccurate to give them a twelfth-century "feudal" meaning.[69] The Normans would do this soon enough. In 1054, Malcolm did not hold Scotland as Edward's vassal. He was king of Scots by inheritance and battle; his obligation to King Edward rested solely on gratitude.

After defeating Macbeth, Siward returned to England carrying with him a great amount of booty and probably believing that his expedition had been a success. The next year he died at York and was buried there in the monastery he had built and dedicated to St. Olaf. His bones were thus to be protected down through the ages by a fellow Scandinavian, an arrangement that suggests that the earl had remained at heart a Dane to his death. The stories of his physical prowess that are based on this aspect of his character and supported by Shakespeare's version of his war against Macbeth give Siward heroic stature. He stands out as the last great earl of the North; in the hands of the romantic, he becomes one of the last Vikings.[70] All this makes it very difficult to reach an accurate appraisal of his importance. If one's view is limited to his lifetime, Siward must be portrayed as a successful earl because he ruled Yorkshire without any known problems from about 1033 to 1055 and because he ended the revolt of the house of Bamburgh. The period of his strong rule gave the North a chance to recover from the turmoil of the preceding period and perhaps resulted in the creation of some bonds with the South. This was certainly the case with the church of Durham, where Siward had curtailed traditional liberties and installed its first southern bishop. Furthermore, he made concrete moves to blunt the growing threat from the Scots by the annexation of Cumberland, which provided protection to Yorkshire and Durham from hostile raids out of the West, and by his support of Malcolm Canmore, which seemed to promise a period of good relations with the Scots.

This is an impressive list of accomplishments, yet we should accept it with caution. According to later tradition, Siward was descended from a line of bears.[71] The attribution of such ancestry may be a direct reference to his physical strength, but Siward's descent from bears can be interpreted in another way: Siward ruled like a bear. He was formidable but lacked insight, and most of his policies depended on force or its threat. He had imposed an outsider on the clerks of Durham, whom they resented. He had become earl of Northumbria by wasting the countryside, and neither his marriage into the house of Bamburgh nor his accommodation with Cospatric, the heir of this family, won the goodwill of the Northumbrians. According to later tradition, they revolted against Siward while he was invading Scotland in 1054. This story should probably not be accepted as literally true, but it rests ultimately on the memory of his unpopularity above the Tees.[72] Siward's rule did nothing to end dissatisfaction in Northumbria; in fact, his actions fed unrest.

Much the same conclusions can be drawn with respect to Anglo-Scottish relations. Siward's policies did not lead to a stabilization of the border; rather, the situation deteriorated as a result of his acts. Even though Macbeth may have been a threat to the North, he was a peaceful neighbor in comparison to the ruler Siward had raised up in his place. Malcolm Canmore's loyalty to his English benefactors lasted exactly as long as he potentially needed their help. After this need had passed, he became a greater threat to the North than any of his predecessors had been, and during the next forty years he repeatedly led armies over the border. If Siward's support of Malcolm is judged by its results, it was a grave mistake. It brought no security to the North, only Scottish armies that pillaged and enslaved the northern peasants.

Finally, the defeat of Macbeth had been won at a high price. In the battle had died Dolfin, Thorfinn's son; Siward, Earl Siward's sister's son; and Osbeorn, the earl's eldest son.[73] Their deaths removed three potential leaders of the next generation; in particular, the losses of the younger Siward and Osbeorn seriously threatened the future of Siward's family. When the old earl died in the following year, he left no adult heir to become earl and defend the holdings and position of his family. The interests of Siward's one surviving son, the young Waltheof, were thus threatened and the way was opened for a disastrous experiment in the governing of the North, an experiment that ultimately culminated in the harrying of the North by William the Conqueror in 1069.

3. The Structure
of Northern Society

The obstacles in the way of forming a picture of northern society prior to the Norman Conquest are great in general and insurmountable on some points. The few surviving pre-Conquest charters are not very informative. Domesday Book would seem to offer an unexampled window into the last phase of Anglo-Saxon society in the North, but it is in reality a treacherous glass. The survey was made twenty years after the battle of Hastings by foreigners who did not understand everything they were recording and whose interest in conditions in 1066 was strictly limited to the question of who held what manor at that date. As a result, Domesday provides only a one-dimensional picture of landholding under King Edward and does not tell what, if any, arrangements the Anglo-Saxon landowners had made with respect to their lands. Because of the terms of the inquest, then, Domesday can contribute little to the discussion of whether feudalism existed in the North prior to the Conquest, and on other basic questions, it is almost as uncooperative. The description of Yorkshire is terse and uninformative; there are few double entries and no important statement of local customs of the sort that are so informative for other parts of England. Beyond Yorkshire, Domesday fails by degrees. Southern Lancashire is described in general and unsatisfactory terms; the sections on northern Lancashire are little more than a geld list; and Northumbria is not described at all. Aside from the light cast by occasional charters, conditions above the Tees are obscure until the compilation of Boldon Book, a custumal of the lands of the bishop of Durham made in 1183, and the beginning of the inquisitions post mortem in the thirteenth century.

These unpromising materials have been the object of a long tradition of scholarship devoted to the explanation of northern society and the Norman Conquest's impact on it. Part of this research has been a reflection of local antiquarian interest, but the subject has also attracted the attention of scholars of the stature of F. W. Maitland, J. E. A. Jolliffe, and Sir Frank Stenton and more recently G. W. S. Barrow and William Rees.[1] The principal reason for this interest concerns what may be termed the "survivals." In general, survivals are strange tenures such as thanage and drengage, unusual renders like cornage, and distinctive traditions of peasant custom that have few clear parallels in the rest of England after the Conquest. They first appear in Domesday's description of southern Lancashire and then in more detail in Boldon Book and the various thirteenth-century surveys. It is usually assumed that these survivals represent direct fragments of northern society from before 1066 and that, if only they can be put together correctly, they will yield at least a general picture of this society. This assumption may well be correct; certainly the method of arguing backward from the known to the unknown is a tool commonly used by Anglo-Saxon and other historians. It is somewhat disquieting, however, since in any such argument the presuppositions govern both the selection of the survival and its meaning. These are usually both clear and logical—if perhaps subject to debate—but often as regards the North they include basic ethnic suppositions such as that some particular custom is distinctively Celtic, Anglo-Saxon, or Danish. Ideas of this nature, particularly if they are coupled with the endless hypotheses of place-name studies, can easily take a historian from the surveys of the twelfth and thirteenth centuries back, not merely to the state of northern society on the eve of the Conquest, but into far earlier times, when the Angles and Celts were struggling for mastery of the province of Upper Britain in the post-Roman period or, in one notable case, to the days before the Celts themselves came to Britain.[2] These chains of reason and supposition are majestic, but they should prompt caution. This chapter will be principally concerned with the investigation of the structure of northern society during the last years of the Anglo-Saxon kingdom and will venture into the years before the Venerable Bede only under duress.

The inquiry must begin with Maitland. In 1890, in an important article dealing with the survivals, he argued that the thanes and drengs who could be found in Lancashire and Northumbria in the twelfth century and later were lineal descendants of pre-Conquest *ministri* and *equites* similar to Bishop Oswald's ridingmen and that the confusion of tenurial custom in the North after the Conquest was the result of the imposition of knight service on the old Anglo-Saxon tenures.[3] Although these conclusions have not been completely accepted, they were extremely important because they pointed in the right direction for further research and stimulated the labyrinthine mind of Jolliffe. He, in turn, created, for all practical purposes single-handedly, the current picture of Northumbrian society. But before he could do this, another ingredient was necessary besides the existence of survivals above the Tees and west of the Pennines; this was what may be called the Yorkshire moat. In a very real sense, the Yorkshire moat in its various guises has made possible the world of Northumbrian scholarship, and Sir Frank Stenton began its excavation in 1910. In that year he published a very good essay entitled "Types of Manorial Structure in the Northern Danelaw." The title seems to indicate that the work covered the Five Boroughs and Yorkshire, but such was not exactly the case. Stenton used Yorkshire Domesday for some important pieces of evidence for his construct of Danelaw society, but on the second page of his essay he cut Yorkshire loose with the assertion "that the harrying of Yorkshire in 1069 makes it impossible to argue with security from 1086 to the conditions of the Confessor's day."[4] Stenton later changed his mind and filled the moat with Danes, but the essential principle with respect to Northumbria did not change. Whether basically unknowable or populated by Danes, Yorkshire did not have to be studied with the lands to the north and west. This meant in practice that any reconstruction of Northumbrian society based on the twelfth- and thirteenth-century survivals did not have to be squared with Yorkshire Domesday.

The importance of this freedom was immense for Jolliffe. In 1926, he devoted forty-two pages of his most abstruse prose to explaining the nature of Northumbrian institutions both before and after 1066. This essay, although very hard to follow at points, covered most of the relevant evidence and was brilliant in its arguments and conclusions. Its general effect is monumental, and it has never been seriously challenged, probably because of his method of investigation. Jolliffe purposed to start at the bottom of society and work up. He submerged himself in the disjointed details of the twelfth- and thirteenth-century surveys and custumals, where no one was likely to follow, isolated the survivals, and combined them in a convincing picture of Northumbrian society. He assumed that peasant custom was functional in terms of the society within which it existed and that one could deduce the general structure of a "primitive" society from its body of custom.[5] Thanks to the Yorkshire moat, he could do this without worrying about the intractable folios of Yorkshire Domesday which, if nothing else, are an embodiment of the opposite principle that society is organized from the top down.[6]

Beyond questions of methodology, Jolliffe's main supposition was that the manor did not exist in Northumbria and Lancashire prior to the Conquest and that the vill was the basis of northern society. By the "manor," Jolliffe meant a village held by a mesne tenant that contained an internal demesne worked by the local peasants for the benefit of the holder of the village. He investigated the subject of peasant custom from the Mersey to the Tweed and found that the obligations borne by the peasants were inadequate for demesne cultivation on a large scale. The northern bonder, a term that may have meant no more than "villager," did indeed owe agricultural labor to his lord, but it was light and seasonal in character, designed to supplement the lord's demesne farming at critical times during the agricultural year. The bonder would usually be required to do one or two days' plowing, perhaps some harrowing, and almost invariably three or four boon days (the gift of a day's labor) in autumn. In addition, the peasants commonly helped cut the hay, carted hay, grain, and the millstone when necessary, and did specified amounts of structural work around the lord's hall and the mill. These obligations were by no means trivial, but they did not include week work (the obligation to work for the manorial lord a set number of days each week) and left the northern peasant free to do his own work for most of the year. The real burden of the peasants, at least on the east coast plain, lay in their renders of grain, malt, and chickens and their payments, originally in kind, for feasts, pannage, and cornage (a cattle render). These renders and services were forinsec (outside) in the sense that they were rendered, not to a demesne or to a manor house within the vill, but to a lord's hall with an attached demesne that was exterior to the vill. That is, groups of these bondage vills were dependent upon a lord's hall. They supported a central demesne with their

labor services, intercommoned on the waste, and formed a jurisdictional unit. Such an agglomeration of unmanorialized, bondage
vills around a central demesne and hall, Jolliffe called a "shire,"
and he argued that this type of organization (hereafter called the
"shire system") was general throughout all the lands of the old
Northumbrian kingdom in 1066 except for the bulk of Yorkshire,
where it had been destroyed by the Danes.[7]

He further thought that the renders and services by which
the peasants supported the lord of the shire were originally (and
inferentially as late as 1066) communal responsibilities and that
they were more like renders to a prefeudal prince than payments
of rent to a landlord. The bonder's obligations were originally public duties. He owed them as a member of the community, and they
did not depend on the amount of land he held. Jolliffe asserted
that, prior to 1066, Northumbria lacked a well-developed theory of
ownership (by which he seems to have meant mesne ownership)
and that the intermediate tenures of thanage and drengage were
ministerial in nature. To the Normans, the thanes and drengs, who
were sometimes associated with bondage vills, seemed to stand
between these vills and the lord of the shire, to hold the vills, as it
were; but Jolliffe was at pains to argue that before the arrival of the
Normans the thanes and drengs did not hold the vills or intercept
any of the bonders' dues and services. They held land within the
vill, not the whole vill, and were responsible for supervising the
collection of the renders in kind and the performance of the
forinsec labor services.[8] They were thus essentially stewards, necessary for superintending the widely dispersed villages of the shire,
but persons of no great consequence, who could not be considered
protofeudal nobles as Maitland had done.

Such was Jolliffe's picture of Northumbrian society. Above
the Tees and west of the mountains the countryside was filled in
1066 with shires, large numbers of bondage vills dependent upon a
central *caput*. These shires were inhabited by a very small number
of great nobles, a ministerial lower nobility composed of thanes
and drengs, and a peasantry that consisted of bonders who still
possessed many of the attributes of freemen.[9] Jolliffe's mastery of
the evidence and his arguments make his construct convincing, but
it is just that—a logical construct. With the ambiguous exception
of the Domesday description of Lancashire, which the Normans
clearly bungled, it touches no evidence from before the coming of

the Normans. This does not mean, of course, that it is incorrect (and Jolliffe's treatment of northern peasant custom seems unassailable), but it does mean that his theory needs two things to be convincing which a simple, direct argument from a body of evidence does not need: Jolliffe required theories that would explain the origin of these institutions and their decline. The first he provided in the closing pages of his essay, where he noted a number of parallels between Northumbrian and Welsh customs and suggested that the unique nature of Northumbrian society had its origin in an extensive mingling of Celt and Angle during the early Middle Ages. Indeed, he thought that in the West this mingling probably resulted from the direct annexation of Celtic principalities by the conquering Angles.[10] This theory of Celtic influence on the formation of Northumbria would adequately explain why the North of England was not like the South, where all the Celts had supposedly fled or been killed, but Jolliffe's picture of northern society still needed a theory of decline that would put it in direct contact with the evidence from after the Conquest upon which all his arguments backward were ultimately based. This was necessary because few examples of functioning shires are found in the surveys and inquisitions. Rather, they are filled with groups of villages that rather look like sections or fragments of vanished shires. To connect these shire segments with the hypothetical functioning shires of 1066, Jolliffe developed a theory of truncation. Baldly put, the Normans truncated the shires. Although they did this in a number of ways, two stand out. The Normans had a well-developed sense of mesne ownership; therefore, grants of the old dependent vills by the tenants-in-chief to their vassals disrupted the traditional system of forinsec works and dues within the shires. Later, the growth of demesne farming during the twelfth century prompted lords to concentrate their energy on parts of the old shires and to liquidate their immediate hold on the more remote villages, whose services and renders were no longer profitable.[11] These two mechanisms were largely responsible for the fragmentation of the shires, and they connect Jolliffe's model of Northumbrian society before 1066 with the evidence of the later Middle Ages.

Given the nature of the evidence, Jolliffe's delineation of Northumbrian society is brilliant. His argument from the High Medieval survivals back to the Anglo-Saxon period are convincing, and his theory of truncation is plausible. His conclusions have not, however, become common in the textbooks,[12] and this is rather curious. One would expect that the more interesting parts of his work would be his general picture of Northumbrian society and his ideas on the impact of the Normans on this system since both are unusual in comparison with southern England. But only one serious attempt has been made to test Jolliffe's ideas in the light of the history of an individual shire (Blackburnshire),[13] and the attention of scholars has been turned elsewhere. In particular, they have been interested in pursuing Jolliffe's theory on the origin of Northumbrian institutions. He thought that the Celts of northern Britain had played a significant part in the formation of Northumbrian society because he saw a number of parallels between Northumbrian and Welsh customs in the high Middle Ages that he believed could not have resulted from the independent development of the two societies. He suggested several specific examples of such parallels, but he did not argue his point in detail, probably because he thought the similarity obvious.[14] That it should have been obvious —at least from a certain point of view—has emerged from the recent discussion of this theme by William Rees and G. W. S. Barrow, who have worked out the points that follow. These may appear somewhat tangential to the subject of northern society, but the quest for Celtic universals has become so involved with the question of Northumbrian institutions that these comparisons must be discussed.

The parallels are impressive. The bondmen of the Welsh commotes owed their prince renders and services that were strikingly similar to those owed by the northern bonders to the lord of the shire. They gave renders of food for feasts (the *gwestfa*) twice a year as did the northern bonders on the east coast plain. They had to support the local serjeants of the peace (the *cais*) by giving them lodging and food (the *cylch cais*). This same duty lay on many of the bonders of the northern counties, where a very similar system of serjeants of the peace existed. The Welsh bondmen and many of the peasants in Durham owed virtually identical structural works for the building of the lord's hall, chamber, and auxiliary buildings, and in both places they often had to feed the lord's horse and dogs. Finally, at least in certain lordships in eastern Wales, the inhabitants were burdened with *commorth*, a cattle render paid every second or third year, and this custom is said to have been a nearly exact parallel to the cornage and other allied cattle payments made in the twelfth and thirteenth centuries by many of the bondage vills, Norman mesne lordships, and even baronies in the lands north of the Tees and the Ribble.[15] These points of comparison establish the marked similarity between Northumbrian and Welsh custom which Jolliffe originally pointed out. In fact, aside from the northern bonder's obligation to help maintain the mill of the shire, the only significant segment of his burdens that has found no place in the comparison with Welsh custom is his seasonal agricultural works, but perhaps even these should be included. Jolliffe thought that the Welsh *maerdref*, that is, the prince's demesne land within the commote that was cultivated by the bondsmen of the dependent hamlets, only developed in the course of the thirteenth century. Glanville R. J. Jones, however, has argued with great determination and some force that the development of both agricultural bond hamlets and the prince's *maerdref* took place much earlier in Wales than has been commonly thought. If he is correct, the shire and the commote become nearly identical institutions through which a dispersed peasantry supported a prince by renders in kind and seasonal works.[16]

Such a conclusion would be more than a matter of mere antiquarian interest. If the shire and the commote are essentially the same institution, as the parallels between them seem to indicate, one would think that the shire must have been originally a Celtic institution. Whether or not one accepts Jones's further argument that this institution, the discrete estate, actually goes back to pre-Roman times,[17] the Anglo-Saxons at least can no longer be pictured as having exterminated every last Celt who did not flee to the hills and mountains of western Britain. Such a reassessment is the intellectual prize to be won by the tedious comparisons of peasant customs. If the method is valid, it offers the possibility of modifying the idea that in its origin England was purely Germanic and un-influenced by any Celtic element. The potential importance of this conclusion, in turn, explains why historians have concentrated on the first part of Jolliffe's theory without questioning his basic picture of Northumbrian society. The latter is altogether too convenient, not to mention too complex, to be tinkered with in this day when the advocates of the Celts, or in the case of Jones, the pre-Celts, are demanding their due in the making of England.

The scope of this discussion has recently been enlarged to

include Scotland, and here the object is the same: to clarify the nature of ancient Celtic institutional arrangements by the isolation and comparison of survivals. Hitherto, this land has been largely protected from such comparisons, even when they seem obvious, by the assumption that Northumbria was entirely Germanic in its structure.[18] This conclusion is, however, unwarranted, and G. W. S. Barrow has pointed out a number of specific parallels between Scottish and Northumbrian institutions as a result of the vantage point he has acquired from editing the charters of Malcolm IV and William the Lion. With respect to eastern Lothian and the Merse, these parallels are not surprising. Both had been part of the Northumbrian kingdom, and Jolliffe himself thought that their institutional makeup was the same as that to the south. Thanes and drengs formed the nobility in this area, and the tenure of the drengs, at least, was ministerial. The thanes of Lothian held shires, and the few examples of early peasant custom that survive from this region show a system of works and renders nearly identical with that found in Northumbria.[19] In addition to reemphasizing these points, Barrow has contributed the observation that the similarities did not stop on the borders of ancient Northumbria. In West Lothian, eastern Stirling, and throughout eastern Scotland generally up to Ross, the native nobility below the earls consisted of thanes in the twelfth and later centuries. These thanes held areas called shires from the king by a tenure that seems to have closely resembled the feudal tenure of fee-farm, and their shires were often identical with the parish. These points are revealing because in Northumbria the thanes were also classed by the Normans with the tenants in fee-farm, and the shires had apparently once been identical with the parish. Barrow further noted that a substantial number of the names of the shires above the Forth were of an early type; and, although the evidence on the thanes is not very detailed, he was unable to find significant differences between them and the Northumbrian thanes discussed by Jolliffe.[20] There was, then, an apparent structural similarity, at least on the upper levels, between eastern Scotland and Northumbria. The possibility of common origins is supported by certain revenues of the Scottish king. He had traditionally the right to collect two nearly universal tributes that were the mainstay of his government and seem to have their parallels both in the North of England and in Wales. Throughout Scotland north of the Forth and the lands of the defunct kingdom of Strathclyde, the king received cain either every year or once every several years. The cain was a food render that in the West consisted of cows, pigs, and cheese; Barrow argued that it was the Scottish equivalent of cornage, the cattle render that many of the Northumbrian bondage vills owed. The second great tribute of the Scottish king was coneveth. It was found in eastern Scotland, including Lothian, and consisted of feasts owed to the king by the populace. Not surprisingly, Barrow saw in it a parallel with the feasts that a number of the bondage vills and drengages in Northumbria and Lothian owed under the name of waiting.[21]

Barrow concluded his initial discussion of these points by suggesting that the king of Scotland's cain and coneveth, the king of England's cornage and waiting, and the Welsh prince's *commorth* and *gwestfa*—not to mention the king of Man's *pecunia* (cattle) and *acconeuez* (coneveth?)—represented a common system of renders and by asking what the relationship was between these hospitality dues that appear to have been widespread in highland Britain.[22] At the time, he did not formally answer this question just as he did not answer similar questions that he posed about the relationships between the Scottish thanes and the Northumbrian thanes, between cain and cornage, or between the system of serjeants of the peace in Scottish Strathclyde and its counterpart in the North of England—but the general terms of his discussion made one answer inevitable: a theory of radical Celtic origins for the institutional structure of the highland zone. Indeed, in his most recent treatment of these matters he has embraced and even gone beyond this position. Barrow has argued not merely that the shires and thanes of Northumbria and Scotland were the same institutions, but that all of eastern Britain from Kent to Scotia had once been subject to a similar system of extensive royal lordship. This system was based on large groupings of dependent villages around a royal center to which they rendered food and labor, and it had existed in Scotland (and, by inference, therefore, in England) before the Picts had been converted to Christianity.[23]

What began as a fairly harmless discussion of the survivals of pre-Conquest Northumbrian society has produced some sweeping conclusions. One is being asked to see in the survivals the fag end of an old royal support system that remained in operation in Wales and Scotland as late as the twelfth and thirteenth centuries and survived in Northumbria in a recognizable form as late as the

Norman Conquest. Up to this date, the structure of society in northern Britain was basically uniform on its upper levels. The countryside of both eastern Scotland and Northumbria was divided into shires held by thanes above the Tweed and by lords of the shire south of this river. These men rendered the great hospitality dues to the king and directly supported the local police just as the men of the Welsh commotes did for their prince. Such is the picture yielded by Northumbrian scholarship and its offshoot, the search for Celtic universals. It is all very symmetrical and rather majestic.

The question, of course, is whether it can be accepted, and I fear that it cannot for two reasons. In the first place, the comparisons of custom upon which this edifice is raised are overgeneralized and ignore certain major difficulties. The cain of eastern Scotland, for instance, was a general food render, principally of grain, not a cow render like cornage.[24] Thus it cannot be identified with cornage, even if the latter was a commutation of old food renders as Rees thought, because there was actually a well-developed system of grain renders in Durham and Northumberland that ran parallel with cornage.[25] Should one conclude that there had been two systems of food tribute in Northumbria or that Rees was wrong about cornage? The latter alternative seems more likely since it is simpler to equate the Northumbrian grain renders with cain, but this does not solve all the problems. Cornage would need a new explanation. The question of why there is no sign of royal cain, cornage, or even peasant grain renders in Lothian and the Merse would still remain.[26] Theoretically this area should provide institutional links between Northumbria and Scotland, but it does not. Waiting is also a problem because it is not altogether clear that it was as common in Northumbria as these discussions imply.[27] Finally, *commorth* was not a general obligation that ran parallel with *gwestfa* in Wales but was restricted to certain lordships along the border.[28] These serious difficulties do not necessarily mean that the attempts to compare Scottish, Northumbrian, and Welsh customs are ultimately wrong, but they do weaken the comparisons by destroying the symmetry upon which they mainly depend for their force.

The second reason why this picture cannot be accepted is that these comparisons are either directly or indirectly based upon Jolliffe's work. His reconstruction of Northumbrian society has gone unquestioned because of its convenience and complexity, but there is reason to believe that it is defective because of his basic approach, that is, his endeavor to reconstruct Northumbrian society from the bottom up. This approach caused him almost completely to ignore the place in society of the men who held the shires, his "lords of the shire," and consequently produced an artificially primitive (prefeudal) impression of Northumbrian society. Furthermore, he described an essentially frozen system. There are no mechanisms for change in this society, and it survives unaltered down to its truncation by the Normans. Both of these are serious flaws. On a theoretical level they limit the validity of his conclusions, and they may be responsible for the difficulties encountered in the comparison of custom. A theory of institutional divergence might clarify the situation, but this is just what Jolliffe's denial of change precludes.

It is one thing, however, to say that Jolliffe is probably wrong and quite another to show where. These difficulties probably cannot be cleared up and a theory of institutional divergence supplied simply by reworking the material he covered. Many of his conclusions seem indisputable, and the real problem is that his evidence is, in effect, one-dimensional. This limitation is inescapable unless some earlier information can be brought to bear on these subjects, and it is here that the Yorkshire moat becomes a matter of the first importance. If the society in Yorkshire in 1066 was not radically different from the one above the Tees, Domesday's description of Yorkshire can be used to supplement and check Jolliffe's reconstruction of Northumbrian society before the Conquest. If, on the other hand, the Danes seriously altered society south of the Tees, such a comparison would not be meaningful.

In other words, it must be determined if the Yorkshire moat will hold water. The concept itself is, in fact, suspicious. This chasm is altogether too convenient for both Northumbrian historians and students of the Danelaw. It allows the former to argue backward from high medieval evidence without any worry that their constructs will be threatened by Yorkshire Domesday, and it permits the latter to ascribe institutions to the Danes without bothering to consider parallel institutions above the Tees. In the face of such wondrous utility, one might well ask for evidence, and here the question becomes very curious. The disquieting truth is that Domesday has been used as the principal direct proof throughout

the Danelaw that the Danes had altered the structure of society.
The reason is twofold. On the one hand, there is practically no
evidence that discloses what effect the Danes had had on native
English society prior to 1066; but, on the other hand, eastern
England appears to be rather different from the western Midlands
and Wessex when these regions are described in Domesday. In
particular, the East is characterized by the soke and by sokemen.
Logically, of course, the restriction of this institution and social
group to eastern England proves absolutely nothing because this
region might have been distinctive before the arrival of the Danes
and because Northumbria, which might have had a similar structure, is not described in Domesday. This last point is of particular
importance because it is doubtful if the Tees had ever formed a
boundary between Durham and Yorkshire, but the distribution of
the soke as it appears in Domesday has nonetheless created the
presumption that the Danes were responsible for the differences
between the Danelaw and the rest of England. Furthermore, this
presumption has been strengthened as the impact of the Danes on
the place names, personal nomenclature, and customary law of
eastern England has been worked out. Within these realms their
influence, whether direct or indirect, was certainly great, thus
facilitating the belief that they influenced the basic framework of
society as well.[29]

In terms of the structure of society, the question of the
Danish impact on eastern England can be limited to the territorial
soke. Was it a Scandinavian creation or a native institution that had
survived the ninth century? Generally speaking, sokes were estates
that consisted of a main village with dependent pieces of property
called berewicks and sokelands. The larger territorial sokes covered
wide stretches of countryside, and the berewicks and sokelands
might be either complete villages or parts of a village. The resemblance between this type of estate and the Northumbrian shire is
obvious, but the identification of the two has been barred by the
idea that the sokes were Danish. In its modern form this hypothesis
is mainly the work of Sir Frank Stenton. His definition of the soke
as an institution would preclude such an identification. He admitted that in some sokes the sokemen owed their lord light agricultural services such as mowing or helping with the harvest, which
were survivals of premanorial conditions and were not derogatory.
"But in general it would seem that the tenant within a soke held his

land by suit of court and a money rent. . . . The territorial sokes of the eleventh century rest upon a great body of custom constraining a lord's dependents, free and unfree, to seek his court, his mill, his fold, his church, to the exclusion of all competing institutions."[30] Stenton emphasized that the sokes were held together by suit, rents, and nonderogatory service; in 1927, he would call it "honorable" service. Sokes were basically jurisdictional units that could not be confused with shires. The main purpose of this definition, however, was not to differentiate sokes and shires, although it incidentally did so. Rather, the nature of the sokes after 1066 had to be in accordance with their origins, which Stenton saw as the direct result of the Danish settlement. He envisaged the Danish invasions as having been a folk migration of free and equal peasant warriors "at least comparable in scale to the later movement from which the duchy of Normandy arose." He thought that they had come in massive numbers and that the territorial sokes had resulted "from the settlement of the rank and file of the Danish armies around the men who had led them in the invasion." The sokelands were the estates these free warriors had occupied; and, for obvious reasons, it would not do to have their supposed descendants, the sokemen, burdened with services inappropriate to their rank. Thus the Danes came to occupy the Yorkshire moat and the lands to the south. There was, as Stenton admitted, no direct proof for this hypothesis,[31] but his prestige was such that it has been accepted. It meant, of course, that Domesday could be taken at face value as describing a society basically altered by a large influx of Danes.

To lay the burden for the creation of this intellectual chasm across the face of England solely on Stenton would be unjust and inaccurate, however, because initially Jolliffe concurred completely. In his work on Northumbria, he investigated the question of whether shire survivals existed in Yorkshire, and he found several examples of them in the West Riding and the western part of the North Riding. The existence of shire survivals in western Yorkshire and their absence from the Vale of York and the East Riding led Jolliffe to conclude that "the line at which . . . [Northumbrian] custom stops is not an early Anglo-Celtic frontier, but a Danish one, that of the kingdom of Anlaf which destroyed Deira, and the break is too abrupt to leave its meaning doubtful."[32] In other words, the Danes destroyed the shire system throughout most of Yorkshire. Somewhat later, however, Jolliffe modified this position.

In an interpretive essay published in 1934, he argued that the territorial sokes were not of Danish origin, that sokes and North-umbrian shires were analogous institutions arising from the pre-feudal stage of Anglo-Saxon society, and that the bonds of suit, rent, and service that held the sokes together were ancient royal dues. This was not exactly a statement that the soke and the shire were the same institution; rather, they were both relics of the "era of the folk" and had originally served the same end.[33] The impli-cation was that Domesday still did not describe Northumbrian institutions.

That this position came very close to enjoying the best of both worlds did not become a serious problem, for Jolliffe's ex-planation of the soke has been largely ignored. This is unfortunate because he was more right than wrong, but it is understandable. His arguments on Yorkshire were either general or ill-conceived, and they were too weak to drive the cohorts of Danish sokemen out of Yorkshire.[34] A good deal of recent work, however, supports the general idea that the territorial soke was an Anglo-Saxon (or Anglo-Celtic) institution. P. H. Sawyer has shown that the Danish armies numbered between two and three hundred men rather than in the thousands, and he has suggested ways a dominant aristocracy of relatively small size could affect place names and law as the Danes did.[35] This discovery is of fundamental importance because it destroys the idea that the Danish invasions represented a folk migration and deprives the sokemen of most of their hypo-thetical Danish forefathers. Even more to the point has been the work of R. H. C. Davis, who has investigated the socage customs of East Anglia, which the Danes are usually regarded as having intro-duced. He would translate "soke," not as "jurisdiction," but as "customs which the aforesaid land owes the king." These customs consisted of hidage, wardpenny, and foddercorn in addition to mowing services, relief, and gersum, and Davis was able to show that sokeland, the land burdened with these services, was pre-Danish in origin: "It is the relic of a period when the land was divided into districts covering several villages, which were admin-istered from a common center and provided the king with his 'feorm' or food rents." He thought that this system had once been much like the Northumbrian shires, the lathes of Kent, or the Welsh commotes, but that its outlines had been obscured by the commutation of the renders and by royal grants to the nobles and the church of the dues and services the sokelands produced.[36]

Davis did his work before Sawyer, and it is therefore understandable why he did not feel that his conclusion that the sokeland was Anglo-Saxon could be extended to the northern Danelaw.[37] He still faced the concept of the Danish invasion as a folk migration and the very real presence of the invasion's latter-day outriders, the philologists; they, in turn, were now burdened with the necessity of explaining why sokeland was Danish in one area and Anglo-Saxon in another. This has never been done, and the only important extension of the discussion beyond certain attacks on Sawyer's theories on the formation of place names, which have sought to reintroduce the idea that the Danes settled in England in large numbers, has been the work of G. W. S. Barrow and Glanville R. J. Jones. On the strength of Davis's definition of soke and morphological similarities, Barrow has denied that there was any difference between the sokes of the northern Danelaw and those of East Anglia and has argued that the Danes could not have created the former because these were only local examples of a system that had once been general throughout eastern England and Scotland. Indeed, Barrow has given evidence from Scotland that may suggest this system had existed before the Picts were converted to Christianity,[38] and Jones's research has been still more ambitious. His interest has been unique in that he has been trying to establish the Celtic origins of the discrete estate. The soke is a regional example of the discrete estate, as is the shire, and Jones has argued that the sokes in Yorkshire were formed when the Celts subjugated the pre-Celtic population of the area.[39] If this idea were correct, it would immediately reduce the theory of a Danish origin of the sokes to nonsense and make their identification as an Anglo-Saxon institution a secondary matter, the result of Anglo-Saxons replacing Celts as the lords of these estates. Unfortunately, Jones has very little evidence to work with, and his arguments are of necessity extremely tenuous.[40] They cannot be taken as established fact, although they may be correct. One immediate result, however, of his determination to prove the Celtic origin of the discrete estate has been his discussion of the Danish place names of Yorkshire. He has argued persuasively that most of them were the result of the Danes renaming Anglo-Saxon villages and were not new creations, and he has hypothesized that the important Danish leaders took over the soke centers and granted out the dependent villages to their followers, from whom most of the *by*-names with a personal name for a first element were derived. This last point is particularly important because it provides a reasonable explanation for the aristocratic implications of the numerous *by*-names of eastern England that have never been adequately accounted for on the basis of a mass migration of free and equal warriors.[41] Furthermore, it would account for the fact that the main villages of the Danelaw sokes have an embarrassing tendency to have English names.[42]

Taken together, the discoveries of Sawyer, Davis, and Jones strongly suggest that the Danes did not significantly alter the institutional structure of the Danelaw and that the soke was an Anglo-Saxon institution. The latest research on the Danes in Normandy has produced similar conclusions[43] and provides new support for Jolliffe's idea that the soke and the shire were analogous institutions. Unfortunately, the issue is not settled. If the soke was a native institution, it becomes important to determine whether Jolliffe's concept of analogy is correct or whether this idea is only a smoke screen, a new version of the Yorkshire moat that will save the primitive simplicity of Northumbria while dragging the Danelaw into the realm of the Anglo-Saxon "folk." Once the influence of the Danes is discounted, the history of the Northumbrian kingdom provides no basis for assuming that Yorkshire was different in its institutional makeup from the lands above the Tees. Two features of its rural structure that are immediately apparent suggest that the distinction might be groundless. First, there are examples of sokes in Yorkshire that were called "shires." Both Howden and (North) Allerton were called shires, and so were Hallam and Sowerby, a division of the Wakefield soke.[44] Second, the verbal identification of sokes and shires is matched by an even more curious phenomenon on the level of peasant custom. Although Yorkshire is not blessed with numerous documents disclosing the nature of local peasant custom, occasional significant examples do appear in the late twelfth and thirteenth centuries. The earliest instances are in the Templars' Inquest of 1185, a document roughly contemporaneous with Boldon Book. One set of these customs, those of Temple Newsham in the West Riding, reveals a very important point. Here the peasants, who held either one or two bovates each, paid yearly 30d. per bovate, 2 hens, and 20 eggs, and during the course of the year they plowed and harrowed for four days, mowed and made hay one day, and did four boon days in autumn. In addition, they were responsible for repairing the mill-pond, bringing new millstones to the village, and washing and shearing the sheep for two days. These customs were not unique. The Templars' Inquest reveals that similar customs were followed at Skelton and Colton, both in the West Riding, and at Alwarthorpe in the East Riding.[45] The thirteenth-century inquisitions post mortem show in more detail that services of the same type were rendered at Harewood in the West Riding, at Kirkby Moorside in the North Riding, and at Burton Agnes in the East Riding.[10] Other examples of the same customary tradition could be cited, but the point of these examples is not to fill thirteenth-century Yorkshire with villages where the peasants followed these customs. Such a picture would be very inaccurate because the harrying of 1069 had destroyed many of the old villages. These lands were redeveloped during the twelfth century by peasants who held them on easy terms.[47] This process and commutation produced a preponderance of rent tenures by the thirteenth century, but the wide dispersal and uniformity of the system of services exemplified by those at Temple Newsham probably mean that these services had been the normal customary system before 1069. Jolliffe unaccountably did not investigate this point although it is of primary importance. His picture of Northumbrian society was based on peasant custom and the renders it yielded, yet the peasants of Yorkshire apparently had been under a very similar system. Except for the grain renders and cornage of the Northumbrian bonder, his services are matched point by point by those of the Yorkshire villein. Both were limited to specific tasks at critical times during the year, and neither were subject to week work.

These points are not conclusive, but the occasional verbal identification of sokes and shires and the probable existence of a common system of customary labor on either side of the Tees before 1069 certainly make Jolliffe's idea that sokes and shires were only analogous open to doubt. In terms of evidence, as opposed to utility, he held this position as a result of his original work on Northumbria that had led him to negative conclusions: "In Yorkshire the system seems to have vanished altogether from the central plain. There is no clear evidence that Howdenshire or Allertonshire were shires in more than name, and on the east the most southern drengage was at Marske, near Middlesbrough. In the west, however, drengage tenures survive in the honour of Richmond, and a number of vills are burdened with forinsec works. The same is true in a less [sic] degree of the soke of Knaresborough, the manor of Thorpe Arch, and the district of Leeds, while cornage is still paid in the fee of Bowes Castle."[48] This distribution of shire survivals was the basis for Jolliffe's initial conclusion that the Danes had destroyed the shire system in Yorkshire, and when he later perceived the similarity between the soke and the shire, it stood in the way of the obvious solution of the problem: the complete identification of the two institutions. His examples of surviving shire customs, principally forinsec labor dues, were few and restricted to western Yorkshire, and therefore—if for no other reason—sokes and shires could not be the same. In actuality, however, this distribution is false. For whatever reason, Jolliffe minimized the examples of Northumbrian custom that he found and failed to discover a considerable body of additional evidence.

In the first place, Northumbrian custom was more common in the western part of the shire than Jolliffe's brief discussion would indicate. As late as the thirteenth century, a number of dependent estates were linked to their manorial centers by forinsec agricultural works that were similar to those rendered by Northumbrian bondage vills to the shire centers, and frequently these works still rested on the vill as a whole, rather than on the individual tenants. The men of Burneston, for example, owed forinsec plowing and reaping at Carthorpe, and the inhabitants of Lofthouse rendered similar works at the manor of Harewood: "The whole township of Lofthus ought to find three boonworks with three ploughs yearly at the lord's food . . . and also thirty-three reapers in autumn for one day at the lord's food." Harewood also received these services from the dependent estates of Newhall and Stubb House, but in these cases the old bondage dues had been attached to the mesne tenures by 1263, the date of the survey.[49] Jolliffe did not note either of these instances, nor did he find that the men of Denton owed plowing and reaping services at Otley as late as 1315 or that five vills owed similar services at Ripon.[50] These were important omissions, but the soke of Knaresborough is, perhaps, the best example of his failure to follow his own leads. He knew of three vills burdened with forinsec works in this estate. Actually, however, eighteen vills seem to have owed boonworks at

Knaresborough, and the old obligation of feeding the lord's dogs, which was characteristic of many Durham villages, was still in force.[51] Finally, the sokemen of Sheffield did hunting and forest services that may have been similar (it is impossible to be certain) to those found in western Durham.[52]

When combined with Jolliffe's examples, these instances of forinsec works establish that shire customs were far from uncommon in western Yorkshire, but the really important point is that his distinction between the west and the rest of the shire will not stand. There are examples of surviving shire customs in the south and the east. Although they seem to be less numerous than in the west, they have a significance beyond their numbers, for there is reason to believe that the harrying was more severe in the Vale of York, the eastern part of the North Riding, and the East Riding than on the flanks of the Pennines, whence many of the western survivals come.[53] The examples are of several sorts. On the one hand, there were household rents and forinsec agricultural services that must have originated in a vanished shire at Kirkby Moorside in the East Riding.[54] On the other hand, a number of Norman mesne tenures bore incidents that had once lain on bondage vills or tenures in drengage. In the far south of the shire, the manor of Stainton was held of the castle of Tickhill by knight service, yet all the men of the manor, free and unfree, had to plow for ten days on the demesne of the castle.[55] This is the sole case in Yorkshire of a type of tenure more common further north that resulted from knight service being imposed on an old bondage vill, but analogous tenures on a lower level existed in the eastern part of the county. In 1255, Osbert de Bolbec held his manor at Levisham in the Vale of Pickering by rent, suit to court, and harrowing at Pickering castle.[56] Jolliffe failed to notice either of these tenures, and this was a serious omission because the twelfth-century charters show that such tenures as that at Levisham were more common than the later inquisitions indicate. The earliest example comes from about 1120–28, when Aschetin de Hawsker received Normanby and Hawsker from the abbot of Whitby to hold by paying 24s. rent and by doing one boon plowing and one autumn boon day each year, and similar tenures are recorded later in the century at Guisborough, at Welbury in the Vale of York, and at Sixtendale in the East Riding.[57] Finally, there is the problem of drengs. Their tenure was an integral part of shire organization, and Jolliffe argued that the survival of drengage in an area indicated that a shire had existed there.[58] In this reasoning he was correct, but he incorrectly maintained that the southernmost drengage in Yorkshire was at Marske on the northeast coast. Deep in the East Riding, three drengs survived into the thirteenth century at Burton Agnes, and several others existed during this period at Driffield and apparently in Howdenshire.[59]

Jolliffe's distribution crumbles in the face of these examples of forinsec services and drengs. Shire customs were more numerous than he thought and were not restricted to the west of the shire. Along with the fact that the general system of customary labor prior to 1069 closely resembled that followed in Northumbria, this discovery strongly indicates that such customs represented the predominant system before the Norman Conquest and greatly increases the probability that the obvious equation of sokes and shires is correct. Actually, one does not need to speak in terms of probability. A number of the examples discussed above show that the dependent members of the territorial sokes, the berewicks and sokelands, were linked to the soke center by the same type of seasonal agricultural services as those that tied the bondage vills to the shire center. Of course, by the time of Domesday, the tenurial arrangements in the county had been disrupted by the harrying, the allocation of lands to the Normans, and an arbitrary reclassification of sokelands as berewicks. These factors create a degree of ambiguity,[60] but the relationships involved are still clear. Denton had been a berewick of Otley in 1086; in 1315, the inhabitants of the vill still performed one day's plowing and one day's reaping at Otley.[61] Ledeston had been a berewick of Kippax in 1086; in the early thirteenth century it owed forinsec plowing at Kippax.[62] Levisham, on the other hand, had been sokeland of Pickering in the eleventh century; it did harrowing at Pickering in 1255.[63] Hawsker had also been sokeland in 1086, and it rendered a day's plowing and reaping at its old soke center of Whitby in the 1120s.[64] Three of the five vills that owed plowing and reaping services to Ripon were classified as either berewicks or sokelands in Domesday,[65] and the same forinsec dependence existed in the manor of Knaresborough. The post-Conquest manor was a combination of the old sokes of Aldborough and Knaresborough. Seven of the nineteen vills that did boonworks had been either berewicks or sokelands in 1086, and the remainder are either not in

Domesday or are deceptively listed with a miscellaneous group of king's thegns.[66]

The soke and the Northumbrian shire were the same institution. This idea may sound radical, but it is in complete accord with Davis's work on East Anglia and provides a foundation for Jones's idea that the Danes mainly took over existing villages. Nor is it in basic conflict with the work of Stenton except on the question of the origin of the sokes. The bulk of his work can endure the idea of an English origin of this institution, and his assertion that the greater sokes were held together by money rents in addition to the several types of suit can be explained as the result of the commutation of old dues. The most serious objection to this interpretation would come from Northumbrian scholars, who would probably raise at least three basic questions, and these must be discussed for their answers will complete the destruction of the Yorkshire moat and seriously change Jolliffe's picture of Northumbrian society.

The questions revolve around the fact that, although the general nature of peasant custom and the forinsec dependence of sokeland are indeed reminiscent of Northumbrian custom, certain other equally characteristic marks of the shire system do not appear in Yorkshire. Domesday, for instance, records only four drengs in Yorkshire, and such individuals should be much more common if the shire system existed south of the Tees.[67] This objection would be wrong on two counts. In the first place, the Domesday commissioners were only interested in putting on record who owned any particular manor in 1066, not who may have been in possession, so that drengs, who did not have a freehold according to Jolliffe, would not have been recorded under 1066. Second, Domesday does record men in possession in 1086 and should note any drengs, but its description of southern Lancashire uses the terms "thane" and "dreng" interchangeably, which means that the small thanes listed in Yorkshire in 1086 may well have been of the same ministerial class as those in Lancashire.[68] This possibility is supported by three facts. First, the four drengs mentioned in Yorkshire are recorded in the very first folio before any mention of thanes, which suggests that the clerks decided to abandon the uncouth title of "dreng" at this point in favor of the more familiar "thane." Second, the small Yorkshire thanes paid the same relief, 40s., as the thanes and drengs of Lancashire.[69] These are important considerations, but the most significant piece of evidence is a long list of some 328 small manors included under the land of the king. These manors form a compact group at the end of the description of the king's larger estates; they were predominantly small, generally ranging in size from one-half carucate to five carucates. They had been held by named individuals in 1066, and their description in Domesday provides no clear reason why they were not listed with the king's thanes.[70] Their absence from this section might be explained by the hypothesis that these manors had not been part of the king's demesne before the Conquest and that they were confiscated estates, but this explanation cannot be true. One of the most important characteristics of the ministerial thanes and drengs on the royal demesne in Lancashire in 1066 was that they paid rent for their "manors,"[71] and the same was true of the small thanes on the royal demesne in Yorkshire. This is clear from the values ascribed to their manors for 1066. These do not represent a real sequence of numbers such as would be produced by even a rough estimation of the yearly value of 328 manors of varying size scattered over the face of the country. Rather, their values in all but an insignificant minority of cases are directly proportional to the number of plowlands they contained. Their values were based on the ratios of 5s., 6s. 8d., and 8s. per plowland or simple multiples and fractions of each figure.[72] This phenomenon is without parallel in Yorkshire except for a group of royal and comital manors valued at the figure of £56,[73] and these figures clearly represent a traditional *feorm* or rent. The men who held these manors were then the equivalent of the ministerial thanes of the West, and the idea that there were no drengs in Yorkshire is specious.

A determined Northumbrian scholar, however, might still not assent, despite the discovery of over three hundred ministerial nobles south of the Tees, and demand to know if the peasants of Yorkshire made the grain renders and cornage payments that were common in Northumbrian bondage vills. These would be serious questions. If the institutional structure of Northumbria was fairly uniform, there should be traces of grain renders and cornage south of the Tees. Neither are found in any number in the custumals and inquisitions, which contain only two examples of peasants burdened with grain renders and but one instance of the payment of cornage (*cougeld*).[74] But at least in the case of the first of these, the grain renders, this is entirely a question of appearance, an impression analogous to Jolliffe's ideas about the distribution of forinsec labor dues and drengs, and just as devoid of substance. For once, literary evidence can throw light on this discussion. The *Chronica Monasterii de Melsa* contains a curious story that when King Athelstan returned from his Scottish expedition, he gave the church of Beverley the right to collect four traves of grain, apparently oats, from each working plow in the East Riding. This render was called hestercorn (*hestornes*). Its collection was a royal right, and its original purpose had been to provide food for the king's horses.[75] This last statement may reflect merely the chronicler's dislike of oats, but the main idea of the account is significant. The grain renders above the Tees were of royal origin,[76] and this story would prove that similar renders had existed in Yorkshire and explain what had happened to them. Of course, the account itself might be doubted, but the *Chronica Monasterii de Melsa* is a serious, if late, source that embodies local material in addition to the works of earlier historians.[77] Furthermore, the matter does not rest solely on its authority. The Hospital of St. Peter of York had a similar tradition that Athelstan granted to the church of York the right to collect one trave of corn from each plow in the province of York.[78] This right passed to the hospital after the Conquest, and both its existence and the existence of Beverley's grain renders are established by later evidence. Beverley's right to its traves was confirmed by both Henry I and Stephen, and St. Peter's traves were confirmed by William Rufus.[79] These charters show that a comprehensive system of grain renders, which probably had consisted of one trave of corn and four traves of oats from each plow, had existed in Yorkshire, and they support the stories about Athelstan granting already existing renders to the church. Both the method of assessment and the political situation in Yorkshire during the tenth century point in the same direction. The levying of the dues on the basis of the working plow looks very ancient, and certainly neither Athelstan nor his immediate successors possessed enough power in Yorkshire to impose a new general tribute for the support of the church. The most likely hypothesis is, then, that either Athelstan or one of the other early kings of Wessex to hold power in the North granted out to the church the old royal grain renders that the kings of Northumbria had once received and the Danish kings of York had continued to collect.[80] These renders in kind would not have seemed very useful to the descendants of Alfred, who never showed any great taste for staying in Yorkshire, and the church in Yorkshire clearly needed to be reendowed after its near destruction at the hands of the Danes.

We come now to the question of cornage, the most debated of all Northumbrian survivals. Its absence from Yorkshire is absolute except at Bowes castle, and no evidence hints that it has gone unnoticed like the grain renders. Yet this is not as serious a problem as it might appear. The cumulative weight of the argument has become great; and, if there is no evidence of cornage in Yorkshire, there is also no sign of it in southern Lancashire, which was clearly a land of shires in 1066. The nonexistence of cornage in the latter area lessens the weight of this objection, and in an indirect way it suggests a solution to the problem. Most of the traditional discussions of cornage have concentrated on the nature of the due, which has inevitably involved a heavy reliance on late twelfth- and thirteenth-century evidence. By this time, however, cornage had assumed different forms. Not surprisingly, the fruits of this approach have been an ever-lengthening list of definitions whose current major representatives are Jolliffe's idea that it was a pasture due analogous to pannage and Rees's theory that it was the equivalent of *commorth*, a Welsh cow tribute paid in lieu of old food renders.[81] The difficulty with such definitions is that they ignore an important aspect of the early evidence in their determination to elucidate the inner nature of the due. The only recent scholar to escape this error is Barrow, who accepted Rees's position and further argued that cornage and the king of Scotland's cain were the same render.[82] This equation represents a major advance, whether it is true or not, because it emphasizes an important aspect of cornage that usually is obscured in the discussion of thirteenth-century details and Celtic parallels: in its earliest appearances, the cornage of northern England was a royal due. The first pipe roll, Henry I's for 1130, shows that cornage was paid to the king in Westmorland and Cumberland, and Henry II's rolls disclose that cornage was a royal due in Northumberland.[83] In Yorkshire and Lancashire, on the other hand, neither Henry I nor Henry II received cornage, and the sum Henry I obtained from Durham in 1130 apparently came to him because he had custody of the temporalities of the bishopric, not as a royal right.[84] The situation was even more complex because there is contemporary evidence that Durham had paid cornage to the king at an earlier date in Henry I's reign, and later sources show that cornage payments were made in northern Lancashire and at Bowes although they did not reach the king.[85] Cornage first appears, then, as predominantly but not exclusively a royal due. It went to the king in the four northernmost counties. In Yorkshire and Lancashire it either did not exist or was found only on the manorial level. This distribution of the right to receive cornage is very curious for it corresponds with the northern limit of the geld in 1066. Most of Cumberland and Westmorland were not under the English king at that date, and Northumbria paid no geld. Yorkshire and Lancashire both did. This is surely significant and suggests that cornage was either an old Northumbrian tribute or perhaps even an ancient royal tribute of the North. It is difficult to tell for certain which it was because there is little evidence that it existed in Lothian.[86] If it did not, as seems most likely, this would suggest that cornage was imposed in the last half of the tenth century after Lothian had been lost. In any case, this hypothesis explains its earliest names, which were not "cornage" but rather the "geld of animals" or the "geld of cows" in the West and the "cornage of animals" in the East.[87] Cornage was the cow tax, not some primitive render attached to the bondage vills. Presumably it had been a general tribute above the Humber, but when the geld was laid on Yorkshire and Lancashire, it either was extinguished in these areas or became a manorial render. Free from the pressure of the geld, it survived in Northumbria and fell to the king when Rufus took over the earldom. Subsequently, Henry I granted the cornage between the Tyne and the Tees to the bishop and monks of Durham.[88]

   If this theory is correct, the absence of cornage in Yorkshire only indicates that the Anglo-Saxon kings had more power there than in Northumbria, and the subject has no particular bearing on whether the soke and the shire were the same institution. In fact, the conclusion that they were the same seems inescapable. This means, in turn, that there is no basis for the assumption that Yorkshire was radically different from Northumbria and that its description in Domesday can be used to check Jolliffe's picture of society above the Tees. But with this determined, it becomes immediately obvious why it was necessary for him to create an institutional discontinuity between Northumbria and Yorkshire. The Yorkshire section of Domesday may not be a mine of information, but it is clear on a number of very basic points that reveal the limitations of Jolliffe's attempt to construct a picture of

Northumbrian society from a selective use of late peasant custom. Three such points stand out. First, the peasantry of Yorkshire was divided into the three usual classes of eastern England, sokemen, villeins, and bordars,[89] and this makes it very unlikely that Jolliffe's assumption that the Northumbrian peasantry consisted only of bonders before 1066 is correct. There is no reason why the class divisions that existed in Yorkshire should have stopped at the Tees. Second, Yorkshire was also the home of a numerous class of land-owners, who ranged in importance from very great nobles to quite humble men with only a few bovates each. Although these men cannot be counted or the extent of their holdings computed except in a few cases because of the way their names were recorded in Domesday,[90] it is still clear that Jolliffe's elusive "lord of the shire" finds only a few peers among them. Third, despite the equation of soke and shire, one cannot say that Yorkshire in 1066 lay under the shire system as Jolliffe pictured it in Northumbria. Sokes there are. The incidents of peasant custom clearly have their origin and rationale in the shire. But the great territorial sokes stand out like islands in a sea of smaller holdings; they do not cover the shire from border to border as Jolliffe would have the shires do above the Tees. The intervening spaces are filled with all sizes of smaller sokes, some of which contain nothing more than a village with perhaps a single berewick or an attached piece of sokeland, and there are also many holdings that consist of only a single village or of part of a village with no dependent berewicks or sokelands. The sokes (the linked entries of the geographers) account for 64 per-cent of the entries in Yorkshire; the single holdings amount to 36 percent.[91] In other words, although the soke is characteristic of landholding in Yorkshire, it varied in size and shared the country-side with a large minority of unitary holdings. The latter and the smaller sokes are explicable in terms of a decayed and fragmented shire system, but they do not conform to the primitive simplicity of landholding which Jolliffe claimed existed in Northumbria before the Normans truncated the shires. Rather, they show that North-umbrian landholding had become complex long before 1066 and that the lands beyond the Tees had not remained some sort of preserve for a timeless Anglo-Celtic society.

Jolliffe seems to have gotten the concept of Northumbria as a land of large shires from Domesday's description of Lancashire as confirmed by the western portion of the early thirteenth-century

Inquest of Knights.[92] These do indeed show that above the Ribble the vill was the basis of society and that these vills were grouped together in large shires that covered the countryside. Earl Tostig's pre-Conquest manor of Preston in Amounderness had contained some sixty-two dependent villages, and his estate of Halton further north had included twenty-two dependent villages. Other manors in the area in 1066 contained twenty-seven, sixteen, and fourteen villages, and holdings made up of a single village or part of a village seem to be entirely absent. These shires of northern Lancashire were truly "princely" shires, and apparently the five hundreds south of the Ribble, which belonged almost entirely to the king, were similar units.[93] The West was, then, full of large constellations of villages belonging mainly either to the king or the earl, and they provided Jolliffe's model. Yet it is doubtful if they were anything more than a local phenomenon. It was shown earlier that Lancashire with the adjoining parts of Westmorland and Cumberland was a late conquest from the kingdom of Strathclyde, and the pattern of landholding that existed there in 1066 is just what one would expect to find in a recently conquered area. Arrangements were simple, and the claims of the king were still strong. Furthermore, it might be hazarded that if primitive simplicity existed anywhere in Britain in 1066 south of the Highlands of Scotland, the lands of the old kingdom of Strathclyde were the place to find it.

There exists no warrant whatsoever to carry groupings of this size over the mountains as the normal form of tenurial pattern, but this is exactly what Jolliffe did. He explained the smaller shires that appear in Northumbrian documents of the twelfth and thirteenth centuries as truncated fragments of large shires that had existed in 1066 and had been universal at that date.[94] He also ignored any evidence that Northumbrian society had become complex before 1066 and was similar to that of Yorkshire. The process through which the bishops of Durham acquired their estates, for instance, is known to a certain extent and could only in the short run have brought diversity to the shires between the Tees and the Tyne. Aside from three royal grants that apparently consisted of a full shire each or of several shires, the bishops were granted villages and small groups of villages by the local nobility, and they purchased groups of villages from the various Scandinavian kings of York and Durham. Some of the estates that were given to them by nobles had been originally purchased by the nobles, and the bishops further complicated the system of landholding by leasing assemblages of villages to members of the Northumbrian nobility.[95] In one notable case, a bishop even gave away a number of estates with his daughter in marriage; although the marriage did not last, several of the villages became hereditary possessions of the woman's descendants by a later husband.[96] Transactions of this sort are incompatible with the social system Jolliffe posited in Northumbria. There is no mention of them in his discussion of Northumbrian society, nor did he consider the peasant groups that existed in Durham in the twelfth century. Boldon Book shows that they were divided into the three broad classes of molmen (firmars), bonders (villeins), and cottars. The similarities between the bonders, the most numerous class, and the villeins of Yorkshire were pointed out earlier, and it seems that a like identification can be made between the molmen and the sokemen. Molmen were perhaps former freemen; certainly they were distinct from the Anglo-Norman firmars with whom they have usually been confused.[97] They were not essentially rentpayers like the latter. Several villages were populated exclusively by molmen, and in a number of others they constituted a normal segment of the peasant population alongside the bonders and cottars.[98] These men held bovates and performed agricultural services that were usually lighter than those of the villeins and were remarkably like those done by some of the sokemen in Yorkshire.[99] Jolliffe seems to have thought that these peasant groups above the Tees had come into existence after 1066,[100] but given the parallels between the molmen and bonders of Durham and the sokemen and villeins of Yorkshire, this is quite doubtful.

In the face of these considerations, it must be concluded that his picture of northern society was oversimplified. His work on peasant custom seems to be sound. But the shires had been truncated and social diversity had developed long before 1066. Had Domesday reached to the Tweed, it would probably have disclosed a society much like the one in Yorkshire. Northumbria would have appeared poorer, no doubt. Perhaps its villages would have been divided between different lords less frequently than those in Yorkshire,[101] but the same social groups and the same basic patterns of landholding would have appeared. Were it not for the difficulties introduced into the study of English institutions by the Danes, this conclusion would have been worked out long ago on the basis of the general similarity between the soke and the shire. That this was not done has been unfortunate. The institutional structure of the North has been obscured by attempts to divine patterns of ethnic institutions, and the actual indications concerning the evolution of northern society that lie in the shire fragments have been ignored except by Jolliffe.

These fragments provide important hints about the evolution of the North's institutions. It is curious, for instance, that Jolliffe's three clearest examples of shires, the Norham-Islandshire complex, Bedlingtonshire, and Heighingtonshire, all belonged to the church. This was evidently not the result of the fact that the church was the only known pre-Conquest landowner to survive the Conquest above the Tees, for the same pattern is observable in Yorkshire. In 1066, the great territorial sokes belonged almost exclusively to the king, the church, and the men who had been, were currently, or could expect to become earls. This suspicious fact is matched by another singular phenomenon. By the time of Boldon Book, Heighingtonshire and Bedlingtonshire both consisted of six villages. Two examples, of course, are not very significant, and Norhamshire comprised only ten villages at this time.[102] But a later survey that includes Islandshire with Norhamshire sets the figure for both at either twenty-four or twenty-six.[103]

If the true number was twenty-four, one might guess that a shire consisted of either six or twelve villages. This figure can be confirmed. Barrow's reconstructions of the shires of Berwick and Coldingham contain twenty-five and twelve villages, respectively. When Cnut gave Staindrop *cum suis appendiciis* to St. Cuthbert, it consisted of twelve vills and was presumably a shire. The lands that Bishop Aldhun leased to three earls contained twenty-four villages, and Athelstan's gift of South Wearmouth was made up of twelve vills. Even earlier (900–915), Bishop Cutheard leased Easington with either eleven or twelve vills to a noble, and it is known that in 655, King Oswy gave the church twelve ten-hide estates, six of which have been identified with a hypothetical shire of Yetholm, itself containing twelve villages.[104] These examples show that the Northumbrian shire was probably a unit of twelve vills or its multiple, but the truly amazing thing is that this unit did not stop at the Tees. If one goes to the trouble to count the berewicks and sokelands of the large territorial sokes in Yorkshire, the same number appears with majestic regularity (see Table 4).[105] This list is not all-inclusive. Several large sokes do not fit the pattern, such as Conis-

Table 4. The Composition of Large Territorial Sokes in Yorkshire

Soke	Berewicks	Sokelands	Total	Holder 1066
Aldborough	3	8	12	King Edward
Easingwold	1	10	12	Earl Morcar
Falsgrave	1	21	23	Tostig
Grindleton	12		13	Earl Tostig
Howden		24	25	King Edward
Kilnsea		11	12	Morcar
Kirkby Moorside	4	8	13	Orm
Knaresborough	11		12	King Edward
Lofthouse		12	13	Earl Siward
Mappleton		11	12	Morcar
Northallerton	11	24	36	Earl Edwin
Pickering	4	18	23	Morcar
Ripon	16	7 or 8	23 or 24	Abp. of York
Sherburn	[23]		[24]	Abp. of York
Tanshelf	5?	6?	12	King Edward
Wakefield	9 or 9	14 or 38	24 or 48	King Edward
Weaverthorpe	3	8	12	Abp. of York
Whitby	1	11	13	Earl Siward
Withernsea		11	12	Morcar

borough and Gilling, which contained twenty-eight and thirty-one vills, respectively, and the smaller sokes based on the unit of six have been left out.[106] But there are enough examples here to show that the big sokes of Yorkshire were based on the unit of twelve.

Numerologists can be expected to have their own suggestions on the meaning of this discovery, but its significance probably reaches no further than the mundane fact that there are twelve months in the year and that this would seem a natural unit to an agricultural people. Twelve villages made a shire above the Tees. A soke center with eleven berewicks and sokelands made a soke in Yorkshire. The berewicks and sokelands were not always complete vills in 1086, but they usually were, and the exceptions probably had been complete in the past. The unit of twelve villages was evidently very ancient. Both Ripon and the Norham-Islandshire complex were pre-Danish possessions of the church. Neither the tax assessment for the Danegeld, the carucates, nor the specifics of landlord right, the berewicks and sokelands, bear any clear relationship to units of twelve in Yorkshire. They play across the face of the units of twelve in an arbitrary fashion that bespeaks the needs and judgments of later ages. The unit itself is probably a relic of the days when taxation went by the village. In Durham this system survived in a number of villages into the late twelfth century, and Jolliffe has argued convincingly that assessment by the village had once been the rule. The principal and oldest burden that lay upon the villages was, of course, the system of renders in kind and the hospitality dues,[107] the English equivalent of the Scottish cain and coneveth, and the grouping of villages in units of twelve had in all likelihood been connected with this system. Such groups may have been the basis for seasonal progresses through the kingdom four times a year with a stop of, say, three days in each shire to eat the food and dispense justice. Alternately, they could have provided the court a regular supply of food in conjunction with the carting dues that lay upon the villages. Other arrangements would have been possible, but it is the general insight into the early function of the shire that is important.

Originally the shires had been nothing more than arbitrary administrative districts of the royal support system of the Northumbrian kingdom. They were the mechanism through which food and, perhaps later, customary labor were extracted from the peasantry for the support of the king and his warriors, and they were not originally Celtic principalities, although they might have been Celtic administrative units which the Northumbrians took over as the basis of their kingdom. Davis has argued that the sokelands of East Anglia were a relic of a prehundredal royal support system,[108] and the Northumbrian shires were probably analogous units. Above the Tees, the power of the kings of Wessex was never great enough to impose the hundred or the wapentake, and the old shires persisted in altered form down to the High Middle Ages. In Yorkshire, however, the new institutions were introduced presumably after the destruction of the Norwegian kingdom, and the shires of the area lost their judicial functions. They had also, it seems, been renamed "sokes" by the Danes; this was not a very serious change, although it has clouded the issue. Later in Scandinavia, *sokn* meant "parish," which was, of course, exactly what the shires had been in an ecclesiastical sense.[109] Furthermore, the original nature of the

Northumbrian shire was not forgotten in Yorkshire. There are occasional examples from after 1066 of wapentakes being called "shires."[110]

If this explanation of the shire is correct, it has important implications concerning the manorial structure of the North. Under the system of landholding and rights that first appears in Yorkshire in 1066 and is later documented in more detail for the North generally, the king received the old renders and works that had characterized the shire system from the great sokes and smaller estates of the royal demesne. Perhaps the sokes held by the earls should also be considered part of the ancient demesne, but on the lands of the church and the nobility these same renders and works went to the landowner, not to the king. They had been submerged to the manorial level: the right to exact them from the peasants constituted the normal prerogative of the landowner in the North. In a very real sense, these rights were the manor between the Humber and the Tweed; how this had come to be is explained by the work of Eric John on the land tenure of early Anglo-Saxon England. He would define the grant of an estate as bookland, not as the grant of the land of the estate itself, but as the grant of the right to collect the royal *feorm* which the peasants owed the king. These grants were made in perpetuity and originally went only to the church. By Bede's time, however, the nobility, which had hitherto had only a life interest in estates, began to obtain bookland, and this type of tenure later became the common way land was held.[111] The significance of this subject lies in the fact that the Northumbrian *feorm* must have consisted of the dues and services produced by the shires. If this identification is correct, grants of bookland provided the mechanism by which the old royal rights of the shire devolved to the landlords of the Northumbrian kingdom and became the basic manorial rights of the North.

This hypothesis clarifies the institutional history of the North in two ways. First, it provides a theoretical background for the landholding patterns of Yorkshire in 1066. The original grants of bookland were probably shires or simple parts of one. Over time, however, the normal mechanisms of Anglo-Saxon land transfer, buying and selling, division among heirs, and gifts to the church, in addition to seizure by the Vikings in Yorkshire and Durham, would produce the complex and fragmented estates of all sizes held by the nobility in 1066.[112] The church, on the other hand, neither divided nor sold, although it was sometimes robbed, so that its shires endured much longer than those of the nobility, and the great sokes of the king and the earls were unalienated sections of the old shire system. The smaller estates held by the king and the church were obtained from the nobility by donation, purchase, and forfeiture for sin in the case of the church and presumably by confiscation in the case of the king.[113]

Second, this hypothesis partially explains why the comparisons of Northumbrian, Welsh, and Scottish customs tend to be inexact. In the early Middle Ages, functionally similar royal support systems had existed in all three areas, but their development over time was very different. The Welsh system lasted intact into the thirteenth century, providing the Welsh princes with food, lodging, and local police. In Northumbria, the shire system was submerged to the manorial level by bookland except on the royal demesne and came to support the nobility and the church instead of the king. Subsequently, new burdens, the king's three works and the geld, were imposed upon Yorkshire, and there are vague traces from after the Conquest that the Northumbrian earls had created a similar system for Northumbria that consisted of army service, fortress repair, and cornage.[114] The Scottish system met a different fate. Like the one in Wales, it lasted into the twelfth and thirteenth centuries although its character had changed by this time. The kings still received their cain and coneveth, but the Scots, who did not develop a tenure comparable to bookland, had achieved the same end by other means. The thanes and earls, theoretically officials of the king, had become hereditary, and they each took a "cut" (*cuit*) of the renders that in a diminished form eventually reached the king. Thus the Scottish royal support system maintained both the king and the nobility by the twelfth century.[115] Given these different histories, it is quite understandable why the comparisons discussed earlier are often misleading. Such a method of institutional investigation is possible, but future attempts will have to be considerably more sophisticated because, even if it is assumed that these three systems were once similar, they diverged very early. Moreover, there is only very slender evidence that the systems really had a common origin and were not the result of the parallel growth Jolliffe thought so unlikely. Finally, the question of the Anglo-Saxon *feorm* must be taken into consideration. In particular, it will have to be determined whether the shire system of

Northumbria was unique in Anglo-Saxon England or whether its outlines are clearer only because of the backwardness of the North.

In conclusion, one very dark subject remains. It seems certain that northern society was far more complex in 1066 than Jolliffe thought and that the existence of bookland in the North was a major cause of this complexity. Bookland was also responsible, in part, for the institutional divergence of the North from Scotland and Wales, but it does not completely explain the landholding system at the time of Domesday Book. In his early work on landholding in the Danelaw, Stenton found that estates were divided between two types of land, inland and sokeland. The former comprised lands described in Domesday as being manors or berewicks and meant that the soil belonged to the lord of the estate. Sokeland, on the other hand, was owned by the person who occupied it, presumably a sokeman, and the lord had jurisdiction only over this land.[116] One might, of course, take issue with this generalized concept of jurisdiction and say instead that the sokemen paid the old royal dues to the lord of the estate, but this does not abolish the distinction between inland, the origin of which is uncertain, and sokeland, which was bookland. Nor was this distinction in its essence the result of some formula imposed on the Danelaw by the Normans. One may suspect that Domesday's employment of the term "inland" represented a southern usage, but the same categories were used in a pre-Conquest survey of some estates of the archbishop of York. The survey was made about 1030 and covers the sokes of Ripon, Otley, and Sherburn. It seems to be based on the assumption that the lands of these estates were either *agenland* or *socnland*. *Agenland* apparently consisted of *inlande* (demesne land in the strict sense?) and *werocland*, a term otherwise unknown.[117] The distinction between *agenland* and *socnland* would seem to be the same as Domesday's distinction between inland and sokeland, or the distinction between inland and *gesette land* found in the Tidenham survey that has recently been discussed by John F. McGovern. He thought that the *gesette land* was property held only by bookright and that inland was held by some inferior tenure as well.[118] This may be true, but one wonders if the emphasis is correct. From bookland a lord received soke, the royal dues. Stenton thought that a lord actually owned his inland, the pre-Conquest *agenland* or the "land which belonged to the hall" in a variant formula of Domesday.[119] If this explanation is right, and it seems to be, then one would suppose that a lord would have a great deal more control over and profit from this sort of land. Furthermore, there is a strong possibility that the differences between peasants were somehow correlated with these tenures. In two instances Domesday gives the population of sokes in Yorkshire in 1066. In Northallerton and its berewicks there were 66 villeins in 1066, and its sokelands were populated by 116 sokemen. At Falsgrave, the other example, the population of the inland is not given, but it is recorded that there were 108 sokemen on the sokeland.[120] If these two entries are representative, one could conclude that villeins lived on inland and sokemen on sokeland. Such a conclusion would be a major step toward bringing the discussion of Anglo-Saxon land law into contact with the social structure of the kingdom, but it can only be stated as a possibility. One and a half examples are not enough to prove it; and, in any case, there remains the question of inland itself. Was it some old secondary tenure, as old as or older than bookland, or was it a new development, an intensive form of noble ownership that had emerged in the tenth century, perhaps connected with sake and soke?

4. THE RULE OF TOSTIG AND THE DESTRUCTION OF THE NOBLES OF YORK

In the North there is a unity to the fifteen years that follow 1055. The cohesiveness is provided by the somber theme of the breakdown of royal government above the Humber and the attendant rush of the northern thegns to destruction. The course and the tragic dimensions of these events could perhaps have been captured in heroic verse, but no known saga maker recorded the fate of the men of the North and the blindness that brought them to it. Only disjointed or partially informed chronicle accounts of these events survive, written by monks who were not able to explain in any detail what happened in the North. Their attention was fixed on the career of William the Conqueror, thus opening the way to the conventional, William-centered accounts of northern resistance to the Norman Conquest. These reconstructions have their value, but, because they focus on the life of William, they tend to isolate events in the North from each other and to obscure their meaning. This court-centered point of view creates its own system of causation and emphasizes the connection between the coming of the Normans and the outbreak of rebellion above the Humber.

The connection did, of course, exist, but the region-based narrative of the preceding chapters has established that royal government in the North was beset by serious problems long before 1066 and that Earl Siward did nothing to improve the situation. This chapter will show that an attempt was made to solve some of these problems on the government level in the decade from 1055 to 1065 and that this attempt not only brought about the collapse of royal authority in the North by 1065 but also was largely responsible for northern resistance to the Norman Conquest. The biographer of Edward the Confessor may have been correct when he linked the expulsion of Earl Tostig from his earldom with the beginning of Edward's physical decline.[1] The old king knew his realm well enough to see the significance of Tostig's failure. It is this failure that links together the years immediately before and after 1066 in the North. Tostig turned traditional resentments and passive disloyalty into actual rebellion and thus created a very difficult political situation that in the end prevented a peaceful extension of Norman power over the North. After 1065, the northern thegns revolted as much because of what had happened to them before the arrival of the Normans as because of what William actually did to them. Their ultimate fear was that their antique world was in jeopardy, and they resisted William with methods appropriate to that world. These came so near to success that they provoked the harrying of the North in 1069.

The immediate origin of this sequence of events dates from the deaths of Osbeorn in 1054 and Siward in 1055 because their deaths made possible a most unfortunate decision respecting the succession of the earldom. Hitherto, northern earls had possessed certain definite attributes of family or ethnic origin, depending on whether they were earls of Northumbria or of York. This is perhaps clearest in the case of the former, whose earls were members of the house of Bamburgh until Siward, and where even after this date the old ruling family maintained its local position. In Yorkshire the situation was more complex, yet even here the earls fell into clearly defined groups prior to 1055. With the exception of Earl Ælfhelm, who was from Mercia, they were either Anglo-Danes and Scandinavians or, less frequently, members of the house of Bamburgh.[2] Never had a West Saxon held direct rule in either province. This practice ended in 1055 with the appointment of Tostig, Earl Godwin's third son, as earl in preference to Waltheof, Siward's young son, or Cospatric, the eldest surviving representative of the Bamburgh family. All that was Danish about Tostig was his name; he had no known connection with the old ruling family of Northumbria. He was, consequently, a complete outsider in the North, and his appointment was in that sense revolutionary. The choice of Tostig stands in serious need of explanation, but on this critical point, there is no direct evidence. His appointment is often assumed to have represented an attempt to integrate the North more closely into the Anglo-Saxon kingdom.[3] There may well be some truth in this idea, and it undoubtedly appeared so to the northerners. Tostig could hardly have been expected to share local concerns. This inevitable disharmony may, however, have been more a result than a preconceived intention, for the choice of Tostig may have been merely a shortsighted attempt at family aggrandizement by the house of Godwin. By the reign of Edward the Confessor, the earldoms of the Eastern Midlands and East Anglia were commonly given to younger members of the families of the earls of Wessex and Mercia,[4] and the appointment of Tostig may have been simply the application of this policy to the North. Tostig was the brother of Earl Harold of Wessex and of the queen, and his acquisition of the North probably represented a major victory over the family of Earl Leofric of Mercia, whose eldest son Ælfgar was exiled at this time, apparently because he, too, wished to follow Siward. Ælfgar had been earl of East Anglia, and at least part of his earldom passed to Gyrth, the next youngest son of Godwin.[5] If this explanation of the elevation of Tostig to the northern earldom is correct, his appointment was probably devoid —at least initially—of any other significance.

Tostig was an unfortunate choice and must have found himself in an unenviable position. He could not have been certain how the northerners would react to their first southern earl, and he was in a weaker position than his immediate predecessors. Had Osbeorn lived and become earl, he would probably have inherited his father's unpopularity above the Tees, yet he would have had, at least, the support of the Yorkshiremen, which had allowed Siward to rule and keep Northumbria quiet. Tostig, on the other hand, fell heir to the problems left by Siward but lacked any important local support above the Humber. Indeed, his effectiveness as earl probably rested on the internal divisions among the northerners and on his own war band that by 1065 numbered over two hundred housecarls.[6] This impressive force was probably the mainstay of his government. To maintain such an army was expensive, and, like Siward before him, Tostig held southern counties as part of his earldom to help defray the cost. From 1055, he was earl of Northampton and probably of Huntingdon as well, and there is evidence that he also held Nottinghamshire.[7] As a result of these possessions, Tostig must have been formidable, even though he was an outsider.

The new earl enjoyed one immediate advantage because he was not from the North. The converse of not having local partisans was the absence of local enemies. Tostig had a freedom of maneuver greater than that of his immediate predecessors, and he used it to try to disarm potential sources of opposition. He entrusted the actual government of the earldom to a local Yorkshire thegn, Copsig,[8] who does not appear to have been linked either to Siward's family or to the house of Bamburgh. Copsig would have been familiar with local problems and customs and may have acted as a buffer between the northern nobility and Tostig. If so, Copsig's appointment was a prudent decision that minimized friction. Tostig may also have tried to improve relations with the clerks of Durham. Certainly by the time of Symeon of Durham, it was thought that Tostig had held St. Cuthbert's church in great veneration and had given gifts to the church. It is also known that Copsig gave several estates in Yorkshire to Durham during this period.[9] Under normal conditions, the giving of land and ornaments was the surest way to win the gratitude of clerks and monks, and these gifts probably represent an attempt to conciliate the clerks of Durham. They were clearly not deathbed bequests.

The attempt to conciliate the clerks probably was not successful. The church normally held its privileges dearer than its property. These privileges were at issue in the North, and on this point Tostig did not abandon Siward's policy. In 1056, Bishop Æthelric resigned Durham and returned to Peterborough, whence he had come some thirty-six years before. Two explanations for this unusual act survive. One source says that he gave up the bishopric because he was weak (that is, he had no local support) and could not properly defend the church's liberty against unnamed evil men.[10] The other account asserts that he robbed the church of a buried treasure and absconded to Peterborough.[11] Whatever the truth, both accounts show that Æthelric was extremely unpopular in Durham. It is also probably significant that he chose to relinquish the bishopric the year after Siward's death. Æthelric had kept his position at Durham only by means of Siward's power; with the death of the earl, he may have found his position untenable. It is even possible that Tostig refused to support him against the clerks. This explanation would be compatible with the first of the two versions of his resignation and consistent with Tostig's gifts to the church. If this was the case, the earl clearly misjudged the situation, however, for he did not allow the clerks to elect Æthelric's successor. Rather, Tostig chose the new bishop, and he selected Æthelwine, Æthelric's brother,[12] who was destined to be unpopular for the same reasons his brother had been. The new bishop was an outsider who had not been chosen by the clerks; in time he, too, would be branded a thief. Tostig did not win the goodwill of the clerks of Durham by this appointment.

Although the appointment of Æthelwine was to prove to be a dangerous mistake, in the years following 1055 the feelings of the Durham clerks probably seemed a distinctly secondary problem to Tostig. He faced much more immediate difficulties with the Scots. During the late 1050s, King Malcolm ceased to be an English client king and became a threat to the North worthy of his ancestors. The quickness of this reversal was partially the result of his success in consolidating his position in Scotland. In 1054, Siward had placed him in possession only of southern Scotland. Macbeth had escaped the battle and retreated to Moray, his native province, where he held out for three more years. Malcolm was able to kill him in 1057, and early in the following year he killed Lulach, Macbeth's stepson, who had been proclaimed king after Macbeth's death.[13] Thus by 1058, Malcolm had eliminated all his immediate rivals and was free to begin raiding the North of England. Certain domestic factors that stemmed from the nature of Scottish society probably urged him to make this decision. The Scots seem to have viewed an invasion of the North principally as an occasion for the forcible transfer of property: they came over the Tweed and out of the hills to steal cattle, take slaves, and collect booty. A king who could successfully lead such bloodthirsty shopping trips gained not only wealth and prestige at home but probably found it easier to govern. Malcolm II had launched his reign with an invasion of England, and his grandson Duncan had done the same within six years of becoming king. When Malcolm began to raid the North, he was, in a sense, only responding to the necessities of a poor kingdom and of a political system based on a warrior king.

These general considerations are undoubtedly important in explaining why Malcolm suddenly turned on his English support-ers. He was not a mere ingrate whom Siward had completely misjudged. Still, he probably came over the border for more concrete reasons. In particular, he had a grievance and was faced with a very promising chance to right it. The grievance was, of course, English possession of the southern part of the Cumbrian kingdom. There was no reason why Malcolm should accept Siward's diminution of his ancestral lands once his need for English help had passed. This need ended with the deaths of Macbeth and Lulach, and Malcolm could attempt the reconquest of Cumberland. This was the flaw in Earl Siward's Scottish policy. Perhaps the dead earl had foreseen this possibility and had thought that a strong earl, such as his son, would be able to thwart Scottish efforts to reclaim Cumberland. Such a hope was not unrealistic because the only major victory the Scots had won against the northern English had been at Carham, where they had faced only the men from above the Tees. After 1055, however, the situation in the North was very different from any that Siward is likely to have envisaged. The North had a West Saxon earl, and his ability to resist the Scots must have been problematical. In fact, the possibility that the divisions between Tostig and the men of his earldom would weaken English resistance was probably a strong inducement for Malcolm to come over the border.

The incursions began in 1058 or early in 1059 and were evidently small raids, perhaps designed to test Tostig.[14] If such was their intention, the earl's response must have been encouraging to Malcolm. Tostig did not respond with raids on Scotland as might have been expected; rather, he chose to negotiate. In 1059, Æthelwine, bishop of Durham, Kynsige, archbishop of York, and the earl journeyed to Scotland and induced Malcolm to come south with them to parley with Edward. Although this collection of dignitaries may have been designed to flatter the vanity of the young king, it could equally well be viewed as an expression of weakness. The English clearly hoped to pacify Malcolm by diplomacy rather than by war. They brought him over the Tweed, and he met Edward somewhere in the North, perhaps at York. The issues discussed at this meeting are not known, but it is likely that Malcolm wanted the return of Cumberland. This demand, if in fact made, was frustrated. Edward gave him rich presents and treated him with honor, but there is no word in the sources that Malcolm received anything more substantial. Tostig was the only one who profited from this meeting because it produced a peace treaty. The king and the earl became sworn brothers, and Malcolm may even have given hostages for his good behavior.[15] The meeting of 1059 was diplomatically a victory for the English. Tostig had won peace for the North, and Malcolm must have gone home with his aims unfulfilled.

This hypothesis is the simplest explanation for what followed. Tostig evidently thought that his sworn brotherhood with Malcolm could be relied upon, for in 1061 he traveled to Rome with Aldred, the new archbishop of York. The North was thus deprived of its two principal leaders, and Malcolm took the opportunity to show his dissatisfaction with the 1059 agreement. He launched a frontal attack over the Tweed, the type of invasion that had become increasingly common as the eleventh century progressed. The Scots laid waste Northumberland and took slaves. They reportedly even ravaged Lindisfarne, and there is circumstantial evidence that Malcolm crossed the Tyne and harried Durham before withdrawing.[16] This invasion is described in only the vaguest terms, but probably the violation of Lindisfarne shows that it was a double invasion from the north and west of the sort Siward had feared. During later invasions, the Scots usually tried to respect the major holy places of the North, but the Cumbrians honored no such restraint. If this supposition of a double invasion is correct, the invasion of 1061 shows the tactical limitations of Siward's annexation of Cumberland. Possession of the western end of the Tyne Gap did not protect the lands above the Tyne against raids from the West.

The chronicle account does not disclose what Malcolm hoped to gain by this incursion, but other evidence suggests that his aim was to recover Cumberland and that he succeeded. This is, of course, a reasonable hypothesis, and it is also the easiest way of explaining the few facts known about the West through the year 1070. As was discussed earlier, Cospatric's charter established that Siward had held power over Cumberland, but the document itself may date from after Siward's death in 1055. Theoretically, it could come from as late as 1064, when Cospatric, the grantor, was killed,[17] and if it were this late, Malcolm could not have recovered Cumberland in 1061. Such a late date is unlikely, however, because there is evidence that the West had been invaded and conquered prior to 1065. Parts of northern Lancashire and the southern sections of Cumberland and Westmorland were surveyed in Domesday, and by this time the villages in the area were derelict. The ravaging of this region, however, cannot be ascribed to any of the disturbances after 1066; in any case, Domesday suggests that these lands were already waste in 1066. Tostig had held most of them before the revolt of 1065, yet they did not pass to his successor Earl Morcar. Tostig was still recorded as their lord in 1066; and since Tostig actually held nothing by that date,[18] the lands must already have been derelict when Morcar became earl. Upon this assumption, William Farrer has suggested that these estates were plundered in the revolt against Tostig in 1065, but this explanation cannot be sustained because the accounts of the revolt do not indicate that the rebels did anything more than kill Tostig's housecarls and rob his treasury before marching south.[19] Northern Lancashire must, then, have been wasted prior to 1065—but after 1055, when Tostig became earl. Given these time limits, the most likely hypothesis is that the area was devastated in the course of an invasion of Cumberland. The occurrence of such an invasion cannot be doubted. Hugh the Chantor records that Siward's western bishopric was destroyed in war, and since the number of Malcolm's invasions was well remembered in the North, this incursion into Cumberland must have been part of Malcolm's first major invasion of the North in 1061. When Malcolm launched his second invasion in 1070, he used Cumberland as his base and attacked Yorkshire over Stainmore. The chronicle that describes the incursion of 1070 says explicitly that Malcolm held Cumberland at this time.[20]

In 1061, then, Malcolm invaded to regain Cumberland, and he struck while Tostig and the archbishop were on their trip to Rome, leaving the North leaderless. There is no word that Malcolm met any organized opposition. He invaded Northumberland, ravaged as far south as Durham, and then moved up the Tyne Gap to take over Cumberland. During this last stage of the campaign, northern Lancashire was wasted to such an extent that many of the estates there remained without a lord until after the Norman Conquest. Late that year or early in 1062, Tostig returned from Rome and found Malcolm in possession of Cumberland. The situation clearly called for military reprisals, but none was forthcoming. The earl's reaction was astonishing: he accepted the loss of Cumberland, and at some date prior to the fall of 1065, probably in 1062, he went to Scotland and made peace with Malcolm.[21] Their agreement, which was a serious setback for the security of the North, left the Scots in possession of Cumberland and marked the abandonment of Siward's efforts to give the North a defensible border. Malcolm's frontier on Stainmore was now within two days' ride of York, and the Tyne Gap stood open. With Cumberland the Scottish king gained the tactical advantage along the border, and he was destined to keep it for thirty years.

The North's poor defensive position during the reign of William the Conqueror had its immediate origin in Tostig's failure to maintain Siward's gains in Cumberland. Since the importance of this failure was probably obvious at the time, Tostig's inactivity requires explanation. At no time did he invade Scotland. Every incident along the border shows the earl temporizing and negotiating, and, because his later exploits reveal that he was a vigorous and warlike man, his refusal to oppose Malcolm is mysterious. His lack of action cannot be explained by the idea that the northerners accepted the validity of the Scottish claim to Cumberland or by the hypothesis that Tostig made expeditions against the Scots that went unrecorded because of the failure of the *Anglo-Saxon Chronicle* for the years 1062 and 1064.[22] In lieu of these two possibilities, the most likely explanation of his inactivity must be that his hold on the North was too insecure to risk an invasion of Scotland. If this hypothesis is correct, the earl was unpopular as early as 1058–59, at most four years after he became earl.

This in turn suggests that Tostig was unpopular in the North from the time of his appointment, which is not surprising given the fact that he was an outsider who lacked any claim to traditional loyalties, and his unpopularity does help to explain the events of 1063 and 1064. In the chronicles the revolt that unseated Tostig in 1065 stands out starkly with little background, apparently unconnected with the historic problems of northern government and explained as the result of tyrannical acts committed by Tostig.[23] Several such acts are specified, but the real question is whether the chroniclers have gotten the sequence of causation right. If Tostig's unpopularity really dates from the early days of his rule, then his "tyranny" actually may have been the result of his attempt to govern a restive nobility.

This hypothesis clarifies one of the most outstanding charges made against the earl. Florence of Worcester says that the northerners rose against Tostig to avenge his treacherous murder of three important Northumbrian nobles. In 1063, he had Gamel, son of Orm, and Ulf, son of Dolfin, assassinated in his own chamber at

York while the two were visiting him under a safe-conduct, and these deeds were followed in 1064 by the murder of Cospatric at the king's Christmas court. This murder was supposedly planned by the queen, Tostig's sister, in the interest of her brother.[24] As the account stands, the meaning of these events is not clear, but when the identities of the dead thegns are considered in the light of Tostig's unpopularity, a different picture emerges. The Cospatric killed at court was Earl Uhtred's youngest son and Earl Siward's collaborator in Cumberland.[25] By the 1060s he was the eldest surviving member of the house of Bamburgh and, as such, had a good claim to be earl of Northumbria. The other two thegns were apparently his associates. Gamel's father, Orm, had married a sister of Cospatric's, and a Gamel is mentioned among Cospatric's relatives and thegns in his Cumbrian charter.[26] Ulf, son of Dolfin, was probably the son of the Dolfin who died fighting Macbeth in 1054 and who was himself the son of Thorfinn, the recipient of Cospatric's charter. These men were the natural leaders of Northumbrian opposition to Tostig's rule, and their murders were exact parallels to Thurbrand's murder of Uhtred, Carl's murder of Ealdred, and Siward's murder of Eadulf. Tostig clearly feared the rivalry of the house of Bamburgh and chose the usual method of stifling Northumbrian separatism when he killed Cospatric, the last of Uhtred's unfortunate sons. It was ultimately, of course, a foolish act. Murder may have been the only convenient way of dealing with the Bamburgh family, but separatism above the Tees had had its origin in Uhtred's murder and had been fed by the murder of Ealdred. Cospatric's death at the king's court was sufficient reason for the Northumbrians to revolt.

The question remains of why the men of York supported the rebellion. The accounts of the event indicate that the North generally rose against Tostig, even though the Northumbrians may have led the way. This is a problem because the union of Northumbrians and Yorkshiremen to achieve a common goal was without historical parallel. Of course, Tostig's general unpopularity above the Humber might have been sufficient to induce the men of York to join the revolt, or perhaps the charge made in the earliest biography of Edward the Confessor applies to Yorkshire. The foreign cleric who wrote this work asserts that the northerners revolted because of the severity of Tostig's law enforcement. He provides a frightening picture of the lack of security on the northern roads and implies that the nobles who led the revolt had themselves lived by robbery and were aggrieved because Tostig had limited their opportunities to practice their occupation. This would be a convenient explanation for the revolt in Yorkshire, but, unfortunately, its details cannot be accepted. First, it is difficult to believe that the harsh treatment of highwaymen produced the popular revolt that drove out Tostig, particularly since the same account says that Siward had also been a stern enforcer of the law.[27] Second, if this explanation were accepted, Tostig would appear blameless of causing the revolt. Such a conclusion is suspicious because the biographer tends to be generally partial to the earl.[28] Finally, it is doubtful if the writer understood the true origin of the brigandage that afflicted the North. I will suggest later that this was one of the results of the loss of Cumberland.

Despite these objections, there still may be some truth in this explanation. At a later point in his narrative, Edward's biographer says essentially that many men charged that Tostig had used the courts to make money.[29] When put this way, the picture of Tostig as the severe and unpopular defender of justice begins to make more sense, for similar accusations are found in other accounts of the revolt. The *Anglo-Saxon Chronicle* says that Tostig was expelled "because first he robbed God, and all those who were less powerful than himself he deprived of life and land."[30] This may mean that he administered justice and levied fines arbitrarily, but it probably refers to the charge found in Florence of Worcester, who says that the Northumbrians (in this case, everyone above the Humber) revolted because Tostig had collected enormous taxes contrary to custom throughout the North.[31] Here is the real cause for the revolt. Taxation reached enough people to produce the type of popular uprising that overturned the earl.

Direct evidence on northern taxation is slight, but clear enough to show that Tostig found it easy to overtax the northerners and that such an attempt was a serious transgression of their privileges. The northern fiscal system survived unaltered into the Norman period as a result of the successful revolt of 1065, and an inspection shows that the northern tax assessment was much lower than that of the rest of England. The earliest clue to this fact comes from the Domesday description of southern Lancashire, which contains the curious statement that six carucates equaled one hide in this area.[32] This equation has usually been treated as an anomaly. Hides and carucates were artificial measures of fiscal assessment, and the two are usually regarded as equivalent terms. Theoretically, one carucate paid as much tax as one hide, hence the absurdity of six carucates paying the same tax as one hide. Unless the carucates of southern Lancashire were exceptionally small, this region had an extremely beneficial assessment. The tax burden might have been light because the area had been part of Edward's demesne in 1065, but this explanation cannot be sustained. Actually, this same equation was more widespread than Domesday admits. William Farrer has shown that in the twelfth century it was in use not only in southern Lancashire but also in northern Lancashire with the adjacent parts of Cumberland and Westmorland, in Yorkshire, and in Durham. All these areas paid geld as part of Yorkshire at the rate of 4d. for each carucate; six carucates thus produced 2s. In the rest of England either one carucate or one hide yielded 2s.[33] Northumberland may not have paid taxes even at the low rate paid by the rest of the North; it had never been assessed in either carucates or hides and thus stood completely outside the Anglo-Saxon fiscal system.[34] Whatever the reason, the North carried a much lighter tax burden than the rest of the kingdom.

This low assessment probably originated when the Norwegian kingdom of York was annexed by Wessex; along with legal autonomy, it was the price of the North's submission. At the time this would have seemed a reasonable compromise, but northern tax privileges must soon have hardened into custom. They were, perhaps, regularized by Cnut, and they survived until Tostig's day as one of the most important distinctions between the North and the rest of the kingdom.[35] They must have stood out as glaring inconsistencies in the Anglo-Saxon tax structure, but it is doubtful if any theoretical preference in favor of equal fiscal burdens prompted the earl to attack these arrangements. His motive was entirely practical. Because of his unpopularity, Tostig needed larger sums of money than were available from traditional sources to support the private army upon which his rule depended. As he was harassed by the Scots and the house of Bamburgh, his expenditures could only have increased so that he was led, on the one hand, to put pressure on the judicial system to produce more fines and confiscations, and, on the other, to levy higher taxes con-

trary to custom. This attack on the fiscal privileges of the North
united the Yorkshiremen with the Northumbrians and produced
the popular support for the revolt of 1065.

The uprising was heralded by the clerks of Durham, who
were no happier with Bishop Æthelwine than they had been with
his brother. They feared that he, too, would rob their church for
the benefit of Peterborough, and a localist party had developed to
forestall this. The leader of the group was Elfred, son of Westou,
who, in addition to protecting the sacred ornaments of the church,
had become the great scourge of the ancient churchyards of the
North. Presumably the clerks had had to endure sophisticated
gibes from their southern bishops concerning Durham's poverty in
sacred relics. To remove this embarrassment, Elfred had devoted
great energy to digging up the bodies of important northern eccle-
siastics and transporting the bones to Durham for proper display.
Until the spring of 1065, his activities had been a natural and
harmless reaction to cultural chauvinism, but in March of that year,
they assumed a political dimension. Some two and one half months
after the betrayal and murder of Cospatric, Elfred brought forth
the body of King Oswin, who had suffered a similar fate in the
seventh century.[36] The parallel between Cospatric and Oswin was
obvious, and the public display of Oswin's body at Durham was
clearly an attempt by the clerks to incite their flock to revolt.
Thus would Tostig pay for his and Siward's infringement of the
privileges of St. Cuthbert.

St. Oswin was unearthed in March of 1065; once the harvest
was in, the North rose in revolt, utilizing the customary northern
tactic for resisting oppression: the sudden raid. Despite this traditional element in their tactics, the precision of the revolt suggests
that it was the result of a carefully framed conspiracy. On 3 October, a group of insurgent thegns entered York by surprise and took
the city. The leaders of this force are otherwise unknown, which
probably indicates that they were from above the Tees. They had
chosen a good moment to strike, for Tostig was absent from the
North. The men of York immediately joined the Northumbrians,
and together they killed the leaders of Tostig's housecarls as they
tried to escape the city. This deed probably destroyed the command
structure of Tostig's men, and the next day the rebels were able to
kill some two hundred of his retainers in Yorkshire and to take all
of the earl's treasure, money, and weapons.[37]

After destroying the hated tools of Tostig's rule, the rebels met together and outlawed the earl. They then invited Morcar, the younger brother of Earl Edwin of Mercia, to be their new earl, and with him at their head, they began to march south.[38] This decision to go south, more than anything else, distinguishes the revolt of 1065 from the later revolts in the North and shows that the rebels had competent, if unnamed, leadership. They were attempting to force King Edward to accept the revolution;[39] the northerners were not so foolish as to stage a local revolt and then wait for the king to ratify their deeds. This aspect of the affair is clear, but their destination and their behavior show that they also viewed the trip south as an integral part of the original revolt. They had already destroyed Tostig's power above the Humber; they must do the same in the South. The rebels apparently crossed the Humber and marched to Lincoln, where they slaughtered more of Tostig's retainers.[40] They were joined by groups of men from Lincolnshire, Nottinghamshire, and Derbyshire, and the whole force moved on to Northampton. Here Morcar's brother Edwin met them with an army drawn from his earldom and some Welsh auxiliaries. The rebels now constituted a formidable force, and negotiations were opened with the king through Earl Harold, Tostig's brother. In the meantime, however, the northerners set about a systematic plundering of Northamptonshire, which had formed part of the earldom of both Siward and Tostig and was now made to pay for the strength it had given to the northern earls. The northern thegns were not oblivious to the relationship between wealth and power. They enslaved hundreds of the men of the area and stole thousands of head of cattle. Perhaps more significant, however, they killed many of the natives, burned their houses, and destroyed their winter supply of corn.[41] These deeds could not have enriched anyone and were clearly designed to impoverish the area. Finally, toward the end of the month, the king agreed to accept the results of the revolt. He could not fight the rebels for a number of reasons, and he consented, therefore, to the appointment of Morcar as earl. Earl Harold did not oppose the replacement of his brother and swore to uphold the settlement. In addition, he—presumably in the name of the king—renewed the law of Cnut.[42] Tostig's attempt to overthrow the fiscal privileges of the North had been abandoned.

Thus the experiment of the first southern earl of the North

ended in disaster. Tostig had failed in his two principal tasks. He had neither maintained the northern border nor succeeded in governing his earldom. His murders and attack on the fiscal system of the North had created such an outrage above the Humber that for once the North had united. The successful revolt that followed ended his rule and its abuses, but it left a legacy of mistrust that weakened the Anglo-Saxon kingdom in the last year of its existence and lasted into the early years of the Norman Conquest to stand in the path of a peaceful extension of William's rule over the North. For ten years before 1065, the northerners had lived under what was to them a foreign earl, who had tried to alter their customs. They did not forget this with the coming of the Normans and were on their guard.

Hitherto, the clarity of the connection between Tostig and northern resistance to the Norman Conquest has not been generally recognized for at least two reasons. First, no one has understood the nature of Tostig's misrule, and consequently the revolt of 1065 has appeared to be the result of straightforward greed and tyranny. The real cause for the revolt, however, was Tostig's attempt to govern the North in the face of northern resistance. Second, the notherners' choice of Morcar as their earl has been misinterpreted. Some scholars have maintained that their selection of a Mercian indicated that they knew that the North could no longer stand alone and that they "were apparently fully conscious of the strong political bonds which bound them to the rest of England." This ingenious theory saves the unity of Anglo-Saxon England from the bodies and devastation of 1065 by emphasizing that the rebels sought the king's approval of their new earl and by asserting that their choice of Morcar served to restore the unity of the kingdom.[43] On a constitutional level, this theory may not be entirely specious, but it cannot be based on the North's choice of Morcar, which is adequately explained on the basis of northern politics. The difficulty the northerners faced in 1065 was that the revolt had been made by both the men of York and the Northumbrians. Therefore it was impossible to choose one of the two available northern candidates and still maintain the unity that was necessary to intimidate Edward the Confessor. The Northumbrians would not have willingly accepted Siward's son Waltheof, nor would the Yorkshire men have been likely to accept Osulf, son of Earl Eadulf, the current representative of the house of Bamburgh. Past antagonism stretching back at least to the days of Earl Uhtred and Thurbrand blocked either man. Given this the northerners could only compromise and choose an outsider. Morcar had no discernible connection with either northern family, and his family had its own differences with the house of Godwin. He was, therefore, a perfect compromise, and his selection left room for an accommodation of the local men that clearly indicates what forces were at work. Osulf of Bamburgh was given the rule of Northumbria under Morcar, and Waltheof was apparently given Northampton and Huntingdon.[44] Thus the choice of Morcar only indicates the paramount nature of local concerns.

The revolt of 1065 was, then, a conservative reaction to innovation and had brought back to power the traditional ruling family of Northumbria and Siward's son. The events of the early months of 1066 show that it had also created new difficulties for government in the North. With the death of Edward the Confessor in January, Harold, Tostig's elder brother, became king, but the northerners, apparently motivated by fear, at first refused to accept him. The source that describes this incident, although somewhat general and rhetorical, says explicitly that they feared being dominated by the South, and the existence of this fear is shown by two Yorkshire coin hoards that were buried at the accession of Harold.[45] Evidently the northerners thought they could expect no better treatment from Harold than they had received from Tostig. Given the succession crisis the king faced, this fear was undoubtedly groundless, but he had, nonetheless, to make a special trip to York to reassure the northerners. Even though he accomplished this by Easter,[46] the incident must still have been very disquieting. The North had threatened, at the very least, to withhold its support from the king, and the whole affair showed that Morcar, who was loyal to Harold, had little control over the men of his new earldom.[47]

No matter how fragile the situation above the Humber may have been, the first attack on the North came from a highly surprising source, given the host of potential invaders who were lurking around the North Sea and the English Channel in the spring of 1066. Upon his exile, Tostig had gone to Flanders, where his father-in-law was count, and he had spent the winter there gathering a fleet for an invasion of England.[48] What he hoped to accomplish with this force is conjectural. He may have been working with either Duke William of Normandy, his brother-in-law, or with King Harold Hardrada of Norway, both of whom intended to conquer England. But there is no real evidence to support either alternative, and it is hard to see how his recorded exploits could have helped either of them—except, perhaps, as a diversion. This is, of course, possible, but it seems more likely that Tostig was working only for himself. He was a bold man; both his successful attempt to intimidate the pope on his trip to Rome in 1061 and his unsuccessful attempt to govern the North show this clearly. The coming year offered rewards for such men, and Tostig probably intended to try his luck.

Early in May he descended on the Isle of Wight and extorted money and provisions from the islanders. He then sailed east to Sandwich, where he impressed some sailors; upon the approach of King Harold, he moved up the coast and entered the Humber, which was apparently the object of his expedition. He did not need to come this far north simply for plunder. Tostig's force is said to have numbered sixty ships; if so, it was clearly large enough to be dangerous to local forces.[49] Such was undoubtedly its purpose. Tostig's foray was not as ridiculous as it usually appears when historians employ it as the curtain raiser for the great invasions of 1066. The real parallels of this expedition lay in the Anglo-Saxon past. Twice during the reign of Edward the Confessor, Ælfgar, the father of Edwin and Morcar, had been exiled and had won reinstatement in his earldom by invading England with forces gathered in Wales and Dublin. The principle behind such action was that if an outcast could wreak enough havoc, the king would be likely to buy him off by giving him back his lands and offices. This must have been Tostig's intention in 1066: he would regain his lost northern earldom by raiding it. Unfortunately for the success of this plan, his arrival in the Humber was anticipated by Earls Edwin and Morcar, who were, after all, the sons of the last successful practitioner of this Anglo-Saxon protection racket. Tostig landed his men in Lindsey and burned several villages, but before he could become a real terror to the countryside, Edwin and perhaps Morcar came up and drove him out of the area. Most of his Flemish ships then deserted him, and he escaped to Scotland with only twelve ships.[50]

In Scotland, Tostig became involved in a much more promising invasion of the North. Even though King Malcolm supported him and his remaining men over the summer, the complete failure of his expedition must have left him with few prospects for the future beyond small-scale piracy. King Harold Hardrada of Norway was, however, planning to invade England that autumn, and, if subsequent events are a true indication of the king's original plans, he had use for a former earl of the North. Harold Hardrada intended to invade Yorkshire and use it as a base for the conquest of the rest of the kingdom. The employment of this essentially tenth-century scheme, which not even Swein and Cnut had used until after they had spent years pulverizing English resistance, may have been due to bold antiquarianism on the part of the Norwegian king, but it was more probably the result of a very contemporary understanding that conditions in the North were far worse than they had been in Ethelred's day. In any case, Tostig agreed to join this expedition, perhaps through the intermediacy of Copsig, his old associate in governing the North, who had already raised a fleet in the Orkneys.[51] This proved to be Tostig's final blunder.

The Norwegian fleet came west in late August or early September. It stopped at the Orkneys, where Harold was joined by a force led by the earl of these islands and by a group of Irish Sea Vikings. Then it moved down the east coast of Scotland, where it was met by Tostig, who became the vassal of the Norwegian king. The fleet now numbered perhaps three hundred vessels, and its prospects for initial success were good. King Harold of England was in the South waiting for Duke William's invasion, and the North was apparently unguarded. Harold Hardrada and Tostig sailed down the coast, entered the Humber by surprise, and disembarked their forces without meeting any opposition.[52] Their ease of movement suggests that Morcar was not in the North at the time, but there may be another explanation. The chronicles probably contain a minor lacuna at this point. None of them say how long the Norwegians were in the vicinity of York before the battle of Fulford Bridge, nor do they explain in any detail what transpired during that time. This is an important omission because it hides the reaction of the northerners to the Norwegian invasion. The little evidence that does bear on this point is discontinuous and perhaps contradictory. Symeon of Durham says that Harold Hardrada took York by force before he fought Edwin and Morcar,[53] but the C version of the *Anglo-Saxon Chronicle* seems to suggest that the Norwegians entered York only after this

battle, implying that the earls were not in York when the Norwegians landed and that they assembled their army in Mercia.[54] If the
Anglo-Saxon Chronicle is correct on these points, the men of York
made no attempt to oppose the invasion, and this, in turn, could
explain the precipitate reactions of the earls and the king when
they learned of the arrival of Harold Hardrada. They faced not
simply an invasion by the greatest warrior in Christendom, but an
invasion that had received local support in the North.

This interpretation is not beyond question, but the invasion
of the Norwegians certainly did become such a specter before
much time had passed. When King Harold learned of their land-
ing, he immediately began to move north. In the meantime, however, Edwin and Morcar gathered an army and, without waiting for
the arrival of the king, engaged the Norwegians in battle at Fulford
Bridge outside York on September 20, 1066. This reckless decision
must have been made in the hope of preventing Harold Hardrada
from consolidating his position, but, in fact, it produced the opposite result. After what is said to have been a long, hard fight, the
Norwegian king routed the earls, who, in their flight, lost more
men to the river Ouse than they had to Harold in the battle. After
this illustration of his power, Harold Hardrada entered York and
allied with the Yorkshire men. They agreed to help him conquer
the kingdom by going south with his army. They also gave the
Norwegians provisions and exchanged hostages with them. The
full implementation of this alliance was averted, however, by King
Harold of England, who was already nearing the North with an
army. He reached Tadcaster by Sunday, September 24, and advanced through York the next day. The Norwegians had had no
news of his coming and had gone east of the city to Stamford
Bridge to receive hostages from the outlying parts of the shire.
Harold was thus able to catch them by surprise away from their
ships and to bring them to battle. In the fight that followed, he
won a complete victory. Both Harold Hardrada and Tostig were
killed, and twenty ships were sufficient to carry away the surviving
Norwegians.[55]

With this victory Harold ended the immediate threat to his
rule in the North and proved his ability as a military commander,
but from the standpoint of the history of the North, these events
have a different significance. Harold Hardrada's plan, despite its
anachronism, had been basically correct. After at most one battle,

and perhaps from his arrival, the men of York had joined his attempt to conquer England. Given an alternative, they no longer saw a need to be governed by the West Saxon monarchy. This was the legacy of Tostig's attack upon the customs of the North. By 1066, political northern separatism existed, and Harold's victory at Stamford Bridge did nothing to end it.

Had Harold enjoyed a long reign, he might have improved the situation through moderate rule. In the days of Ethelred, ethnic factors may have been partially responsible for the preference of the men of York for the cause of Swein and Cnut, but since that time the problems of the North had been basically political. the revolt of the Bamburgh earls, the unpopular rule of Siward in Northumbria, and finally Tostig's attempt to govern the North. The northerners had allied with Harold Hardrada not because he was Scandinavian, but because they distrusted government from the South. Since this was essentially a political problem, Harold might have been able to quiet northern fears. What Harold in fact did before he left York was more prosaic. Morcar had failed either to control or to defend Yorkshire, and Harold apparently entrusted the shire to Mærlesweïn, an important noble in the northern Danelaw.[56] The source of this information is not beyond question, but it is probably correct. Morcar is called an earl in the chronicles after September of 1066, but he never again is connected with events in the North. This probably means that he had no power above the Humber. Certainly all the northern revolts were led by local nobles.

After installing Mærleswein, Harold went south to face Duke William of Normandy, who had landed while Harold was on his northern campaign. On October 14, the duke completely defeated Harold's army at Hastings, and King Harold himself disappeared into legend. With him went any chance that the problems of the North would find a peaceful solution. During the remaining months of 1066, William consolidated his position in the South by receiving the submissions of the earls, of most of the important churchmen, and of London; and on Christmas day, Archbishop Aldred of York crowned him as the successor of the Anglo-Saxon kings. This meant disaster for the North. As king, William inherited all the problems of northern government that had been created before his arrival, but he lacked the necessary knowledge, if not the will, to deal with them.

Before returning to Normandy in March of 1067, William made his first attempt to provide government for the North, and a worse choice is difficult to imagine. He gave the earldom of Northumbria to Copsig, Tostig's old associate, who had submitted to William at Barking in early 1067.[57] This was an incredible decision: Copsig had been an agent of Tostig's government and had taken part in the earl's invasion of 1066. Furthermore, if the stories of Tostig meeting Harold Hardrada at the mouth of the Tyne are true, Copsig had probably supported himself by piracy at the expense of the very men whom he was now called upon to govern.[58] Any one of these deeds was enough to make Copsig unpopular in the North; it is exceedingly difficult to imagine what William thought he was doing. To make any sense out of the situation, it is necessary to posit that Osulf, who had held Northumbria under Morcar, had refused to submit to William and that Morcar was no longer the earl of the North. Otherwise, the appointment of a new earl would have been a direct provocation both to the Northumbrians and to Morcar. Beyond this, only conjecture is possible. Perhaps the most likely explanation is that William was trying to be conciliatory by sending a near native to be earl, but that he had inaccurate knowledge of the revolt of 1065 that came from Tostig. The latter had spent the winter of 1065–66 in Flanders, where he could have been in communication with Duke William. Tostig is said to have charged in another context that the northern revolt had been the result of a conspiracy headed by his brother Harold;[59] and, if William believed this, the appointment of Copsig would not have seemed absurd. On the other hand, Copsig himself may have been partially responsible for the decision. He was clearly adept at survival, having lived through the revolt of 1065, Tostig's invasion of 1066, and probably the battle of Stamford Bridge; there is no knowing what a man of his talents may have told the new king.

Whatever role misinformation may have played in making Copsig earl, it clearly did not affect his behavior, for he had no illusions about the necessities of his government. In early February 1067, he came north with a band of retainers and took the traditional first step toward establishing one's rule above the Tees: he sought out Osulf, the current representative of the house of Bamburgh. He probably intended to kill or capture Osulf, but failed. Copsig only succeeded in driving him into the hills where he began the easy task of gathering an army. The return of Copsig convinced the Northumbrians, if they had any doubts, that they could expect no better treatment from William than they had received from Edward the Confessor. The new earl had crossed the Tees as an invader in the direct tradition of other Yorkshire men who would have ruled Northumbria—Thurbrand, Carl, and Siward—and more recently, of course, Tostig. Within five weeks, therefore, Osulf was able to raise an army with which to administer the equally traditional solution to the problem. On March 12, he surprised Copsig at a banquet in Newburn. The earl tried to save himself by fleeing to a church, but the Northumbrians set the church on fire. When Copsig was at last forced out, Osulf cut off his head.[60]

The sending of Copsig into Northumbria had been clearly a mistake both for the earl, who had lost his life, and for William, whose authority had been flouted. The earl's personal unpopularity and his attack on Osulf were undoubtedly the major causes of the revolt, but certain evidence suggests that the Northumbrian revolt of 1067 was an echo of the revolt of 1065 on another level. William the Conqueror's most pressing need in early 1067 was booty. His mercenary army had not followed him to England just because they believed in the validity of his claim to the throne. He needed money to pay off his soldiers, and in 1067 he levied a heavy geld to supply it. The collection of this money from Northumbria must have been Copsig's first responsibility; indeed, the promise that he could collect it may have been the chief factor that prompted William to appoint him earl. Copsig had, after all, substantial experience in extracting money from the North. No source says that the Northumbrians rose against the earl because of the tax, but this may well have been an important factor in their revolt. The two events were separated by only a short period of time. William imposed the tax sometime between Christmas of 1066 and his return to Normandy around February 21, 1067. Copsig went north in mid-February and was killed about five weeks later on March 12. The Northumbrians had revolted in 1065 in part over unjust taxes, and they threatened to do the same in 1072–74 over another attempt to collect taxes above the Tees.[61] Furthermore, the geld of 1067 struck the North as being outrageous. The version of the *Anglo-Saxon Chronicle* written at York notes that William had promised to rule in the manner of his best predecessors, then says:

"All the same he laid taxes on the people very severely." The Peterborough version, on the other hand, mentions this tax in a matter-of-fact way and only in passing.[62] Given these factors, it is quite possible that William's first geld provided the Northumbrians with an example of Norman tyranny that was quite as frightening as the return of Copsig and reminiscent of the rule of Tostig.

From two points of view, then, William's dealings with the North must have raised the specter of Tostig's attack on the privileges of the North, and it is no wonder that Osulf was able to move through the Northumbrian countryside at the head of a small army without anyone warning Copsig of his approach. As at York in 1065, the sympathies of the people were with the rebels. Ironically, however, William was spared the full consequences of his mistakes by events in Northumbria. The killing of Copsig marked the beginning of a revolt that was directly analogous to the one of 1016, but this withdrawal from William's lordship soon ended in an ignominious fashion. In the fall of 1067, Osulf, who was evidently trying to maintain the normal functions of government, was killed while attempting to bring an outlaw to justice, and this event gave William the opportunity to reestablish his authority above the Tees without military intervention. Upon his return from Normandy in December, the king sold the earldom of Northumbria to Cospatric, son of Maldred, who was an adventurer appallingly suited to the chaos that was now developing above the Humber. His father Maldred had been the brother of King Duncan of Scotland, the father of Malcolm III, and his mother had been a daughter of Earl Uhtred and his third wife, a daughter of King Ethelred.[63] Cospatric was, consequently, closely connected with both Scotland and Northumbria, and it is impossible to say which connection he valued more. In any case, he was able to go north and establish himself as earl, theoretically under the lordship of William.

The fact that the king had sold him the earldom probably indicates that William was uncertain whether he could extract a regular income from Northumbria, and the events of 1068 show that this fear was not without foundation, for the same sequence of taxation and revolt occurred as in 1067 except on a wider scale and unobscured by other factors. William levied his second geld at some date between early December 1067 and late March 1068.[64] In the spring, Edwin and Morcar revolted, and the northerners joined with them. Indeed, the North is said to have been the main center of trouble in 1068,[65] and the current geld was probably responsible. One of the basic laws of northern political behavior was that it took a specific outrage to bring the northern thegns into the field. This had been true of every revolt since the first cause célèbre, the murder of Uhtred in 1016, and it continued to be true through the last northern revolt in 1080. Only in 1068 do the chronicles make the North rise spontaneously. Since this is at variance with the northerners' usual behavior and since it is clear that William's government and soldiers had left the North untouched until this point, the most probable explanation is that the king's demands for money provided the northerners with the necessary concrete example of Norman tyranny.

The revolt that materialized was entirely in accordance with this explanation. It was essentially negative, a rejection of William's power, and did not, at least in its initial stages, represent an attempt to drive the Normans out of England. The *Anglo-Saxon Chronicle*'s laconic description of the beginning of the rebellion caught its spirit accurately: "Then the king was informed that the people in the North were gathered together and meant to make a stand against him if he came."[66] William was faced in the spring of 1068 with a general revolt of the North that aimed at denying his authority. The situation was particularly ominous because the rising was led by the existing governmental authorities above the Humber, Cospatric, his new earl of Northumbria, and Mærleswein, both of whom apparently preferred battle to trying to tax the men of their earldoms. The only important man in the North known to have opposed the revolt was Archbishop Aldred, who had had firsthand experience with William's power, but he could do nothing.[67] The rebels knew, of course, that the king would come North and made preparations against the event. They probably decided to hold the Humber-Aire line, a tactic that could deny William access to most of the North and was followed in 1069,[68] but beyond this their plans are a matter of conjecture. They may have thought that they could withstand the Conqueror with the help of Mercia; this alliance had worked against Edward the Confessor in 1065. Furthermore, Edgar the Atheling had escaped from William's control by the spring of 1068, and some may have wished to crown him king. Alternatively, the northerners may have hoped for foreign aid. English malcontents had been seeking the intervention of King Swein of Denmark, who had a claim to the throne; and King

Malcolm of Scotland seems to have been planning an invasion of the North for the summer of 1068.[69] None of these possibilities materialized. While the northern thegns, posturing in heroic fashion, lived in tents to avoid the enervating effects of houses and fortified suitable places along the Humber and in the swamps and woods of the West Riding, William acted quickly. Any military calculations of the northerners that were based either on their revolt against Edward or on a memory of the long campaigns of Ethelred's reign were soon proved false. The king first went to Warwick, where he built a castle, which induced Edwin and Morcar to abandon the revolt. He then advanced to Nottingham and erected a second castle. These two successes demoralized the northerners, who were now without domestic allies as they found the king bearing down upon them. Cospatric, Mærleswein, and Edgar the Atheling fled to Scotland with several important thegns, and the men of York submitted to the king, who entered the city and raised a castle within its walls.[70] Thus, without a single battle, William had overcome the revolt of 1068. It had been a fiasco, and the northerners' brave talk of the springtime about standing against the king had only resulted in the exile of their native leaders and the imposition of direct Norman rule by midsummer. They had been shown to be militarily ineffective, and William's triumph seemed complete.

These were the lessons the revolt of 1068 seemed to teach, but both were in reality deceptive. William's only accomplishment in 1068 was to set the stage for the debacle of 1069. Such military power as existed in the North had not been destroyed. The northerners had submitted because their allies had deserted them. In these circumstances, they judged it wise to recognize the king and thereby avoid the reprisals that would follow a military defeat, but they had not been cowed. Their refusal to meet William in the field was as much the result of their conception of warfare as of the size of his army or his military reputation. Although the northerners occasionally fought regular battles as at Carham in 1018, their taste usually ran to rural ambushes, raids, and surprise attacks on settlements. The history of the North after 1000 establishes this beyond dispute. While such tactics may have struck the Normans as treachery incarnate, they were an effective adaptation to the small population and broken terrain of the North. No invader with a large army was likely to stay in the North for long, and upon his departure, the thegns who had been skulking in the woods and hills could reemerge and follow the tactics used by Osulf in 1067 or by the northern rebels in 1065. The employment of such means of resistance was in turn the reason why so many members of the house of Bamburgh had been killed through treachery by men wishing to govern the North; false promises were literally the only means to catch them. In 1068, William himself may have tried to employ this device. While in York, he sent the bishop of Durham to Scotland to make a peace treaty and probably to get Malcolm to disgorge the leaders of the northern revolt, who had taken refuge in Lothian, or more probably in Cumberland, but despite the assertion of Orderic Vitalis that Malcolm swore fealty to William through ambassadors,[71] Æthelwine of Durham clearly failed to accomplish very much. Malcolm did not expel the northerners, and Cospatric, Mærleswein, and Edgar the Atheling remained at large to lead future revolts.

These men were a threat because William's success in 1068 provided the provocation for renewed insurrection. The revolt of 1068 had resulted from William's failure to govern the North through its native leaders, who had, in fact, led the resistance to the king. He was thus left with no realistic alternative but to replace them with Normans. Consequently, he built a castle, garrisoned it with five hundred picked men under William Malet, and entrusted the government of Yorkshire to Robert fitz Richard.[72] This decision was understandable given the situation, but it led to disaster nonetheless. The imposition of direct Norman rule coupled with the gelds of 1067 and 1068 must have struck the men of York as a direct parallel to the government of Tostig. Furthermore, the Normans apparently acted rapaciously. Dark rumors come out of this period about the imprisonment of Yorkshire thegns and the confiscation of their estates, and these stories apparently have some basis in fact, for William Malet, the governor of York castle, definitely had acquired estates in the shire before the fall of 1069. The same general picture of Norman behavior is suggested by the existence of an immense treasure inside York castle by autumn.[73] This money had clearly been extracted from the surrounding countryside, and its collection coupled with the taking of native lands by whatever means was shortsighted and provocative.

The actual spark that set off the new revolt occurred in Northumbria. By the winter of 1068, Norman control of Yorkshire must have seemed secure enough for William to make an attempt to bring the lands above the Tees under his control, and to accomplish this he appointed a new earl, Robert de Comines, and sent him North with seven hundred men. In January, Robert and his men crossed the Tees and entered Durham, where they killed and plundered peasants who were unlucky enough to be in their path. This action must have confirmed the worst fears of the residents of Durham concerning the real meaning of the Norman Conquest, and they devised a stratagem to deal with the invaders. As Robert approached, they left the city and hid in the surrounding countryside. Bishop Æthelwine warned him upon his arrival that the Northumbrians were laying a trap, but he took no notice, perhaps feeling that William's easy triumph at York the previous summer had shown the mettle of the northerners. Robert entered the city and allowed his men to plunder the houses, which was probably what the Northumbrians had hoped would happen. After night had fallen, the natives assembled and broke through the town's gates without warning. By this time the Frenchmen were scattered throughout the city, undoubtedly in a state of complete disarray. Exhausted by the day's plundering, confused, and disorganized in a strange, dark town, they could offer no effective resistance, and the Northumbrians slaughtered them all except for one or two survivors: Earl Robert himself was cut down in traditional fashion as he tried to escape the burning house in which he had sought refuge.[74]

The successful massacre of the Norman force at Durham signaled the beginning of the last general rising of the North, and the Normans were now to learn the maddening nature of northern tactics. A band of rebels caught Robert fitz Richard, the governor of York, away from the protection of York castle and killed him and a group of his retainers. The castle garrison was the only remaining Norman force above the Humber, and they were in the greatest jeopardy. Cospatric, Mærleswein, and Edgar the Atheling had returned from Scotland when the insurrection began, and they moved on York with an army, which was soon strengthened by Archil, the greatest Yorkshire thegn, and the four sons of Carl. The presence of Cospatric and the sons of Carl in the same army was of grave significance. Carl had killed Ealdred, Cospatric's uncle; Carl's father Thurbrand had killed Uhtred, Cospatric's grandfather. The union of men who had every reason to hate one another was an appalling indication of the degree of northern hostility to the Normans, and William Malet quickly felt its force. The rebels entered York and, in alliance with the men of the city, besieged the castle, whose defenders sent word to William that unless they were relieved, they would suffer the fate of Robert de Comines and Robert fitz Richard. The king responded to this threat as quickly as he had to the revolt of 1068. He moved north and surprised the besiegers within the city walls before the castle fell. There followed a shadowy encounter between the king and the northerners in the streets that ended in the relief of the castle and the flight of the rebels. Either as part of this battle or after its conclusion, the Normans ravaged the city and plundered the churches.[75]

The chronicles describe this expedition as a victory for the king, but actually his success was only partial. He had kept possession of York and inflicted a tactical defeat on the northerners. To strengthen his hold on the city, William stayed there for eight days and built a second castle, which he entrusted to William fitz Osbern.[76] The choice of this man, perhaps William's most trusted and capable subordinate, probably indicates that the king realized the limitations of his recent victory. It had produced no political agreement with the northerners, and they were still in revolt. All their important leaders had escaped the battle in the city and had retreated to the hills with their men to await the departure of William. This came soon enough, leaving William fitz Osbern waiting for the counterattack of the rebels. He, however, was a more formidable opponent than either Robert de Comines or Robert fitz Richard had been, and he probably had the further advantage of knowing what to expect from the northerners, who had already conducted four surprise attacks on cities or towns since 1065. When they did indeed try to repeat this tactic, William fitz Osbern was not caught unprepared. They assembled in the hills sometime after Easter, intending to renew the siege of the castles, but before they could reach the city, he caught them in the open and defeated them.[77]

This victory relieved the immediate pressure on York, but it did not end the revolt, whose leaders were still free and commanding the survivors of the two recent defeats. Indeed, the Norman leaders must have been coming to the realization that they were facing a basically impossible situation in the North. Their defeats of the rebels had neither destroyed the latter's military strength nor proven their tactics unworkable. After each defeat, the northerners had only retreated to lurk in the hills awaiting a new Norman mistake, and the mechanics of this situation are probably illustrated by the behavior of the Norman force William sent to avenge the killing of Earl Robert de Comines and his men. This army left York in the late spring or summer and advanced as far as Northallerton in the North Riding of Yorkshire. Here the Normans were surrounded by a dense fog that prompted an immediate retreat to York. Symeon of Durham says that St. Cuthbert had sent this fog to protect the men of Durham and that the Normans realized its supernatural origin.[78] In fact, they must have feared an attack by the northerners in the fog, and whether such was likely is beside the point. In an open field on a clear day, the Normans did not fear the rebels; when conditions were otherwise, they did.

The main hope of the northerners by this time was probably that they would receive outside aid. It must have been known in the North by the summer of 1069 that King Swein of Denmark was planning to send an expedition to England that fall. His ambition to claim the English throne had been encouraged by English money, and it is likely that much of it had come from the North.[79] All that the northerners had to do was to hide in the hills until autumn, when they could emerge with a good chance of driving the Normans from the North. They presumably thought that Swein would go on to defeat William later, perhaps after several years of war on the model of the fighting of Ethelred's days.

Unfortunately for the North, only the first part of this plan worked. The Danish fleet duly arrived in the fall, led by Swein's brother Osbeorn and two of the king's sons. It consisted of two hundred forty ships and included warriors from Poland, Saxony, and Frisia in addition to Danes. Theoretically, this force was large enough to challenge William the Conqueror himself, particularly given the English allies it would assuredly find, but this possibility was mocked by subsequent events. The Danes had come to England to fight an antique campaign. They slowly plundered their way up the coast and entered the Humber on September 8. By this time, their sluggishness had destroyed any chance of surprise, one of the main advantages of a seaborne attack, and William had been able to warn his men in York of their approach. The advance knowledge did not save York, but the Danes' aversion to pressing an advantage was an ill omen for the North, nonetheless. The northern rebels also knew that the Danes were coming, and Edgar the Atheling, Mærleswein, and Waltheof, Siward's son, had gathered a fleet of their own from unknown sources. They, too, evidently thought that seaborne raids offered the best hope of beating William, and the initial encounter seemed to confirm this idea. When the Danes arrived in the Humber, the rebels joined them. Archbishop Aldred suddenly died. He was the man who had crowned William and presumably foresaw the destruction to come. The Danes waited several days in the Humber to give Cospatric with the Northumbrians and a group of rebels from Yorkshire, led by Archil and the sons of Carl, time to join the main force. When this was accomplished, the composite host moved up the estuary toward the city. As they approached, the Normans fired the houses near the castles which they feared might be used to fill up the ditches around the castles, but they did their work too well, for the flames spread to the rest of the city and York burned. The next day the Danes and rebels marched into the still burning city with the leaders of the North in the van. They caught the Normans in the streets, and the outcome was as decisive as in Durham in January. The entire Norman force was either killed or captured.[80]

To understand the strange and awesome events that followed this victory, it is necessary to put aside hindsight. Neither the northerners nor the Danes knew that they were soon to be the object of William the Conqueror's most brutal campaign. Nor is there evidence that the Danes had come to England to fight a major battle with William in the fall of 1069. Had that been their intention, it would have been far simpler to land in southern England and offer battle. The taking of York had cost time and men, and it had brought them no immediate accretion of strength. The destruction of William's power above the Humber had satisfied the immediate aims of the rebels. The Northumbrians are known to have gone home for the winter,[81] and it is likely that the Yorkshire men did the same. The Danes were thus left in possession of York, and this had probably been their goal from the beginning. They had come to England to destroy Norman power in the North and to establish a base there for the subsequent conquest of the rest of the kingdom. This is the simplest and most reasonable explanation for their actions, and it is supported by the fact that King Swein did arrive in the Humber in the spring, intending to launch a campaign.[82] He found then that he was too late and that his expeditionary force was in a pitiable condition. The reason was simple and only partially the result of the acts of William the Conqueror: the cost of taking York had been too high. Because of the fire the Normans had set, the city had been nearly destroyed, and this had put the Danes in a bad position. With York intact, they could have shut themselves up behind its walls and snugly waited for spring, and William could have done little. To besiege the city would have required that the Normans spend the winter in the open, which would probably have broken their health and would have failed in any case, given Danish control of the Ouse and Humber. To take York by assault would have been extremely dangerous. The Danes and the northerners were equal— if not superior—to the Normans in hand-to-hand fighting. But for the burning of York, William would have faced these grim alternatives.

As it was, the plans of the Danes were seriously upset. October and William the Conqueror were both advancing against them, and their behavior, which seems aimless in the pages of Orderic Vitalis, was largely the result of this quandary. They needed a place to spend the winter, but William would not give them time to establish one. Initially they tried to salvage as much of their original plan as possible by going down to the Isle of Axholme at the head of the Humber and fortifying it as a winter base. This attempt was frustrated by William, however, who had launched a late fall campaign. The destruction of York had given him a chance to fight the Danes in the open, and he had seized this opportunity with the fury and vindictiveness of a man who has narrowly escaped a fight for his life. William reached Lindsey with an army before the Danes' fortifications were complete, and he was consequently able to enter the swamps and drive them back across the Humber into Yorkshire. This defeat did not make them desist from their plan, however. Once the king had left the area to deal with a secondary revolt in Staffordshire, the Danes recrossed the Humber and moved into Lindsey to establish a camp. There a Norman force, which the king had left behind, fell upon them by surprise and dispersed them for a second time.[83]

These two encounters were a serious setback for the Danes, who still lacked a winter base, and they must have made it obvious to William that they had no intention of fighting a major battle.

The possibilities opened to him by this knowledge meant doom for the North. After being driven out of Lindsey, the Danes had returned to Yorkshire, and it was rumored that they intended to reoccupy York. This was an admission that their situation had become very serious, and William, who had returned from the West, followed them into the North. The Yorkshire men were not caught entirely unprepared by this development, however. They occupied the northern bank of the river Aire and held it against the Normans for three weeks. Perhaps they thought they could hold this position all winter, although it is more likely that the Aire represented an extemporized line of defense. Neither the northerners nor the Danes seem to have made any preparations in case the Normans crossed the river, and when this occurred, all organized resistance disappeared. William forded the Aire far upstream and moved directly on York through the hills. By the time he arrived, the Danes had abandoned the indefensible city and were apparently lying in the Humber aboard their ships;[84] they were now in an untenable position. William's relentless pressure had made it impossible for them to establish a base either north or south of the Humber, and winter had come. They could not go home, nor would they fight. Osbeorn, the Danish leader, therefore admitted his defeat and came to an agreement with William. The king gave him money and promised that the Danes could forage along the coasts of the North; Osbeorn promised to depart in the spring without fighting.[85]

This ignominious conclusion to the Danish invasion left the North exposed to the full fury of William the Conqueror's wrath. The rebels had evidently retreated to the hills when the king crossed the Aire, assuming, no doubt, that this invasion would lead to no more permanent results than his earlier trips north had. William could be expected to rebuild the castles, but with the coming of spring, they could issue from their dens to attack them, probably in alliance with the Danes, who might have forgotten by then their promise to go home. If the northerners reasoned in this way, they were completely mistaken, for William the Conqueror was not to be tricked again. He had learned the nature of northern tactics from the revolts of 1068 and 1069, and he now adopted a plan that would make it impossible for the North to revolt after his departure. Leaving detachments to watch the movements of the Danes and to repair the castles, he entered the hills to hunt down and kill the rebels. The success of this operation may have been strictly limited by the rebels' knowledge of the terrain of the North, but this made little difference in the long run because the main Norman effort was reserved for the peasants, who were completely unprotected with their leaders hiding and the Danes neutralized. William sent groups of soldiers throughout the Vale of York and the major river valleys with orders to harry the peasants, and this ghastly tactic finally brought "peace" to the North. The Normans massacred many peasants outright, but the large number who must have escaped were ultimately doomed as completely. The soldiers burned the villages and the grain from the last harvest; they also made certain that no crop would be planted in the spring by destroying the plows and other tools of the peasants and by wantonly slaughtering the livestock.[86]

The most intense destruction took place in Yorkshire, but the Northumbrians did not escape completely. William held a macabre Christmas court in the burnt-out shell of York to which he had brought all the visible paraphernalia of his kingship to symbolize the legitimacy of the continuing slaughter. He then dislodged a group of rebels from Holderness and moved to the Tees, where he received the submissions of Cospatric and Waltheof. The termination of their defiance did not save the Northumbrians, however. William crossed the river with the intention of wasting the countryside, but the situation in Durham was somewhat different than that in Yorkshire. The villages were empty. The peasants, knowing what to expect from the Normans, had escaped to the hills and forests with their herds and movable property, and the bishop and clerks had fled to Lindisfarne, leaving Durham deserted. William was consequently unable to destroy native society above the Tees as completely as in Yorkshire. The Normans marched in two major groups through eastern and central Durham to the Tyne, where they destroyed Jarrow. Then they devastated the Tyne valley and perhaps southern Northumberland as far west as Hexham, but their impact on this sparsely populated land was too small to warrant a long stay. Sometime in January, William led his army back to the Tees by way of the Roman road through the Pennine foothills and continued on to York. There he garrisoned the castles and made arrangements for the government of the North before striking west over the Pennines to harry Cheshire.[87]

When the spring of 1070 arrived, the northern rebels did

not emerge from the hills to continue their revolt. They had resisted the Norman Conquest because they had feared a basic re-
definition of the relationship between the North and the king. This
fear had its origin in Tostig's murders and taxes, and it had been
intensified by William's appointment of Copsig, by his gelds, and
by the imposition of direct Norman rule in 1068. In 1070, this fear
was no longer important. The harrying of the North had been an
attempt to produce an artificial famine, and it had succeeded. Few
details survive, but the general picture is clear. The chronicles
agree that there was no food in the North for those who lived
through the military operations of the winter of 1069–70. Some of
the greater nobles survived, but the mass of the peasantry faced a
grim future in which mechanisms let loose by the harrying continued the destruction long after William had left. After eating their
domestic animals and horses, some peasants sold themselves into
slavery to avoid starvation. Others joined the bands of outlaws
that formed in the free zone and plundered villages that had
escaped the Normans. Many starved to death; according to Symeon
of Durham, the roads and huts of the North were littered with
decaying bodies that spread disease among the living. There is
even evidence that the harrying upset the balance between human
society and nature so that the wolves came down from the hills to
feast on the bounty of William the Conqueror.[88] Substantial numbers of northerners apparently tried to escape this nightmarish
world by fleeing to the South and perhaps to Scotland. Their presence is recorded as far away as Evesham, but this expedient did
little good, for many died or became slaves nonetheless.[89] These
conditions ensured that the North would never again threaten
William's control of England. He had solved the political problem
of the North by destroying native society in Yorkshire and by
severely damaging it in Durham.

5. Government by
Punitive Expedition

Under the very eyes of the Danes, who wintered in the Humber, Yorkshire had been turned into a wasteland. By spring, their army, probably demoralized by failure and certainly half starved as a result of the Norman tactics, was no longer a dangerous fighting force.[1] Nor did a native army reappear to try to capture the castles in York. To this extent the harrying of the North was a complete success; it had ended the last significant threat to William's possession of the Anglo-Saxon crown; but its effects should not be exaggerated. William had done his best to destroy native society in Yorkshire in order to solve his immediate problem during the winter of 1069, and in certain respects the destruction strengthened royal control over Yorkshire. Yorkshire could no longer be used as a base for a Scandinavian attack on the rest of the kingdom. This unhappy shire could not even support its own inhabitants. Furthermore, Yorkshire could now be integrated into the Anglo-Norman kingdom in a way that the old earldom had never been. The earldom was, of course, suppressed, and the royal demesne was soon bloated with confiscated estates to provide the sheriffs, who now administered the shire, with a sound financial base.[2] These were important considerations, but the limitations and negative effects of the harrying were just as pertinent, if not more so, in the years following 1070. Although most of the men of York were now just as dead as the heroic age, a number of years passed before either of these truths gained currency across the North Sea. Despite the harrying of the North, Scandinavians would still dream from time to time of reenacting antique feats of plunder and pillage in England, and some actually would come to try. Moreover, if the men of York could not aid invading Danes, neither could the peasants of Yorkshire support very many Normans. In 1070, the redevelopment of Yorkshire lay many years in the future.

The situation in the North was more complex than historians have usually portrayed it. The harrying of the North established William as the most powerful and feared dispenser of political authority in the North, but it did not give him complete control or render his authority unassailable. His power was limited and his authority open to attack because the old political and military realities of the North reasserted themselves in 1070 and the years that followed.

William's first two appointments suggest that he understood his weakness in the North. The archbishopric of York and the earldom of Northumbria were vacant in 1070, and the king filled both positions during the year. To the first he appointed Thomas, a canon from Bayeux and a protégé of Bishop Odo, the king's half brother.[3] Thomas did not, however, succeed to all the old privileges and liberties of the position. Lanfranc, the archbishop of Canterbury, made a successful attempt with the king's support to limit Thomas's freedom by demanding a profession of obedience from him. This demand and its repetition at the consecration of later archbishops of York led to a bitter controversy between York and Canterbury that lasted into the twelfth century. The later stages in this dispute were marked by polemics and forgeries and form an unedifying episode in ecclesiastical politics, but in the beginning, serious issues were involved concerning the general nature of the church in England.[4] The question also had important political implications in 1070. Hugh the Chantor, the early twelfth-century historian of York, asserted that Lanfranc defended his demand for a profession of obedience from Thomas before the king with the argument: "It was expedient for the unity and solidarity of the kingdom that all Britain should be subject to one primate; it might otherwise happen, in the king's time or in that of one of his successors, that some one of the Danes, Norwegians or Scots, who used to sail up to York in their attacks on the realm, might be made king by the archbishop of York, and the fickle and treacherous Yorkshire men, and the kingdom disturbed and divided."[5] Lanfranc's argument was not simply a device to further his own ecclesiastical aggrandizement but was based on a real possibility. The Danes took York in 1075, and in 1085 they prepared an expeditionary force that caused William the Conqueror great anxiety. Moreover, in the spring of 1070, the year of Thomas's appointment, King Swein entered the Humber to take command of the remnants of his fleet. He intended to violate Earl Osbeorn's promise of the previous winter to depart England in peace, or so the survivors of the harrying thought. In the words of the *Anglo-Saxon Chronicle*, "The local people came to meet him and made a truce with him—they expected that he was going to conquer the country."[6] Some four or five months after the harrying of Yorkshire, the men of York were still prepared to support a Danish invader; and, although nothing serious happened in 1070, the incident shows that Lanfranc's fear that the Normans could not keep the Danes out of Yorkshire had some foundation.

Norman weakness in the North is shown even more clearly in William's other appointment in 1070. Sometime after Christmas of 1069, he had received the submissions of Cospatric and Waltheof on the banks of the Tees; presumably around this time, he reinstated the former as earl of Northumbria.[7] This act of forgiveness was uncharacteristic of the Conqueror's dealing with landed English rebels, and it was a sign that he had no realistic hope of depriving Cospatric of power or of controlling Northumbria. William cannot have had much faith in Cospatric, who had been in rebellion since he purchased the earldom from the king in 1068. In 1070, however, the castles at York were the de facto northern limit of William's realm, and fifty miles of empty countryside separated them from Durham.[8] Even kings of the stature of Cnut had had trouble governing Northumbria, and the harrying made this task doubly difficult for William. He could not play the old game of using the men of York to keep the Northumbrians in check and therefore he was forced to recognize Cospatric, the current representative of the house of Bamburgh, as earl. This decision may have been distasteful to the king, but the establishment of some agreement with Cospatric, no matter how hollow, was far preferable to the alternative of Cospatric submitting to his cousin Malcolm Canmore or ambushing a new Norman earl.

The difficulty of exercising power beyond York led William to maintain the Northumbrian earldom; but there was a dark side to this situation for the Northumbrians. The ruin of Yorkshire may have insulated them from Norman power, but it left them to face the Scots alone. This, too, became obvious in 1070, when Malcolm

launched his second invasion of the North. He was still in possession of Cumberland, which he had won from Tostig in 1061, and
he now showed how this flanking position could be used against the
English. Sometime during the summer, the Scottish king led an
army, probably mainly composed of Galwegians, into Cumberland.
This force then moved up the Vale of Eden, across Stainmore, and
down into Teesdale, where it began to plunder the countryside.[9]

Malcolm's intentions on this occasion, as on most others,
are obscure. His invasions may have been only large raids conducted to gain booty and slaves. Yet this idea, whose principal
recent exponent was R. L. Graeme Ritchie, has been rejected by
John Le Patourel in general terms and seems especially difficult to
sustain in the case of the invasion of 1070.[10] Malcolm's armies did
undoubtedly come for plunder, but if this was the only consideration, the 1070 invasion was ill-conceived. Yorkshire had already
been wasted by the Normans, and the Scots could have gotten
more booty further north. Both the route Malcolm's army took
during the first stage of the invasion and the fact that this was
the only known Scottish invasion between 1000 and 1200 that originated solely in the West were highly unusual. The main element of
most Scottish invasions was a thrust over the Tweed. In 1070,
Northumbria was left untouched at first. Given the configuration
of the border, this must have been intentional, and it probably
means that Malcolm hoped to isolate Northumbria further by
completing the destruction of the North Riding. Perhaps he hoped
to detach the earldom once he had shown the Northumbrians that
he could conduct a campaign in Yorkshire. Cospatric was, after all,
his cousin, and might be willing to change sides.

Initially the invasion went fairly well. The Scots plundered
and burned down the south side of Teesdale and moved east into
Cleveland, which they also wasted. The Normans apparently did
not respond; but after Malcolm was in Cleveland, something went
wrong with his plans. The Scots crossed the Tees into Hartness and
began to ravage up the coast toward Wearmouth.[11] This violation
of Cospatric's earldom destroyed any chance that Malcolm might
reach an understanding with the earl and jeopardized the expedition's booty. The Scottish attack on Durham was illogical from the
standpoint of either politics or plunder; the most likely explanation
for this incursion is that Malcolm had lost control of his army.
This was always a danger with a Scottish army, particularly one

with Galwegians in it, and the king's soldiers may have gone into Durham to find more abundant booty or simply to obtain food. In any case, Cospatric immediately struck back. He did not elect to meet the Scots in the field, for he was in no position to repeat the deeds of Uhtred or of Eadulf that had resulted in the decoration of Durham's walls with the severed heads of defeated Scots. Instead Cospatric led a counterraid up the Tyne gap into Cumberland, where he stole the booty Malcolm had gathered in Teesdale and sent back over Stainmore. This raid enraged Malcolm, who, in retaliation, ordered his men to kill or enslave everyone who fell into their power. The Scottish king apparently viewed Cospatric's conduct as a breach of faith in some sense, but alternatively he may only have reacted in frustration because whatever political aims he may have had were now impossible.[12] The enmity that had arisen between Malcolm and Cospatric reduced the 1070 invasion to the status of a raid. The Galwegians committed atrocities and filled Scotland with English slaves. Cospatric harassed them with sallies from Bamburgh and remained William's earl.[13]

This in itself is somewhat curious. Cospatric's behavior probably cannot be explained on the basis of loyalty to William. He may simply have feared Malcolm more than he did William even though he and the Scottish king were first cousins and the earl had spent time in Malcolm's court. Or Cospatric's behavior may reflect the strength of the political bond that united Northumbria with the Anglo-Saxon crown, particularly when the Northumbrians were faced with Galwegians. There is not sufficient evidence to draw a conclusion. Cospatric clearly was in a difficult situation because the destruction of Yorkshire made a defense of the North impossible. Reinforcements could not be obtained from Yorkshire to help beat back the Scots, and the only other source of aid, a royal expedition, could not make good this deficiency. Even if the king found it convenient to send an army north, it would inevitably arrive too late.

Indeed, it is very hard to make sense out of Cospatric's political position between 1070 and 1072. His recorded acts, although scanty, seem to have been proper. In 1070, he defended his earldom, and in 1071, he followed William's orders concerning the bishopric of Durham. Æthelwine, who had become bishop under Tostig, had been outlawed late in 1069, and in 1071, William gave the bishopric to Walcher, a secular priest from Lotharingia, whom the king had invited to England to fill the post.[14] This appointment was another sign that Northumbria was not secure enough to be used as patronage for one of the king's faithful clerks. William did what he could, of course, to get Walcher started. He sent the bishop to York under the care of a housecarl named Eilaf with an imposing group of magnates and ordered Cospatric to conduct him on to Durham; the earl complied. Cospatric's behavior, however, had another side. The king's enemies were not necessarily his enemies. Several of the leaders of the revolts against William were still at large, and they were using the Northumbrian ports. In 1070, Edgar the Atheling, Siward Barn, and Mærleswein were at Wearmouth with a considerable body of followers, and Bishop Æthelwine took ship for Flanders from the same port several months after he was outlawed.[15] All these men eventually joined Malcolm in Scotland, and the next year Siward Barn and Bishop Æthelwine with a large body of men came south again and joined Hereward on Ely.[16] They almost certainly stopped along the Northumbrian coast, and, although the brief descriptions of these movements do not connect them in any way with Cospatric, it is very difficult to believe that the earl's old allies were sailing up and down the coast of his earldom without at least his tacit consent.

In 1072, William the Conqueror tried to put an end to the ambiguity and chaos in the North. He had been unable to respond to Malcolm's invasion for two years because of troubles in the fens with the remnants of King Swein's fleet and with the English rebels on Ely. By 1072, these difficulties were past, and some action above the Tees was necessary as the last step in the consolidation of his power over the Anglo-Saxon kingdom.[17] The extent of William's plans is not, however, self-evident. Undoubtedly he wanted to punish Malcolm for his invasion or invasions and to force him to abandon his policy of harboring Anglo-Saxon rebels and allowing them to use his kingdom as a base for operations in England. The latter aim would require the creation of a political understanding with Malcolm. Ritchie has asserted that the preceding objectives constituted his only aims and that William had no intention of conquering Scotland in 1072. Ritchie's argument depends entirely upon the inherent difficulties in conquering Scotland—the lay of the land, the distances, and the absence of strong points that had to be defended.[18] These considerations were probably irrelevant to William's intentions in the summer of 1072. The king did not know that Malcolm would refuse battle, nor can it be assumed that he was well informed on the geography of Scotland. In fact, there is not enough evidence to say with any certainty how ambitious William's plans were in 1072, and the idea that he wished to conquer Scotland is just as likely as is its opposite.

If, however, William did hope to accomplish great things in 1072, these plans did not last long. During the summer, he collected an army of cavalry and a fleet, and after mid-August he began to move north along the east coast. With him was Eadric the Wild, presumably to give advice on how to deal with Celts. The fleet was perhaps intended to bring supplies and also to act against Anglo-Saxon pirates in the Scottish ports. The invasion went smoothly but not too successfully. William crossed into Lothian, but apparently Malcolm refused battle. With the Scots withdrawing before them, the Normans marched through Lothian and crossed the Forth into Scotland proper, where they "found nothing that they were any better for," a commentary on the poverty or at least the pastoralism of the northern realm.[19] By this time, William was probably feeling frustrated and exposed. His fleet may have had some success against the pirates, but otherwise he had accomplished nothing. His penetration into Fife had produced no battle. His army had collected little plunder, and he was by now some 230 to 250 miles from York, his nearest base. His position was perilous, for behind him all the way to the North Riding, the dales of northern Britain lay athwart his line of retreat, and Malcolm was king of the heads of these dales, a sobering lesson in geography. With autumn advancing, William chose to negotiate. The two kings met at Abernethy, where they came to an understanding. Malcolm accepted William as his overlord by doing homage, gave hostages, probably including Duncan, his eldest son, and apparently promised to expel Edgar the Atheling, his brother-in-law, and other prominent English rebels.[20] William withdrew from Scotland, no doubt after promising to respect Malcolm's borders.

This agreement may have fallen short of the Conqueror's expectations, but it had some value. On his way south, the king plucked its first fruit—Cospatric. Once back in Northumbria, he deprived the earl of his office on the charges that the latter had been involved in planning the death of Earl Robert in 1069 and that he had helped kill Normans at York later in the same year; these deeds had presumably been forgiven on the banks of the

Tees two years earlier. Before William's agreement with Malcolm, the deprivation of Cospatric might have had serious repercussions, but in the late fall of 1072 it provoked no native uprising or Scottish invasion in support of the earl. Because of the Conqueror's agreement with Malcolm, Cospatric could not even stay at the Scottish court, as was his custom, and had to go into exile in Flanders.[21] William did not, however, change his policy with respect to the earldom. His expedition had been an impressive demonstration of his power that had won him the submission of Malcolm and had allowed him to expel Cospatric. His actual control of the North depended upon his presence there, and William could not stay, even if he wanted to, because there was not enough food in southern Northumberland to support his troops.[22] Because he could take no radical action, he appointed another native earl. His choice fell on Waltheof, Siward's younger son, whose mother had been a daughter of Earl Uhtred.[23] Waltheof was thus, like Cospatric, related to the house of Bamburgh through the female line and therefore could be expected to possess personal authority in Northumbria. William may have contemplated his appointment for some time. Alone among Edward's earls, he had enjoyed lasting favor from William. Waltheof had been allowed to keep his father's old earldom of Huntingdon and Northampton, and he had been accorded the unparalleled privilege for an Anglo-Saxon of marrying within the Conqueror's family. His wife was Judith, the daughter of William's sister Adelaide.[24] These honors were probably intended to ensure that the new earl of the Northumbrians would be a faithful adherent of the king.

William may have been satisfied as he crossed the Tyne on his way south. In a sense, his achievement was superficial, but the limits of the possible were narrow in the North in the 1070s. With Yorkshire a wasteland and few Norman landholders above the Tees, his power was very limited. He had obtained Malcolm's homage, gotten his enemies expelled from Scotland, and installed a new earl, who was bound to him by strong ties. All these arrangements fell apart within three years, but William had had little choice. He may even have realized the fragile nature of the situation, for he did not pass into Yorkshire before he had left behind something more substantial than the promises of Malcolm and the loyalty of Waltheof. His army stopped in Durham and built Bishop Walcher a castle where he could find relief if the natives proved recalcitrant.[25] Even this turned out to be a failure in the end, but through no fault of William, who crossed the Tees, never to return.

One can hardly blame the Conqueror. It must not have been pleasant for him to be faced with problems whose insolubility was primarily the result of his own deeds. The church at Durham had a tradition that had been turned into a miracle story by Symeon's time that William had crossed the Tees at a dead run that fall through fear of St. Cuthbert or, more specifically, through dread of damnation. It is tempting to see in this story a reflection of the fact that in 1072 William came to understand the consequences of his acts.[26] Alternatively, the story may only mean that St. Cuthbert's monks believed that he should have understood and feared for his soul because they knew about the harrying. Indeed, they undoubtedly knew more than their historian, Symeon of Durham, chose to explain in detail. His special concern was the history of St. Cuthbert's church and, to a lesser extent, important events that had occurred in the North. These were interests that could exclude much, yet even his works contain hints that conditions were far worse than political and military events alone would indicate. What did he mean, for example, when he said that William built Durham castle so that Walcher and his men would have protection *ab incursantibus*?[27] This vague phrase might refer to Scottish invasions or to the type of raid characteristic of northern rebellion; probably, however, Symeon sought to indicate a more mundane reality of the last decades of the eleventh century, a reality that has escaped historians because it did not often fall within the categories of events of interest to the chroniclers and therefore received only a scant description. Individually, the notices of this phenomenon are not too informative, although some are highly suggestive. In combination, they show that one of the most serious results of the Conquest on the North was an intensification of the threat from the free zone to the agricultural communities of the east coast plain. That is, the number of outlaws increased dramatically, and the origin of this development lies in the years before 1066.

As late as the reign of Edward the Confessor, one of the North's outstanding problems was the large-scale brigandage made possible by the wild conditions of the free zone. Robbers were so numerous that travelers went in groups of twenty to thirty men and still found no security when Siward was earl, and Tostig is said to have made war on these brigands with some success.[28] The only specific example of his campaign, however, shows that the problem went beyond the inherent lawlessness of the Northumbrians. Tostig once captured a notorious outlaw, named Aldan-hamel, who had been plundering, burning, and killing in Northumbria for a long time; after his capture, Aldan-hamel's family and friends tried to ransom him, but to no avail.[29] This is hardly an account of the bringing to justice of a common highwayman. The uncouth name, presumably a mangled version of a Norse or perhaps Anglo-Saxon original, his crimes, which seem to have been raids, and the attempted ransom indicate that this outlaw was a man of some standing from the hills or from the West who had lived by raiding Northumbria.

If this interpretation of Aldan-hamel is correct, it has extremely important implications for northern history during the eleventh and early twelfth centuries because it suggests that the famed lawlessness of the North was produced in part by predatory incursions of the inhabitants of the shores of the Irish Sea and of the hills of the northern free zone. Such raids would provide a reasonable explanation for the formidable level of brigandage under Siward, and Tostig's war against the robbers could be understood as an attempt to thwart raids from the West.[30] This idea fits in very well with two pieces of information from this period. First, in 1065, Tostig held nearly all of northern Lancashire with the adjoining parts of southern Westmorland and Cumberland south of the mountains, and he had probably held the great sokes centered on Gilling and Catterick opposite Stainmore.[31] These two groups of estates commanded the most important routes south and east from Cumberland and were probably intended as a barrier against raids. Second, this explanation is supported by the only contemporary description of Tostig's campaigns against the Scots: "[They] harassed him often with raids rather than war. But this irresolute and fickle race of men, better in woods than on the plain, and trusting more to flight than to manly boldness in battle, Tostig, sparing his own men, wore down as much by cunning schemes as by martial courage and military campaigns."[32] The Galwegians, whom this writer called "Scots," raided the North, and Tostig replied with the ambushes and stratagems appropriate to this kind of warfare.

Although the information on these raids is very general, it is unlikely that they were restricted to Yorkshire's border with

Cumbria. Aldan-hamel had been active above the Tees, and this is not surprising because Northumbria's western border was rather different from what it is usually conceived as being. A good border for Northumbria was a frontier that lay far back in the hills on a line similar to that which existed in the thirteenth century.[33] With such a line, the Northumbrians would have some protection against raids from the West and certainly warning of their approach, but in this period they did not enjoy these advantages. Twelfth-century evidence indicates that the Cumbrians had expanded far to the east in the days of their power and that the Northumbrians' border with their descendants, the Galwegians, was a north-south line. During the reign of King David, all the inhabitants of Scotland south and west of the Clyde were known as Galwegians, and, according to G. W. S. Barrow, Galloway "in its widest sense" comprised all of Scotland south of the Clyde and west of Teviotdale.[34] Barrow's definition is probably somewhat conservative. Jocelin of Furness says that Cumbria ran from sea to sea like Hadrian's wall, and this outrageous statement contains some truth. Jocelin was presumably thinking of mid-twelfth-century conditions, and his statement can be confirmed in part for he also says that St. Kentigern's bishopric, Glasgow, was coterminous with the kingdom.[35] This is significant because David's Cumbrian inquisition makes the same identification between Cumbria and Glasgow and adds that the former lay *inter Angliam et Scotiam*.[36] Nor was this *inter* restricted to the West. In the early twelfth century, Teviotdale was apparently subject to Glasgow.[37] This does not, of course, bring Cumbria quite to the North Sea, but it does in general confirm Jocelin's conception of the extent of Cumbria. Furthermore, three aspects of the feudal history of the northern end of the free zone amplify his conception. First, despite Rufus's conquest of Cumberland in 1092, Gilsland, which was centered on the western end of the Tyne gap, remained subject to the Scottish king until the reign of Henry II.[38] Second, there is no evidence whatsoever that North Tynedale was part of England until the reign of Henry I at the earliest and more probably the reign of Henry II. Third, the barony of Langley, which occupied the South Tyne west of Corbridge, was a creation of Henry II.[39] The North of England was, then, much smaller and less defensible than is usually assumed. Until 1092, Northumbria's border with Cumbria probably ran north from the Rere Cross on Stainmore to the Tweed and included on the Cumbrian side the bulk of the northern free zone; even after this date the Scots held a large salient that protruded down to the South Tyne.[40] As late as the reign of Henry II, Northumbria consisted of the eastern coastal plain with the immediately adjoining hills. Corbridge and Hexham stood on the border. Because of this north-south frontier, Aldan-hamel would not have required exceptional energy to carry on his plundering and burning. He need not have lived outside the modern boundaries of Northumberland.

This border must always have been a source of danger for the Northumbrians during times of internal weakness or rebellion. Earl Eadulf had had to ravage the Cumbrians during his rebellion against Cnut, and during his unpopular rule, Tostig had struggled against raids from the West.[41] After 1066 such disturbances became even more serious because the Norman Conquest distracted and weakened the traditional governmental powers on the east coast plain to a degree unparalleled since the ninth century. Unheard-of events occurred in the North. In 1067, Osulf of Bamburgh, the killer of Copsig, was killed by an outlaw. When Bishop Æthelwine and his men tried to return to Durham in 1070 from Lindisfarne, where they had fled to escape William, their numbers and the presence of St. Cuthbert's body did not prevent their being plundered and harassed by a certain Gilmichael, *quidam ultra amen Tinam praepotens.*[42] Later in the same year, Malcolm raided the North Riding and Durham from Cumberland, a tactic with no recorded parallel since the days of Norwegian power in the North.

The harrying added a new dimension to the problem of Northumbrian security because the destruction of stable society in Yorkshire was followed by the appearance of robbers below the Tees. Probably most of them were native Yorkshire men who had taken to brigandage to avoid either starvation or William's "forgiveness." Symeon of Durham says that throughout the 1070s travel across the empty countryside that separated Durham and York was extremely dangerous on account of outlaws and wolves, which faced the same problem of survival as the nobles once the peasants and their animals were destroyed. Other accounts confirm Symeon's information.[43] The founders of Selby, ten miles from York, were harassed by outlaws who lived in the woods during the 1070s, and Hugh fitz Baldric, the sheriff of Yorkshire, is said to have had to travel around the shire with a small army because hostile Anglo-Saxons were still at large.[44] Finally, the monks at Whitby had trouble with outlaws during the 1070s and were so regularly robbed by outlaws from the woods as late as the reign of William Rufus that they tried to settle elsewhere.[45]

These examples show that brigandage was a serious and enduring problem in the aftermath of the harrying. The surviving peasants must have enjoyed little security. Domesday shows that the notices of rapine recorded in the chronicles do not give the true dimensions of the problem. One of the most curious features of this document's Yorkshire folios is its account of the Pennines and Lancashire above the Ribble. These have been interpreted as showing that Yorkshire west of roughly the four-hundred-foot line and the adjacent parts of northern Lancashire were almost entirely uninhabited in 1086, but such a view is mistaken.[46] The Normans did not actually survey many of the Pennine villages and all of northern Lancashire, probably because they did not control these areas.[47] There is narrative evidence for this hypothesis. During the early 1070s, Archbishop Thomas of York had Bishop Wulfstan of Worcester perform episcopal functions in parts of his diocese because these areas were still unsubdued, and the areas in question can only have been the West.[48]

This discovery completes the melancholy picture of the North in the years immediately after 1069. The harrying had, apparently, activated the southern free zone by filling the hills with disinherited rebels turned outlaws, and the isolated examples of brigandage in the literary sources were only outliers of a much larger area that ran south from the Cumbrian border through the Pennines into northern Derbyshire and in which Norman power was not firmly established as late as the end of William's reign.[49] William had, then, won his crown at a terrible and lasting price for the North. Norman rule was restricted to the east coast plain and to the western plain as a result of the harrying. Between there was brigandage. The harrying also made it extremely difficult to control Northumbria on a regular basis and impossible to keep the king of the Scots and the Cumbrians from raiding the North, particularly because the Cumbrian border was so far east. These were the basic problems that confronted Norman rule in the North during the rest of the eleventh century. They could not be solved until a numerous Norman aristocracy that could control Northumbria and fight the Scots was established beyond the Humber.

Such a group could not be created until Yorkshire was redeveloped, and this took time both because of the magnitude of the task and because the danger to peasants from outlaws based in the free zone had to be contained first. In the meantime, the events of northern history proceeded from an outré mixture of traditional problems in an acute form and Norman weakness. The North was violent and unstable, and it is no wonder that William never crossed the Tees again and came only once more to York. The Abernethy understanding could only fall apart.

Although this occurred by degrees between 1072 and 1080, the first signs appeared in 1074. When the Abernethy agreement was less than two years old, Edgar the Atheling sailed back to Scotland from Flanders with his followers. He probably was invited by Malcolm,[50] who either had decided that he could safely harbor his brother-in-law or was plotting to disrupt the North again. The latter would be the more likely of the alternatives if 1074 was also the year when Malcolm invited Cospatric to come to Scotland from Flanders and gave him the earldom of Dunbar in Lothian, an event that was clearly a prelude to trouble in Northumbria. But although the return of Edgar and Cospatric would logically fit together, Cospatric's reappearance in the North cannot be dated with any precision.[51] It may have happened in 1074; in any case, the reception of Edgar was a clear violation of the understanding between Malcolm and William and showed that the former had not been too impressed by the Conqueror in 1072. This incident did not, however, lead to any serious problems in the North because of two unforeseen events. While Edgar was in Scotland, the French king offered him a castle on the Channel from which he could harass William. Edgar accepted, but on his way south he lost all of his ships in a storm somewhere along the English coast. This disaster ended the Atheling's open opposition to the Conquest. He regained Scotland but now sought and obtained a reconciliation with William, presumably because he had lost too many followers to remain a plausible rebel.[52]

The Atheling's defection from the forces of disorder was not, however, very important. He had never been dangerous except on the theoretical level. Nevertheless, the events of 1074 raise two curious questions: why had Malcolm risked William's displeasure for no apparent reason and how had Edgar managed, despite shipwreck, his own incompetence, and the Normans, to escape back to Scotland, particularly since some of his followers went on foot?[53] The fact that these questions cannot be definitely answered suggests that some important aspect of the northern political situation in 1074 was not recorded in the chronicles, and the same difficulty is encountered in the events of 1075. In that year, Earl Waltheof of Northumbria, whom William had appointed only three years previously, went into open revolt in company with the Breton earl of East Anglia and the Norman earl of Hereford. The motives of the participants in this bizarre coalition were probably disparate; but, although historians have realized this, no one has produced a convincing explanation of why Waltheof joined the revolt.[54] This is not the fault of the historians who have studied the revolt, but stems directly from the primary Anglo-Norman chronicles, whose writers either did not know why Waltheof had revolted or deliberately minimized his role because his headless corpse had begun to perform miracles, a sure sign of innocence.[55] The embellishment and outright fabrication necessitated by this point of view would not have been possible if the real reason for Waltheof's revolt had been current in the South in the late eleventh and early twelfth centuries.

Some important event or situation of 1073 or 1074 has been left out of the major chronicles. Only its ramifications, which together amount to the collapse of most of William's authority in the North, are visible. Fortunately, this gap can be filled, although not with the exactitude one might wish. Symeon of Durham knew what had happened, but he buried the event in one of St. Cuthbert's miracles in the defense of Northumbrian property, where it has successfully eluded historians. This miracle shows that Waltheof had excellent reasons for joining the revolt of Earls Ralph and Roger; indeed, he had no choice. William the Conqueror had blundered badly—in 1073 or more probably in 1074, he decided to levy a tribute or tax on Northumbria and sent a certain Ralph above the Tees to collect it.[56] The miracle describes the imposition of this tax as uncustomary, and given the reaction of the Northumbrians to demands for money in the past, the result might have been easily anticipated. But these Northumbrians were on their best behavior in a miracle story; and, in any case, credit, especially credit for defying the king, belonged to St. Cuthbert. Kept alive by this necessity, Ralph went about his business levying the tribute, but on the night before it was to be collected, he foolishly dropped his guard and went to sleep. Cuthbert duly appeared to Ralph in a dream, chided him severely for taxing his flock, and intimated that he would be punished. Ralph awoke sick the next day. He had lost all interest in gathering the tribute and only wished to escape Northumbria alive. After he had made appropriate signs of reverence to St. Cuthbert, this was granted to him. Upon his departure he regained his health, but, needless to say, he carried with him no money.[57]

Although Cuthbert was a powerful saint, this story must be a twelfth-century monk's way of saying that William had tried to tax Northumbria, probably believing that he had accomplished more in 1072 than he actually had, and that the Northumbrians had driven out the tax collectors. Waltheof was inevitably involved because he either had been a party to the expulsion of Ralph or had failed to protect him. Either way, he was effectively in revolt against William. Furthermore, Waltheof made the now traditional Northumbrian gesture of defiance of southern authority. He sent a raiding party of Northumbrians over the Tees in search of the sons of Carl, who were now to pay for their father's killing of Waltheof's grandfather on his mother's side, Earl Ealdred. Siward's son had changed sides in the old battle between Bamburgh and York, but this paradox did not save the sons and grandsons of Carl. The Northumbrians caught them at a banquet and killed most of them.[58]

The innuendoes of this deed may have been lost on the Normans, but the basic meaning was unmistakable. William's authority in the North had collapsed in 1074, and it was entirely his own fault given the Northumbrians' sensitivity on the question of tribute. Their behavior was entirely consistent with what they had done in 1065 and during the early revolts against William. The only question involved—and this is perhaps the reason why William felt he could safely levy the tax—is understanding how they had the effrontery to defy him again, especially with the harrying only four years past. Furthermore, they were now faced with the same old difficulty as in past revolts. It was one thing to drive out the agents of an unpopular southern government, but quite another to avoid paying for doing so.

This problem presumably bothered Waltheof, and he may have been more active in the events of 1074 and 1075 than the chronicles indicate. In particular, Edgar's return to Scotland and

Malcolm's willingness to receive him with honor were probably connected with Waltheof's revolt and may represent the first steps in an unsuccessful attempt by the earl to obtain aid from this quarter. Waltheof is also likely to have been seriously involved in the planning of the revolt of 1075, if only because he greatly needed aid. His momentarily successful defiance of William can only have encouraged Ralph and Roger, and he may have convinced them to revolt rather than the opposite as the chronicles assert. Finally, the rebel earls invited a Danish fleet to come to their aid, and although Ralph and Roger are expressly said to have been responsible for this, it is more likely the work of Waltheof or at least accomplished through his intermediacy.[59]

A respectable coalition that offered Waltheof more hope than he had had any right to anticipate in 1074 had been brought together by the spring of 1075. Unfortunately for the earl, it vanished as quickly as it had been formed. The rebels were undone by a failure to coordinate their actions that stretched from the English borderlands to Denmark. No one was on time in 1075 except William's representatives. The arrival of the Danes was delayed by a conflict between the sons of Swein Estrithson, who had died in April of 1074. Ralph and Roger took the field anyway, but they were unable to unite their forces. Roger remained penned up in the West, and Ralph's revolt quickly contracted to the inside of his castle at Norwich which was besieged by William's forces for three months.[60] Waltheof, the victim, no doubt, of a growing sense of desperation, seems to have stayed in the North waiting for the Danes. Rumors were current, to be sure, that the North was in revolt, and Lanfranc ordered Walcher to be prepared for the arrival of the Danes.[61] Yet, as the revolt in the South collapsed, Waltheof apparently remained inactive because he realized that the Northumbrians could not act alone, and when the failure of the Danes to arrive had clearly undone the revolt, he capitulated. According to one version of the *Anglo-Saxon Chronicle*, the earl crossed to Normandy to seek William's pardon and offered the king treasure, presumably the tribute that had been withheld in 1074. To Waltheof this sign of submission may have seemed sufficient atonement; but, if so, he was forgetting the fate of Earls Uhtred, Ealdred, and Eadulf. His was to be no different. William dissembled until they had returned to England and Waltheof's safe-conduct had presumably expired. Then he had the earl cast into prison.[62] About the same time the Danes finally arrived with a fleet of two hundred ships. They could do nothing against the Normans by themselves; after a perfunctory cruise up the Humber to York, where they sacked the cathedral, they left the kingdom.[63]

Thus the great coalition of 1075 faded away. Military events had made a mockery of the real danger posed by the alliance between the rebels and the Danes, and William's authority was again unchallenged in the North. Ralph de Gael, the former earl of Norfolk, however, had removed his revolt to Brittany. The development of a dangerous situation there[64] probably induced the king to treat the Northumbrians moderately. Waltheof, who had risen far too high in the royal favor to be forgiven, was beheaded; but the royal punitive expedition that might have been anticipated was not sent into the North.[65] By the next campaigning season, William had a more pressing use for his soldiers than burning out Northumbrians, so they went unpunished for once. The king merely appointed a new earl, and his choice was as conciliatory as possible short of selecting another member of the house of Bamburgh, whose representatives had not been notable for their loyalty. No new Norman earl was placed over the Northumbrians; rather, the king built upon the one remaining pillar of public authority above the Tees. Bishop Walcher was allowed to buy the earldom.[66] He had remained both alive and loyal since his appointment in 1071, an impressive accomplishment for an outsider above the Tees; and his selection was the easiest solution to the problem of Northumbrian government in 1076, for any other choice would have risked an incident. Furthermore, William seems to have made an attempt to bolster Walcher's prestige. He restored to Durham an old estate that had been lost, granted some new property, and confirmed the ancient laws and customs of the bishopric,[67] presumably including a promise that Walcher's rule was not to be disturbed by any threat of royal taxation.

This makeshift arrangement functioned with some success for five years, but it is difficult to form a very clear impression of the nature of Walcher's government or its popularity with the Northumbrians. He was fondly remembered by later monks at Durham, and Symeon portrays him as an honest, upright man who diligently performed his episcopal duties.[68] Walcher's support of the revival of monasticism in the North could account for Symeon's appraisal, although there is no compelling reason to believe that it does.[69] Rather, it seems likely that certain aspects of Walcher's character were edited out. The bishop was clearly an exceptionally ambitious man. Why else would he have undertaken the care of St. Cuthbert's testy flock, not to mention the government of Northumbria? Furthermore, if he really did buy the earldom, one must suppose that he intended to get his money back. Walcher had not come into Northumbria just to be a good bishop, even though he may have been one; and he was sufficiently political-minded to grasp the basic truth that to survive above the Tees he had to come to terms with the house of Bamburgh. From an early date he had adopted a certain Ligulf as his principal adviser. Ligulf was an important landowner, who had retired to his Northumbrian estates in the face of the Conquest and was married to a daughter of Earl Ealdred. He was, thus, like Cospatric and Waltheof, connected with the Bamburgh family, and his presence in the bishop's council must have provided a link with the native aristocracy. Walcher is said to have performed no important secular act without his consent,[70] and this policy of accommodation and respect for Northumbrian tradition was probably responsible for his survival. There was, however, another side to the bishop's government. Even Symeon of Durham does not suppress the fact that Walcher's household knights often plundered and occasionally killed the natives and that Walcher did nothing to stop them. This dangerous policy could be expected to provoke the Northumbrians and is extremely difficult to account for. The usual explanation, an extrapolation from Symeon, is that Walcher was incapable of controlling his soldiers.[71] Alternatively, Walcher's soldiers may have acted on the bishop's orders, conceivably in response to native opposition or out of arrogance, situations Symeon would not have felt free to mention since either would have put the bishop in a bad light.

Whichever of these was actually the case, Walcher's government did arouse the resentment of the Northumbrians; and, even without the misdeeds of his soldiers, this was probably only to be expected given the circumstances that had surrounded his acquisition of the earldom in 1075. William's conciliatory settlement of the rebellion of 1074–75 is unlikely to have impressed on them the inadvisability of defying Norman power, but it is impossible to tell how serious this problem was between 1075 and 1079. In the latter year, however, an event occurred that may have been prompted by the weakness of Walcher's government and increased his difficulties with the Northumbrians. In August of 1079, Malcolm Canmore finally decided that he could safely ignore the Abernethy agreement entirely and launched his third invasion of the North. Certain general considerations that had nothing to do with the North were undoubtedly involved in this decision. In 1077, Malcolm had defeated the ruler of Moray, his chief domestic rival, and this victory had freed him from internal dangers. Furthermore, William the Conqueror was fighting his son Robert in northern France that summer and must have seemed only a very distant threat. Malcolm probably also judged that Walcher would be able to put up no serious resistance. Certainly this proved to be the case. In mid-August the Scots came over the border and freely plundered Northumberland for about three weeks. Walcher neither met them in battle nor launched counterraids as Cospatric had done in 1072, and the Scots were able to return home with many slaves and much booty.[72]

This invasion set the stage for the last outrage of the Northumbrians. Walcher's failure to provide even a nominal defense for Northumberland apparently ended his prestige. By spring, Ligulf, Walcher's native collaborator, became uncooperative in council. Ligulf was the natural leader of any resistance to Walcher, and his disaffection was, therefore, serious. Unfortunately, the resulting event is obscure because the only coherent account of the incident, that of Florence of Worcester, explains it as a personal conflict between Ligulf and two of Walcher's subordinates, his chaplain Leobwin and Gilbert, the bishop's kinsman who managed the secular government of the bishopric. According to Florence, Leobwin had been jealous of Ligulf for some time and decided to kill him after Ligulf had opposed him in the bishop's council.[73] Since Ligulf was the current link between the Bamburgh family and Northumbrian government, however, one may legitimately doubt whether the incident was this simple; but even if it was, the Northumbrians had lost too many members of the house of Bamburgh ever to believe that the event that followed was not an official act of Walcher's government.

A classic sequence ensued. Gilbert, who had agreed to do the deed, attacked Ligulf's hall by surprise in the night and killed him along with most of his household.[74] The use of this tactic should probably be understood as a sign that Walcher and his men were already faced with a serious situation, although Gilbert and

Leobwin may have been so arrogant that they disregarded the provocative nature of their action. In either case, the murder of Ligulf was a fatal mistake because whether or not the Northumbrians had been contemplating a revolt, they had now been provoked by the traditional act of oppression, the murder of a member of the house of Bamburgh by an agent of the king. Their reprisal was equally traditional. Walcher had shut himself up in Durham castle after the murder, but he soon consented to a meeting with Ligulf's relatives at Gateshead, which offered a convenient gathering place for Northumbrians from either side of the Tyne. Presumably he had been offered some hope that peace could be restored, but the meeting was a trap. When Walcher arrived at Gateshead with a hundred knights on 14 May, he found that the Northumbrians would come to no agreement. He then with some naivety retired to the church. The Northumbrians first killed all of his retainers who had remained outside, then cut down Gilbert and the bishop when they tried to escape, and finally burned down the church to get at Leobwin. The killer of the bishop was Eadulf Rus, the son of Cospatric who had been killed by Tostig in 1064.[75]

In a fundamental sense, the massacre at Gateshead was the last incident in Northumbrian history because the Northumbrian nobility had finally overreached itself. The rebels did go down to Durham, where they besieged the castle, but they were unable to take it by assault and withdrew on the fourth day of the siege.[76] Probably they reasoned that the castle garrison was too small to be a serious threat; in any case, their major objective, the destruction of Walcher and the instruments of his government, was already accomplished. In 1080 as in past revolts, the Northumbrians had acted in response to a specific outrage. Once this was avenged, there was nothing else for them to do. They may have reasoned, with the events of 1075 in mind, that the worst they could expect would be the imposition of a new earl, and their failure to press the siege of the castle, which was within their means, may have been an attempt to limit the provocation they gave the king.

If this was the case, it was a futile gesture. The Northumbrians were undone by their lack of imagination. After lifting the siege they had gone home.[77] This time William did not simply appoint a new earl. He had been doing that since 1067, when his first earl had been killed. In 1080, he made a determined attempt to take Northumbria in hand; and, even though the measures that followed are not known in detail, they seem to have been part of a comprehensive plan. First, the Northumbrians were punished for the killing of Walcher and his men. At some date during the summer, William's half brother Odo led an expedition into Northumbria to harry the countryside. No chronicler describes the details, but Odo's purpose seems to have been to kill Northumbrians. The Normans slaughtered and maimed both the guilty and the innocent, and they were apparently able to weaken the native nobility seriously, killing or driving into exile many of its members.[78] This was an extremely important event. It was the final solution to the old problem of governing the Northumbrians that stretched back to the days of Cnut's conquest of England. There would be no more native revolts above the Tees because in 1080 the Northumbrian nobility had joined the nobles of York.

Odo's expedition solved one aspect of the general political and military problem the North posed, but it did little to ensure that the Normans could keep control of the area. The Northumbrian nobility had at least demonstrated little inclination to go over to the Scots except in extremis, and with them gone, some action against Malcolm was clearly necessary. William met this need with a second expedition in 1080. In the fall, he sent his son Robert into Scotland with an army. Ritchie has asserted that the purpose of this move was entirely diplomatic, that it was a "demonstration in force" designed to bring about a reconciliation with Malcolm,[79] but there is no proof that this was the intention. William and Robert may have hoped for a decisive battle that would simplify the situation in the North, and all that is known for certain is that a battle did not take place. Robert led his army through Lothian to Falkirk, where he met Malcolm. The Scottish king would not fight, and Robert was faced with the choice of chasing him further or negotiating. Robert chose the latter. The two men renewed the Abernethy agreement, and Malcolm gave more hostages for his good behavior. Then Robert returned to Northumbria *nullo confecto negotio.*[80] This phrase of Symeon's suggests that the outcome of Robert's expedition was thought to be unsatisfactory.

Robert had accomplished all that could be realistically hoped, and, like his father in 1072, he did not leave the Northumbrian landscape as he had found it. On his way south, Robert stopped on the north side of the Tyne opposite Gateshead and built a new castle, the Newcastle as it would become in time. The erection of this castle had a multiple significance. On the one hand, its location across from the spot where Walcher and his men had been massacred stood as a warning to the remaining Northumbrians. On the other hand, it was a tangible sign that Norman England now extended to the Tyne. Some historians would also add that the location of this castle was an admission that the lordship over the country north of the Tyne was debatable, or perhaps even Scottish,[81] but neither of these suppositions is true except perhaps in a military sense. Newcastle could defend Durham but not Northumberland.

Yet this observation, despite its descriptive truth in 1080 and for many years to come, obscures the fact that Newcastle was probably intended as a base for the new regime William created in Northumbria after the conclusion of the military operations of 1080. Robert had secured freedom for the North from major Scottish invasions, and Odo had crushed native opposition to Norman rule. Thus William could integrate Northumbria more closely into the kingdom than it had been in the past by introducing Normans into the ecclesiastical and secular government of the earldom. Before the year was out, William de St. Calais, a trusted administrator of the king, obtained the bishopric of Durham, and around the same time, a certain Aubrey became earl of Northumbria.[82] To succeed, however, Aubrey needed a stronghold between Durham castle, which belonged to the bishop, and Bamburgh, the ancient fastness of the earls, which was nearly forty-five miles above Gateshead. Newcastle provided one. It was a secure bridgehead into Northumberland, the necessary preliminary to the exercise of political and military power above the Tyne.

Moreover, Newcastle did not stand alone. The expeditions and appointments of 1080 that brought the formal conquest of Northumbria were matched to the south by the beginnings of an assault on the free zone. This was a task of the utmost importance because the creation of a strong North depended upon the extension of Norman control into the hills. Until this was accomplished, the peasants would still be subject to brigands, and it would not be too important who was earl or bishop, as was soon illustrated when William's new earl of Northumbria resigned the honor and went home because he either could not control the earldom or thought it was worthless.[83] This curious incident forced William to appoint another earl, Robert de Mowbray, and confirmed the need for the

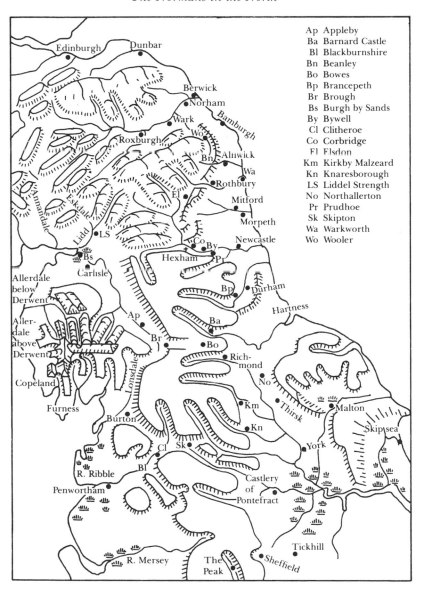

Ap Appleby
Ba Barnard Castle
Bl Blackburnshire
Bn Beanley
Bo Bowes
Bp Brancepeth
Br Brough
Bs Burgh by Sands
By Bywell
Cl Clitheroe
Co Corbridge
Fl Elsdon
Km Kirkby Malzeard
Kn Knaresborough
LS Liddel Strength
No Northallerton
Pr Prudhoe
Sk Skipton
Wa Warkworth
Wo Wooler

Edinburgh
Dunbar
Berwick
Norham
Wark
Bamburgh
Roxburgh
Wo
Alnwick
Bn
Wa
Rothbury
Annandale
Eskdale
El
Mitford
Lidd
LS
Morpeth
Newcastle
Bs
Co By
Carlisle
Hexham Pr
Allerdale below Derwent
Bp
Durham
Hartness
Aller-dale above Derwent
Ap
Ba
Copeland
Br
Bo
Rich-mond
No
Furness
Km
Thirsk
Malton
Burton
Kn
Skipsea
Cl Sk
York
R. Ribble
Bl
Penwortham
Castlery of Pontefract
Tickhill
R. Mersey
The Peak
Sheffield

policy, which had probably already begun, of establishing a series of compact fees at the mouths of the major breaks in the southern Pennines and in other places that were subject to the incursions of outlaws and pirates. Some of these fees were explicitly known as castleries, and all of them were exceptionally compact units. Their purpose was defensive in the sense that they were designed to control communications, and some of them, notably those adjoining the hills, were intended as bases for expansion.[84] Their lords usually possessed formidable judicial powers that included infangthief, the right to have a gallows, the right to the goods of condemned fugitives, the assize of bread and ale, and the return of writs except for pleas of the crown.[85] Taken together, these powers amounted to effective police power. They were all that a baron needed to be a terror to outlaws and robbers, and herein probably lay the principal day-to-day function of these fees. They were established to provide law and order in vulnerable districts. A castlery was not simply an area organized for the support of a castle; it was also the area subject to the castle.

The oldest of these units around the Pennines was in the south and probably dated back to the days when the marcher earldoms had been formed. Henry de Ferrers's castlery of Tutbury dominated the roads that converged on Derby from the northwest and blocked the major river valleys of the southern end of the Pennines,[86] and there was a similar, although smaller, unit west of Nottingham, where the holdings of William Peverel, which may also have been a castlery, covered the city against the west.[87] These two fees had probably been formed in the early 1070s to secure communications around the southern end of the free zone and to contain raids from this area. Hereward the Wake, it will be remembered, was killed by knights from Tutbury, according to Geoffrey Gaimar.[88] Tutbury and the honor of Peverel also presumably served as the direct archetype for the fees William created in the North around 1080.

This late date for the establishment of the castleries and similar districts in Yorkshire may seem surprising, but it is apparently correct. W. E. Wightman has argued from the details of their description in Domesday that they were formed late in William's reign, probably as an aid to Robert de Mowbray, and his reasoning is convincing.[89] Moreover, Symeon of Durham specifically states that the countryside of Yorkshire remained uncultivated and empty for nine years after the harrying, and the most probable explanation for the passing of these conditions is that William had begun to create defensive districts at critical spots in the North in 1079–80.[90]

Two castleries and three exceptionally large and compact fees were established to protect the lowlands of the North from the various threats that surrounded them (see map). There was, on the one hand, the danger of piracy along the coast; and Holderness, the area most exposed to this danger, was given almost in its entirety to Drogo.[91] On the other hand, there was the more serious threat from the wild parts of Yorkshire, the fens and the mountains; and three large lordships, Tickhill, Pontefract, and Richmond, were established in settled regions adjoining these areas. In the far south of the West Riding and in the neighboring parts of Derbyshire and Nottinghamshire, Roger de Busli was given a compact fee (Tickhill) through which the roads from York passed south and which abutted three dangerous areas, the Pennines on the west, the fens at the head of the Humber on the east, and Sherwood Forest on the southeast.[92] North of Roger's land, Ilbert de Lacy's castlery of Pontefract stretched continuously from the Pennine foothills to the fens on either side of the Aire. Pontefract dominated not only all the roads running north-south, but also the entrance of the Aire gap, which was the easiest passage through the Pennines from their southern end to the Tyne gap far to the north.[93] The next important passage through the mountains above the Aire gap was Stainmore in the North Riding, and it was blocked by Count Alan's castlery of Richmond, a solid block of 199 manors on the eastern slopes of the Pennines and the edge of the Vale of York.[94] Richmond, Pontefract, and Tickhill closed the easiest exits from the Pennines and together provided security for the Vale of York. In the West the functions of these fees and of Holderness were combined in the lordship of Roger of Poitou, who held all of Lancashire between the Ribble and the Mersey along with the western flanks of the Pennines around the approaches to the Aire gap. Roger's fee was in reality a military salient intruded between the free zone and the Irish Sea pirates. Finally, by 1086, a new royal castle had been raised far up the Derwent valley at the Peak in Derbyshire.[95]

The creation of these lordships around the Pennines was the most important development in the North in the 1080s because they offered the hope that the danger from the free zone could be contained and ultimately destroyed. Unfortunately, however, the daily activities of men such as Ilbert de Lacy or William Peverel, not to mention Earl Robert de Mowbray in the wilds of Northumberland, were not gaudy enough to attract the attention of the chroniclers, and nothing is known of them. Indeed, hardly anything happened in the North outside the ecclesiastical sphere between 1080 and 1087 according to the chronicles. There were no murders, revolts, or invasions, and Norman power was uncontested, at least during the daylight hours and away from the woods. The only exception was the threatened Danish invasion of 1085, which probably provoked the devastation of Holderness by the Normans, but in the end the Danes did not come.[96]

This rare period of peace survived the Conqueror's death in 1087. The military activities connected with the baronial revolt of 1088 were limited to southern England, and even though Earl Robert and Bishop William were among the rebels, there were only minor repercussions in the North. Malcolm did not invade either because he was getting old or because he was waiting to see how Rufus would fare against the rebels, and Robert de Mowbray obtained a complete reconciliation with the king. The only ones to suffer were William de St. Calais and the clerks of Durham. The former, who may have done some local raiding, was exiled as a result of the revolt, and the latter had to endure the fiscal tedium of one of Rufus's agents until the bishop's restoration three years later.[97] With this exception, the tranquillity of the North remained unbroken until 1091, when open warfare with the Scots broke out.

This appearance of tranquillity may be deceptive, however, because there is a possibility that the settlement of the baronial revolt of 1088 brought a basic change in royal policy in the North. Certainly there was need for change. William the Conqueror had achieved the destruction of serious opposition to Norman rule in the North but little else, and when Rufus became king the Normans above the Humber were still in a weak and unsatisfactory position. With their settlement limited to below the Ribble in the West and probably to south of the Wansbeck in Northumberland,[98] they were potentially at the mercy of the Scots because the border was as disadvantageous as ever and the redevelopment of Yorkshire had only begun despite the creation of castleries around the southern free zone. This area itself was still for the most part unsubdued, and the peace of the North depended on the homage of Malcolm Canmore, a volatile substance.

The Normans in the North cannot have been pleased with the situation. But in one respect it was susceptible to immediate improvement: the Scottish danger could be eliminated quickly if Rufus disregarded his father's understanding with Malcolm. Malcolm's homage to William has usually been considered from the standpoint of whether it compromised the independence of the Scottish kingdom, and this is unfortunate because the arrangement was as much in Malcolm's interest as in William's. The Scottish king did homage and thereby accepted a position of political subordination that meant little in practice; William, however, must have guaranteed him against general Norman aggression or infringements on the border. In fact, the meeting of 1080 is said to have included a definition of the border, although its precise terms are unknown.[99] This understanding was to Malcolm's advantage for it, in effect, froze the border and indirectly limited Norman settlement to areas that were not too exposed to the sudden eruptions of Scots and Galwegians. A breach with Malcolm was, therefore, in the interest of the northern nobles if they could be assured of royal support in the hostilities with the Scots that would follow, and it is likely that Rufus gave such a promise in 1088. As a result of the baronial revolt of that year, the marcher lords seem to have obtained the abrogation of similar guarantees William had given to the Welsh princes, and it is unlikely that the northern rebels, especially Robert de Mowbray and Roger of Poitou, would have been satisfied with less.[100]

This can only be offered as an hypothesis, however, because there is an important gap in the chronology of events in the North under Rufus. At some point the king resumed his father's policy of establishing well-enfranchised lordships along the edges of the free zone, but exactly when these baronies were created can only be guessed. In the instance of Skipton in Craven, this is not a serious problem. Skipton stood at the head of the Aire, and although it was of great importance because it split the southern free zone and ensured direct communications with the West, its establishment had only internal significance. Rufus's other new baronies, however, were all on the Scottish border. In the West, he gave Ivo Taillebois a new lordship composed of Ewecross Wapentake, southern Westmorland, and southern Cumberland. These lands provided the basis for the later baronies of Burton in Lonsdale, Kendal, and Copeland, and if Furness was included, as is likely, they constituted a continuous strip of land running from the north-western exit of the Aire gap to the Irish Sea. Ivo's lands covered all the routes north into Cumbria and all the trails from northern Lancashire over the Pennines from the Aire gap northward. If this land was given to Ivo before 1092, it originally formed a frontier castlery analogous to Richmond.[101] Rufus created similar lordships along the east side of the Pennines. Guy de Balliol obtained upper Teesdale, where he built Barnard Castle, and the barony of Bywell in the Tyne valley.[102] It is also possible, although not likely, that Rufus gave Redesdale to Robert de Umfraville, who held this valley by the tenure of guarding or keeping it from the outlaws.[103] Bywell and Barnard Castle had a similar purpose. They blocked either the two or the three most obvious passages above Richmond from Cumbria into Northumbria and were of the utmost impor-tance for protecting the coastal plain. Rufus's fees were, moreover, squarely on the Cumbrian border, or in the case of Ivo's lands, what was the border before 1092; and, if they were formed prior to 1092, they were a direct provocation to Malcolm Canmore and a sign that the spirit of Abernethy was dead.

This problem of timing is important because of the chain of events that began in 1091 and led to great political changes in northern Britain. In that year, Malcolm Canmore shattered the peace of the North by invading Northumbria. The question is whether he did this for his own reasons, such as to aid Edgar the Atheling who had been deprived of his estates in Normandy, or whether he had been baited into it just as Rhys ap Tewdwr, the king of South Wales, was being baited in these same years by the marcher lords of Wales.[104] Probably the latter was the case, although it is impossible to be certain. The invasion of 1091 was, at least, extraordinary. Not only did Malcolm invade Northumberland in May, a very bad time of year for an army to find provisions in the North, but he apparently hoped to take Durham, something not attempted by the Scots since Duncan's expedition in the 1040s and which, if successful, would have resulted in the collapse of Norman power above the Tees. The invasion of 1091 was a serious attack, not a raid or a diplomatic gesture as has been suggested,[105] and it indicates that Malcolm either felt himself to be in an exceptionally strong position, which is unlikely, or that he had become alarmed at the growth of Norman power in the North. In either case, his bold stroke did not work, though the reasons are far from clear. The Scots entered Northumberland in May. They then moved south, bypassed or took Newcastle, and penetrated as far as central Durham. At this critical point, however, the oldest descriptions of these events become contradictory. The account usually followed by historians, a summary of Malcolm's raids in the *Historia Regum*, says that Malcolm was confronted by a small group of knights at Chester-le-Street just north of Durham and quickly withdrew.[106]

Other sources, including a different passage in the *Historia Regum*, indicate that this is not what happened or, at least, not all that happened. The main narrative in the *Historia Regum* directly associates the failure of Malcolm's invasion with the arrival of William Rufus's retaliatory expedition in the North in the fall, and one of St. Cuthbert's miracles indirectly explains what took place.[107] It indicates that Durham was, in fact, besieged for some time in 1091 and that the opposing knights did nothing to drive away the Scots, who finally fled for no apparent reason.[108] The befuddlement of invading armies and of historians who would trace their movements was, of course, one of St. Cuthbert's most important abilities, but in this particular instance the writer goes too far. To complete the miracle, he adds that Bishop William was restored the same hour that the Scots decamped.[109] The bishop's appearance out of nowhere would have been a miracle indeed; but, in fact, it is known from other sources that William de St. Calais was reinstated in the fall of 1091 by Rufus, his brothers, and a large Norman army that was on its way north to fight Malcolm.[110] They were the ones who saved Durham, and this in turn means that the Scots had stayed in Northumbria throughout the summer of 1091.

The implications of this incident for Norman power in the North were ominous, and even if Rufus had not hitherto been pursuing a policy hostile to the Scots, he now embarked on one. The English king had come north that fall with an army and a fleet to force a military decision, and when it became clear that the Scots had already retreated out of Northumbria, he followed them into Lothian. Not unpredictably, this direct approach failed in 1091, just as it had in 1072 and in 1080. Malcolm would not give battle, and Rufus's chances of ever catching him were completely destroyed when he lost his supply fleet. The Norman army was soon cold and starving, and the invasion ended in the usual way. Malcolm and Rufus met in Lothian, perhaps with a well-fed and properly clothed Scottish army lurking in the nearby hills, and negotiated a renewal of the Abernethy agreement through the intermediacy of Edgar the Atheling and Duke Robert. Malcolm swore fealty to Rufus, who promised to return the twelve vills Malcolm had held under William the Conqueror. Then Rufus went south.[111]

This settlement did not end the matter, however. Rufus was apparently unhappy with the results of his invasion of Scotland,[112] and he may even have felt that he had made a fool of himself. In any case, the basic problem with the Scots still remained, and to solve this problem, he tried in 1092 a new tack that combined force with deceit. His first move was to conquer Cumberland. The expedition by which this was accomplished is described in little detail, but it seems to have been a well-conceived effort to take and hold the area. In 1092, Rufus led an army north and drove out Dolfin, the lord who had ruled Cumberland. With this accomplished, the king had Carlisle restored and a castle built there. Peasants with their families and livestock were brought in from the South to support the garrison.[113] Presumably this was necessary because the local inhabitants had not been able to practice settled agriculture on any scale with the Galwegian threat to the north and the back side of the free zone to the east and south. The castle, town, and peasants were, then, a unit. Carlisle was a self-supporting military colony that would significantly improve the configuration of the northern border. It could close the Vale of Eden, thereby protecting Yorkshire and Lancashire, and it could to some extent hinder movement through the Tyne gap.

These were, however, potentialities in 1092. At the time, Carlisle was only an isolated strong point whose lines of communication were unprotected and which could not defend itself for long. Indeed, its immediate use proved to be diplomatic rather than military. The military colony at Carlisle functioned as either a bargaining point with Malcolm or bait to bring him out into the open. This is evident from Malcolm's strange behavior in 1093. Despite the fact that the conquest of Carlisle is usually assumed to have been an act of naked aggression directed against Malcolm, he gave no sign for some time that he viewed it as such. He did not try to stop Rufus in 1092, nor did he invade the North during the normal campaigning season of 1093. Rather, in September of 1093, Malcolm came south peacefully, laid one of the foundation stones for Bishop William's new cathedral at Durham, and then went on to visit Rufus at Gloucester.[114] His behavior is puzzling; his unusual restraint must mean either that the situation was ambiguous in some sense or that an important factor has been misunderstood. Malcolm was not the man to come meekly to Rufus to ask for the return of Cumberland. Indeed, the *Anglo-Saxon Chronicle* says that he came south to demand that Rufus fulfill the terms of some agreement, and this agreement must have concerned Cumberland.[115] This suggestion, however, is no help unless one assumes that Rufus had promised to give back Cumberland, uncharacteristic behavior for the Red King but consistent with a transitory vow to reform himself which the king had made when he thought he was dying during the summer of 1093.[116]

The existence of such a promise from Rufus may account for Malcolm's forbearance. Yet it does not explain why Malcolm did nothing in 1092, and another hypothesis is more likely. Scholarship on these events has been marred by a basic error concerning the status of Cumberland. In 1092, Rufus had driven a noble named Dolfin out of Cumberland. The prevailing opinion is that this Dolfin was the eldest son of Earl Cospatric, who had once been earl of Northumbria and was later earl of Dunbar under Malcolm, but no direct evidence whatsoever supports the identification of the Cumbrian Dolfin with Cospatric's son.[117] It might be suggested as plausibly that the Cumbrian Dolfin was a descendant of the Dolfin, son of Thorfinn, a Cumbrian noble, who had died fighting against Macbeth in 1054.[118] This new identification is important because the idea that Dolfin was Cospatric's son is the only support for the belief that Cumberland was under the Scottish king in 1092. The last date when this is known to have been true is 1070, and after that there is simply no information on the question, although it may be relevant that Malcolm's invasions of 1079 and 1091 do not seem to have included contingents from the West.[119] Furthermore, the *Anglo-Saxon Chronicle* says that Dolfin ruled the area—not that he held an official position from Malcolm or owed obedience to the Scottish king.[120]

The assumption that Cumberland was Scottish has no support but silence. The contrary hypothesis that it had fallen away from the Scottish kingdom at some date after 1070 and was ruled independently by a local noble does less violence to the *Chronicle*'s description of the conquest of the area and makes sense of the events from the fall of 1091 to the early winter of 1093. When the Abernethy agreement was renewed in Lothian in 1091, Rufus had undertaken to restore Cumberland, which was ruled by a native noble, to Malcolm. The twelve vills (shires?) that Florence says Rufus promised Malcolm may represent Cumberland.[121] The next year Rufus did drive out Dolfin, and Malcolm had no reason to suppose that the English king would not honor the rest of the agreement. Of course, he did not. Consequently, in the late summer of 1093, Malcolm came south to demand that Rufus keep his promise. The chronicles, however, leave no doubt that Rufus behaved very badly on this occasion. The *Chronicle* says that he would not fulfill the agreement or even see Malcolm.[122] Florence adds that Rufus demanded Malcolm's submission to the judgment of Rufus's court, presumably over the question of Cumberland, and that Malcolm refused to plead except before a mixed court on the border.[123]

Malcolm had been tricked. Rufus was in possession of Cumberland, and if Malcolm could have it at all, it would be as a fief from William Rufus, an unacceptable condition. The incident may have been contrived to humiliate the Scottish king or to drive him into making a blunder, and there is some support for this idea. Orderic Vitalis believed that the destruction of Malcolm Canmore was brought about by treachery, although he laid the blame on Earl Robert de Mowbray rather than on Rufus.[124] In any event, Malcolm did make a serious mistake after his meeting with the English king. He returned to Scotland in a rage and collected an army even though it was late fall. Then sometime in early November, he invaded Northumberland, probably with the ultimate intention of taking Carlisle, but his reaction had been anticipated. Earl Robert de Mowbray was waiting for him with an army in Northumberland, and this is an indication that Rufus had retained Carlisle to lure Malcolm south of the Tweed, for it is very difficult to believe that Earl Robert normally kept—or could even afford to keep by himself—a large enough army on hand in mid-November to fight the Scots in the field. Malcolm was entering a trap. The earl awaited the Scots south of the Aln, and after they had crossed the river, he fell on them by surprise. In the battle that followed, the bulk of the Scottish army was either killed or drowned in the swollen river while trying to escape. Malcolm himself and Edward, his designated heir, were also killed.[125] Thus William II's machinations reached a successful conclusion. Malcolm Canmore had finally given battle, and his death opened unusual possibilities to the English king and ultimately led to the passing of the old political structure of northern Britain. Judged from the standpoint of the events that followed, Malcolm appears to have been a man who had held back time by his own existence. Of course, this is both the nature of politics and an exaggeration.

Rufus was now confronted with an unparalled situation in the North. Robert de Mowbray had killed the reigning king of Scots, his heir, and most of their army. The ensuing internal political conflicts in Scotland gave the English king the opportunity to neutralize Scotland by backing contenders for the throne. In this sense the situation was similar to the one that had led to the establishment of Malcolm Canmore as king by Siward and Edward the Confessor, but circumstances were particularly promising in 1093. Malcolm had been prepared to ignore Scottish custom regarding the succession, which would have made his younger brother Donald Bane king after his death, by having himself immediately succeeded by Edward, his eldest son by Margaret.[126] The death of Edward and, more important, given the number of sons of Malcolm and Margaret, the destruction of Malcolm's army, which probably had included many of his closest supporters, made this impossible. Donald Bane, who had been alienated from his nephews by his brother's attempt to disinherit him, was consequently able to become king late in 1093, and he ensured that he would not be challenged by the sons of Malcolm and Margaret by expelling the Anglo-Saxons whom Malcolm had received during the Norman Conquest and who had presumably been an important source of his strength.[127] These disasters ruined the hopes of Malcolm's sons by Margaret and made Donald Bane a weaker king than his brother.

They also greatly improved the chances for success of Rufus's attempt to solve the Scottish problem—insofar as politics could solve it—by setting up his own king of Scots. Even before Donald Bane's purge of the Anglo-Saxons had driven Malcolm's sons by Margaret into William II's hands, he had had a suitable candidate for the Scottish throne. During the reign of William the Conqueror, Malcolm had given up Duncan, his eldest son by his first marriage, as a hostage. In 1093, Duncan was serving in Rufus's army, and his chances of ever becoming king were very small because he apparently had been declared a bastard and thereby removed from the line of succession to the Scottish throne as envisaged by Margaret.[128] Duncan was, therefore, a perfect tool for Rufus, a candidate who would owe the Normans everything if he could be placed on the throne, and after his father's death Rufus accepted Duncan's homage and gave him an army with which to claim his inheritance.[129] The dispatch with which this was accomplished strongly suggests that this operation had been considered in advance. Between November 13, the date of Malcolm's death, and Christmas, not in 1094 as is continually asserted, Duncan was able to raise his army, enter Scotland, and drive out his uncle Donald.[130] Rufus and Duncan had evidently been prepared for Malcolm's death, and the speed of Duncan's campaign perhaps indicates that he used the same soldiers Robert de Mowbray had employed against Malcolm. This, of course, is only a suggestion; and, in any case, the attempt to set up a vassal king of Scots dependent on Norman arms was only momentarily successful. Soon after becoming king, Duncan lost most of his army in an ambush and continued to rule only on the condition that he not bring Anglo-Saxons or Frenchmen into Scotland to serve in his army. This stipulation rendered him powerless, and in 1094 he was killed by Donald, who again became king.[131] This failure did not cause Rufus to abandon the plan, but it was three years before a new pretender could be sent over the border.

In the interval, another event took place that revealed the ramifications in Northumbria of Malcolm's death and of the distracted conditions of the kingdom of the Scots. In 1095, Earl Robert de Mowbray revolted. This was an unparalleled event. No Norman had felt sufficiently at home in the North to revolt before, and the very possibility that the earl of Northumbria could consider breaking with the king depended on the absence of danger from Scotland. Furthermore, the same factor may have been ultimately responsible for his revolt in a direct sense. The early chronicles do not ascribe very intelligible motives to Robert, but one charter may contain the key to his behavior. The record of a concord made between the earl and the bishop of Durham in 1094 shows that Rufus had extinguished the earl's judicial rights over St. Cuthbert's estates. If this charter is genuine, which it seems to be, it provides a sufficient motive for Robert's revolt.[132] Rufus had probably decided that he did not need such a powerful Northumbrian earl with Duncan on the Scottish throne, and this hypothesis is supported by the fact that Robert did not hold Newcastle in 1095.[133] The earl refused to agree to this diminution of his power.

Conditions in Northumbria, however, do not explain the downfall of Robert. Had he been alone, he would probably have accepted the reduction of his privileges, but he seems to have been a member of a widespread conspiracy that involved many nobles, especially those of the Welsh border. Their aim was to overthrow Rufus, and the plot must have been formed early in 1094 before the great Welsh revolt of that year and while Duncan was still alive.[134] Once the Welsh revolted, however, most of the conspirators abandoned the plan—except for Robert de Mowbray. He stood no chance alone, and the most likely explanation for his defiance of the king is that he had been betrayed and that Rufus had decided to make an example of him. Robert was a very convenient example in 1095 because he had recently inherited the extremely wealthy estate of his uncle Geoffrey, bishop of Coutances.[135] By Easter of 1095, when he would not come to court, the earl was a marked man; and after he had failed to appear at Whitsuntide, Rufus led an army into Northumbria, where he had little difficulty taking the earl's castles and capturing the earl. Only Bamburgh, which was held by Robert's wife, held out for long, and she eventually yielded when the besiegers threatened to mutilate her husband.[136]

Clearly times had changed, and perhaps the surviving Northumbrian nobles were amused. Rufus had easily suppressed the revolt despite the isolation of Northumbria. Robert's men had all been conveniently assembled in castles, and the opportunities the North offered for irregular warfare had been ignored, although this may not have been the earl's intention.[137] Furthermore, Robert de Mowbray survived the revolt, something no Northumbrian earl, except for Cospatric, had managed to do in the eleventh century. The earl went off to a dungeon for the next thirty years. This commonplace baronial revolt had, however, a significance beyond its comparison with past revolts. The earldom had lost its regional political significance in 1080 when the Northumbrian nobility had been destroyed in the aftermath of the revolt against Walcher. Now it had lost its military utility. If the Scots had been so little to be feared that Robert could revolt, then Rufus had no need of a Northumbrian earl, and he did not appoint a new one. The earldom of Northumbria was abolished after this revolt, or taken into the king's hands as some Northumbrian monks liked to think.[138] The distinction made little real difference. The king took over the demesne of the earls, and henceforth, Northumberland would be ruled by sheriffs. This, of course, represented a fundamental change in the position Northumbria had occupied within the kingdom. The suppression of the earldom ended, at least in theory, the administrative and judicial isolation of Northumbria except on the estates of St. Cuthbert, and it created the novel possibility that royal power could be directly exercised above the Tees by more prosaic means than the punitive expeditions and murders that had characterized relations between the northern earls and both the Anglo-Saxon and the Norman kings. In terms of the future, Rufus's failure to appoint a new earl destroyed the threat that a line of Norman earls would become entrenched above the Tees and pursue the independent policies of their predecessors.

The finality of the situation depended upon the continued weakness of the Scots. Should a new leader of the stature of Malcolm III arise among them, they could force the revival of the earldom out of military necessity and perhaps even reverse Rufus's conquest of Cumberland. Indeed, these possibilities were apparent in 1095, for Rufus did not leave the North, or was not long gone, before he took steps to ensure that the Scots would not become a threat to the North in the foreseeable future. By late August of 1095, if not earlier, he had begun his second attempt to establish a vassal king of Scots, and this endeavor was probably directly connected with his expedition against Earl Robert. A charter made at Norham on August 29 records a land grant to Durham by Edgar, Malcolm III's third son by Margaret. The charter discloses that Rufus had already given Lothian and Scotland to Edgar, and it is likely that something more tangible was involved than the Red King's recognition of Edgar's right to be king and a symbolic investiture because the charter records Edgar's gift to Durham of two large estates in the Merse. Unless these gifts were anticipatory, which is unlikely, they indicate that Edgar already controlled the valley of the Tweed, and the most probable explanation is that Rufus or his agents had established Edgar above the Tweed after the fall of Bamburgh.[139] In 1095, then, Rufus could safely suppress the earldom because he had installed a new marcher lord beyond it. This time the plan worked despite the precedents against it. In 1097, Rufus was able to send Edgar the Atheling into Scotland with an army to put his nephew into possession of the rest of his kingdom, and for once the Atheling acted effectively. He defeated Donald Bane in battle, drove him out of the kingdom, and then installed Edgar as king "in fealty to King William."[140] All this, of course, had been done before, but this time it led to important results. Contrary to any expectations that might have been based upon the fate of Duncan II or the perfidy of Malcolm III, King Edgar both survived and remained loyal to the Normans. While he reigned, the North lived in peace with the Scots, and during this period ties were established between the Scottish and Norman royal families that ensured the continuance of peace for thirty years after Edgar's death. This abnormal period of peace, in turn, allowed the Normans to consolidate the hold on the North they had already won and, in a very important sense, to extend their rule

6. The Impact of the Normans on the Northern Village

The preceding narrative shows that the North was conquered in three stages and that the first two were completed by the death of William the Conqueror. At this date, Norman nobles were established in southern Lancashire and along the east coast plain from the south of Yorkshire north through Durham into southern Northumberland. They had not yet ventured in any numbers into northern and central Northumberland and northern Lancashire or into the Pennines, but on the plains their power was supreme— if not unchallenged in the north and in the mountains. This chronology of their expansion is an important improvement upon traditional accounts of the subjugation of the North that make the establishment of Norman power automatically follow either the harrying of 1069 or the punitive expedition of 1080 and ignore the territorial limits of this power even in the 1080s and 1090s. An understanding of the local importance of the house of Bamburgh and of the threats inherent in the North's western border make the extent of Norman expansion more understandable. Still, my account is traditional in a sense. It benefits from a regional point of view and from the inclusion of the pre-Conquest history of the North, but the process described is familiar in its general outlines. It is the narrative of the replacement of native landowners by Frenchmen and the consolidation of the latter's power by means of the castle, the church, and the knight.

Aside from the slaughter, the establishment of this new aristocracy was the most important immediate result of the Conquest. Before the extension of Norman settlement into Cumberland and Northumberland can be profitably traced, it is necessary to take a closer look at the settlement of the Normans in Yorkshire and Durham from the standpoint of a basic question that is usually shunned: did the Norman Conquest represent a straightforward substitution of one upper class for another, or did its effects reach deeper in the social hierarchy? In the parlance of Conquest studies, the basic problem is to determine whether these new landlords simply' stepped into the shoes of their Anglo-Saxon predecessors and ran their new estates according to local custom or whether they made basic changes in the management and organization of their estates.

Those familiar with the general body of literature on the Norman Conquest will consider this an unfruitful line of inquiry because it is generally assumed that the Normans were content to continue the level and type of agricultural exploitation that had existed in King Edward's day. Recent research has shown that they may perhaps have raised rents or demanded higher farms from their manors and that, on occasion, they may have increased the amount of labor they received from peasants by insisting on strict definitions of services;[1] but these qualifications have not shaken the great unvoiced assumption that the greater Norman barons were basically gentlemen, that is, that their greed did not cross class lines. Perhaps Frank Barlow best summed up this view on the subject in a recent appraisal of the effects of the Conquest:

> The new landholders acquired all the rents and services which their predecessors had enjoyed. In an economic context the change of lords made little difference to the agricultural producers, the farmers and their labourers, the small-holders and the stock breeders. There were many rough actions and misunderstandings; there may occasionally have been new men with new ideas. Sometimes there was a determined effort to restock under-exploited estates. There may have been a general movement to require full economic rents. But the . . . major barons were mostly absentees. . . . [They] may have pressed heavily on their stewards, reeves, and other agents to increase revenue from their estates; but they had no revolutionary means of exploitation.[2]

This characterization of Norman economic behavior may be correct in general, but at least one recent historian, R. Welldon Finn, has held the opposite view that the Normans demanded increased labor dues from the peasants where possible.[3] Even if the prevailing view is an accurate description of the way the Normans dealt with their estates in southern and midland England, it only proves that they were reasonably satisfied with their new manors and is not a sign that they were either unwilling or unable to reorganize estates that did not meet their expectations. The greater Norman barons were mainly parvenus who were still concerned with enlarging their landed wealth;[4] they could not necessarily be expected to respect peasant custom when it was not in their interest to do so. Specifically, one might wonder if the Normans behaved in the same way above the Humber as they had in the South since in the former region their new "manors" were at best lightly exploited relics of the shire system and more often were wholly or partially waste. They might be expected to have taken a different line in such circumstances, and there are hints in the works of historians of the North that they did. These are vague and imprecise, but they are nonetheless a useful balance to the prevailing opinion. Stenton's early work on the estates of the northern Danelaw in the eleventh century led him to the belief that some process was occurring through which the greater sokes were breaking up and the smaller ones amalgamating "to produce an intermediate type of estate, an estate forming an intermediate agrarian unit, in which the features characteristic of the later manorial economy might find room for development."[5] What Stenton meant by "process" and "development" is not obvious, but they would seem to be open to the interpretation that the Normans were restructuring the sokes. The same conclusion is suggested by some of the work of T. A. M. Bishop. In 1934, he made a statistical study of the vills in the Vale of York and found that those vills with demesne land in 1301 had contained some population in 1086, whereas those vills with no demesne land in 1301 had been waste in 1086. On the basis of this pattern, he concluded: "The social depression which had been suffered after the conquest by the population of Yorkshire will account for the prevalence of a manorial institution in those vills where any population survived."[6] This is a stronger statement than Stenton's although it is not clear whether Bishop thought that the Normans had introduced the manor into Yorkshire or had simply continued it. He probably held the former view because he suggested in passing in this article that there might have been a "sudden and limited expansion of the manorial system within a short period after the conquest."[7] Certainly by 1948 he was of this opinion. In that year he stated this position clearly, albeit in a forbidding footnote on the next to the last page of his essay: "I assume that such burdens as the medieval peasantry of Yorkshire endured were fastened on them between the years 1069 and at latest 1100: the period of a rebellion, a punitive expedition, entry into possession by a foreign military caste, social degradation of the inhabitants in comparison with those of the rest of the northern Danelaw, compulsory migration, and the creation of conditions antecedent to the manorial system in a mild form."[8] Finally, Jolliffe believed that the Normans introduced demesne farming in Northumbria during the twelfth century.[9] The opinions of all three of these scholars are invalidated to some extent by the fact that a mild form of manorialism had existed throughout Northumbria in 1066, but it is not certain that this discovery completely explains the phenomenon they noted. Consequently, their views create a sufficiently strong prima facie case to justify pursuing this line of inquiry despite the general presumption that the Normans simply installed themselves in the economic structure they found, caulked its seams, and preserved traditional forms of organization.

     In the North this model has a certain unreality, in any case, because in many villages little of the traditional rural structure remained for the Normans to respect. During the terrible winter of 1069–70, much of northern society was destroyed in Yorkshire and Durham, and an understanding of this event and its results must stand at the base of any realistic attempt to determine the nature of the Norman settlement of the North. Unfortunately, the extent of this destruction above the Tees is unknown, but as late as the time of Domesday, marks of the harrying were still evident in Yorkshire, where the countryside was studded with empty villages. H. C. Darby and I. S. Maxwell found that "over one-half of the vills of the North Riding and over one-third of those of the East and West Ridings were wholly or partially waste."[10] The remainder of the vills had some population in 1086 but not necessarily as much as in 1066. These figures are too low because they include only those vills explicitly described as waste or as containing waste, but not those vills without recorded population yet not described as waste. Other statistics in this vein could be easily supplied, but perhaps a more meaningful impression of the extent of the destruction can be gained from a comparison with Nottinghamshire, which was smaller than any of the ridings of Yorkshire and itself contained a large swath of poorly developed land. In 1086, there were more people living in Nottinghamshire than in any two of the three ridings of Yorkshire, and the population of that shire (5,573) was more than double the recorded population of either the East Riding (2,362) or the North Riding (2,014). Plow teams show the same picture of desolation. The figure for Nottinghamshire (1,969) was more than twice as large as the figures for the East Riding (791) or the North Riding (847) and substantially in excess of the number recorded for the West Riding (1,292).[11]

These low numbers were not the result of the fact that the upland areas of Yorkshire could never have borne intensive settlement. Even on the lowlands of the shire both men and beasts were spread thinly in 1086. Throughout the Vale of York there were only a few areas where the recorded population reached 2 men per square mile. In Holderness the figure was 3.6, and nowhere except for a narrow belt of land running from the lower Wharfe south past Tanshelf and Doncaster to beyond Tickhill (the Limestone Hills) were there as many as 4 men per square mile. In Nottinghamshire, on the other hand, nearly two-thirds of the county had between 5 and 10 people per square mile, and in the East Riding of Lincolnshire, which lay just across the Humber from Holderness (3.6), the population ranged from 9.8 to 13.7. Whether one multiplies the Domesday figure for population by a factor of 4 or 5 to obtain the actual population, Yorkshire was still nearly an empty land seventeen years after the harrying, and oxen were as rare as men. Throughout the Vale of York there was no more than 1 team per square mile except southwest of York (1.2), and this density was only exceeded by more than two-tenths in the core of Richmond (1.8) and the Limestone Hills, where it varied between 1.4 and 2.2. In the North Riding of Lincolnshire there were generally over 2 plows per square mile and in the Trent lowlands of Nottinghamshire, between 2.6 and 4.7.[12]

These comparisons convey an impression of the effects of the harrying in real terms and make it impossible to believe, as has been asserted by W. E. Wightman, that the lowlands of Yorkshire had undergone "a pretty full" recovery by 1086.[13] They also automatically exclude much of the shire from the bounds of any theory of Norman economic inertia. To be of value, many estates above the Humber had to be revived. Yet beyond this general point, the meaning of Domesday's figures is not clear because it is not certain that they can be taken entirely at their face value. Some rebuilding had presumably taken place between 1070 and 1086, the date of Domesday's description, but this document's Yorkshire folios fail to give any intermediate value for manors between 1066 and 1086. This omission hides the original extent of the waste in 1070 and effectively screens the Normans' initial dealings with their new estates and creates uncertainty with respect to Yorkshire's population in 1086. Two major alternatives could account for these figures: development in place or forced immigration. The population of the shire in 1086 could have been composed of survivors of the harrying and their children, who had stayed in their ancestral villages and redeveloped them under their new Norman lords. If this was the case, there would be a direct relationship between conditions in 1070 and in 1086 except that the areas of waste would have shrunk somewhat by the later date. Alternatively, the Normans may have brought in immigrants from undevastated parts of the shire or from beyond its borders to revive completely depopulated villages. If this happened on any scale, there would be little connection between the situation in 1070 and that described in Domesday.

Two important attempts have been made to deal with this complex problem. The first was offered by Bishop, who in 1948 suggested an ingenious theory based on the second of the two alternatives.[14] His ideas were buttressed by an impressive statistical analysis of Yorkshire Domesday, and they were revolutionary in the sense that, if accepted, they would have forced a reevaluation of the stereotype of Norman economic behavior. Bishop began by pointing out that the distribution of waste villages was not uniform in 1086. In the lowlands there were both waste vills and inhabited vills, yet the higher parts of the shire, the Pennines, the Moors in the North Riding, and the Wolds, were covered by great, unbroken bands of uninhabited or waste vills. The obvious inference from this uneven distribution of waste would be that the Normans had harried the highlands more effectively than the plains, but Bishop did not draw this conclusion. Rather, he asserted that the Normans had harried only the plains and river valleys in 1069 and had not penetrated the Pennines, the Moors, or the Wolds. This assertion, for which he provided no proof, was the foundation of his theory. If it were accepted, then one had to suppose that there had been extensive population movements of some sort within Yorkshire between 1070 and 1086. In particular, Bishop argued that the Normans had made an attempt to revive agricultural production on the Yorkshire plain by initiating population movements from the unwasted highlands down onto the lowlands. The sporadic distribution of waste in the lower parts of the shire was a sign that certain vills had been redeveloped by their Norman lords—not that the Normans had spared an occasional vill in 1069–70—and the bands of waste in the uplands were the result of a forced exodus carried out by the Normans in hope of increasing their agricultural profits. Bishop believed that this theory was supported by three patterns he had discerned. First, a number of villages on the plain contained a populated estate belonging to one Norman lord and a waste estate belonging to another lord. He rejected the possibility that the lord of the populated estate might have simply usurped all the peasants in a partially waste village and argued that such populated estates had been redeveloped by their lords. Second, a number of other vills contained excess plow teams in 1086 as compared to 1066, but their values had fallen from 1066. Bishop believed that these vills were recently resettled and perhaps expanded. Finally, and this was his major proof, he thought that as a general rule only those fiefs that contained both upland and lowland holdings had recovered to any significant extent by 1086.[15]

This fascinating theory, which would dispel some of the obscurity that hangs over Yorkshire during the critical period from 1070 to 1086 and hides the Norman settlement of the county, is unfortunately false. Darby and Maxwell have raised four main objections to it in their geographical analysis of Yorkshire Domesday. First, it was not "intrinsically improbable," as Bishop thought, that the Normans had wasted the uplands. These settlements were more in need of subduing than the plain because of their remoteness. Second, they pointed out that this theoretical consideration was supported by the Domesday returns from Cheshire. These give a value for each manor not only for 1066 and 1086, but also for the intermediate date when the Norman lord took possession and show that the Normans had harried both the uplands and the lowlands in this shire but that the uplands had not recovered as quickly as the lowlands. Third, they were unable to substantiate Bishop's claim that only those individual fiefs had recovered that contained both lowland and upland vills. Finally, they pointed out

that there were occasionally great differences in population between two estates of a single lord in the same village. Such instances
dull the significance of the cases of unequal development of manors
lying in the same vill but belonging to different lords, which Bishop
interpreted as a sign of colonization.[16]

These points are well taken and leave Bishop's theory quite
doubtful.[17] The same conclusion is supported by the findings of
my inquiry. Northern resistance to the Norman Conquest was
based upon hit-and-run tactics in which the woods and hills played
a crucial role as concealed places of assembly and refuge. Their
reduction was necessary for the Normans to control Yorkshire, and
Orderic Vitalis specifically states that William pursued the rebels
into the hills and woods during the winter of 1069.[18] It might
still be doubted that the Normans did as thorough a job wasting
the difficult country of the uplands as they did the plain, but
the unbroken bands of seemingly uninhabited vills that appear
in Domesday are to some degree an illusion, for they resulted
from the failure of the Domesday clerks to obtain information
on the specifics of population and waste for many of the Pennine
villages.[19] They cannot, therefore, be taken at face value, and the
most likely hypothesis is that there was a sporadic distribution of
waste in the uplands just as there was on the plain. These considerations strike at the heart of Bishop's theory by showing that his
assumption that the uplands had escaped the harrying is false and
that the impression that they were without population in 1086 is
doubtful.

Despite their objections to Bishop's theory, Darby and Maxwell concluded their discussion of this issue by suggesting that
there might, indeed, have been some population movement from
unwasted to wasted vills, but that there was insufficient evidence to
be certain.[20] That the latter was a serious reservation is shown by
their failure to enlarge upon the question of what sort of redevelopment they envisaged. Although their suggestion saved the theoretical possibility of redevelopment, it was a tacit admission that
there was little sign of any. This may seem surprising, but only
from the standpoint of compartmentalized thinking. In terms of
economics, there should have been a movement under way by 1086
to revive the better land of Yorkshire; but in terms of the military
situation, or perhaps more accurately the police situation, it is
hard to see how such a movement could have made progress in

much of Yorkshire. Until the last years of William the Conqueror and probably beyond, the Pennines and Moors were the seats of outlaw bands that were reinforced along the coast by pirates and in the northwest probably by raiders from over Stainmore. Isolated colonists could have hoped for little security, and the most promising sites for redevelopment would have been those near still populated vills that could afford some protection. Not until the establishment of such defensive bulwarks as Richmond and Pontefract, which occurred late in William's reign, did these conditions begin to pass.[21] General efforts at redevelopment may then have begun, but, if so, they are unlikely to have made enough progress by 1086 to leave a clear mark in Domesday. The question, then, has been misconstrued. The Normans may have made an attempt to increase the amount of land under the plow, but only in areas where it was fairly safe to do so, that is, in areas with a significant continuity of habitation.

Bishop uncovered the clue to what actually happened although he failed to interpret it correctly. The general statistics discussed earlier indicate that the countryside of Yorkshire was far from recovery in 1086. Most of its villages were either waste or underpopulated, and only a few had come through the Conquest unchanged. Bishop, however, pointed out that certain overstocked manors were an exception to this rule. These were villages in which the number of plows at work in 1086 exceeded the number of plowlands (the land that could be worked by one plow) traditionally ascribed to the vill. By inference, such vills also had a larger population in 1086 than in 1066. Bishop cited the example of Handsworth to illustrate this phenomenon. It had land for 7 plows, yet there were 8½ plows at Handsworth in 1086. A substantial number of similar cases existed in Yorkshire at this date, despite the general condition of the shire, and they were very significant. Bishop, however, did not investigate them closely because his attention was attracted by another characteristic of Handsworth. Its yearly value had fallen from £8 in 1066 to 40s. in 1086, and Bishop thought that this decline in value was significant because it indicated that the twenty-one peasants at Handsworth were recent colonists who "had not yet advanced far in clearing and cultivation." He further theorized that the excess teams here and in other vills of this type were either engaged in clearing or were transient and would in the future move to waste vills,[22] but this interpretation cannot be accepted. The values of manors in Yorkshire were subject to variation as a result of too many possible causes to be used as an index of the date of colonization,[23] and, in any case, the obvious inference from the excess team and a half is that the arable land of the village had been expanded, not that there was a floating corps of plowmen.

At one point in his article, Bishop raised the possibility of plotting the overstocked manors on a map, but he dismissed it because he was more concerned with the supposed relationship between upland waste and populated manors in the lowlands within individual fiefs.[24] Had he pursued the idea, he would have found the clearest signs Domesday can provide of Norman estate development in Yorkshire during the years 1070 to 1086. A map of the overstocked manors shows that these estates were distributed in a highly singular fashion across the face of the shire. They were not spread evenly over the plain or even limited to it as Bishop's theory would suggest they should have been (see map 6). Rather, great stretches of prime land in Holderness and much of the Vale of York were completely without them, and there were a number of them on the unrewarding soils of the Howardian and Hambleton Hills and in the Sandstone Hills. Moreover, the overstocked manors tended to stand in groups, not in isolation. The majority of these manors were located in four main areas: in the Aire valley and the land to the south, in Richmond below the Swale, and around the edge of the Southern Wolds, plus a complex area that comprised the Howardian and Hambleton Hills with the valley of the upper Derwent and the adjoining fringes of the Vales of Pickering and York (hereafter called the "Howardian Hills and vicinity"). Nor is this tendency of the overstocked manors to be found in groups their only peculiarity. Domesday's description of the fief of Ilbert de Lacy consistently names his Anglo-Saxon subtenants in 1086. His fief was situated on either side of the Aire in the largest concentration of overstocked manors in the county, and the estates of his Anglo-Saxon tenants show nearly as strong a tendency to have excess teams as those of his Norman tenants. Finally, of the eighty overstocked manors in this area, sixty-seven had fallen in value.

The manors with excess plows were, then, concentrated in a few areas. In the one area where Anglo-Saxon subtenants are named, their estates also tended to be overstocked, and in the same area, which contained the greatest number of such manors in the

Distribution of Overstocked Manors in Yorkshire in 1086

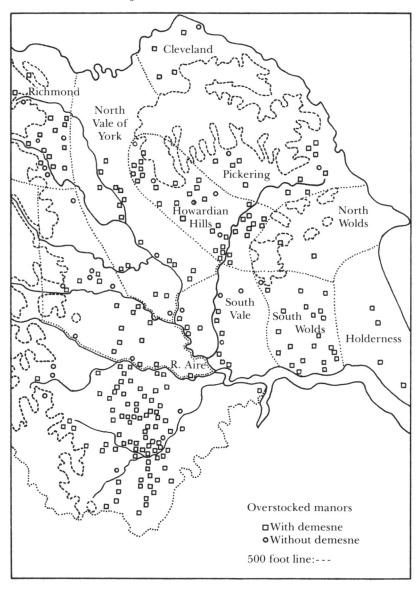

Cleveland

Richmond

North
Vale of
York

Pickering

Howardian
Hills

North
Wolds

South
Vale

South
Wolds

Holderness

R. Aire

Overstocked manors

□ With demesne
○ Without demesne

500 foot line: - - -

shire, there had been a general fall in value. Bishop's theory cannot explain these patterns, but they are explicable in terms of the hypothesis that the Normans restricted their efforts at redevelopment to only a few relatively secure areas. In a sense, "redevelopment" does not accurately describe the process that occurred. The areas where there were concentrations of manors with excess teams in 1086 were areas that either had not been harried in the winter of 1069 or had not been ravaged so severely that the continuity of life had been broken. In these areas the Normans increased agricultural production in an attempt to augment their own wealth by expanding the arable of existing villages and probably by redeveloping nearby waste holdings. This is the meaning of the extra plows. Nor is there any need of an elaborate hypothesis to explain where the Normans got the peasant labor for this expansion. All discussions of this question have ignored the single most likely source of "colonists": the refugees. The harrying of the North displaced thousands of peasants by destroying their livestock, agricultural implements, and winter food supply—not to mention their seed corn for 1070—and set in motion a population movement that reached the Midlands and ultimately even Scotland. The object of this migration was to find food and probably the chance to sell themselves into slavery, a poor man's alternative to starvation, aside from brigandage, in a society that lacked credit mechanisms. Initially these refugees would have gone to the undevastated parts of Yorkshire, where the local Norman and Anglo-Saxon lords gave refuge to the most desirable, young men and women in their teens and those with special skills, and sent the rest on their way because the stream of starving peasants represented as much of a threat to the local economy, particularly to livestock, as an opportunity to acquire cheap labor. Probably, in fact, some small villages that had escaped the Normans were destroyed by their passage.

Although this line of reasoning is compelling, some index of continuity is desirable as a support for the hypothesis that the concentrations of overstocked manors were located in areas that had not been too severely wasted in 1069 rather than in areas that had been completely redeveloped after that date. Since Domesday does not give any manorial values in Yorkshire for an intermediate date between 1066 and 1086, this problem cannot be approached directly, but functioning of rural churches served by resident priests can be used as an indirect source of this information because they are unlikely to have survived at a very much greater rate than the peasantry. This should be true irrespective of whether the Normans burned down churches in 1069. Actually they may have done so if the Yorkshire peasants followed the usual northern expedient in times of danger—flight to the churchyard with all the movable property circumstances allowed. But even if the Normans resisted the temptation provided by such convenient gatherings, the relationship should still hold because it stems directly from the nature of churches as parasitic service institutions. With the destruction of the economy in an area, the disruption of normal patterns of life, and the death or dispersal of the inhabitants, the churches in the area would cease to exist because both their reason to be and their income would be gone. Furthermore, in a devastated area later colonized, a functioning church would be one of the last things to be created since the population would have to reach a fairly high level in terms of numbers and prosperity before a church could be supported. These considerations, of course, do not form a firm basis for statements about individual churches, but they are valid for groups of churches. Regions in which functioning churches were recorded in 1086 had either been spared or not too seriously disturbed in the harrying of the North. Therefore, the distribution of churches provides a general index of the continuity of local habitation.[25]

If overstocked manors were in fact located in areas that had not suffered overwhelming destruction, there should be a correlation between the number of overstocked manors in an area and the number of functioning churches there. High numbers of the former should be found with high numbers of the latter, and the opposite should also hold true. This relationship does exist (see map). If the shire is divided into suitable areas suggested by the distribution of overstocked manors, topographical factors, and feudal geography, and if these areas are ranked according to the number of overstocked manors and functioning churches in each, a marked correspondence emerges (see Table 5 and compare A with B).[26]

The correspondence between A and B is close enough to establish that the relationship in question exists and to show that the areas where there were numerous overstocked manors had not been harried too severely. There is not, however, complete agreement between the two rankings. With the second position in the

Distribution of Functioning Churches in Yorkshire in 1086

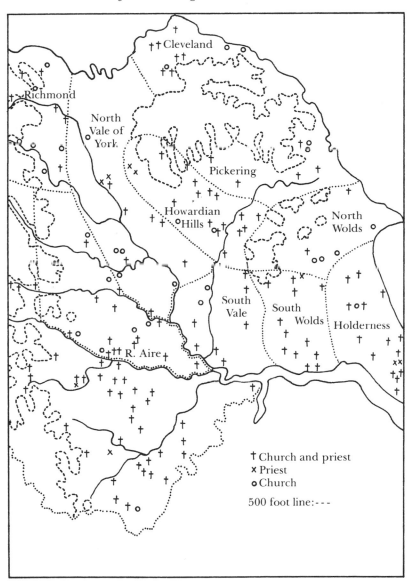

Cleveland

Richmond

North
Vale of
York

Pickering

Howardian
Hills

North
Wolds

South
Vale

South
Wolds

Holderness

R. Aire

† Church and priest
✗ Priest
○ Church

500 foot line: - - -

Table 5. *Overstocked Manors and Functioning Churches
in Yorkshire in 1086*

Regions	M	C	A	B	A'	B'
I. Below the Aire	87	37	1	1	1	1
II. Above the Aire	23	14	3	3	3	3
III. Pennines	0	3	11	9	8	8
IV. Richmond	19	6	5	7		
V. N. Vale of York	19	9	5	5	5	5
VI. S. Vale of York with H. Levels	14	7	6	6	6	6
VII. Howardian Hills and vicinity	39	16	2	2	2	2
VIII. Cleveland	5	7	8	6		
IX. Vale of Pickering	13	5	7	8	7	7
X. N. Wolds	2	2	10	10		
XI. S. Wolds	22	13	4	4	4	4
XII. Holderness	4	16	9	2		

Key:
M = The number of overstocked estates
C = The number of functioning churches
A = The ranking of the overstocked estates
B = The ranking of churches

A' and B' = The revised rankings of A and B, each corrected by the deletion of those areas harried twice in 1069–70.

rankings slight discrepancies begin to appear, although from the standpoint of the ranking of the overstocked manors, there is an exact correspondence through position six. This is not, therefore, a serious matter since the proposition at issue is only that there should be large numbers of functioning churches in areas that contained numerous overstocked manors, not that there should always be large numbers of overstocked manors in areas where churches were numerous. Most of the discrepancies could be accounted for as the result of the inevitable inaccuracies introduced into the rankings by the small numerical bases that appear toward the end of the ranks. Still, this explanation can hardly apply to Holderness, which was ninth in overstocked manors but second in functioning churches. This difference is not due to some trick of the numbers, and it suggests an explanation for the discrepancies between the two rankings. They are the result of the simplicity of the model. Despite the prominence the harrying of the North claims in a discussion of Yorkshire, various parts of the shire endured other episodes of destruction after 1069. Holderness and the eastern part of the North Wolds had probably been devastated as late as 1085 to deny supplies to a threatened Danish invasion, and Richmond and Cleveland had been harried by the Scots in 1070.[27] Such incidents as these could be expected to introduce confusion into the basic data. If these areas are excluded from the rankings, a rather different result emerges: there is a perfect correspondence between both ranks for the seven areas wasted only once in 1069–70 (compare A' with B').

This agreement and its absence when the four fringe areas are included in the calculations can best be explained by the following hypothesis. In the winter of 1069, William only began to harry Yorkshire after he had crossed the Aire, and the land to the south of this river only suffered from the enforced stay of his army as it waited to force the line of the river. This undoubtedly produced a good deal of local destruction but far less than the harrying proper that commenced once the Normans were beyond the Aire and the Danes had retreated to their ships. The Normans then thoroughly wasted two great swaths of land, judging from the survival of functioning churches. One included the Vale of York, Richmond, and much of the region above the Aire, and it ran an indeterminate distance into the Pennines. The other area comprised the Vale of Pickering, the Northern Wolds, and Cleveland. Aside from the South, the Howardian Hills, the Southern Wolds, and apparently Holderness escaped the full fury of the destruction.[28]

This hypothesis is entirely in accord with what little is known from chronicles about the harrying and with the distribution of waste in 1086. The first great band of destruction in central Yorkshire would have been produced by the systematic harrying conducted in December of 1069, and the second would have been the result of William's later movements. Specifically, after Christmas the Conqueror moved east from York to dislodge a group of rebels from Holderness and then went north to the Tees, presumably along the coast.[29] During the course of this campaign, the Northern Wolds, the Vale of Pickering, and Cleveland would have been harried. This reconstruction of the harrying is supported by a significant feature of Darby and Maxwell's maps of the waste in Yorkshire in 1086. These show that the waste in central Yorkshire above the Aire included a high degree of totally waste villages such as would have been produced by the methodical operations in December and that the waste in the east was more often only partial, a reflection apparently of William's haste to cross into Durham as winter deepened.[30] Finally, this theory accounts for the existence of a less heavily wasted strip of land running from the western end of the Moors down through the Howardian Hills and the middle Derwent to the Southern Wolds and Holderness. This area was on the edge of both phases of the harrying but the direct object of neither.

Once the Norman armies had departed, peasants fled the blasted stretches of countryside, and many of them went initially to the less devastated regions. South of the Aire and in the other inland areas that had not suffered too greatly, some of their number were used by the Normans to expand agricultural production and to redevelop waste vills during the 1070s. Most were probably forced to move on. Those peasants, however, who had fled to the northern part of the shire and to Durham met a different fate. In the spring of 1070, Malcolm Canmore suddenly erupted into Yorkshire. He came over Stainmore and ravaged Teesdale and Cleveland before crossing into Durham.[31] Of course, by this time there was not much left to plunder, and the Scots consoled themselves by turning the raid into a slaving expedition. This may even have been their intention from the beginning since the taking of slaves was a common feature of later Scottish raids. They were able to take advantage of the conditions created by the harrying to enslave large numbers of refugees who had assembled in some of the areas through which they passed, and Symeon of Durham believed that they were so successful that every Scottish household had the convenience of an English slave as a result of this expedition.[32] Perhaps many of the refugees were not unwilling to go. This last episode was, in turn, responsible for the failure of the relationship between overstocked manors and functioning churches to hold true on the northern edge of Yorkshire.

The Normans increased agricultural production by expanding the arable in localities where large segments of the native population had survived and which had been the object of population movements set off by the harrying. They may also have redeveloped waste villages near these secure areas, but they probably did not risk their oxen and seed in isolated attempts at reclamation until the 1080s at the earliest. Generally speaking, there is a fairly direct relationship between what happened in Yorkshire in 1069–70 and the situation described in 1086. A complex form of development in place had occurred, and Domesday can be more or less taken at its word without the help of convoluted hypotheses.

This much is sufficiently clear, but it is imprecise in that it ignores the fundamental question of how the Normans organized their "increased agricultural production." This is a matter of overriding importance for understanding the significance of the Norman Conquest of the North. Whether this settlement represented merely the substitution of one landholding group for another, or whether its effects went deeper, ultimately depends on how the Normans obtained wealth from their new manors. In theory they had a clear choice. Either they could organize their expanded (and repopulated?) manors on the basis of shire custom and realize an increased revenue indirectly because the manorial population was now larger or they could adopt a more direct system. In many cases the Normans apparently chose the latter alternative. In the 1070s, there was no compelling reason why they should stay within the limits of Northumbrian custom, and the evidence already discussed shows clearly that they abandoned it in at least one basic respect. What occurred in the overstocked vills during the 1070s was not predominantly an expansion of the area under the plow to meet the needs of a more numerous village community, although there were instances of this; it was in most cases a direct expansion or creation of demesne land for the benefit of the lord of the village. In 1086, there were some 220 overstocked manors in Yorkshire. Of these, 179 contained demesne land, and in one-third (60) of these, the plows belonging to the lord of the manor exactly accounted for the excess plows of the estate and were clearly recent intrusions. Moreover, if those overstocked manors in which the plows of the peasants were only one-half plow greater or smaller than the number of plowlands attributed to the manor are added to this group, then the clear examples of manorialization increase from 33⅓ percent to 44 percent of the overstocked manors containing demesne land. This group consisted of old bondage vills that had been manorialized by the Normans. The other overstocked manors with demesne are more complex than this group, but they had probably been subject to the same development. One of two conditions was found in them. Either the number of demesne plows exceeded the increase in the total number of plows (24 cases) or it was less than the total increase (72 cases). The former condition probably represents the expansion of a preexisting demesne, and the latter is perhaps the result of a general enlargement of the arable with or without the creation of a new demesne. Alternatively, individual manors in either group could have been formed by the revival of waste villages. Finally, only 12 of the 41 manors that still lacked demesne in 1086 and were less valuable than the rest had been granted to undertenants by this date.

In Yorkshire, the Norman Conquest did not represent the simple substitution of one group of landholders for another. The Normans broke with northern tradition by increasing the amount of land tilled directly for their benefit. Probably this meant that they would be wealthier in time than their predecessors, but it had immediate social ramifications because it was combined with a preference for one specific manorial form. At least this is suggested by what little can be learned from Domesday about a second aspect of the way they organized their estates. Of course, Domesday was not a custumal, nor did it define the terms it used to describe the peasants. But it seems to record a great social depression in Yorkshire that was principally marked by the almost complete disappearance of sokemen. There were, for instance, over three times as many sokemen in Nottinghamshire in 1086 as in all of Yorkshire, and the meaning of this comparison cannot be explained away by the suggestion that sokemen had not been numerous in Yorkshire in 1066. The populations of two sokes, Northallerton and Falsgrave, are given for 1066, and these two estates contained more sokemen (224) at that date than the North and East Ridings combined in 1086.[33] The Yorkshire sokemen had almost vanished as a significant class. This was an important social change, but what is usually not pointed out is that the fall of those sokemen and even villeins who had lived through the harrying was not as great as economic considerations alone might have dictated. In the years immediately after 1069 the problem that faced the burned-out peasants was survival. There were too many people for the weakened agrarian economy to feed; and because of the slaughter of oxen and the destruction of agricultural implements, recovery is not likely to have been rapid. Indeed, the situation may have worsened during the early 1070s until enough people starved to death or left for the economy to stabilize. In these circumstances the Normans could have set what terms they wished for the refugees, but they seem to have acted with some restraint. When the population of Yorkshire was finally recorded in 1086, there were no serfs at all in the shire and only a small number of bordars. This is significant because it means that the Normans had not chosen to cultivate their new demesnes with either serfs or a naked use of hired labor. The only possible exception is the West Riding, where bordars accounted for 33 percent of the population. Some of the survivors may have been reduced to the status of bordars there, but this is uncertain. The percentage of bordars in the population is impressive in comparison with the percentages of bordars in the North and East Ridings, 16 and 19 percent, respectively, but it is not much larger than in neighboring Derbyshire, where bordars were 27 percent of the population.[34]

Throughout the North and East Ridings the bulk of the population consisted of villeins in 1086. This class made up 79 percent of the recorded population in the former and 73 percent in the latter. Even in the West Riding they were 54 percent of the population; and, if grouped with the sokemen, who were more common here than in the other two ridings, they and the sokemen were nearly twice as numerous as the bordars.[35] Given the forces let loose by the harrying, this preponderance of villeins was clearly artificial. If Domesday's employment of the term "villein" (*villanus*) was at all consistent with later northern usage, their existence had been fostered by the Normans, and this phenomenon requires explanation. At the minimum, of course, it means that the Normans preferred to have their demesnes cultivated by the customary labor of villeins, the holders of one or two bovates presumably, rather than by either serfs or bordars. But beyond this obvious point, one is nearly in the dark on the basis of the Yorkshire evidence. Theoretically, the large numbers of villeins could be explained within the terms of Northumbrian society. The Normans had a greater need for peasant labor than their predecessors. Villeins yielded more free labor than either sokemen or bordars, so the Norman lords maintained surviving villeins and established indigent sokemen and villeins (and bordars?) as villeins. This line of reasoning could provide a rationale for groups of overstocked manors such as those of Hugh fitz Baldric that contained almost exclusively villeins (1 sokeman, 385 villeins, and 7 bordars to be exact[36]) and could explain those numerous (72 out of 179) overstocked manors with demesne that show an increase in the number of peasant plows. Both could be understood as attempts to increase the amount of customary labor available by the multiplication of the villein population.

This line of explanation may contain some truth, but a limited body of evidence indicates that the social depression of the Yorkshire peasantry may also have been the result of an arbitrary act of power and greed. A survey of Ripon, Otley, and Sherburn, estates of the archbishop of York, has survived from around the year 1030, and when its description of these estates is compared with their description in Domesday, radical changes are obvious. These are least pronounced at Ripon, where the two accounts substantially agree except for five pieces of land that appear as sokeland in 1030 but as berewicks in 1086.[37] Given the size of the Ripon estate and the amount of time between the two surveys, this change might not be judged significant were it not for the fact that the same type of transformation reappears at Otley and Sherburn on a much greater scale. In 1030, the estate of Otley consisted of the head village and sixteen dependent villages. Otley and six of the villages were divided between *agenland* and sokeland, and the remaining ten villages were entirely sokeland.[38] By 1086, however, there was no sokeland dependent upon Otley. It and fourteen of the sixteen villages mentioned in 1030 are listed, but they are all described as berewicks.[39] The accounts of Sherburn reveal the same phenomenon. In the early survey it had twenty-two dependent villages and parts of twelve more villages. Six of these properties were divided between *agenland* and sokeland; the rest were entirely sokeland. Domesday, however, describes Sherburn as having only berewicks.[40] In both of these estates the rights of sokemen had been annulled. By 1086, their land belonged to the archbishop, and the Normans probably were responsible for this transformation of sokelands into berewicks. Furthermore, this act of tyranny seems to have affected the status of the peasants. Sherburn's population in 1086 consisted of 8 sokemen, 101 villeins, and 122 bordars.[41] The Normans did not simply preserve villeins and set up refugees as villeins; they created them by fiat.

There is little evidence, moreover, that the Normans changed the nature of villeinage itself. The obligation to perform week work was not one of the ancient burdens that lay upon the northern peasantry, but two examples of it are known in Yorkshire.

At Carlton and East Hardwick, dependent members of the manor of Tanshelf, the peasants who held bovates had to work two days a week during forty-seven weeks of the year and six days a week "during the five weeks of autumn" on the old central demesne at Tanshelf, and at Buttercrambe on the Derwent the bonders worked four days a week from Whitsunday to Martinmas.[42] These examples are unique, but they are disquieting, nonetheless, because they come from the two areas with the highest concentration of overstocked manors in 1086 and from vills that seem to have been overstocked.[43] This might be only coincidence, but it probably means that at least in these two instances the Normans had imposed heavier labor obligations on the villeins to make possible the cultivation of enlarged demesnes.

Bishop was the first to point out these examples of week work in Yorkshire. He believed that the Normans had, indeed, imposed this obligation around Tanshelf (he did not discuss Buttercrambe), but he rejected an economic interpretation. Rather, he thought that it "must be considered to have been imposed by an exceptional effort of social and economic oppression, from a motive other than that of mere economic exploitation: a motive presented by the strategic importance of the Aire crossing in the vicinity of Pontefract."[44] Given only two examples of week work in Yorkshire, this might seem a reasonable idea, particularly since Bishop had misinterpreted the evidence of an expansion of demesne farming, but even without this information Bishop's interpretation ignores the basic problem that week work may have been more common at an earlier date than the thirteenth-century inquisitions indicate. By this period labor services had been commuted into money payments to a great extent in Yorkshire, and commutation may hide old obligations to perform week work. This is not just a theoretical possibility. Within a restricted area, comparable obligations should have been commuted for roughly similar payments, although complete agreement could not be expected because of the bargaining process and variation in the value of bovates, money, and labor. Furthermore, the payments made as commutation should stand in a close relationship to the money value of uncommuted villein services in cases where the services themselves were originally similar, provided, of course, that commutation had not been carried out too long ago. These considerations are important because of the dim light they throw on commuted peasant custom in the vicinity of Buttercrambe. If these payments are compared with the combined value of the rent, renders in kind, and customary works of the villeins of Buttercrambe, a suspicious pattern emerges. In manors that had contained demesne land in 1086, the payments ranged from 9s. 2d. per bovate to 13s. 4d. with the value of the rent, renders, and works at Buttercrambe (9s. 11d.) falling well within these limits. The rate at the manor of Helmsley, however, where there had been no demesne in 1086, was only 5s., half the common rate of 10s. found in the vills that had been manorialized in 1086 (see Table 6). This pattern shows that the obligations of the villeins of Buttercrambe were not unique in their scale, and it probably means that the Normans had imposed heavy labor duties on the peasants in the surrounding villages.

Unfortunately, this line of inquiry cannot be extended to the shire at large because of the uncertainties inherent in the method. Yet its results seem solid in the neighborhood of Buttercrambe, and this means that the general absence of week work in the inquisitions is not necessarily significant. Indeed, this example and the mentality reflected in the social depression of the sokemen, the preference for villeins, and the expansion of demesnes make it likely that the two known examples of week work were not exceptional acts of oppression. Rather, it looks more as if the first generation of Norman lords used their power to establish a seignorial regime that approximated the textbook manor and in many cases

Table 6. *Bovate Rates in the Vicinity of Buttercrambe*

Date	Manor	Bovate Rate	Manorialized in 1086
1271–72	Burton-le-Willows	10s.	X
1282	Buttercrambe	(9s. 11d.)	X
1258–59	Catton	9s. 2d.	X
1285	Helmsley		
	West Newton (a member)	5s.	
	Pockeley (a member)	5s.	
1285	Howsham	10s.	X
1245–46	Skerpenbeck	10s.	X
1267–68	Skerpenbeck	13s. 4d.	X

Source: *YI*, 1: nos. VIII, XLVI, LX, LXXI; 2: no. XXIX.

included the imposition of week work on the villeins. That the Normans took this last step, of course, can only be stated as a probability on the basis of the Yorkshire evidence, but some uncertainty is to be expected given the agricultural history of the shire during the twelfth century. The creation of manors was a movement inevitably limited in its scope and duration. Only during the 1070s and early 1080s did conditions make possible the imposition of new burdens on the peasants of Yorkshire. Once these years of starvation and exodus had passed, the Norman lords no longer held the upper hand. If they were to redevelop their remaining waste estates, they had to attract peasants by offering them easy terms, and Bishop has shown that revival along these lines did take place in the long run.[45] A secondary effect was to encourage the widespread commutation that hides the older burdens of the Yorkshire peasantry.

To determine whether the Normans changed the nature of villeinage in more than a few instances, we need some way of getting around the effects of thirteenth century commutation. Although this is apparently impossible in Yorkshire, Durham is another matter. The agrarian history of the lands between the Tyne and Tees is not so subject to this complication both because much of the land belonged to the church and because this area was not harried to the same extent as Yorkshire.[46] Only limited rebuilding was necessary above the Tees after the harrying; and, if a brief expansion of manorialism accompanied the Norman Conquest here, its chances of leaving traces in the records were much better than those of the parallel movement in Yorkshire. In particular, it should be visible in Boldon Book, Durham's twelfth-century custumal, which provides an incomparable chance to study northern peasant custom.

Even though the various scholars who have worked with Boldon Book have not discovered any sign of manorial development, their failure is not decisive. The exclusion of Durham from Domesday precludes a straightforward collation of the manorial forms of 1086 and later peasant custom. There are no overstocked manors here to serve as the obvious starting point for an investigation. Furthermore, the scholars who have studied this document have had their own concerns, and these have overpowered Boldon Book. Gaillard T. Lapsley, for instance, was interested in the survivals, and he based his division of St. Cuthbert's villages into classes of forest, pastoral, and agricultural villages principally on the presence or absence of cornage.[47] Jolliffe followed a similar line. He was almost entirely preoccupied with the insight the survivals in Boldon Book could throw on conditions in the North before 1066. Beyond this date his only interest lay in establishing a connection between the integral shires and the complex manorial forms found in later records. These concerns led him to his theory of truncation and an unsupported assertion that demesne farming had increased in the twelfth century, accompanied around Durham by the imposition of week work on the peasants.[48] Regrettably, he did not pursue this idea since it was only a logical necessity of his theory of truncation, not a question that basically concerned him. Finally, M. M. Postan, who ignored Jolliffe, based his analysis of Boldon Book on the false assumption that Durham had been manorialized on a Midland pattern since time immemorial, and this curious mistake led him to interpret Boldon Book backward.[49]

Actually, the information on demesne farming in Boldon Book is one of its clearest aspects. The document is not a description of peasant farming or a self-conscious repository of ancient Northumbrian custom, even though information on both subjects can be derived from it. Boldon Book is an account of the manorial rights of the bishop, a list of the renders in kind, payments, and customary labor he could claim each year from the manors he held directly and a record of the farms of manors held by tenants. Although at first sight this information represents a confusing maze with its welter of detail, close study reveals general patterns in the vills that were not at farm, and the most important of these was the distinction between villages with a demesne and those without one. This was the critical factor that differentiated villages in twelfth-century Durham. General internal organization and peasant custom were correlated with the presence or absence of demesne land in a village except in late-functioning shires such as Heighingtonshire.

Two systems for harnessing peasant labor for the support of the landlord were in operation in Durham at the time of Boldon Book. The one that has traditionally attracted the most attention was a survival from the old shires, and it was usually found in villages that lacked demesne land. These villages were not completely uniform, of course, but Butterwick can stand as a fair example of the type: "Buterwyk [Butterwick] renders 32 shillings and 9 pence cornage and 1 milch cow and 8 scot-chalders of malt and the same of meal and the same of oats. And every plough[team] of the villeins ploughs and harrows 2 acres at Sedgefield. And the villeins do 4 boon-days for every house with 1 man. And they cart a tun of wine and the millstone of Sedgefield. The dreng keeps a dog and a horse and goes on the great hunt with 2 hunting-dogs and 5 ropes, and does suit of court and goes on errands."[50] This was the classic bondage vill. Butterwick lacked a demesne, and its inhabitants, who were all apparently bonders aside from the dreng, performed light agricultural duties in another village. At the time of Boldon Book, seven other villages had the same characteristics, and six villages without drengs belonged to this type.[51] The five villages that contained molmen (firmars) also should be added to this group because their only distinction was the payment of a farm assessed on the bovate in lieu of the grain renders, cow render, and cornage payments that were made by the bonders in the other villages.[52] The only exception to this general rule that the custom of the shire was found in vills without demesnes was a small number of villages that had presumably been the centers of groups of bondage vills in days gone by. Aside from Heighington, they had been shorn of their dependent villages by 1183, but their internal arrangements still bore the mark of the shire. Demesnes were either small or defunct except in Heighingtonshire, and the peasants either paid compositions for part of the old dues or were subject to the usual heavy renders in kind and formalized but limited obligations to perform customary labor.[53]

The system was different in the manors where the second customary tradition was followed. Despite the prominence shire custom has claimed in most discussions of Boldon Book, by this date a number of villages in Durham had big demesnes, and in these villages a customary tradition, which was an integral part of extensive demesne cultivation and had no discernible roots in Northumbrian custom, was in force. Villeins subject to this system of obligations performed week work. The customs of the men of Boldon, where there was a demesne of four plows, typify the system: "In Boldona [Boldon] there are twenty-two villeins, every-one of whom holds 2 bovates of land of 30 acres . . . and works through the whole year three days in the week except Easter and Whitsunweek and thirteen days at Christmas."[54] There were also twelve cottars at Boldon who held twelve acres each and had to work two days a week throughout the year except on the three festivals mentioned above.[55] Altogether, the bishop had at his disposal ninety days of unpaid work each week throughout most of the year for the upkeep of the demesne at Boldon and for other manorial tasks. Nor was the situation at Boldon unique. The peasants in nineteen other villages were subject to the same customs as their fellows at Boldon.[56] In several other manors with large demesnes the peasants did week work also, although the obligations were somewhat different from the three days a week required in the Boldon villages. In most of the other villages the villeins seem to have held only one bovate, and they worked two or three days a week from Lammas to Martinmas and one or two days a week during the remainder of the year.[57] Finally, there were three villages inhabited exclusively by cottars burdened with week work.[58] Jolliffe dismissed all these villages in one brief and ambiguous sentence that hid both their number and their importance, and Lapsley classified most of them as pasture vills because their inhabitants paid cornage.[59] Only Postan accorded them their true importance, but he failed to understand their meaning.[60] In fact, the manors in which the villeins did week work were the most heavily exploited manors in Durham. They accounted for most of the demesne land that was not at farm and were subject to a regime that was diametrically opposed to the shire system customs followed in the villages without demesnes. The latter was predominantly a system that gathered in the products of peasant labor and only a limited amount of direct labor. The former yielded huge amounts of free labor. This fundamental distinction divided the Durham peasantry.

The line of cleavage ran even deeper than this discussion would suggest. There was no simple opposition of shire custom and week work in St. Cuthbert's villages that might be explicable in terms of alternative systems for exploiting the peasants. Although the difference between the two customary traditions was real, the situation described in Boldon Book had another dimension that had implications of the gravest social importance. Boldon Book contains clear examples of bondage vills where the peasants were burdened with shire customs, but equally clear examples of villages with demesnes and peasants burdened with week work are harder to find because the accounts of such manors are long and confusing and bear an obvious resemblance to the bondage vills. Again the situation in Boldon was typical:

> [The villein] . . . does in autumn four boon-days at reaping with his entire household except the housewife . . . and they [the villeins] reap moreover 3 roods of oat-stubble . . . and harrow it. Every plough [team] of the villeins, also, ploughs 2 acres and harrows them, and then they have once . . . a dole . . . from the bishop, and for that week they are quit of work, but when they make the great boon-days they have a dole. And in their works they harrow when it is necessary, and they carry loads . . . and when they have carried them every man has a loaf of bread, and they mow one day at Hoctona [Houghton] . . . and then they have a dole. And every two villeins build one booth for the fair of St. Cuthbert. And when they are building lodges and carrying loads of wood they are quit of all other works.
>
> The villeins in their work every year ought to make, if need be, a house 40 feet in length and 15 feet in breadth.[61]

In addition to their week work, all of these obligations rested upon the villeins of Boldon, and this is significant because these services were nearly a parallel of those of the villeins of Heighingtonshire, Jolliffe's standard example of shire custom, and of those found in less detail in the bondage vills.[62] Furthermore, the villeins of Boldon made the same renders as the peasants in bondage vills. They gave hens and eggs, wagonloads of wood, and cornage; even the old grain renders were represented by certain rents and an oat render.[63] This situation was typical of all the manors in which the peasants did week work except for the three manors inhabited solely by cottars. In all instances the peasants were not subject just to week work; they were burdened with all the renders and works of shire custom as well.

This underlayer of shire custom shows that the Boldon villages and the other villages with big demesnes had once been typical Northumbrian villages. Furthermore, it means that there were not only two customary traditions in Durham in the twelfth century but rather two distinct levels of peasant exploitation, and the heavier of the two, the manor with week work, had been superimposed on the lighter, the Northumbrian bondage vill. In light of the expansion of demesne farming initiated by the Normans in Yorkshire, the explanation of this situation is all too obvious:

Walcher and his men had manorialized the Boldon villages and imposed week work on the peasants. Boldon Book records the impact of manorialization on the level of peasant custom in Durham, just as Domesday Book disclosed its general outline in terms of manorial structure in Yorkshire. Furthermore, the two examples of week work from Yorkshire link these two descriptions for they come from overstocked vills and exhibit the same combination of week work and shire custom as the Durham examples.

Probably most of the Boldon villages and the other villages in this category had been devastated by the Normans in the course of William's march to the Tyne after Christmas of 1069. The uniformity of custom exhibited by the twenty Boldon villages is indicative of a recent, common origin. If they had been manorialized piecemeal, in separate acts of power, diversity probably would have resulted. The most likely occasion when they all could have been restructured was immediately after the harrying of the North. Of course, very little is known about where the Normans went above the Tees, but the peculiar distribution of villages with week work generally fits in with the few details known about William's movements. Orderic Vitalis says that William traveled to the Tees after driving some rebels out of Holderness,[64] which probably means that he marched north through the eastern end of the Vale of Pickering, skirted the Moors along the coast, and crossed into Durham from Cleveland. Symeon of Durham picks up the narrative when the Normans are across the Tees. He says that William divided his force, that Durham was abandoned out of fear of the Norman advance, and that the church at Jarrow was burned.[65] Finally, Orderic concludes with the information that the Normans returned to the Tees from Hexham through some very rugged country.[66] These details are meager but sufficient. The villages with big demesnes and peasants who did week work were not scattered at random over the face of the county; they were predominantly arranged in north-south lines except in the area just south of the Tyne (see map). They all lay on or near a hypothetical line of march running north from Preston on the Tees, dividing to pass on either side of the raised ground in eastern Durham before reuniting in the vicinity of Jarrow, and then running west toward Hexham. From Hexham the line runs south to the Tees either by the old Roman road through Ebchester and Langchester, or perhaps through the hills to the upper Wear valley

Manorial Types in Durham at the Time of Boldon Book

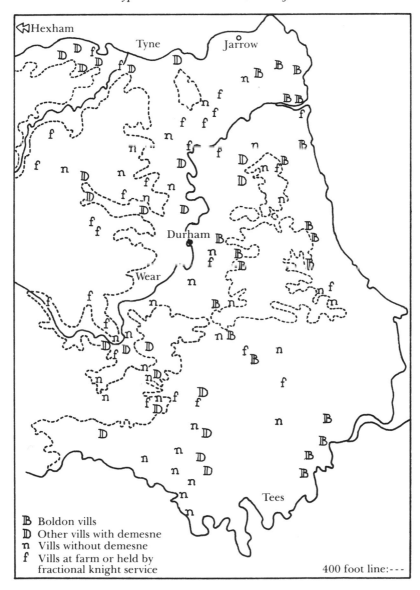

$\triangleleft$ Hexham

Tyne   Jarrow

Durham

Wear

Tees

𝔹 Boldon vills
𝔻 Other vills with demesne
n Vills without demesne
f Vills at farm or held by
　fractional knight service

400 foot line:- - -

and down this valley to the Roman road. The correspondence between the distribution of the manor in Durham and what is known of William's movements during the harrying is too exact to be coincidental. The villages with demesnes were the ones the Normans destroyed in January of 1070.

The ensuing events seem clear. The Durham peasants are known to have fled when the Normans crossed into the bishopric.[67] Although they saved their lives and perhaps their oxen, many faced a grim future. The inhabitants of the devastated villages returned to find their food taken, their homes burned, and their tools destroyed. Somehow they had to rebuild and bring their fields back into production while avoiding starvation, and it is doubtful if they made much progress before Walcher and his knights appeared in 1071. He took advantage of their plight by setting up demesnes in the wasted villages and by imposing week work on the peasants. In return, they received food, tools, and seed. Presumably the particular social mix in a given village—molmen, villeins, and cottars; villeins and cottars; or just cottars—reflects how desperate conditions were in that village in 1071. For many—all the villeins and most of the cottars—week work was the price of credit. This was the meaning of Symeon of Durham's statement that during this period many men "truly sold themselves into perpetual servitude, provided that they could maintain a certain miserable life."[68] Week work not unreasonably appeared to be slavery to men accustomed to the light or indirect customs of the shire, especially when it was added to their old customs.

This hypothesis lays a heavy burden on the shoulders of Bishop Walcher, but evidence from Northumberland is conclusive on his responsibility. One can scan Jolliffe and other modern discussions of Northumbrian custom and find no examples of week work above the Tyne. The peasants of Northumberland appear under the undisputed, although sometimes decrepit, sway of shire custom, and this seems quite reasonable since the Normans had little impact on this area before the reign of Henry I, and the creation of manors was a phenomenon associated with the years shortly after the Conquest. This picture is generally correct, but not entirely accurate. Despite the preponderance of shire custom, there were a few instances of peasants burdened with week work above the Tyne. The bonders in at least four of Tynemouth's villages did two days of week work except at Christmas, Easter, and

Whitsuntide. The villeins of Grindon in Norhamshire performed two days of work with a second man each week throughout the year,[69] and the bonders at Acklington, a member of the barony of Warkworth, were liable to three days of week work.[70] These examples are not numerous enough to challenge Jolliffe's general picture of peasant custom in Northumberland, but they do have a direct bearing on the introduction of the manor into Durham. They all exhibit the same underlayer of shire custom as the Boldon vills and the villages with week work in Yorkshire, and this in itself suggests a Norman origin for the week work. Moreover, they have one notable thing in common: they all were probably in Walcher's possession at some time between 1071 and 1080. Norhamshire, of course, was one of the most ancient endowments of St. Cuthbert, and it would have fallen to Walcher as bishop in 1071. Warkworth and Tynemouth, on the other hand, were part of the demesne of the earl in this period,[71] but Walcher held this position also from 1075 to 1080 and was presumably in possession of these estates. He is, then, the single thread that unites the three anomalous examples of week work from above the Tyne, and these villages must have been manorialized under his rule.

Taken together, the evidence from Yorkshire, Durham, and Northumberland provides an insight into the somber nature of the Norman Conquest of the North. The Normans did not simply dispossess a large number of Anglo-Saxon thanes and continue to collect the old revenues. Rather, they altered the manorial structure in many northern villages. Until the Conquest, the northern manor had consisted of the right to receive the old renders and customary works of the Northumbrian shire from a particular group of peasants. These were important rights and had served to support a numerous class of landowners in 1066, but they were predominantly an indirect system for drawing off wealth from the peasantry. They produced substantial renders in kind, a certain amount of general purpose work (such as errands, carting, the maintenance of the mill), and only a limited quantity of customary labor for the cultivation of the lord's demesne. The Normans did not accept this system where they could avoid doing so. In the 1070s they had all the advantages over the peasants—superior force, judicial power, and supplies of grain and oxen—and they used this power to introduce a different manorial regime. Capitalizing on the desperate conditions they themselves had created, they increased demesne cultivation and imposed week work on the peasants where circumstances were favorable. These innovations were a radical departure from northern custom, particularly since week work was simply added to the existing obligations. They meant that the holders of these manorialized villages would be wealthier than their predecessors and that the peasants would be poorer. The Norman settlement of the North was founded upon an exceptional act of economic brigandage, an act whose effects passed from generation to generation except in Yorkshire, where widespread commutation intervened to ease the burden.

7. Henry I's New Men in the North

One writer has said that, although Rufus won the North, Henry I consolidated Rufus's gains.[1] Yet to distinguish between the achievements of Rufus and Henry in this way gives the establishment of Norman power in the Far North (Northumberland, Cumberland, and Westmorland) an air of continuity and inevitability that the process did not in reality possess. Rufus won certain short-term advantages that might easily have passed away and had, indeed, done so once, and, for several reasons having little to do with the North, Henry realized the potential in the situation Rufus had left him. Even this statement, however, falls short of the truth in two important respects. Henry was, in fact, a conqueror in the North although he did it by proxy, and his consolidation resulted in a fundamental shift in northern power relationships in favor of Northumbria and the recreation of conditions not seen in the North since before the Viking invasions.

This appraisal of events in the North between 1100 and 1135 should not be understood as an attempt to minimize William Rufus's contribution to the creation of stability in the region. His accomplishments were real but they were limited to a single area. The Red King's domain was diplomacy and war, and through these means he had achieved nearly everything he could have desired short of the conquest of Scotland. The building of the castle at Carlisle offered some protection to the lands to the south if only because any future Scottish invasion would have as its first object the recapture of Cumberland. The ending of the Northumbrian earldom removed the threat that a line of Norman earls would pursue the semiautonomous and sometimes rebellious policies made possible by the isolation of Northumbria, and the killing of Malcolm Canmore allowed Rufus to establish a friendly king of Scots. These were important improvements in the northern political situation, but Rufus's ascendancy was fragile and easily reversible. Siward, the last great warrior to rule the North before the coming of the Normans, had followed a policy remarkably similar to that of Rufus. He, too, had taken over Cumberland and installed his own king of Scots, Malcolm Canmore. This first attempt to pacify the Scots through good relations with their king had fallen apart as soon as Malcolm was secure in Scotland, and Edgar presented the same danger. Of course, such a reversal may not have been a realistic possibility for the Scottish king before 1099. The accounts of Edgar the Atheling's expedition of 1097 that put him on the Scottish throne say only that the Atheling drove out Donald Bane, not that the latter was captured or completely neutralized; and it is likely that King Edgar faced some opposition or at least potential danger from Donald between 1097 and 1099, when the latter was finally captured and blinded.[2] The threat from Donald ensured Edgar's loyalty to Rufus until 1099, and it is not surprising that in that year the Scottish king consented to come south and carry the sword at Rufus's crown-wearing in London.[3] But no one could have known with any certainty that Edgar would remain faithful to the Normans. Because of Donald's xenophobic expulsion of the Anglo-Saxons, Edgar was perhaps less powerful than his father. Yet he apparently brought some Anglo-Saxons back into Scotland with him, and there is no evidence that his rule was particularly weak because his subjects viewed him as a "usurper."[4] Had Edgar lived long enough to consolidate his position, he might well have come over the Tweed to waste Northumberland and demand the restoration of Carlisle. Rufus was, after all, no more of a convincing benefactor to Edgar than Siward and King Edward had been to his father.

Rufus's real failure in the North, however, did not spring from the paradox that he had sought peace with the Scots by supporting Duncan and then Edgar while he retained Cumberland. Rather, the flaw in his achievement lay in the fact that he apparently did very little to ensure the retention of Cumberland. It had been won by an army from the South, and Malcolm Canmore had been defeated and killed by another army specially brought north. Both of these incidents were part of a deliberate plan to lure

Malcolm Canmore into the open and defeat him. They were hardly typical of the Normans' real strength in the North, which had been demonstrated more accurately in 1091, when Malcolm had plundered Northumbria as far as the city of Durham and escaped scot-free. Until a Norman aristocracy was established in the Far North, Scottish raids could not be contained, and there is no evidence that Rufus established many nobles there even though he had control of Cumberland for nine years and of Northumberland for five years. He did apparently install sheriffs or analogous officers in the region. From 1095, Robert Picot was sheriff of Northumberland, and W. son of Theoderic and a mysterious "G." are addressed successively in writs referring to Carlisle.[5] Yet the identities of these three men are unknown, and although the writs in question mention their barons and lieges, these shadowy figures are doubtful evidence for the existence of a Norman landholding class in either area. If their inclusion in the addresses of these writs was not conventional, they were probably the armed retainers of the sheriffs. Even in the early thirteenth century, when the Norman equivalent of the Mayflower syndrome was well established, none of the tenants-in-chief in Cumberland claimed that their families had gotten their lands before 1100, and the assertions of some of their peers in Northumberland that their ancestors had held *post conquestum Anglie* are utterly doubtful.[6] The claim itself is anachronistic. No Norman could have gotten or kept land above the Tyne before the campaigns of 1080. Earl Robert de Mowbray might conceivably have created some baronies between 1080 and 1095; but with the possible exception of Herbert de la Val, the first lord of Callerton, a small barony on the south coast, there is no evidence that any of Mowbray's men were reconciled with Rufus.[7] Moreover, none of the supposed early holders of the baronies in question is mentioned in or witnessed either King Edgar's grant to Durham or the several charters made by Rufus while he was in Northumberland in 1095.[8] The only exception is William de Merlay, the first lord of Morpeth, whom Gaimar mentions in his account of Mowbray's revolt. But Gaimar's description of this revolt is confused and at variance with the older accounts, and his story about Rufus besieging William de Merlay is unsubstantiated by the other sources.[9] Nor is there mention in the charters of William de Merlay or any other of the founding barons between 1095 and 1100. This silence even encompasses Guy de Balliol, lord of Bywell, whose descendants claimed that Rufus had given him the family lands.[10] Most of these men do appear in documents made after 1100, which, along with their absence before 1100, suggests that the thirteenth-century claims were inflated. With the probable exceptions of Bywell and Callerton and possibly of Morpeth, none of the baronies in Northumberland originated before 1100. Combined with the evidence of the more modest Cumbrian barons, this means that the barons of Robert Picot, W. son of Theoderic, and "G." were the household knights of these officials. Circumstances in the North had not changed significantly from the 1080s, when Bishop Walcher maintained a private army of over one hundred men and Bishop William de St. Calais is said to have kept a force of comparable size.[11] The Normans were still castlemen who lived in large groups behind their walls and ditches and subsisted on the tribute of sullen villagers. This is not a romantic image. When Bishop William de St. Calais died in 1096, a number of Durham peasants took the opportunity to decamp into Northumberland with their cattle. Others went into Yorkshire either to find refuge in the southern free zone or, more likely, to advance themselves by taking part in the redevelopment of the wasted countryside.[12]

When Henry became king, Norman settlement had scarcely advanced beyond its limits at the death of William the Conqueror. Above Durham, which was probably fairly well in hand despite peasant dissatisfaction, Robert Picot controlled Newcastle, Tynemouth, and Bamburgh. In the West, someone held Carlisle for the king, but on either side of the mountains, the countryside—or whatever was left of it after the revolts and Scottish raids of the eleventh century—was unoccupied by Normans except in Durham, where Agerius de Cornford appears by 1095, and perhaps in the very southernmost part of Northumberland.[13] The limited extent of Norman settlement in the North at this date is, in fact, surprising; and, although there was more involved than this, it resulted from the fact that the border counties were unattractive to the Normans because of the brigandage made possible by the free zone and the configuration of the Cumbrian border and because of the threat of Scottish invasions. These dangers had not passed away as if by magic. Even later in his reign when he had done much to pacify the North, King Henry enlarged his bodyguard when he crossed the Humber, and at least in 1100 there was no certainty that King Edgar would not resume the raids that had characterized

Northumbrian-Scottish relations since the early years of the eleventh century.[14] The Scottish monarchy was not yet dependent upon the Normans in any fundamental sense, and there is no evidence of any Norman penetration into Scotland either as members of the court or as landholders before 1100,[15] which is not surprising given the sparseness of Norman settlement in the border counties.

The accomplishments of Henry I in the North were to alter basically this set of circumstances. The fortuitous conjunction of Henry's own experiences during the 1090s, his political needs and methods after becoming king, and extremely good fortune with respect to the Scottish royal house enabled him to transform the scattered outposts of Norman power which Rufus had left behind. When he died in 1135, the position of the Normans in Yorkshire had been consolidated, a Norman aristocracy had been installed in the border counties, and King David had taken the first steps in establishing a Norman aristocracy in Lothian and Cumbria. These developments laid the foundations for the societies that existed in the North and in southern Scotland during the High Middle Ages, and there was a unity to their formation. Unfortunately, however, the connection between these developments has been obscured by the gaps separating local studies, English history, and Scottish history. The subject provides an appalling example of how modern points of view can annihilate the past. Because of this problem and because the basic factor that allowed Henry to settle Normans in the Far North lies outside medieval history as it is usually conceived, the outlines of this development must be reconstructed piece by piece. Certain questions, such as the curtailment of the northern free zone, must be left in abeyance for a time, and the same evidence must sometimes be studied from different perspectives. This may prove tedious, but since the demands of English and Scottish history have succeeded in turning the question of the North into a malodorous onion, it can only be peeled layer by layer.

The easiest way to approach the problem initially is on the level of royal politics. Henry I was not immediately secure upon his accession. He had become king only through a seizure of the English crown that nullified his elder brother Robert's right to succeed Rufus, and he was not popular with the great Norman families with estates in both England and Normandy, who may have preferred Duke Robert to Henry and who certainly feared for their lands in the struggle that was to develop between the two brothers.[16] This combination of factors was either dangerous or potentially so until 1106 and to an extent even later, and two of the ways Henry tried to strengthen himself were of extreme importance for the North. The more obvious of these was his marriage. Late in 1100, he took as his wife Maud, the daughter of Malcolm Canmore and Margaret, Edgar the Atheling's sister. This marriage has usually been seen as the symbolic beginning of a reconciliation of Normans and Anglo-Saxons; or, upon the assumption that Henry was disturbed by the theoretical weakness of his claim to the throne, it has been explained as an attempt by Henry to create a link between himself and Edward the Confessor.[17] Yet the immediate point of the marriage more likely was diplomatic, for it marked an alliance between Henry and Maud's family, and the retailing of prophecies concerning the return of green trees is unnecessary to explain its utility. The new king was a shrewd diplomat, and he was acutely conscious of the dangers that could threaten a state from its frontiers. Since the late 1080s he had been lurking around the western marches of Normandy, first as lord of the Cotentin and later as the protector of Domfront. At times he had been in close association with Robert of Bellême, a master in the art of frontier disruptions, and with Hugh the Fat, *vicomte* of Avranches and earl of Chester.[18] From experience and probably from his own dreams, Henry knew the threats to orderly government that such areas could pose, and his marriage with Maud must be understood in this context. It ensured that Edgar, his most powerful neighbor in Britain, would not invade the North to recapture Carlisle or to support Duke Robert, and it performed the same function after Duke Robert was captured and imprisoned. During his later continental wars, Henry was not distracted by Scottish invasions as his father and brother had been. The marriage ensured that the relationship with the Scottish king that Rufus had established as the provider of armies would endure even though it was no longer a real necessity for the sons of Malcolm and Margaret.[19] When Edgar died in 1107, his younger brother Alexander became king "with King Henry's consent" but without the intervention of a Norman army. He remained at peace with Henry,[20] and their relationship may have become closer. Alexander married one of Henry's illegitimate daughters, and in 1114 he actually led an army, probably but not necessarily composed of Scots, in Henry's invasion of Wales.[21]

Very little is known about this unparalleled incident, but it would seem to have prefigured the nature of English-Scottish relations after 1124. In that year, David, Malcolm's youngest son, who was bound by ties of taste, friendship, and patronage to Henry I, succeeded Alexander. Henry's marriage to Maud, then, gave the North a long period of peace—insofar as kings could give peace in the North. For thirty-five years there were no Scottish invasions, a remission without parallel since 1000, and during these years Normans settled in the border counties and under King David in southern Scotland. David's cooperation made the movement possible because the northern free zone could not be reduced without the help of the king of Scots.

Another of Henry's solutions to his early political problems had a very direct influence on the settlement. His response to the disaffection of the greater Norman nobles was to create a new nobility—a party of nobles who owed their position in the upper reaches of society to him. This tactic was noted at the time by Orderic Vitalis, who, as a spokesman for the old nobility, asserted that Henry had raised these men from the dust. Although this idea has passed from Orderic into modern accounts of Henry's reign as a commonplace, the creation of Henry's new nobles has not yet been the object of a comprehensive investigation.[22] In general terms, the phenomenon is clear. His new men led his armies, kept his castles, and ran his government and were rewarded with the spoils of feudal government and with land. This was a matter of the greatest importance for the North because in 1100 there was more land above the Humber that could be granted out as patronage than in any other part of the kingdom. The border counties were largely unoccupied by Normans; and in Yorkshire, where William the Conqueror had installed his own supporters during the 1070s and 1080s, plenty of land was available from the royal demesne and forfeitures. To a remarkable degree, the Norman settlement of the North was the result of Henry's gifts of land to his friends.

In Yorkshire, the introduction of Henry's new men resulted in a minor tenurial revolution. Early in the reign, some of the established nobles received grants of land and privileges that appear to have been designed to win their loyalty and were probably local examples of the favoritism such already established families as the Giffards, Clares, and Beaumonts enjoyed in the south.[23]

Robert de Lacy, the lord of the castlery of Pontefract, for instance, had become sheriff of Yorkshire by 1102, and around the same time he obtained either the grant of Bowland and Blackburnshire in Lancashire or the transformation of preexisting mesne tenures of these lands into tenancies-in-chief.[24] Henry also gave the soke of Bridlington to Walter de Gant, an important landholder in Lincolnshire and the East Riding, and he probably granted the great soke of Wakefield to William de Warenne, who already held Conisborough and was earl of Surrey.[25] Robert, Walter, and William were all men whose support was worth having, and their cultivation by the king to some extent blurs the line between the old and new nobility. The real rewards, however, went predominantly to men more closely connected to the king. Shortly after Tinchebrai, Henry gave Robert de Brus some eighty manors from the royal demesne, chiefly in Claro Wapentake, and another thirteen estates that had been part of the Mortain fee, and between this date (1106) and about 1118, Nigel d'Aubigny, another new man, obtained the forfeited estate of Robert de Stuteville.[26] In Yorkshire the Stuteville lands consisted of two large groups of manors, one centered on Kirkby Malzeard in the West Riding and the other stretching from Thirsk east into the Vale of Pickering.[27] These two grants were perhaps the most striking of Henry's creations, but in a number of other instances he reworked the tenurial structure of the shire. Early in the reign, for example, Geoffrey fitz Pain, an important new man, obtained Warter, which had been royal demesne; and between 1115 and 1118 he was rewarded with the barony of Hunsingore.[28] The history of Pontefract, however, provides the most flagrant example of Henry's devices. The king's initial attempt to win Robert de Lacy's loyalty apparently failed, and Robert forfeited Pontefract for unknown reasons at some date between 1109 and 1118. Henry then gave the honor to Hugh de la Val, presumably to ensure his support in northern France; when the latter died prior to 1129, the king gave Hugh's widow to William Maltravers, a prominent royal minion, and sold him the estate for a term of years.[29] Finally, the three mainstays of Henry's new regime in the North, Walter Espec, Eustace fitz John, and David, all became important landholders in Yorkshire. David, who was the youngest son of Malcolm Canmore, held Hallamshire (Sheffield).[30] Walter Espec and Eustace fitz John were Henry's northern justiciars. Walter was given a large barony around Kirkham and Helmsley; and Eustace, who was the farmer of Aldborough, Knaresborough, and the escheated honor of Blyth (Tickhill) during Henry's later years, obtained the lordship of Malton.[31] Even these examples do not exhaust the list of Henry's changes in the tenurial structure of the shire, for the king diverted the descent of a number of other estates to his own candidates or inserted subtenants of his choice into established baronies.[32] By 1135, the king had brought into being a group of nobles who owed their rise to him, rivaled in power the descendants of the Conqueror's barons, and controlled the government and most of the important castles of the shire.

Beyond Yorkshire, the impact of Henry's patronage was even more complete. The Northumbrian countryside was apparently considered royal demesne. This was, of course, a legal fiction typical of Norman justice, but it was useful to Henry, who filled the Far North with his supporters. In southern Durham he gave Hartness to Robert de Brus and probably Greatham to the Bertrams, and above the Tyne he created a line of baronies running to the Tweed.[33] In the Tyne valley and the hills to the north, Walter de Bolbec, who probably benefited from a connection with the Giffards, received Styford, and in the same region Robert de Umfraville obtained Prudhoe, which was probably augmented before 1135 by the grant of the serjeanty of Redesdale.[34] To the east and north, Henry apparently gave Mitford to William Bertram or his father, and he may have given the neighboring lordship of Bothal to a son of William.[35] Mitford, Bothal, and Morpeth, which may have been an older lordship, dominated the lowlands of Northumberland from the Tyne to the Coquet. Beyond them six new baronies were created. Morwick and Hadestone, which adjoined the royal demesne at Warkworth, went respectively to Hugh fitz Eudo, perhaps the son of Henry's *dapifer* Eudo, and to Aschantinus de Worcester, who had custody of the Durham episcopal manors after Ranulf Flambard's death.[36] North of these fees, Henry established Alnwick, the greatest of the Northumbrian baronies, for Eustace fitz John and Ellingham for Nicholas de Grenville.[37] Finally, the king brought Norman settlement to the Tweed. Robert de Muschamp, who may have been the steward of Walter de Gant, was given Wooler in the Till valley, and Walter Espec received Wark on the Tweed.[38]

West of the mountains the tenurial structure of the countryside was also established during Henry's reign, and here again the process represented the endowment of Henry's followers. Probably after 1106, the king gave the lordship of Carlisle, which encompassed the Vale of Eden with the Cumbrian lowlands north of the Derwent, to Ranulf Meschin. Ranulf was the son of the *vicomte* of the Bessin and had led the van of Henry's army at Tinchebrai.[39] He, in turn, established two baronies, Burgh by Sands and Liddelstrength, on the Galwegian border; and he seems to have tried to install his brother William in Gilsland. This attempt did not succeed because Gille, the native lord of the area, held out against the Normans till around 1156, but William did not go without land.[40] Henry gave him Copeland (also called Egremont or Allerdale above Derwent) on the southwestern coast of Cumberland.[41] Copeland was the westernmost member of a string of lordships that ran around the southern side of the Cumbrian dome and the western side of the Pennines, and these, too, all went to Henry's supporters. Furness was part of the honor of Lancashire. Nigel d'Aubigny received Kendale and Burton in Lonsdale, the lordship created by Rufus for Ivo Taillebois.[42] Skipton passed to William, Ranulf Meschin's brother, when he married the daughter of Robert de Rumilly; and the forest of Bowland and Blackburnshire, members of the castlery of Pontefract, were held successively by Robert de Lacy, Hugh de la Val, and William Maltravers.[43] Finally, around 1120, Lancashire itself was given to Stephen of Blois, Henry's greatest political creation. It may have belonged to Ranulf Meschin prior to this date, although this is not certain.[44]

Throughout England's northernmost counties the creation of a Norman landholding class was primarily the work of Henry I after 1106 through dispensation of the king's patronage. Even in Yorkshire, where a Norman aristocracy had been established during the 1070s, forfeitures and the abnormal extent of the royal demesne enabled him to install a large group of his own supporters who intensified the French presence in the shire. In the lands beyond, including those parts of Durham not held by St. Cuthbert, Henry created the territorial aristocracy by granting fiefs to his supporters. Henry's patronage was not limited entirely to Normans. Natives played a secondary but important part in the process. The first sign of this fact comes from a Northumbrian writ of about 1103 that reveals that Henry had replaced Robert Picot, Rufus's sheriff, with two Northumbrians, Ligulf and Aluric.[45] Sub-

sequent writs and other documents show that Ligulf administered
the part of Northumberland dependent upon Bamburgh, and
Aluric, the part dependent upon Corbridge.[46] This return to the
use of native officials presumably indicates that Henry had decided that Northumberland was best governed in these early years
through local men, but the system was continued even after his
new men had come into the area. Around 1118, Aluric and Ligulf
were replaced or followed by Ligulf's son Odard of Bamburgh,
and he was succeeded about 1133 by his son Adam.[47] The reliance
on a line of native sheriffs long after any obvious need for their
collaboration is curious, and the usage had a parallel in Cumberland, where another Odard, apparently the son of Hildred, the
farmer of Carlisle, was sheriff in 1130.[48]

    The reemergence of natives in the North was, in fact, a
notable feature of the years between 1100 and 1135, and the king
exhibited a strange and somewhat contradictory personal taste for
northern Anglo-Saxons. For a period during the 1120s he employed as his confessor Prior Athelwold of Nostell, who had originally been lord of Pocklington in the East Riding.[49] Henry took as
one of his mistresses the daughter of Forne son of Sigulf, who
was apparently a Yorkshire man; and he both rewarded and employed these northerners.[50] In 1133, Athelwold became the first
bishop of Carlisle.[51] Forne's daughter eventually was married to
Robert d'Oilli, one of the king's constables, and Forne himself rose
mightily. He was a minister of the king in Yorkshire during the
1120s and later in Northumberland, and Henry rewarded him
with a small estate in Yorkshire and, more important, the barony of
Greystoke in Cumberland.[52] In addition to these lands, Forne also
apparently acquired Coquetdale in Northumberland, Coniscliffe
in southern Durham, and probably large possessions in upper
Teesdale from King Henry.[53] He was, in reality, a Northumbrian
new man, and there were other examples. Adam son of Swane, for
instance, who was descended from a family that had held land
around Pontefract since before the Conquest, received an extensive lordship east of the Eden in Cumberland and land in Lancashire from Henry I, and his younger brother Henry acquired
Edenhall and Langwathby in Cumberland.[54] The king's native
sheriffs were also rewarded for their services with land. Henry
gave Gamelsby and Glassanby with other lands in Cumberland to
Odard and Hildred, and he created two baronies in Northumber-

land, Embleton and Dilston, for Odard son of Ligulf and Richard son of Aluric.[55] A group of nine Northumbrian villages near Bamburgh and the vills west of Rothbury that later became the barony of Hepple were left in the hands of natives as thanages, and there seems to have been an analogous group of serjeanties in Cumberland.[56] Finally—and these were perhaps the most curious grants of all—Henry reestablished the sons of Cospatric in the North. Cospatric II, the youngest son of the old earl, received the great serjeanty of Beanly in Northumberland; and Waltheof, Cospatric I's second son, obtained Allerdale below Derwent in Cumberland.[57] These grants to natives are numerous enough to show that being a native was not a bar in the North to entering the king's service under Henry I. One might be tempted to conclude that these grants represented reconciliation between Saxon and Norman in practice, but such an idea would be highly doubtful. Henry may conceivably have had a personal weakness for natives, as evidenced by his Yorkshire mistress and his confessor, and such a predilection would fit in with a certain type of romanticism concerning the Anglo-Saxon past which the king's new men sometimes affected.[58] Yet Henry's native new men usually received second-rate land. If this was reconciliation, the price was cheap. In fact, it seems more likely that they were simply useful on the local level and that by employing them Henry's patronage tapped another source of disaffected men whose gratitude could be relied upon. The result of Henry's land grants was, in any case, the creation of a hybrid aristocracy in the North, and the chief characteristic of these men was that they owed their fortunes to him. They were his men, whether Anglo-Saxon or Norman, and they were unrivaled from Cheshire and the honor of Tickhill north. Their establishment represented the territorialization of Henry's party.

The creation of a Norman landholding class in southern Scotland can be viewed as an extension of the same process. This was certainly true chronologically. Normans appeared on both sides of the Tweed during roughly the same years even though this is usually overlooked because of the ideological width of the Tweed or on the assumption that Normans were in Northumberland and Cumberland earlier than they actually were. Furthermore, King David's reasons for bringing Normans into Scotland can only be explained in terms of his early education and his relationship with Henry I. David, or David fitz Malcolm as he should be called, was in reality one of Henry's new men, although his high descent and his eventual accession to the Scottish throne tend to blind Scottish historians to this fact. He was born around 1085 and spent only some eight years in his parents' household before the circle was broken in 1093 by the death of his parents and Donald Bane's purges. At this time, his elder brothers and sisters evidently took him to England, where he was reared among the Norman boys of the court.[59] The seriousness and religious attitudes he later exhibited may go back to his childhood with St. Margaret, but in most other respects his stay among the Normans was of critical importance in the formation of his character. David spent his adolescence being educated by Normans to be a Norman, and according to both William of Malmesbury and Orderic Vitalis, he became one in his tastes and behavior.[60] This, of course, explains in cultural terms why he was later to surround himself with Normans, and it has been taken as the chief reason for the coming of the Normans into Scotland.[61] The Norman Conquest of this kingdom is explained as a matter of royal taste. Yet this approach, evidently because it seems a sufficient explanation, has obscured how David first became important in Scotland through the work of Henry I. After his sister's marriage to Henry, David became a member of the royal household, and he witnessed several royal acts. He was, however, important because of his sister. He signed as "David the Queen's brother," and no one was likely to have thought that he would ever become king of Scots.[62] David was the seventh son of Malcolm Canmore, and even though four of his elder brothers had been killed or otherwise eliminated by 1100, the probability was that one of his two remaining brothers, Edgar and Alexander, would have a son who would supersede him. To understand David's relationship with Henry, one must forget the knowledge that these men had no sons. In the early 1100s, David was a young man with no great prospects, which may have recommended him to Henry, who had spent his own youth in similar circumstances, and in 1107 the king became David's benefactor. In that year, King Edgar died, and he apparently left David either the lordship of southern Scotland or the royal estates in this region. David, however, was not put in possession of this bequest until Henry threatened to send an army against King Alexander, who was reluctant to honor Edgar's wishes.[63] This incident is hard to explain in terms of Henry's Scottish policy, but unless one assumes that Maud's demands for justice for her youngest brother were truly formidable, it means that Henry feared that Alexander could not be relied upon and had decided to weaken his power by establishing David in Lothian and Cumbria. David first rose in the world probably because of his usefulness in keeping the Scots weak.

Between 1107 and 1124, David was Henry's marcher lord in southern Scotland. The second great improvement in his fortunes was probably an outgrowth of this position. On the one hand, David needed sufficient material resources to function effectively; and, on the other hand, there was the necessity of ensuring his loyalty. Both problems were solved in 1113, when Henry gave him Maud de Saint-Liz for his wife. She was the daughter of Earl Waltheof, Siward's son, and Judith, William the Conqueror's niece; besides these genealogical attractions, she was the heiress of the earldom of Northampton and the honor of Huntingdon.[64] David's marriage with Maud made him one of the most important nobles in England, bound him even more closely to Henry, and gave him the lordship of a number of the Normans who would later become important in Scotland. Henry had, in fact, revived the old pattern of a Northumbrian earl holding the earldom of Northampton except in this instance the earl in question ruled the lost province of Lothian. It is also probably no coincidence that the earliest stories of how Lothian had been lost to the Scots were inserted into the chronicles during the reign of Henry I. These accounts, which are contradictory in their details, carried the inference either that Lothian was a fief of the English crown or that it had been improperly acquired by the Scots,[65] and they may have been intended as the basis for a revived English claim of the province although they may only reflect a feeling at Durham that Lothian should have been part of England. From 1107 until 1124, David was Henry's man in both a personal and a tenurial sense. The Normans who accompanied him around Lothian and Cumbria were predominantly drawn from the earldom of Northampton or from Henry's patronage network.[66] These were the men who staffed his government and received lands in Scotland; and after David became king in 1124, the same pattern persisted. During David's later years, few Normans entered Scotland.[67]

The value of the ties between David and Henry was not restricted, however, simply to the maintenance of peace between England and Scotland or to the provision of David with suitable companions. Henry I's greatest accomplishment in the North was the containment, division, and reduction of the northern free zone, an achievement which made estates in the region valuable enough to be granted out as rewards for his supporters, and ended the concentration of the Normans around a few military and administrative strong points such as Newcastle, Bamburgh, and Carlisle. David's cooperation in this process was of funda- mental importance. At first sight, David's role is not particularly obvious, of course, for in Northumbria, the eastern margin of the free zone appears to have been contained by methods similar to those employed further south, which owed little to Earl David. In Teesdale, Guy de Balliol built Barnard Castle in the early twelfth century, and Brancepath above the Wear is probably of a com- parable date.[68] To the north, Henry created two new baronies, Styford and Prudhoe, at the mouth of the Tyne gap, and Robert de Umfraville apparently built a castle at Prudhoe. In addition, Nor- man control was pushed up the North Tyne to its junction with the Rede. The valley of the latter was given to Robert de Umfraville on the condition that he close it to robbers, and he accomplished this by the erection of Elsdon castle. The line of motte-and-bailey castles between Hexham and the junction of the Rede and the North Tyne, that is, Gunnerton, Wark on Tyne, and Bellingham, presumably also dates from this period.[69] Elsdon and the castles on the Tyne controlled all the important routes out of the northern free zone south of Coquetdale. The latter was apparently protected by a royal castle at Rothbury. The upper reaches of the Aln and Beamish were dominated by Cospatric's serjeanty of Beanly, which he held by the tenure of guaranteeing the good intentions of outsiders entering Northumberland through his estates. The valley of the Till was blocked by the barony of Wooler, which probably had a castle at Wooler, and by Walter Espec's lordship of Carham.[70] Walter's castle at Wark-on-Tweed defended an important ford over the Tweed, and to the east, Bishop Ranulf's new castle of Nor- ham, which he had built to protect Norhamshire from raiders, performed a similar function.[71]

　　These castles along the eastern edge of the free zone from the Tees to the Tweed gave the east coast plain a measure of protection against raids. Although this attempt to contain the east- ern free zone is easily visible, the more important work was done in the West. The key to creating peace in the Far North was the

control of communications through the hills, and this was established by Ranulf Meschin, the lord of Carlisle, and by Earl David.
Presumably Ranulf's work came first. When he received Cumberland, Carlisle was an exposed strong point, but probably by 1120,
when he gave up his northern lordship to become earl of Cheshire,
and almost certainly by 1135, Carlisle had been linked with Richmond by castles at Appleby, Brough, and Bowes, and its communications with Lancashire had been secured by the castle of
Burton-in-Lonsdale.[72] The former castles in particular were very
important because they controlled the Vale of Eden–Stainmore
route and split the Pennines. Furthermore, Ranulf blocked the
Galwegian border with two new baronies. Burgh by Sands controlled the fords across the Solway, which were the most practical
route to the north, and Liddel covered the route around the edge
of the hills.[73] These lordships and castles put the Normans in a
much better position to control movements through the southern
part of the old Cumbrian kingdom, but to be really effective, they
needed to be extended beyond the border. This was Earl David's
contribution. According to local tradition at Glasgow, David had
been sent by God to punish and restrain the Galwegians, and he
accomplished this by creating around the western flanks of the
Scottish part of the free zone three large lordships modeled upon
Carlisle.[74] He gave Liddesdale to Ranulf de Soules, Eskdale to
Robert Avenel, and Annandale to Robert de Brus.[75] These military
districts covered all the dales between Cumberland and Annandale. The latter contained the Galwegians of Nithsdale and provided the basis for keeping the Roman road to the Clyde open.[76]
Eskdale and Liddesdale dominated the trails leading to Teviotdale
and to the North Tyne. Together these fees split the northern
free zone and prevented east-west raids. They were, moreover,
matched by a series of military districts in the north that protected the Midland valley of Scotland just as the southern lordships
shielded Tweeddale and Northumberland. David gave Cunningham to Hugh de Morville and North Kyle and Renfrew to Walter
fitz Alan.[77]

    The effect of the activities of Ranulf Meschin and Earl
David was the fragmentation and containment of the northern free
zone. This was a necessary condition for the revival of northern
society on both the English and Scottish parts of the east coast
plain, and there is a curious parallel between David's career and

the appearance of Normans above the Tyne. This pattern can only be stated tentatively, of course, because of the extremely limited nature of the evidence. There is practically no evidence that Norman landholders were established in Northumberland during the first decade of Henry I's reign. A shadowy "Graffard," who apparently held land around Tynemouth, is mentioned, and two writs refer to Guy de Balliol. But the second of these, a writ issued in 1105, strongly suggests that there were no other important Norman landholders along the Tyne, and beyond Graffard and Guy, no outside settlers are mentioned except for a mysterious colony of Flemings, who seem to have been established somewhere above the Tyne.[78] After King Edgar's death, however, this situation changed. David vanishes from Henry's charters between 1108 and 1112, which presumably means that he was spending most of his time in Scotland, and at the end of this period two significant pieces of evidence concerning Northumberland appear. First, in 1111, Henry removed the Flemings from the shire; and second, in the same year, Robert Muschamp, the lord of Wooler, is mentioned in a writ. This suspicious coincidence is repeated later in the 1110s. From about 1116 through 1121, David again fails to attest any of Henry's acts; and during roughly the same years, about 1114–21 and 1116–20, respectively, neither Robert de Brus, who probably already was lord of Annandale, nor Ranulf Meschin witnesses a royal charter.[79] The simultaneous absence of these three men is not likely to have been the result of chance, and it probably means that during these years they were busy in the West bringing order to the Galwegian march. Furthermore, at the end of this period, Eustace fitz John, Walter Espec, and Forne son of Sigulf, the three principal agents of Henry's government in Northumberland, all appear above the Tyne, as do Walter de Bolbec and Robert de Umfraville.[80] In 1121, moreover, Bishop Ranulf built Norham castle, and between 1119 and 1124, Berwick and Roxburgh, the first Scottish burghs, appear.[81] Finally, in 1122, King Henry himself came north and surveyed Cumberland and Northumbria.[82] If the pattern this evidence discloses can be relied upon, the attack upon the northern free zone was at least contemporaneous with the settlement of Normans in Northumbria and Tweeddale, and it probably preceded settlement in the East. David's activities were clearly central to the process, even though their exact nature remains hidden.

The Norman settlement of the border counties and of southern Scotland cannot be explained except in terms of the political needs of Henry I and his relationship with Earl David. Henry brought the Normans north either directly or through David, and with the aid of David he created the conditions that made their settlement possible. The lands of the old kingdoms of Northumbria and Cumbria were settled as a unit. Yet this conclusion raises a fundamental question that cannot be answered satisfactorily within the framework of political history. If this chronology is correct, one must ask why the Normans had not taken lands in the Far North before 1110. They had come to England to get estates, to become greater lords than they were; and their behavior in southern England and elsewhere in Christendom establishes that they had few scruples, and these largely restricted to the church, that could stand for long between them and land in the hands of natives. Judged by their actions elsewhere, their neglect of Northumberland, Cumberland, and even Scotland till the early twelfth century is an enigma, which is probably why their late arrival above the Tyne has been largely overlooked. They should have been there; and despite the fact that Henry I's diplomatic and political needs provide a convincing explanation of why he gave Normans land in this area, his reasons were not unusual. Both William the Conqueror and William Rufus had wanted a quiet North so that they could concentrate their strength in Normandy, and the need to reward followers with land was not new in 1100. There is no sign that the Conqueror or Rufus had more lands at their disposal than men willing to occupy them. The idea that estates in the region were not very valuable because of the insecure conditions there is more helpful, but it only pushes the problem back geographically. Why had the Normans not moved into the hills and mountains of the free zone before 1100? The cooperation Henry received from David was, no doubt, convenient in this endeavor, but it was not essential. Ranulf Meschin could have pushed into Galloway. No answer to this question is apparent because the explanation lies in an unexplored area.

In reconstructing the history of the Norman Conquest the usual topics of investigation are the diplomatic, political, and administrative activities of the kings, the question of feudalism, and military history. Ecclesiastical history is also normally included so that the famous triad of castles, knights, and monks tends to dominate our conception of the Conquest. This is, of course, inevitable because to varying degrees these were the questions that interested chroniclers or were mentioned in charters. In the case of the North, this point of view dates back to the 1090s, when a certain Boson, a knight of Bishop William de St. Calais, is reported to have had a vision that could be favorably compared with the concluding paragraphs of many modern works on the Norman Conquest. Boson had the privilege of witnessing through a vision a supernatural slide show that revealed that the significance of the Norman Conquest of the North lay in the replacement of Northumbrian spearmen on fat horses by armored knights riding chargers, the substitution of monks for married priests, and the building of the castle and cathedral at Durham.[83] One might add that Boson should also have seen peasants laboring under a more intensive manorial system to support the new regime, but his picture of the effects of the Conquest is still strikingly modern. Unfortunately, however, such a point of view cannot explain why the Normans failed to pass beyond Durham until late in the life of this perceptive knight, because the reason lies in the mundane. Twelfth century writers usually took this realm for granted, and modern accounts of the Normans either ignore the day-to-day reality of their lives and in particular the fact that they functioned in terms of an agricultural society or relegate this subject to generalized discussions of manners and morals or to abstract Domesday studies. This is unfortunate because the Norman settlement of the North was a colonizing process; and, as in most such ventures, mundane considerations played an important role in determining its course and scope.

I have deferred the question of the effects of the mundane until now despite its relevance between 1070 and 1100 because the most important clue to its solution comes from an obscure corner of Scotland during the reign of King David. As observed earlier, he was responsible for bringing Normans into Scotland, but very little evidence on this subject has survived. To a remarkable degree, the history of this event is based upon deductions from a limited group of charters. In terms of twelfth-century Scottish history, this small body of evidence is regrettable, but in a roundabout way it is favorable to the present investigation because in Scotland peripheral information concerning the Normans, which in England receives little emphasis, stands out clearly. Specifically, settlement patterns seem to have existed among the Normans who took land in Scotland, and this phenomenon is most striking in the Southwest. The men whom David planted around the Galwegian border formed a very interesting group. Their enfiefment showed the importance of David's possession of Northampton and his connection with Henry I, for they either held land in David's Midland honor or, as in the case of Robert de Brus, were Henry's new men. Moreover, these men all came originally from the same region in France, Lower (western) Normandy or the borders of Brittany. Walter fitz Alan's father was from Dol, and Robert de Brus was from Brix south of Cherbourg. Morville is near Brix, and Soules (now Soulles) is in the vicinity of St. Lô. Robert Avenel apparently belonged to an important family of the Avranchin.[84]

That all these men came from the same area might be explained as the result of the fact that Henry I's patronage network had originally been based on western Normandy.[85] But while this consideration is obviously relevant, David's land grants in eastern Scotland show that it was not the only factor involved. The Normans to whom he gave land in Tweeddale, Lothian, and Fife were of diverse origins. A number of them cannot be traced to northern France even by conjecture; and of these, William of Lamberton is perhaps the most remarkable, for he took his name from the village of Lamberton near Berwick. Others in this group can be traced to England although in some instances not by very far. Walter de Ridale (Tweeddale), for instance, was from Northumberland, and William de Sommerville (Lannarkshire) and Walter of Lindsey (Lothian) cannot be followed south beyond the castlery of Pontefract and northern Lincolnshire, respectively.[86] The other men in this group, Robert Corbet (Teviotdale), Berenger Engaine (Teviotdale), and David Olifart, were from Northampton, but the origins of their families beyond that point are unknown. The remaining men came from different parts of northern France. Hugh de Morville and Robert Avenel, who both held land in western Scotland, also got land in the East, and Simon fitz Michael (Fife) was a Breton, judging from his name.[87] Robert de Bourneville (Lothian) apparently came from near Caen, and Gervais Ridel (Lothian) is said to have stemmed from Blayne in Guienne prior to his establishment in Northampton.[88] The rest came from the East. Richard Comin (Peebleshire) is said to have been from Comines near Lille, and Geoffrey de Melville (Angus?), William Maule (Perthshire), and Robert de Umfraville (Stirlingshire), the lord of Prudhoe and Redesdale in Northumberland, all were eastern Normans.[89] Finally, three dependents of the War-renes from eastern Normandy, Alexander de Saint-Martin, Hugh Giffard, and Bernard de Balliol, received land in Lothian after the marriage of Ada de Warenne to David's son Henry.[90] David's Normans in eastern Scotland formed a heterogeneous group. As in the West, the importance of the king's connection with Northampton and with King Henry's friends is noticeable. Yet there was no exclusive concentration of western Normans in this part of Scotland as there was on the borders of Galloway, and this discovery makes the latter arrangement more suspicious than it seemed in isolation.

This pattern might be accidental, and it would be difficult to rule out such a possibility on the basis of the Scottish evidence, which is limited with respect to the West. But if the distribution of Normans in Scotland has some meaning and is not the result of chance, one might expect to find a similar distribution in the border counties of England. If this question is pursued, significant results emerge. Of the baronies in Northumberland, three, Hepple, Langley, and Warkworth-Rothbury, were established too late to be considered here.[91] Four of the remainder, Beanly, Dilston, Embleton, and Gosforth, were held by natives when they first appeared, and the holders of five other early baronies, Bolam, Bothal, and Hadestone along with Mitford and Wooler, have not been traced to Normandy although they were apparently Normans.[92] This group includes men who took their names from places in England, such as Aschantinus de Worcester and Gilbert of Newcastle, and men with ambiguous names, such as the Bertrams or Robert de Muschamp. Eight men remain after these deductions, and they were nearly balanced between eastern and western Normans. Robert de Umfraville (Prudhoe and Redesdale), Walter de Bolbec (Styford), and probably Nicholas de Grenville (Ellingham) came from eastern Norman families, and Guy de Balliol (Bywell) should be grouped with these men although Bailleul-en-Vimeu was a few miles east of the Norman border.[93] Hugh fitz Eudo, on the other hand, stemmed from west central Normandy, if he really was the son of Eudo de Ria, and there were two men, Walter Espec (Wark) and Eustace fitz John (Alnwick) whose families came from the West.[94] Finally, Herbert de la Val may have been from the West, although this is not certain.[95] The origins of the Northumbrian barons establish that the group of men who received land from

David in eastern Scotland were not unusual. The landholders between the Tyne and the Tweed were drawn from families of both
Upper and Lower Normandy with the former in a slight majority,
and their number included a substantial group of men who cannot
be traced to Normandy.

In Cumberland, however, quite different results emerge
that have a direct bearing on David's western Normans, and this
information is of critical importance because it shows that the
Northumbrian and eastern Scottish evidence cannot be taken as
revealing the composition of a "normal" Norman landholding class
in this part of Britain. The tenurial structure of Cumberland was
the work of Ranulf Meschin and, after 1120, of Henry I; and they
enfiefed a very interesting group of men. Seven of the men who
received land were natives, which, given the size of the area, was a
large group; four of the Frenchmen cannot be traced to northern
France. These men were different from their eastern peers such as
Gilbert de Newcastle or David's Northamptonshire men because
three of them, Guy the Hunter, Richard Redere, and Walter the
Chaplain, were obscure because of their own lack of status rather
than their possession of an English place name. Furthermore, the
fourth man, Thurstan de Reigny, was clearly French even though
he has not been traced.[96] None of these men has been shown to
have come into Cumberland as the result of secondary immigration, such as certainly took place on the east coast. This is
curious, but the really important point is that there were no Normans at all from Upper Normandy in Cumberland. Ranulf was the
hereditary *vicomte* of the Bessin, and six of the seven men who
received land from him and Henry I were from Lower Normandy
and Brittany.[97] The only exception was a solitary Fleming, Turgis
Brundis, the lord of Liddel.[98] This same pattern is discernible just
south of Cumberland. Burton in Lonsdale and Kendale were apparently held successively by Ivo Taillebois from west-central Normandy and by Nigel d'Aubigny from western Normandy. The
tenurial history of Skipton in the Aire gap is similar.[99] Its first lord
was Robert de Rumilly, who came from Remilly in Lower Normandy, and its second holder was William Meschin, lord of Allerdale above Derwent and the brother of Ranulf Meschin.[100] In
Lancashire above the Ribble, where most of the countryside was
taken up by honorial demesne manors, thanages, and serjeanties,
the only important lordship was the fee of Lancaster, whose first

holder, a certain Gilbert, seems to have been a retainer of William Meschin, and the only identifiable landholder in Furness during the reign of Henry I was Michael le Fleming.[101] The concentration of western Normans in Scottish Cumbria was not an anomaly. English Cumbria and the region just to the south were also settled by men from Lower Normandy and Brittany; and the two Flemings, who might be taken as exceptions to this pattern, have their parallel in Scotland, for either King David or his successor, Malcolm the Maiden, settled a Flemish colony along the headwaters of the Clyde above Lanark.[102]

The combination of evidence from the northern counties of England and from southern Scotland establishes that there was an east-west split in the settlement of Normans within the region during the reign of Henry I and David. The lands of the old kingdom of Strathclyde or Cumbria (in its widest sense) were settled by men from Lower Normandy and Brittany with some Flemings. Along the east coast plain, on the other hand, a composite nobility was established that included men from all the former areas, men whose families can be traced only to southern England, and Normans from Upper Normandy who probably formed the predominant faction. Furthermore, the nobility William the Conqueror installed in Yorkshire was similar in its composition to the later nobility of Northumbria and Lothian.[103] This settlement pattern, which appears to be without exception, is so clear-cut that it must reflect the operation of some selective factor, and since this distribution of Normans ignores national boundaries and is not explicable in terms of Henry I's patronage, this factor must have been exercised by the Normans who settled in the region. Indeed, in this selective factor lies the link between the mundane and the coming of the Normans into the Far North.

At first sight, the bizarre arrangement of Normans in the North may seem to correspond with nothing more significant than the boundaries of the old kingdom of Strathclyde in the days of its greatest power or, to the nonromantic, with a north-south line from the headwaters of the Ribble to the Scottish Highlands, but this distribution does have a meaning. It corresponds with a basic agricultural division of the North that was reflected in a number of differences between the agricultural systems of the east coast plain and the West. The characteristics of these regions were probably complex even in the early twelfth century. They certainly were later, but for the moment they will be discussed in terms of the distinction that was of most immediate significance to the Normans. This was the question of northern cereal production. From this standpoint, the North was transected by the oat bread line. This term is entirely a matter of convenience and was chosen in memory of Samuel Johnson, who was of the opinion that oats were eaten only by horses and Scots.[104] The line defined that part of the North in which spring crops (oats and barley) were predominant over winter cereals (wheat and rye), and it was not absolute in the sense that there were no exceptions to its sway. Nevertheless, it was a fundamental division of northern farming, and it can be seen most clearly in the mid-eighteenth century just before the advent of modern transport and the industrial revolution severed diet from the confines of regional agriculture. In the 1760s, Arthur Young, that great apostle of agricultural improvement, toured the North. As was his custom, he wrote an account of his journey from which a rough map of the bread types of the North during this period can be constructed.[105] This information should not be understood as necessarily applying to the "better" people on the wrong side of the oat bread line, for they belonged in terms of food to a wider world, nor does it correspond completely with what was being grown in that "superior" grains that did not appear in the bread were sometimes grown locally. But the bread types do reveal the cheap local grains, those grains that did best in the neighborhood. Such a map shows that the consumption of wheat bread was largely restricted to the southern part of the east coast plain. North of the Vale of York in Durham and southern Northumberland, rye became an important bread grain in the local diet although wheat was also used; and from Morpeth on the Wansbeck north, wheat and rye were both replaced by bread made from a combination of barley and peas. As might be expected so close to Scotland, oatmeal in the form of porridge also occupied an important place in the Northumbrian diet.[106] The really surprising point, however, is that reliance on spring crops was not confined to northern Northumberland. In the eastern flanks of the Pennines in Yorkshire, oatmeal seems to have been the primary bread grain, and spring cereals were unrivaled in the West. In lowland Cumberland, the local bread was made from oats and barley with some rye, and in Westmorland and Lancashire oat bread or oatcakes (clap bread) was the common bread.[107] The same was true, of course, in southwestern Scotland, and the English oat bread area apparently ended in Cheshire, although there was another zone of barley bread running down toward Newcastle-under-Lyme west of the Pennines.[108] Arthur Young's journals show that the North was divided by a line that ran from the Wansbeck south through the hills into the West Riding, and to the north and west of this line the usual bread grains were oats and barley. This distribution of bread types can be confirmed by the Board of Agriculture reports of the early nineteenth century which show Northumberland divided between a northern area of barley-peas bread and a southern rye area and the West still in general confirmed in its taste for oat bread.[109]

The oat bread line had probably cut across the North since prehistoric times. This is not to say that the situation in the mid-eighteenth century can be carried backward without alteration. The exact location of the line had undoubtedly shifted from time to time with fluctuations in the climate, developments in agricultural practice, and changes in taste. Such minor alterations are shown by the fact that in 1698, Celia Fiennes, another journal writing traveler, did not encounter clap bread until she had penetrated Amounderness as far as Garstang or by the probability that northern Lancashire was in an area of barley bread in the sixteenth century. There were also favored areas beyond the line in the East where wheat could be grown in the Middle Ages, and from the late sixteenth century spring wheat was occasionally grown in the West.[110] Furthermore, it is clear that winter wheat was grown on a limited basis in Lancashire before this. But these are the exceptions that are inevitable in agriculture. F. J. Singleton has collected evidence that illustrates the reliance of the agricultural system in Lancashire on spring crops, principally on oats, from the eighteenth back to the thirteenth centuries, and he has shown that the structure of the field system in Lancashire was based on their growth.[111]

Singleton's research supplies a surprisingly direct link between conditions in Arthur Young's time and those of the High Middle Ages; and to a certain extent, the same correspondence can be found in the East. A portion of the Lay Subsidy Roll for 25 Edward I dealing with the West Riding has survived, and it discloses in enough detail what crops were being grown in the countryside south of the Aire and to a lesser extent around Ripon to make possible the construction of a crop sequence map (see map).[112] This map reveals that the cultivation of wheat was limited to the lower parts of the area, generally to land below 250 feet and to the valley floor of the Calder. On either side of the zone where wheat was grown, there were belts of villages in which rye took the place of wheat; and finally, on the higher ground toward the west there were a number of vills where only oats were grown. This is remarkable proof of the age of the distribution of bread types as they were revealed in the eighteenth century, and it is probably a correct assumption that in the thirteenth century, the oat bread line continued on to the north through the edge of the Pennines just as it did later. To the east of the line there is, of course, little need to establish the importance of wheat and rye. The Lay Subsidy shows their cultivation in the late thirteenth century, and they are accounted for in the pipe rolls of Henry III and John.[113] In Durham, where the growing of wheat cannot, perhaps, be assumed so lightly, it is known that the episcopal demesne manors yielded 2,065½ quarters of wheat and 5,236½ quarters of oats in 1211, and Boldon Book shows that wheat was produced on these manors in the 1180s.[114] Finally, the oldest fairly general evidence that throws any light on this question, Henry II's pipe roll for 1172, apparently reflects the oat bread line. In that year the king sent 200 skeps of wheat and 100 skeps of oats to Ireland from Yorkshire. From Northumberland, however, he could only dispatch 300 loads of oats and from Cumberland, 200 loads of oats.[115]

   This does not necessarily mean that no wheat was grown in Northumberland and Cumberland in 1172, but it is good evidence that there was no surplus of this grain that could be sent out of these shires. And this should not be particularly surprising. Both areas were beyond the economic or large-scale limit of wheat cultivation as defined by H. Dudley Stamp. According to Stamp, these limits are the 60-degree isotherm for July in the north and the 30-inch rainfall line in the west.[116] Currently Durham and Lancashire are on the edge of the area marked off by these criteria. The 60-degree isotherm runs in a southwest tending arc through northern Yorkshire, and the 30-inch rainfall line stretches north-south across the eastern slopes of the Pennines. Lowland Yorkshire is mostly within these limits, and eastern Durham is just on the other side of the line in terms of temperature but not of moisture. Much of the Pennines are excluded on either ground.

Crop Sequences in the West Riding in 1297

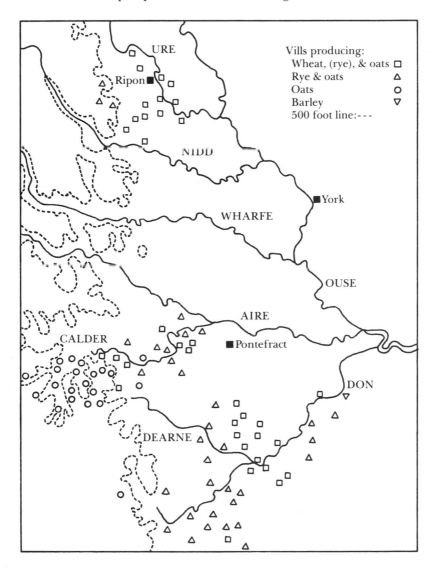

Vills producing:
Wheat, (rye), & oats □
Rye & oats △
Oats ○
Barley ▽
500 foot line:- - -

URE

Ripon

NIDD

York

WHARFE

OUSE

AIRE

CALDER

Pontefract

DON

DEARNE

In the West, Lancashire and Westmorland are mostly below the 60-degree isotherm for July but only barely, and all of the area, especially to the east and northeast, receives more than 30 inches of precipitation yearly.[117]

There is a remarkable correspondence between Stamp's criteria for wheat cultivation and the historical oat bread line. Wheat can be grown north of Stamp's limits, but it becomes an undependable crop liable to an alternation of good yields and poor except in a few favored spots mainly on the very eastern margins of Scotland.[118] This problem of dependability—or economic production—is the basis for the similarity of the eighteenth-century bread types and the crop distributions in the Middle Ages. The common local breads of the 1760s were the cheap breads made from grain that grew well under local conditions. These were not necessarily the only crops that could be grown in the neighborhood if one were prepared to take risks; but the medieval peasant could not afford risks. For him, crop failures meant ruin and starvation. The northern peasant had to grow crops that could be expected to do well year after year, and this necessity produced the crop sequences that have been encountered. Rye will endure the cold better than wheat. Barley can be grown further north than rye, and oats will withstand more moisture than either barley or rye.[119] Furthermore, there is some evidence that the northern peasant's criteria for growing wheat prior to 1066 were closer to Stamp's theoretical requirements than to either the eighteenth-century distribution of bread types or the situation that existed in the twelfth century. Despite the general similarity of shire custom throughout the North, there were some important differences between its demands in Yorkshire and Northumbria that seem to reflect the pre-Norman oat bread line. In Yorkshire, for example, the old grain renders of the shire—insofar as their composition can be reconstructed—apparently were made up of oats and corn, presumably either rye or wheat.[120] Above the Tees, on the other hand, these renders consisted of oats and barley either in their raw state or as malt and meal, and it is probably a fair inference that the Northumbrian peasants did not normally grow wheat, for had they done so these grains almost certainly would have been included in their dues.[121] The number of boon plowings required of peasants each year points in the same direction. In Yorkshire, peasants usually had to do two free days of plowing a year, one in the fall and another in the spring.[122] In Northumberland, however, they did one plowing a year at oat seed time, and in Durham the oldest tradition required plowing only once a year.[123] Both Northumbrian grain renders and boon plowings indicate that the oat bread line had run somewhere through southern Durham or northern Yorkshire during Anglo-Saxon times, and there is evidence that it had at least one outlier in Yorkshire. In the reign of William the Conqueror, Holderness is said to have yielded nothing but oats.[124]

The question of the oat bread line is important for understanding the Norman Conquest of the North for the simplest reason: the Normans came to England for land—but not for any land. This is what we forget as members of an industrialized society separated from the countryside by supermarkets and a commercial system of food distribution that blurs regional differences. In the eleventh and twelfth centuries such differences determined what most men ate, and this was of direct concern to nobles because they had specific expectations with respect to food. Nobility was expressed and enjoyed in a standard of living, and although this aspect of noble status is often lost sight of in favor of other questions such as lordship or judicial privileges, in the settlement of new lands it was a matter of the first importance. A noble standard of living was both a question of taste and a matter of status; and, as it always is with status, there were requirements. For example, wine was important. R. Dion has shown that good wine was an important symbol of nobility and that the necessity of serving wine to one's guests and dependents led to the extension of viniculture in France.[125] The consumption of venison that had been killed by one's own hand was probably another such symbol, and the right kind of bread certainly was.

For the French nobility in general this meant bread made from wheat (*frumentum*), and the Normans were no exception to this rule.[126] It is, in fact, doubtful whether they ate any other type of bread or, at least, thought that they should. In the lists of provisions for royal castles, wheat and wine occupied the place of honor, and when Richard fitz Nigel wrote his account of how the old royal farm had come to be paid in money rather than in produce, he assumed that the only bread grain it had yielded had been wheat.[127] The assumption is, of course, questionable, but it did reflect Norman feeling on what the farm should have provided. In the early Norman maintenance allotments bread made from wheat occupied a dominant position, and the meaning of such allotments in Norman society stands out clearly in the rules that governed the royal court under Henry I. At court, all bread was made from wheat. In Henry's reign a bushel of wheat, or as the Normans called it, "a bushel of Rouen," yielded three grades of bread. In order of descending fineness, one could obtain from each bushel 40 lord's simnel loaves, 140 salted simnel loaves, and 260 ordinary loaves, and the type of bread members of the royal court received each day depended upon their rank. The chancellor, for example, was given "1 lord's simnel loaf, and 2 salted simnel loaves, and 1 sextary of clear wine, and 1 sextary of ordinary wine." The steward, however, obtained only "2 salted simnel loaves, and 1 sextary of ordinary wine," and the various service personnel of the court were given something called "customary food" which presumably consisted of ordinary loaves and ordinary wine.[128] With the *companaticum* (side dishes of meat, poultry, and fish), these allotments constituted the diet of the nobles at the court, and they illustrate two very important points concerning the Norman nobility. First, despite their wealth, bread was the primary item in their daily diet; and second, the quality of one's bread was a symbol of personal status.

There was a direct connection between this aspect of nobility and regional agriculture. Indeed, this was the basis for the settlement patterns discovered in the North. William the Conqueror's followers hoped to be rewarded with land, but land that did not grow wheat, and particularly land where wheat could not be grown, was of little use to them. Such acres would not make them greater nobles. In southern and central England this was not, of course, a serious problem because within these areas the land and its produce met the expectations of the Normans, but in other parts of the British Isles this was not necessarily the case. To illustrate this point in general, one need only recall Gerald of Wales's description of Ireland:

> The land is fruitful and rich in its fertile soil and plentiful harvests. Crops abound in the fields and flocks on the mountains. . . . The island is, however, richer in pastures than in crops, and in grass rather than grain. The crops give great promise in the blade, even more in the straw, but less in the ear. For here the grains of wheat are shrivelled and small, and can scarcely be separated from the chaff by any winnowing fan. The plains are well clothed with

grass. . . . Only the granaries are without wealth. What is born and
comes forth in the spring and is nourished in the summer . . . can
scarcely be reaped in the harvest because of unceasing rain.[129]

In other words, Ireland was a pleasing land except that wheat did
poorly there, and this single consideration clouded Gerald's view
of the island.

It might be objected, of course, that Gerald was the spokesman for a later generation of Normans and that such considerations did not restrain the Conqueror's rude barons, but in the
north evidence shows that this was a matter of fundamental importance from the beginning. The Norman settlement of the North
cannot be explained without reference to the question of what kind
of land the Normans wanted. In literary evidence, this point is
made explicitly in a story concerning Odo of Champagne, the third
husband of William the Conqueror's sister Adelaide. William apparently gave him Holderness, which had been forfeited by Drogo,
its first holder, late in the Conqueror's reign. Shortly afterward,
however, Odo and Adelaide had a son, and Odo was soon petition-
ing the Conqueror for more land. According to the story, his
reason was very simple. Odo disliked Holderness because it produced nothing but oats, and he wanted some wheat-bearing land so
that he could feed the child. William is said to have agreed to the
request. This story is admittedly late, but it probably represents an
authentic family tradition of the lords of Holderness, who were
descended from Odo.[130] And even if Odo's reputed aversion to
feeding his son oatcakes is not historical, other evidence shows the
same attitude at work among the Norman nobles who settled above
the Humber and indicates that it restricted their settlement.

The clearest proof comes from Ilbert de Lacy's castlery of
Pontefract in the West Riding. This nearly solid block of territory
stretched from the fens west of the Ouse up into the Pennines.
Because of unique circumstances, the actual distribution of Norman settlement within his fee can be determined clearly. First,
Domesday consistently names the Anglo-Saxon undertenants who
held of Ilbert, information not usually available elsewhere, and
second, Pontefract lay just to the north and at some points inside
the area covered by the late thirteenth-century crop sequence.[131]
This conjunction makes it possible to compare the crop sequence
with the populated estates belonging to Ilbert, and such a com-

parison reveals an important phenomenon (see map). In 1086, Ilbert's Norman undertenants held manors only in the central part of the castlery, almost exclusively on land below 250 feet, and their manors corresponded closely with the area within which wheat was grown at the time of the crop sequence. On either side of this central block of estates, the villages either were held by natives or were held directly by Ilbert and contained no demesne land. These peripheral strips corresponded generally with the areas in which rye and oats were later grown. What had happened is clear. Ilbert and his vassals had only taken direct possession of that part of the castlery in which wheat either was being grown or could be grown, and they had left the less desirable land to Anglo-Saxons.

Within the castlery of Pontefract, Norman settlement did not cross the oat bread line during the reign of William the Conqueror because the land to the west was unattractive and valueless to Ilbert's men, and the same was true all along the eastern flanks of the Pennines in Yorkshire, although in most other areas it is

The Populated Estates of Ilbert de Lacy

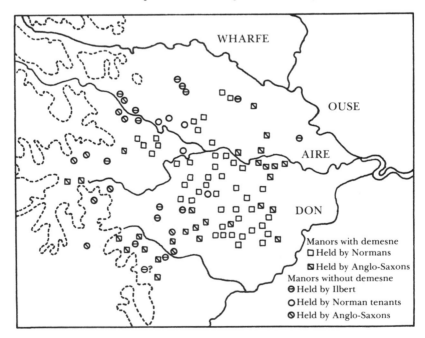

impossible to tell whether there was a band of Anglo-Saxon lords to the west of the Normans as there was in Ilbert's fee.[132] Probably this was a common phenomenon, however, for some signs of a similar pattern can be found in William de Percy's estates south of Ripon and in Richmond, and a very similar arrangement is visible in the description of Henry de Ferrers's estates in Derbyshire (see map, p. 224).[133] Despite the clarity of this pattern, it does not represent the only reaction of Normans to the oat bread line. In a sense it is an exaggerated example of what happened, for around the Pennines the Normans were faced with poor soil and rapidly increasing elevation that brought in its train an ever-decreasing growing season and increasing rain.[134]

Elsewhere the oat bread line did not bring Norman settlement to an immediate stop. Roger of Poitou, for instance, is said to have disliked Lancashire, which is understandable since it was probably an oat bread area, but he managed to attract a few Normans into the region.[135] The details of his enfiefments, however, indicate that this was a difficult process and that he was none too successful. In 1086, Roger's Norman tenants formed only a small group that numbered fifteen men if no two of them had the same name.[136] With two exceptions, they were obscure knights of no standing, and they all settled south of the Ribble. Furthermore, it is likely that most of them gave up their lands and left.[137] Lancashire was, in fact, so unattractive to Normans that Roger was forced to rely heavily on natives. Nineteen natives were holding land south of the Ribble in 1086, and there were probably others who are hidden by Domesday's incomplete description of Lancashire.[138] By 1094, a hybrid aristocracy unquestionably existed in this area, and the early thirteenth-century surveys reveal that a large number of thanages had survived the coming of the Normans into Lancashire. These thanes held, moreover, by fee farm, and this probably means, as Jolliffe has suggested, that Roger of Poitou simply terminated the old renders and works of the shire in favor of rents because the former were valueless to him.[139]

In Lancashire, Norman settlement faded out between the Ribble and the Mersey rather than coming to an abrupt stop as it did around the Pennines, and the pattern was similar in Northumbria. Durham was probably on the very southern edge of the oat bread area—or barley bread area—in the late eleventh century if the later grain renders of the bondage vills accurately repre-

Henry de Ferrers's Estates in Derbyshire

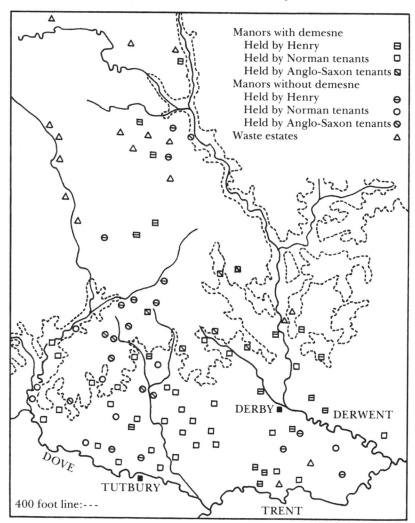

sent agricultural production prior to the Conquest. Nevertheless, Normans were established in this area before 1100, and their settlement was apparently made feasible by changing the manorial structure of Durham. Bishop Walcher, it will be remembered, was responsible for radically expanding demesne farming in a number of St. Cuthbert's villages and for imposing week work on the peasants of these villages; and although this can be explained as a straightforward act of economic exploitation, it is likely that it also represented an attempt by the bishop to obtain direct control over what the peasants were growing.[140] This is suggested by the fact that at the time of Boldon Book, wheat production in Durham was almost entirely confined to the demesnes of villages that had been manorialized by Walcher. Furthermore, even at this late date, most of the unmanorialized vills either were administered by drengs or were farmed by their inhabitants.[141]

In general, the first wave of Norman settlement in the North went as far as the oat bread line—the limit of dependable wheat cultivation as expressed in peasant breads. In southern Lancashire and Durham, the Normans may actually have crossed the line, but in both of these border areas wheat could be grown even though it had not played an important role in peasant agriculture prior to the Conquest. Moreover, in these areas the Normans altered the old manorial system of the North. In Lancashire the shire system was scrapped, and in Durham the element of demesne farming was intensified. These changes, although different in their specifics, both represented attempts to improve local traditions of peasant agriculture that were unacceptable to the Normans.

Where wheat could not be grown, the Normans did not take lands, and this was one of the basic reasons for their weakness in the North between 1070 and 1100. The Normans' dietary expectations kept them out of the free zone that occupied the most intractable part of the oat bread area and shielded northern Lancashire, the Vale of Eden, and the Cumbrian lowlands from their settlement. Estates in these regions held little value for Normans, and their reluctance to establish themselves on the other side of the oat bread line was the chief reason why they had difficulty controlling the free zone. During the reigns of William the Conqueror and William Rufus, the southern free zone was contained by castleries, but it was not occupied. In Yorkshire, where the east coast plain could support a numerous baronage, containment had some success, and in Durham, which was fairly well protected against raids from the West by the mass of the northern Pennines, it also worked. Beyond these limits, Norman power remained tenuous until after 1100. Rufus was unable to consolidate his hold on Carlisle by the establishment of a local baronage, and this failure combined with the inability of the Normans to penetrate the free zone restricted Norman settlement in Northumberland.

There was land above the Tyne that was worth having from the Normans' point of view. Wheat can be grown as an aristocratic crop north of Durham, especially in the Merse, Lothian, and the coastal fringe of southeastern Scotia proper. The only difficulty with its cultivation in the dry parts of this region is the danger of occasional failures, a threat that kept peasants from growing it but did not restrain nobles if they were sufficiently determined. This the Normans were; and the risk, therefore, was no insurmountable barrier to their settlement above the Tyne. They simply had to be prepared to pay a very high price for wheat in certain years.[142] Of course, this was a theoretical consideration in the eleventh century. Peasant agriculture undoubtedly produced unappealing crops; and, given the preponderance of renders in kind over labor dues in Northumbria, the introduction of the cultivation of wheat on any scale would have been difficult unless a noble were prepared to follow Walcher's example. Still, this problem was ultimately solved by the second generation of Normans in England; therefore, the real bar to Norman settlement in lowland Northumberland must have been the insecurity of the east coast plain vis-à-vis the free zone. Above the Tyne this plain becomes progressively narrower and more exposed. It is backed by the hills of the northern free zone all the way to Tweeddale, and beyond this break, the coastal plain of Lothian is similarly confined by the eastern extension of the southern highlands. In agricultural terms —and these were the terms that interested the Normans—the Far North consisted of this restricted plain, and as long as the northern free zone and the West were unsubdued, the agricultural communities of the coastal plain were of little value. Indeed, there were no monasteries, mints, or known towns of any size between the Tyne and the Forth in the eleventh century. This in itself is symptomatic of a small and impoverished rural population, and other evidence confirms this deduction. The miracles of St. Oswin disclose that the countryside of southern Northumberland was so poor in the late eleventh century that Norman armies could not feed themselves there, and the same was true of the Merse, which was potentially a richer area, for in 1138, King Stephen had to withdraw from there because his army could not find food.[143] Earlier, King Edgar is known to have given away on two different occasions deserted estates in the Merse and to have provided the recipients with oxen for their redevelopment. These terms suggest that the general neighborhood was underdeveloped, and conditions in Lothian may not have been much better. Most of the Norman and Anglo-Saxon expeditions into Lothian were accompanied by fleets that were presumably used to carry supplies. This was certainly the case in 1091. When Rufus lost his grain fleet in that year, a number of his knights and horses died of hunger.[144]

The east coast plain above the Tyne was in this state because it was vulnerable. As long as the Tyne gap and the valley of the North Tyne were in native hands, the Galwegians could be at the gates of Hexham without warning, and the fear that resulted from this insecurity dominates Northumbrian descriptions of their western neighbors. All that is really known about the Galwegians in this period is that they were a semipastoral people who somewhat resembled the Welsh in their manner of fighting and their customary organization, but in the hands of the historians from Hexham they become monsters. The Galwegians (Picts) are uniformly portrayed as a morally debased people, who cruelly committed unthinkable blasphemies and atrocities. At home they were thought to live after the manner of beasts. This charge lacks substance in the early accounts except for the report of an ill-advised attempt by the Galwegians to sacrifice a bull to St. Cuthbert.[145] When the Galwegians came out of the hills, however, the Northumbrians painted a grim, if generalized, picture. The Galwegians desecrated churches, took slaves, and killed for the fun of it. They were especially prone to slay the old and the sick, husbands in front of wives, and babies. The latter were ripped from the womb or thrown into the air and impaled on spears. Afterward, the Galwegians drank their blood. Finally, in the best accounts of this ilk, the Northumbrian women are led off into the west tied together and naked to face a fate worse than death (which does not go undescribed).[146] That these accounts are hysterical and soon became conventionalized cannot hide the fact that they rested on absolute dread. They are the usual result of contact between agriculturalists and a semipastoral folk given to plundering and slaving from an inaccessible homeland. The problem was not new. When the Romans had at last come to understand the difficulty of controlling the northern free zone, they had built a wall through the Tyne gap and written off the rest of the North.

During the reign of Henry I, this problem was solved—or at least greatly reduced. He and King David installed a Norman aristocracy in Cumberland and eastern Galloway that began the work of establishing law and order on the local level and sealing in the Galwegians. In view of the previous discussion of the Norman preference for wheat-producing land, this extension of Norman settlement may seem mysterious, if not contradictory; but there was a simple reason why Henry and David could achieve what had escaped William the Conqueror and Rufus. On a practical level, the nobility of northern France was not entirely homogeneous in its criteria for land. The Breton settlement of Richmond during the reign of William the Conqueror suggests that this was the case, and an investigation of the matter discloses that Henry I and his new men had special significance for the North. A political division had existed among the Norman nobles under William the Conqueror, at least in that the nobility of Lower Normandy had not benefited from the distribution of English lands to the same extent as the nobles of Upper Normandy; this was presumably the reason Henry cultivated men from the former area in the days before he became king.[147] He could turn the disaffection in Lower Normandy to his advantage. Once he was king, the fact that his political debts and his patronage network were based on this area had important consequences for the North because western Normans and their neighbors in Brittany had wider standards with respect to land than did the great men of the East. It was not a matter of their not sharing the same concepts of nobility; the Lower Normans valued wheat highly as an article of food and as a symbol of their status. Their numerous grants of yearly gifts of wheat to the monasteries of the area prove this conclusively, but they illustrate another point. These gifts, examples of wheat being used as money, and tenures based on the yearly payment of a stated quantity of wheat, show that while this grain was highly prized, it was also rare.[148] Indeed, there is literary evidence to this effect. Prior to the Conquest, the bishopric of Coutances was so poor that Bishop Geoffrey's household had to subsist on black bread, and this was not simply because of an absence of estates.[149] In terms of cereal production, much of Lower Normandy and the adjacent section of Brittany was poor land, and the common bread grains were rye and oats.[150] Because of their poverty, nobles from this region were more flexible than nobles from Upper Normandy. They would take land that would not grow wheat.

Furthermore, many nobles from the region probably were anxious to obtain estates elsewhere and knew the value of land in the oat bread area. The Breton massif and its eastern extension, the lands that later bore the Norman bocage, were poor lands. They are wet, and the soil is generally acid, leached, and infertile.[151] These lands apparently were so poor in places that the agricultural system would not support all the local nobles. During this period, many Bretons became mercenary soldiers because of the poverty of eastern Brittany; and, according to Orderic Vitalis, Robert Guiscard and his followers left the Cotentin for the same reason.[152] In many instances, then, it is likely that western Normans and Bretons had compelling reason to leave home, and they were probably peculiarly fitted to deal with the oat bread area. In his account of William the Conqueror's early invasion of Brittany, William de Poitiers says that the Bretons normally ate little bread and that they relied principally for their livelihood on their herds and flocks rather than upon cultivation of land. Furthermore, William had to withdraw from Brittany on this occasion because he could not find enough wheat to feed his army.[153] These were, of course, conditions reminiscent of the North, and to a lesser degree they applied to western Normandy. Both the higher parts of Brittany and the Norman bocage were areas of infield-outfield farming. Peasant labor dues were light, and livestock raising was very important.[154] These conditions were very similar to those found in northwestern England and western Scotland, and the fact that Henry's new men were familiar with such an agricultural system, at least in principle, meant that they could utilize land worthless to an eastern Norman.[155]

The relevance of this difference among the Normans is obvious. Henry's new men would take land the first generation of Norman nobles had despised. This is why no eastern Normans settled in Cumberland and western Scotland. What the Lower Normans and Bretons would not take could be given to Flemings, who were accustomed to rye and oat bread and who were concerned, in any case, with raising sheep.[156] The residue, in northern England at least, went to Henry's Anglo-Saxons. Thus one returns in the end to the original point, although with more precision.

Peace with Scotland and the establishment of a French aristocracy above Durham and Lancashire were a direct result of Henry's politics. For his own reasons, he brought to England a group of men who were able to breach the oat bread line. Norman settlement of the east coast plain from the Tyne to the Forth followed.

8. CONCLUSION

By 1135, the year of Henry I's death, the theme that has united this study—the destruction of northern society and its rebuilding—was complete in its essentials. There were, of course, unfinished tasks, but in most respects the North of the high Middle Ages had come into existence by this date. The region's old problems had been largely solved, and the northern barons faced new difficulties such as the Galwegians' reaction to the intensification of Lowland culture, which the Norman settlement represented, or the question of the political relationship between Norman Scotland and Norman England. We have, in fact, reached a familiar world, a world whose birth has been dated too early, misunderstood, or simply taken blithely for granted because of the way eleventh- and twelfth-century English history has been written.

Court-centered history is not an adequate medium for re-covering the past, even in England. When written from a regional point of view, the history of the North between 1000 and 1135 assumes a different shape than that found in accounts that inexorably advance reign by reign with the deeds and worries of a southern king as their focus. The findings of this study show that the latter approach has obscured the nature and continuity of the North's problems, distorted the accomplishments of several kings, and even failed to notice a number of important developments in northern history. In particular, the prominence normally accorded the Norman Conquest, that great child of court history following its inherent trend toward biography, needs to be modified and the concept itself expanded as it concerns the North. The idea that the Conquest was a primary causative factor that had completed its work by 1070 has artificially severed the history of the North after 1066 from what went before and beclouded the history of the Norman settlement of the North. The idea that the northern

thanes resisted the Conquest because it was a conquest being carried out by Normans and the assumption that once the northerners
were crushed in the reprehensible but effective harrying Norman
settlement immediately followed are false. Before 1066, the North
had, in fact, been changing in the direction it later followed. After
that date, the old northern world did not pass away entirely for
some years, William the Conqueror notwithstanding, and Norman power was not firmly established throughout the North for
many more.

During the first eighty years covered by this study, northern
political history was dominated by a clash between the regional
nobility and the kings. In the most general terms, this conflict
was the result of the kings' attempts to govern the North and
the northerners' progressively more desperate efforts to resist the
king or his agents. There was little real correspondence between
the self-interest of the two parties. The North was poor, politically
and fiscally privileged, and in need of defense. It was also remote
from the Anglo-Saxon kings' center of power and interest, and
they were concerned with it only as a source of danger to their
authority or as a means of maintaining the equilibrium of the
kingdom's political system. Between 1000 and 1066, the North
was ruled by setting the northerners against each other and by
unpopular earls whose power was bolstered by the earldom of
Northampton.

By the fall of 1066, the opposition aroused by such measures
above the Humber had become so powerful that the bond between
the northern nobility and the king had nearly dissolved, and this is
of great importance in understanding the course of the Conquest.
The northerners had no way of knowing that William the Bastard
and his mercenaries represented the wave of the future, and they
reacted to him not as a new phenomenon that had radically altered
the political order but in accordance with the lessons of their past.
Every king since 1000 had oppressed either Northumbria or York.
Ethelred had controlled the Danes of York with the Northumbrians. Cnut had reversed the relationship, and Edward the Confessor
had governed the North through Siward, who had been unpopular
in Northumbria, and through Tostig, whose rule had provoked the
great northern revolt of 1065. These precedents gave the northern
thanes every reason to expect the worst from William simply because he was king; and he, unfortunately, lived up to their fears.

His appointments, gelds, and confiscations were reminiscent of Tostig's rule and clear evidence that he would ignore the traditional ruling families of the North and trample on the area's privileges. In combination with his castles, these measures provoked the revolts of 1067, 1068, and 1069. In these insurrections, the northerners employed the tactics that had worked for them in the past: surprise attacks aimed at destroying the agents of southern government. Northern resistance to the Conquest was an extension of the regional nobility's pre-Conquest resistance to the king, and its object was to reject William's authority, not to undo the Conquest. William, however, did not understand this; and when the northern revolt merged with the Danish invasion in the fall of 1069, he destroyed the immediate threat to his power which the latter represented and solved the old problem of resentment in Yorkshire to West Saxon rule by the harrying. Despite the prominence of this event in most accounts of the Conquest, however, it did not give the Normans control of the North. Rather, it activated the free zone that made the redevelopment of Yorkshire a slow process, and this in turn was a serious barrier to the extension of Norman power beyond York. For ten years the Conqueror was forced to govern Northumbria through a succession of natives, and this policy had little success because the nobles above the Tees had not been cowed by the harrying. True to their past, they answered new Norman outrages by revolts in 1074–75 and 1080, and the last of these led William to destroy the Northumbrian nobility.

In a political sense, this was the end of the Norman Conquest of the North. It was also the last episode in a conflict that stretched back to the early eleventh century and perhaps into earlier times. A conception of the Conquest that turns on the elimination of the old nobility between the Humber and the Tweed, however, is incomplete. Until after 1100, Norman power in the North was weak because the Normans did not immediately spread to the old limits of the Anglo-Saxon kingdom or into the Northwest. The establishment of the new territorial aristocracy was not the simple substitution of one group of nobles for another. It was in reality a colonization with two stages; and during the first of these, the expectations of William's followers determined the scope and nature of the Conquest quite as much as their king's victories. The Norman nobles wished to transplant their culture to England, and in an important respect they were unable to do this in parts of the North. In their culture, bread made from wheat was a primary sign of nobility, and the corollary of this was that land that would not grow wheat was little esteemed. In the North, wheat either would not grow or did poorly in several areas, and this directly limited the extent of Norman settlement. William's men took estates in Yorkshire, Durham, and southern Lancashire. In the first two of these shires, they exploited the desperate conditions produced by the harrying to impose on the peasants a more rigorous manorial regime than the one in force before 1066, and at least in part their objective was to establish a system that would give them control over what the peasants planted. Where wheat could not be grown, the Normans did not settle. William I and William II therefore had to contain the free zone rather than conquer it, and Cumberland and Northumberland remained without territorial aristocracies after 1092 and 1080, respectively. The first was on the wrong side of the oat bread line, and the second was too vulnerable to depredations from the West to be worth settling. Finally, the fact that the border counties were unoccupied was one of the principal reasons why the Conqueror and Rufus were forced to deal with the Scots by means of diplomacy and intervention in their internal affairs.

Between 1070 and 1100, the Norman Conquest of the North was impeded by the culture of the barons of Upper Normandy, who were the most trusted and rewarded of the Conqueror's followers, and this barrier was not removed until a shift in Norman politics occurred. When settlement pushed forward around 1106, it encompassed the border counties and southern Scotland as well because these areas could best be occupied together. This accomplishment was the Normans' most important contribution to the North. For political reasons, King Henry brought to England a group of western Normans and Bretons who were willing to take lands on the other side of the oat bread line, and he established these men in northwestern England and through Earl David in Galloway. Their settlement shielded the East from the Galwegians and closed the routes through the hills. Once this was done, Norman nobles pushed up the east coast plain from the Tyne to the Forth and even into Fife.

As a concept, the Norman Conquest usually consists of two parts, the establishment of effective Norman power and a radical break with the past or a turning point. In terms of these criteria, the movement that brought Normans to the Tweed and beyond marked the true end of the Conquest of the North. This colonization fundamentally altered the region. In a negative sense, the problems that would complicate the future stemmed directly from the nature of the second stage of settlement. In the West this was not a spontaneous migration, but was the establishment of a specific group of men, King Henry's supporters, and they were numerous enough to contain the Galwegians, but not to conquer all Galloway. This was a serious shortcoming because the Galwegians reacted to foreign penetration of their land in a violent fashion. Before 1135, southwestern Scotland became the seat of an antidynastic and—given the nature of David's rule—antiforeign revolt that was the harbinger of several later revolts, and during the invasions of Stephen's reign, the Galwegians came out of the hills to torture and kill the Lowlanders of the North whose increasing strength threatened their world.[1] Furthermore, the willingness of Henry's followers to take land in the West was largely a function of their poverty, and one piece of evidence shows that they did not automatically pass on their taste for the West to their wealthier descendants.[2] Throughout the rest of the century, the marcher lords of Galloway had to be continuously replenished by newcomers. Finally, for the next two centuries, Anglo-Scottish relations would be bedeviled by the fact that the border divided a single nobility.[3]

These problems notwithstanding, however, it is difficult to exaggerate the positive results of the second stage of colonization. Had isolated Norman barons pioneered in Northumberland and Lothian, they probably could have done no more than recreate the depressed conditions that had existed there before 1066, but by subjugating the West, the Normans revived a set of circumstances not seen since the years when Northumbrian power was at its peak. The security thus gained was the basis for the redevelopment of the old Northumbrian lands on both sides of the border. Even before 1135, Henry's new men began to fill the North with burghs and monasteries, and King David was engaged in the same task in Lothian and Tweeddale. Moreover, the taming of the free zone enabled the monks and nobles to send their sheep into the hills, a most fortuitous circumstance given the industrial complex that was emerging in Flanders in this period. These developments need to be investigated both in the light of the reduction of the free zone and from the standpoint of their function in Norman colonization of the North, but in general terms they clearly amounted to nothing less than the successful transplanting of Norman culture to the lands between the Humber and the Forth.

In creating the peaceful conditions that made this possible the Normans surpassed their immediate predecessors and even the Romans, who had not been able to master the Northwest for long, but the triumphs of the second period of Norman colonization also have an ironic element. The Normans did not, in fact, surpass the pre-Viking Northumbrians. For a time they, too, had mastered both the East and part of the West, and their culture had flowered until their kingdom was laid in ruins by the Danes in Yorkshire and the Norwegians in the West. The North did not recover from the effects of these depredations until Henry's supporters breached the oat bread line, and here one encounters a curious phenomenon. Norman colonization of the North was to some extent a reverse migration, or perhaps one should say that it followed an old pattern. Recent research has found that Danes from eastern England played a major role in the Scandinavian colonization of Upper Normandy and that Norwegians from the Irish Sea littoral were dominant in the settlement of Lower Normandy.[4] The descendants of the latter supported Henry I against the Upper Norman establishment and tamed the West, and the significance of this is not limited solely to its irony. The repetition of this pattern suggests that the importance of the oat bread line (or at least the cultural divisions with which it corresponded) was not limited to the episode of medieval colonization studied in this book and that this factor must be considered in any attempt to explain the distribution of Scandinavian settlement in Britain and in Ireland.

Abbreviations and Selected Short References

ASC / *The Anglo-Saxon Chronicle: A Revised Translation.* Edited and translated by Dorothy Whitelock, David C. Douglas, and Susie I. Tucker. New Brunswick, 1961.

Boldon Book / "Text to the Boldon Book." Edited and translated by Gaillard T. Lapsley. In *The Victoria History of the County of Durham,* edited by William Page. Vol. 1. London, 1905.

Capitula de Miraculis / *Capitula de Miraculis et Translationibus.* In *Symeonis Monachi Opera Omnia,* edited by Thomas Arnold. 2 vols. Rolls Series, vol. 75. London, 1882–85.

Codex Diplomaticus / *Codex Diplomaticus Aevi Saxonici.* Edited by John M. Kemble. 6 vols. London, 1839–48.

EHD, 1 and 2 / *English Historical Documents.* Vol. 1, *c. 500–1042,* edited by Dorothy Whitelock. London, 1955. Vol. 2, *1042–1189,* edited by David C. Douglas and George W. Greenway. London, 1953.

ESC / *Early Scottish Charters prior to A.D. 1153.* Edited by Archibald C. Lawrie. Glasgow, 1905.

ESSH / *Early Sources of Scottish History, A.D. 500 to 1286.* Edited and translated by Alan O. Anderson. 2 vols. Edinburgh, 1922.

EYC / *Early Yorkshire Charters.* Edited by William Farrer and C. T. Clay. 12 vols. Yorkshire Archaeological Society Record Series, extra ser. Edinburgh, 1913–65. In progress.

Florence of Worcester / Florence of Worcester, *Florentii Wigorniensis Monachi Chronicon ex Chronicis.* Edited by Benjamin Thorpe. 2 vols. London, 1848–49.

Fordun / John of Fordun, *Chronica Gentis Scotorum.* Edited by William F. Skene. The Historians of Scotland, vols. 1 and 4. Edinburgh, 1871–72.

Gaimar / Geoffrey Gaimar, *L'Estorie des Engles*. Edited and translated by T. D. Hardy and C. T. Martin. 2 vols. Rolls Series, vol. 91. London, 1888.

Lancashire Pipe Rolls / *The Lancashire Pipe Rolls and Early Lancashire Charters*. Edited by William Farrer. Liverpool, 1902.

Orderic Vitalis / Orderic Vitalis, *The Ecclesiastical History of Orderic Vitalis*. Edited and translated by Marjorie Chibnall. Vols. 2–5. Oxford, 1969–75.

Pipe Rolls of 31 Henry I / *Magnum Rotulum Scaccarii, vel Magnum Rotulum Pipae de Anno Tricesimo-Primo Regni Henrici Primi*. Edited by Joseph Hunter. Record Commission. N.p., 1833.

Pipe Rolls / *The Great Rolls of the Pipe of the Reigns of Henry II, Richard, and John*. Multivolume. Pipe Roll Society. London, 1884–1955.

RRA-N, 1 and 2 / *Regesta Regum Anglo-Normannorum, 1066–1154*. Vol. 1, *Regesta Willelmi Conquestoris et Willelmi Rufi, 1066–1100*, edited by H. W. C. Davis. Oxford, 1913. Vol. 2, *Regesta Henrici Primi*, edited by Charles Johnson and H. A. Cronne. Oxford, 1956.

RRS, 1 and 2 / *Regesta Regum Scottorum*. Vol. 1, *The Acts of Malcolm IV, King of Scots, 1153–1165*, edited by G. W. S. Barrow. Edinburgh, 1960. Vol. 2, *The Acts of William I, King of Scots, 1165–1214*, edited by G. W. S. Barrow and W. W. Scott. Edinburgh, 1971.

Symeon of Durham, *HDE* / Symeon of Durham, *Historia Ecclesiae Dunhelmensis*. Vol. 1 of *Symeonis Monachi Opera Omnia*, edited by Thomas Arnold. Rolls Series, vol. 75. London, 1882.

Symeon of Durham, *HR* / Symeon of Durham, *Historia Regum*. Vol. 2 of *Symeonis Monachi Opera Omnia*, edited by Thomas Arnold. Rolls Series, vol. 75. London, 1885.

YI / *Yorkshire Inquisitions of the Reigns of Henry III and Edward I*. Edited by William Brown. 3 vols. Yorkshire Archaeological and Topographical Association, record ser., vols. 12, 23, and 31. Leeds, 1892–1902.

NOTES

Chapter 1

1. Although it contains a number of errors, the best account in many respects is still John Hodgson Hinde, *A History of Northumberland in Three Parts*, pt. 1, written from a regional point of view.

2. See D. P. Kirby, "Strathclyde and Cumbria," pp. 77–94; and P. A. Wilson, "On the Use of the Terms 'Strathclyde' and 'Cumbria,'" pp. 57–92.

3. F. M. Stenton, *Anglo-Saxon England*, pp. 33–34.

4. Dorothy Whitelock, "The Dealings of the Kings of England with Northumbria in the Tenth and Eleventh Centuries," p. 70.

5. T. W. Freeman, H. B. Rodgers, and R. H. Kinvig, *Lancashire, Cheshire, and the Isle of Man*, pp. 27–28.

6. Donald Nicholl, *Thurstan Archbishop of York (1114–1140)*, pp. 16–17.

7. For a delightful introduction to Northumbria before the Viking invasions, see Peter Hunter Blair, *Northumbria in the Days of Bede*. Consult Alfred P. Smyth, *Scandinavian Kings in the British Isles, 850–880*, for the history of the Viking kingdom of York and its relations with the Irish Sea Vikings; see also Wilson, "The Terms 'Strathclyde' and 'Cumbria,'" pp. 73–74.

8. See Marjorie O. Anderson, "Lothian and the Early Scottish Kings," pp. 98–110; G. W. S. Barrow, "The Anglo-Scottish Border," pp. 32–35; Alfred P. Smyth, *Scandinavian York and Dublin*, 1:107–13.

9. William of Malmesbury, *Willelmi Malmesbiriensis Monachi de Gestis Pontificum Anglorum Libri Quinque*, p. 209.

10. J. E. A. Jolliffe, "Northumbrian Institutions," p. 31; Stenton, *Anglo-Saxon England*, p. 91.

11. F. M. Stenton, "The Danes in England," pp. 233–38. For a general introduction to the debate over the size and impact of the Viking settlements see Gillian Fellows Jensen, "The Vikings in England."

12. Stenton, "The Danes in England," pp. 216–18.

13. William Farrer, "Introduction to the Yorkshire Domesday," p. 134.

14. Stenton, "The Danes in England," pp. 243–46; Bertie Wilkinson, "Northumbrian Separatism in 1065–1066," p. 504, n. 2.

15. Eric John, *Orbis Britanniae and Other Studies*, p. 46.

16. R. L. Graeme Ritchie, *The Normans in Scotland*, pp. 27, 29. Most of the Scandinavian settlement in Durham was restricted to Sadberge wapentake; see V. E. Watts, "Place Names," pp. 258–61.

17. See Jolliffe, "Northumbrian Institutions," pp. 1–42; William Rees, "Survivals of Ancient Celtic Custom in Medieval England," pp. 148–68; G. W. S. Barrow, "Northern English Society in the Early Middle Ages," pp. 1–28.

18. Stenton, *Anglo-Saxon England*, pp. 505–6.

19. H. H. E. Craster, *The Parish of Tynemouth*, p. 52.

20. Gaillard T. Lapsley, *The County Palatine of Durham*, pp. 25–27.

21. *EHD*, 2:517.

22. See *Anglo-Saxon Charters*, ed. P. H. Sawyer; John, *Orbis Britanniae*, p. 62.

23. Frank Barlow, *The English Church, 1000–1066*, p. 105. Sometime between 1020 and 1023, Bishop Edmund sought Cnut's approval for his election, but this was after the fact. The first bishop to be dependent (apparently) on royal approval was his successor Eadred, who is said to have purchased the bishopric in 1042 (Symeon of Durham, *HDE*, pp. 86, 91).

24. Consult the earl lists in *De Primo Saxonum Adventu*, pp. 382–83; in *De Obsessione Dunelmi*, pp. 215–18; and in Symeon of Durham, *HR*, pp. 197–98. The conventional attribution of the latter to Symeon will be followed only for purposes of clarity. The list in *De Primo Saxonum Adventu*, p. 383, suggests that Earl Eadulf Evil-child was appointed, but he is not mentioned in the other sources. See Stenton, *Anglo-Saxon England*, pp. 417–18.

25. *The Chronicle Attributed to John of Wallingford*, ed. Richard Vaughan, pp. 45, 54; Whitelock, "Dealings with Northumbria," pp. 71–77.

26. Whitelock, "Dealings with Northumbria," pp. 77–82; on Thored see pp. 78–79.

27. Ibid., p. 80; *ASC, s.a.* 975 ABCDE, p. 78; *s.a.* 1006 CDE, p. 87.

28. Ibid., *s.a.* 993 CDE, p. 83; Florence of Worcester, 1:150–51.

29. *Encomium Emmae Reginae*, ed. Alistair Cambell, pp. lvi–vii, 18–19; *ASC, s.a.* 1013 CDE, p. 92.

30. *ASC, s.a.* 1006 CDE, p. 87. The only English source to describe the invasion of 1006 is *De Obsessione Dunelmi*, pp. 215–16. It says that the invasion and siege took place in 969, a date which is corrupt, but this deficiency is made good by the *Annals of Ulster*, which describe a battle between the English and Scots in 1005(6). This date falls within the limits appropriate to the participants (*ESSH*, 1:525). Bernard Meehan has recently denied the existence of this encounter because it was not mentioned

by Symeon of Durham in the *HDE*, because its description in *De Obsessione Dunelmi* has certain details in common with Symeon's account of the siege of 1040, and because he believes that Uhtred was earl long before 1006 (*De Obsessione Dunelmi*, p. 216, says he became earl after this victory) ("The Siege of Durham, the Battle of Carham and the Cession of Lothian," pp. 15–17). Meehan prefers to interpret the story of the invasion of 1006 and the accounts of the battle of Carham in 1018 as misdated and misplaced reflections of a real battle between Uhtred and Malcolm in the West, an encounter only recorded by the fourteenth-century chronicler John of Fordun. These arguments are not convincing. See nn. 31, 32, 48, and 50.

31. Edmund Craster, "The Patrimony of St. Cuthbert," pp. 194–95; *De Obsessione Dunelmi*, pp. 215–16. The fact that this encounter is not mentioned in Symeon of Durham's *HDE*, a point raised by Meehan, "The Siege of Durham," p. 15, is hardly a serious objection. It assumes that Symeon provides a complete political narrative of events in Northumbria, but this is not the case. As his title says, his work is a history of the church of Durham, and he mentions little that is unconnected with this subject. Moreover, he had practically no information on the tenth and early eleventh centuries other than the names of the bishops. He covers the years from 900 to 1018 in twelve pages of the printed text and devotes six of these to the semimiraculous founding of Durham in the 990s. He then moves directly to the battle of Carham in 1018 without noticing any events for the first seventeen years of the eleventh century (*HDE*, pp. 72–84).

32. Presumably the statements that the heads of the Scots were put up on stakes in both 1006 and 1040 is the similarity that caused Meehan to think that the account in *De Obsessione Dunelmi*, pp. 215–16, was based on Symeon's account of the later siege in the *HDE*, pp. 90–91 ("The Siege of Durham," p. 15). The problem of when Uhtred became earl of Northumbria is somewhat more serious. Meehan, presumably following Whitelock, notes that Symeon calls Uhtred "earl" in his account of the founding of Durham in 995 (ibid., p. 16; Whitelock, "Dealings with Northumbria," p. 82; Symeon of Durham, *HDE*, p. 82). It is unclear, however, how much weight should be placed on this statement. Symeon gives no sign that he knew the names of the Northumbrian earls before Siward, and this isolated reference to Uhtred, particularly when it occurs in connection with the founding of Durham, is hardly strong evidence that he was earl before 1006. Furthermore, he does not begin to witness charters until 1009 (Whitelock, "Dealings with Northumbria," p. 82, n. 4). On the other hand, it would not be unlikely that Uhtred, as heir to his father, had occupied a subordinate position during his father's later years. There certainly were subordinate earls in the North in this period (ibid., p. 78; *ASC*; *s.a.* 1006 CDE, p. 87).

33. *De Obsessione Dunelmi*, pp. 216–17.

34. *De Obsessione Dunelmi*, pp. 217–18. It is, of course, possible that Uhtred's battle in Cumbria lies behind this statement. See Fordun, p. 182.

35. *ASC*, *s.a.* 1014 CDE, p. 93; *s.a.* 1015 CDE, p. 94; *s.a.* 1016 CDE, pp. 94–95; *De Obsessione Dunelmi*, p. 218. See note 41 for a discussion of the date of this murder.

36. *De Obsessione Dunelmi*, pp. 216, 218–19. With some differences of detail, this story is also found in *De Primo Saxonum Adventu*, p. 383; and in Symeon of Durham, *HR*, pp. 197–98.

37. Whitelock, "Dealings with Northumbria," p. 82. Meehan dates it 1073–76 in "The Siege of Durham," pp. 18–19.

38. Symeon of Durham, *HR*, p. 147; *De Obsessione Dunelmi*, pp. 216–17; *EHD*, 1:433.

39. Symeon of Durham, *HDE*, p. 83; *Historia de Sancto Cuthberto*, pp. 213–14; H. H. E. Craster, "The Red Book of Durham," p. 526.

40. *De Obsessione Dunelmi*, p. 218.

41. *De Primo Saxonum Adventu*, p. 383. The account in Symeon of Durham, *HR*, p. 197, says it was done *permittente Cnut*, and Florence of Worcester, 1:172, combines both accounts. In a recent essay, Archibald A. M. Duncan has tried to resolve the conflict in the sources between the date of the battle of Carham (1018) and the statement found in the *HR* (but nowhere else) that Uhtred led the Northumbrians in this encounter. He endeavored to do this by arguing that the apparent statement in the *ASC*, *s.a.* 1016 CDE, pp. 94–95, that Uhtred was killed as he went to submit to Cnut in 1016 was "parenthetic" and actually referred to an event that took place in 1018 or somewhat later ("The Battle of Carham, 1018," pp. 21–25). Needless to say, this is not the natural reading of this passage, and Duncan's only support for his ingenious suggestion, other than his demonstration that the chronicler did on occasion make such anticipatory references, is his argument that in 1016 the killing of Uhtred was not in Cnut's best interest because he needed to win the Northumbrians' support (ibid., pp. 23–24). This is perhaps true, but such an observation ignores the enmity that had already arisen during the ten years of Uhtred's rule over the Danes of York. Cnut's supporters in York wanted Uhtred dead in 1016, and Cnut could only agree.

42. *De Obsessione Dunelmi*, p. 218.

43. Whitelock, "Dealings with Northumbria," pp. 82–83.

44. Ibid.; Stenton, *Anglo-Saxon England*, p. 418. Hinde, on the other hand, thought that the Northumbrians went into revolt in 1016, *A History of Northumberland*, pp. 162–64.

45. *De Obsessione Dunelmi*, pp. 218–19. Meehan would date the cession somewhat earlier ("The Siege of Durham," pp. 18–19). Cf. Anderson, "Lothian," pp. 104, 111.

46. *De Primo Saxonum Adventu*, p. 382. See Anderson, "Lothian," pp.

104–10, on this source and its relationship with the later versions found in Roger of Wendover and John of Wallingford.

47. Symeon of Durham, *HDE*, p. 84; *HR*, pp. 155–56. *Annales Lindisfarnenses et Dunelmenses*, ed. Georgius H. Pertz, *s.a.* 1018, p. 507.

48. Stenton moved the battle back to 1016 on the grounds that names are better remembered than dates, and he denied that it had any role in the Scottish acquisition of Lothian (*Anglo-Saxon England*, p. 418). Duncan successfully defended the traditional date (1018) and argued that Uhtred gave Lothian to the Scots after he was defeated at Carham and that Cnut had him killed after this encounter rather than in 1016 ("The Battle of Carham," pp. 22–24, 27–28). See note 41. Barrow, who tried to deal with the Scottish acquisition of Lothian in terms of a broader range of evidence than that afforded by these narrative sources, felt that the cession of 973 probably recognized a fait accompli and that Carham had no importance in determining the border ("The Border," pp. 31–34). Meehan denied that the battle of Carham ever took place ("The Siege of Durham," pp. 12–13, 16); his argument is not convincing, see Duncan, "The Battle of Carham," pp. 20–21. Meehan also felt that Eadulf Cudel's cession was a fiction that rested on a confusion of Eadulf Cudel with Eadulf Evil-child, who may have been earl in 973, the supposed date of the first cession ("The Siege of Durham," p. 17).

49. Anderson, "Lothian," pp. 110–11. The *HR* is a composite work. For this period it is based on the chronicle of Florence of Worcester to which a northern chronicler, probably in the 1160s, added notices of events in the North. Most of these additions are of great value. See Peter Hunter Blair, "Some Observations on the 'Historia Regum' Attributed to Symeon of Durham," pp. 77–78; and Derek Baker, "Scissors and Paste," pp. 83–124. The chronicler had, however, few detailed, local materials covering the period before Edward the Confessor's reign (in this respect the *HR* resembles Symeon's *HDE*), and he mentions no earl before Siward in his additions except for his assertion that Uhtred was present at Carham (*HR*, pp. 155–56). Standing by itself, this statement is highly suspect. The *Anglo-Saxon Chronicle* puts Uhtred's death under 1016 (see note 41), and the compiler of the *HR* himself copied verbatim into his manuscript Florence's account of Uhtred's death in 1016 (*HR*, p. 148). The compiler of the *HR* clearly had no knowledge of the earlier earls of Northumbria at this stage of his work, and his statement that Uhtred was at Carham should carry no weight. Eventually he did obtain a short account of the earls of Northumbria which he inserted under the year 1072. This list, however, contained no dates for the earls that would have allowed him to correct his error (*HR*, pp. 197–99). This list was also used by Roger of Hoveden (Anderson, "Lothian," p. 104).

50. For Symeon's knowledge of the earls of Northumbria see note

32. Carham is not the only example of Symeon failing to provide the Northumbrians with secular leadership. In his account of Duncan's defeat at Durham in 1040, he does not disclose who defeated and drove away the Scots (*HDE*, pp. 90–91). Indeed, it is a small wonder that he recorded Carham at all. Symeon does not mention Malcolm III's invasion of 1061, William's harrying of Durham in 1070, and Malcolm's invasions of 1070, 1079, and 1091, presumably because Cuthbert failed to act on these occasions.

51. *De Obsessione Dunelmi*, p. 219.

52. *Codex Diplomaticus*, 4:nos. 741–80 and 781, also see no. 730. A "Siward minister" witnesses in company with Carl in 1032 and by himself in 1033 and 1035 (ibid., no. 746; 6:nos. 1318, 1332).

53. Ibid., 4:no. 742, is witnessed by an *Eadredus dux*, but this charter is spurious (*Anglo-Saxon Charters*, ed. Sawyer, no. 1221).

54. *Codex Diplomaticus*, 4:nos. 687, 719; 6:nos. 1306, 1308–10.

55. Anderson, "Lothian," p. 111.

56. Symeon of Durham, *HDE*, p. 85.

57. Ibid., pp. 85–86; Barlow, *The English Church*, p. 230.

58. Symeon of Durham, *HDE*, p. 86.

59. *De Obsessione Dunelmi*, p. 219.

60. *ASC*, *s.a.* 1031 DEF, p. 101. This account links the Scottish expedition with Cnut's journey to Rome, but the latter took place in 1027 (ibid., p. 101, n. 5). This does not necessarily mean that the Scottish expedition is misdated.

61. *Historia de Sancto Cuthberto*, p. 213.

62. Symeon of Durham, *HDE*, pp. 90–91.

63. *ESSH*, 1:583. The people who were the object of this raid were actually called *Brittones* rather than Galwegians (Symeon of Durham, *HR*, p. 198).

64. *ASC*, *s.a.* 1041 CD, p. 106; Symeon of Durham, *HDE*, p. 91; *HR*, p. 198.

65. Symeon of Durham, *HR*, pp. 197–98.

66. *Annales Dunelmenses*, *s.a.* 1043, p. 508.

Chapter 2

1. Frank Barlow, *Edward the Confessor*, p. 89.

2. That Siward maintained a body of housecarls is shown by the fact that some of them were killed in his battle with Macbeth (*ASC*, *s.a.* 1054 D, p. 129).

3. *ESSH*, 1:595, n. 2; Edward A. Freeman, *The History of the Norman Conquest of England*, 2:376–77.

4. This figure is conjectural. In 1065, the northern rebels killed over two hundred of Tostig's retainers. If this figure can be taken seriously,

it suggests that Tostig had more than two hundred retainers, and Siward is unlikely to have had a smaller body of men (Florence of Worcester, 1:223).

5. *De Obsessione Dunelmi*, p. 219.

6. See the descent of the lands that Bishop Aldhun gave to Earl Uhtred with his daughter in ibid., pp. 215–17, 219–20.

7. There is not enough evidence to tell how the earldom descended from one member of the house of Bamburgh to another prior to the eleventh century. The succession after 1000 is highly suggestive, however. Earl Waltheof was followed by his son Uhtred, and Uhtred was succeeded, not by his son Ealdred, but by his brother Eadulf Cudel. After the latter died, the earldom passed in turn to two of Uhtred's sons, Ealdred and Eadulf. His third son, Cospatric, did not become earl, but the chronicler who records this fact clearly assumed that it would have been normal for Cospatric to have been earl in his turn. On the basis of this evidence it can be concluded that these two generations did not follow the rule of primogeniture (ibid., passim; *De Primo Saxonum Adventu*, pp. 382–83; Symeon of Durham, *HR*, pp. 197–98).

8. *De Obsessione Dunelmi*, pp. 219–20. The northern earl lists do not mention Siward's elder son, Osbeorn, and this presumably means that he had a different mother than Waltheof, who is frequently mentioned.

9. This is shown by the fact that Waltheof continued the blood feud when he became earl, but from the side of the house of Bamburgh. He had some of his henchmen kill a number of the sons and grandsons of Carl (ibid., p. 219).

10. Symeon of Durham, *HDE*, pp. 79–80.

11. See ibid., pp. 56ff.

12. *De Obsessione Dunelmi*, pp. 219–20.

13. Symeon of Durham, *HDE*, p. 91; *HR*, p. 162. The *Annales Lindisfarnenses et Dunelmenses*, ed. Georgius H. Pertz, *s.a.* 1043, p. 508, says that this visit took place in 1043.

14. Symeon of Durham, *HDE*, p. 91; *HR*, p. 162.

15. Symeon of Durham, *HDE*, p. 91; *HR*, p. 162.

16. Symeon of Durham, *HDE*, p. 86; H. H. E. Craster, "The Red Book of Durham," p. 528. The absolute chronology of the death of Edmund, the appointment of Eadred, and the succession of Æthelric varies somewhat in the sources. Both Symeon's *HDE*, p. 91, and the *HR*, p. 162 (but see pp. 162–63) seem to agree that Edmund died in 1042 and that Eadred was then bishop for ten months. The major discrepancy concerns the date when Æthelric became bishop. The *HDE*, p. 91, says this occurred in 1042, but the *HR*, pp. 162–63, says 1043. The latter may be following the *Annales Dunelmenses*, *s.a.* 1043, p. 508, which states that all these events took place in 1043 along with Siward's invasion of Northumbria. The *ASC*, *s.a.* 1041 D, p. 106, on the other hand, indicates that

Æthelric became bishop in 1041. This entry is, however, unclear and is only in the D version of the chronicle (ibid., p. 106, n. 6). Furthermore, all the Durham sources agree that Æthelric only became bishop after Hardacnut's death in June of 1042.

17. Symeon of Durham, *HDE*, p. 91.

18. D. P. Kirby, "Strathclyde and Cumbria," p. 86; P. A. Wilson, "On the Use of the Terms 'Strathclyde' and 'Cumbria,'" pp. 71–74; G. W. S. Barrow, "The Anglo-Scottish Border," p. 24.

19. See Wilson, "The Terms 'Strathclyde' and 'Cumbria,'" pp. 71–74; Kirby, "Strathclyde and Cumbria," p. 88.

20. F. M. Stenton, *Anglo-Saxon England*, pp. 331–32; Alfred P. Smyth, *Scandinavian York and Dublin*, pp. 75–86; cf. David M. Wilson, "Scandinavian Settlement in the North and West of the British Isles," pp. 99–107.

21. Wilson, "The Terms 'Strathclyde' and 'Cumbria,'" pp. 90–91; Smyth, *York and Dublin*, pp. 79–86.

22. F. T. Wainwright, "Æthelflæd Lady of the Mercians," p. 63; Stenton, *Anglo-Saxon England*, pp. 332–33; Smyth, *York and Dublin*, pp. 94, 107–9. Smyth's reconstruction of Ragnall's movements in 1018 depends upon his assumption that the sacking of *Dunbline* (Dunblane?) occurred in 918 rather than in 912, the year it appears under in Symeon of Durham, *HR*, p. 93. It seems more likely that the two invasions were separate incidents and that in 918, Ragnall stormed up the Tyne Gap, rather than the Midland Valley of Scotland, and defeated the Northumbrians and Scots who were awaiting him at Corbridge. For discussions of the sources for these events see Smyth, *York and Dublin*, pp. 93–103; and F. T. Wainwright, *Scandinavian England*, pp. 163–79.

23. Stenton, *Anglo-Saxon England*, pp. 332–33; Wainwright, "Æthelflæd," pp. 63–66; *ASC, s.a.* 919 (922) A, p. 67; *s.a.* 920 (923) A, pp. 67–68; Edmund Craster, "The Patrimony of St. Cuthbert," pp. 186–90; *Historia de Sancto Cuthberto*, p. 210. A similar attempt to control the movement of the Norse through the southern Pennines seems to have been made in Derbyshire; see P. H. Sawyer, "The Charters of Burton Abbey and the Unification of England," pp. 30–34.

24. *ASC, s.a.* 927 (926) D, pp. 68–69, n. 1.

25. *EHD*, 1:506.

26. *ASC, s.a.* 944 ABCD, p. 71; *s.a.* 945 ABCD, p. 72.

27. Barrow, "The Border," p. 24; A. M. Armstrong et al., *The Place-Names of Cumberland*, pt. 3, p. xxvi. The reconstruction of Cumbrian history after 945 found in Kirby, "Strathclyde and Cumbria," pp. 84–92, is based mainly on Fordun and cannot be trusted.

28. Stenton, *Anglo-Saxon England*, pp. 361–63.

29. *ASC, s.a.* 966 DEF, p. 76; F. M. Stenton, "Pre-Conquest West-

morland," pp. 218–19, argued that this raid was "an act of private violence," but this is not likely given the general nature of the North's western frontier.

30. Alan O. Anderson, "Anglo-Scottish Relations from Constantine II to William," pp. 4–5.

31. The grant is recorded in *De Primo Saxonum Adventu*, p. 382. For the later, inflated versions of this story see Marjorie O. Anderson, "Lothian and the Early Scottish Kings," pp. 106–10. Archibald A. M. Duncan assumes that the relationship between Lothian and Cumbria functioned in the opposite way and that the Scottish acquisition of Lothian between ca. 960 and 1018 "virtually ended" the independence of the Cumbrians (*Scotland*, p. 98).

32. *ASC, s.a.* 973 (972) DE, p. 77; Armstrong, *Place-Names of Cumberland*, p. xxvi.

33. Anderson, "Anglo-Scottish Relations," pp. 4–5.

34. *ASC, s.a.* 1000 CDE, p. 85; *EHD*, 1:541–42. The idea that the English had lost control of Lancashire after Athelstan's death is supported by the fact that the archbishops of York did not maintain their possession of Amounderness.

35. Anderson, "Anglo-Scottish Relations," p. 5; Duncan, *Scotland*, pp. 94–95.

36. Anderson, "Anglo-Scottish Relations," pp. 2–4; 2, n. 2. For Constantine's attempts to defend the Northumbrians, see Wainwright, *Scandinavian England*, pp. 163–79, and Smyth, *York and Dublin*, pp. 93–113. Duncan has suggested that the Northumbrian earls sought Scottish protection during this period (*Scotland*, p. 94). It is sometimes said that Constantine's successor Malcolm I invaded the North about 950 (ibid.). The account of this incident is garbled, however (it suggests that Constantine was behind the invasion); and Malcolm was certainly allied with the English in 952 (*Chronicle of the Kings of Scotland*, in *ESSH*, 1:452; *Annals of Ulster*, in *ESSH, s.a.* 952, 1:451).

37. Anderson, "Anglo-Scottish Relations," pp. 2–5. Anderson, however, emphasizes (p. 5) that the Scots accepted a subordinate position in the alliance with the Anglo-Saxon kings after 945 in order to keep Cumbria. This suggestion seems very unlikely since there is no good evidence that they actually controlled Cumbria.

38. *De Obsessione Dunelmi*, pp. 215–16.

39. Symeon of Durham, *HDE*, p. 84; *HR*, pp. 155–56; Barrow, "The Border," pp. 24–25; cf. Duncan, *Scotland*, p. 98. The suggestion that Malcolm made his brother the ruler of Cumbria depends upon an ambiguous notice in an Irish chronicle. The *Tigernach Annals*, in *ESSH*, 1:578, record that in 1034, "Suibne, Kenneth's son, king of the Galwegians died." Suibne, son of Kenneth, has not been connected with the family of Mal-

colm, son of Kenneth, or even of Boite, son of Kenneth, because he is called the king of the Galwegians. No other source mentions him, and it seems only a remote possibility that a brother or cousin of Malcolm II would be ruler of this distant area. Such a view would be justified except that it probably rests upon an anachronism. In the early twelfth century, the term "Galwegians" covered all the people living in Clydesdale and the lands to the west and south (Wilson, "The Terms 'Strathclyde' and 'Cumbria,'" pp. 90–91). If this is the usage of the *Tigernach Annals*, then Suibne was the ruler of the Cumbrians. It might be objected, of course, that this is a very early example of the use of the term "Galwegians" to cover Cumbrians, but this can be answered with the suggestion that the latter would look like Galwegians (the *Gall-gael*) to the Irish earlier than to the Scots given the initial coastal settlement of the Irish Sea Vikings. Furthermore, there is really no good evidence for the separate existence of a Galwegian kingdom. It is then likely that Suibne ruled the Cumbrians, and there is no good reason for not identifying him with the Scottish royal house.

40. Symeon of Durham, *HDE*, pp. 90–91; *HR*, p. 198. The sequence of events is conjectural. Anderson, "Anglo-Scottish Relations," p. 9, says that Eadulf attacked Cumbria first and that Duncan raided in retaliation. This is not impossible, but it is unlikely. It is difficult to imagine any motive for Eadulf's raid other than revenge, given the poverty of Cumbria. Furthermore, it is very improbable that Eadulf would engage in provocative actions while he was already in revolt against the English king.

41. Cnut's Scottish expedition is mentioned in the *ASC*, s.a. 1031 DEF, p. 101, where it is misdated and described in the vaguest terms. There is no mention of any fighting, and the entry is scant proof for anything more elaborate than a trip north by Cnut through which he obtained a nominal Scottish submission. Furthermore, Malcolm broke this agreement quickly (ibid.). There is no record that Cnut took any action in response, which is not surprising given the situation in Northumbria. There is also a possibility that the Northumbrian earls had allied with Malcolm. This hypothesis would greatly simplify the political history of the North during this period, but the only evidence that points in this direction is the marriage of Malcolm's grandson Maldred to a daughter of Earl Uhtred, supposedly before 1018 (*De Obsessione Dunelmi*, p. 216).

42. *Prose and Verse Chronicles Inserted in the Chronicle of Melrose*, in *ESSH*, s.a. 1003 and 1034, pp. 576–77.

43. *Annals of Ulster*, s.a. 1032 and 1033, p. 571. It is equally possible that Macbeth killed Gillacomgain since Macbeth's father had been killed by Gillacomgain and the latter's brother (*Tigernach Annals*, s.a. 1020, p. 551). This alternative would not mean, however, that the killing was not done in Malcolm's interest. Macbeth's marriage to Gillacomgain's widow, however, probably means that he had no part in the killing of her husband.

44. *Prose and Verse Chronicles*, s.a. 1003, p. 576; *Tigernach Annals*, s.a. 1034, p. 578; see n. 39.

45. *Chronicle of the Kings of Scotland*, s.a. 1040, p. 581.

46. See *ESSH*, 1:576, n. 7; and Anderson, "Anglo-Scottish Relations," p. 9, for a discussion of these points. Fordun says that Duncan had married a kinswoman of Siward (1:187). Although this statement is commonly accepted, it has no contemporary support and may be untrue.

47. R. L. Graeme Ritchie, *The Normans in Scotland*, p. 4, n. 1; Duncan, *Scotland*, p. 115, n. 27.

48. The three main Northumbrian sources all say that Uhtred gave his daughter by his third wife, Ethelred's daughter, to Maldred: *De Obsessione Dunelmi*, p. 216; *De Primo Saxonum Adventu*, p. 383; Symeon of Durham, *HR*, p. 194.

49. *The Chronicle of Melrose from the Cottonian Manuscript, Faustina B. ix in the British Museum*, ed. Alan O. Anderson and Marjorie O. Anderson, s.a. 1050, p. 23.

50. Ritchie, *Normans in Scotland*, p. 4, n. 1.

51. Fordun, 1:187; Florence of Worcester, 1:212.

52. See *Anglo-Saxon Writs*, ed. F. E. Harmer, pp. 419–24, 531–36, for the text, notes, and bibliography. See also H. W. C. Davis, "Cumberland before the Norman Conquest," pp. 61–65. For the alternative (Scottish) interpretation consult *ESSH*, 2:37; and John C. Hodgson, *The Parish of Edlingham*, pp. 24–26.

53. *Anglo-Saxon Writs*, ed. Harmer, pp. 423–24.

54. Ibid.; Davis, "Cumberland," pp. 62–63.

55. *Anglo-Saxon Writs*, ed. Harmer, pp. 423–24.

56. Cf. *ESSH*, 2:37; Hodgson, *The Parish of Edlingham*, pp. 24–26.

57. *Anglo-Saxon Writs*, ed. Harmer, pp. 423–24, 559.

58. Hugh the Chantor, *The History of the Church of York, 1066–1127*, p. 32. As early as King David's Cumbrian inquisition, the bishopric of Glasgow is equated with the kingdom of the Cumbrians (Wilson, "The Terms 'Strathclyde' and 'Cumbria,'" p. 85); this identification apparently preceded the later "inflated" territorial claims of the bishops of Glasgow (ibid., p. 83) and is probably the reason Hugh calls these men bishops of Glasgow. In a sense he is guilty of an anachronism. Although he regards this church as the predecessor of the revived bishopric of David's time, its ultimate fate fits a church centered in Cumberland much better than one located at Glasgow. It is not likely that Macbeth would have allowed an ordination by York, and Hugh says that after these two bishops, the church was destroyed (that is, rendered vacant) by war. This war should be identified with Malcolm's reconquest of Cumberland in 1061 or later in the decade (Hugh the Chantor, p. 32).

59. *Anglo-Saxon Writs*, ed. Harmer, p. 562. The identification of this

Cospatric with Uhtred's youngest son is generally accepted by English historians. It is ultimately based on the arguments of Davis, "Cumberland," pp. 63–65. Some Scottish and northern historians prefer to identify him with Cospatric son of Maldred: *ESSH*, 2:37; Hodgson, *The Parish of Edlingham*, pp. 25–27; Duncan, *Scotland*, pp. 98–99. Such an identification necessitates dating the charter after 1055, but this is unlikely. See note 60.

60. Siward died in 1055, but the passage in which he is mentioned is defective. One cannot tell on its basis whether he was alive when the grant was made; see *Anglo-Saxon Writs*, ed. Harmer, p. 534. It might be observed, however, that it is hard to imagine what good a dead earl's protection would have been to Thorfinn.

61. *Annales Dunelmenses*, *s.a.* 1046, p. 508; *Tigernach Annals*, *s.a.* [1045], p. 583 and n. 6, n. 7.

62. The use of fleets on invasions of Scotland was common. Athelstan had one in 934, as did Siward in 1054, and William in 1072 (*ASC*, *s.a.* 934 ABCDEF, p. 69; *s.a.* 1054 D, p. 129; *s.a.* 1072 DE, p. 154). When William Rufus invaded Scotland in 1091, his fleet was wrecked in a storm; probably as a result, his army suffered from a lack of provisions (Florence of Worcester, 2:28).

63. *Annales Dunelmenses*, *s.a.* 1046, p. 508.

64. Gaimar, ll. 5045–46. Dorothy Whitelock, "The Dealings of the Kings of England with Northumbria in the Tenth and Eleventh Centuries," p. 86, n. 4, says that Gaimar used a lost northern source at this point.

65. Florence of Worcester, 1:210.

66. Gaimar, ll. 5043–46. Gaimar is the best source for Siward's trip to Scotland in 1053, and he does not mention any fighting. On the other hand, Henry of Huntingdon describes two military expeditions. The first was supposedly led by Siward's son Osbeorn, who was killed. The second was Siward's successful expedition (*Henrici Archidiaconti Huntendunensis Historia Anglorum*, p. 194).

67. *ASC*, *s.a.* 1054 CD, p. 129; *Annals of Ulster*, p. 593, and n. 2.

68. *ASC*, *s.a.* 1054 CD, p. 129; Florence of Worcester, 1:212.

69. See Anderson, "Anglo-Scottish Relations," p. 10, where Malcolm is portrayed as Edward's vassal.

70. See Ritchie, *Normans in Scotland*, pp. 4, 7.

71. *Life of Waltheof*, in *ESSH*, 1:597, note.

72. Ibid., p. 594, note. This account contains bald errors. The Scottish king whom Siward aids is named Donald. He is a combination of Duncan, Malcolm, and the latter's brother Donald, all in one. Furthermore, this account asserts that the Northumbrian rebels killed Siward's son Osbeorn.

73. *ASC*, *s.a.* 1054 CD, p. 129; *Annals of Ulster*, *s.a.* 1054, p. 593.

Chapter 3

1. F. W. Maitland, "Northumbrian Tenures," pp. 625–33; J. E. A. Jolliffe, "Northumbrian Institutions," pp. 1–42; F. M. Stenton, "Types of Manorial Structure in the Northern Danelaw," pp. 3–93; Stenton, "The Danes in England," pp. 203–46; see Stenton, *Preparatory to Anglo-Saxon England*, pp. vii–xiv, for a bibliography of his works; G. W. S. Barrow, "Northern English Society in the Early Middle Ages," pp. 1–28; William Rees, "Survivals of Ancient Celtic Custom in Medieval England," pp. 148–68. See also G. W. S. Barrow, *The Kingdom of the Scots*, pp. 7–68. This book is principally a collection of his previously published articles, but its first chapter ("Pre-feudal Scotland: Shires and Thanes") is a new discussion of many of the questions I am investigating here.

2. For the most blatant examples of this approach, see Rees, "Ancient Celtic Custom," pp. 148–68; and Glanville R. J. Jones, "Basic Patterns of Settlement Distribution in Northern England," pp. 192–200.

3. F. W. Maitland, *Domesday Book and Beyond*, pp. 308–9; Maitland, "Northumbrian Tenures," p. 632.

4. Stenton, "The Northern Danelaw," p. 4.

5. Jolliffe, "Northumbrian Institutions," p. 4.

6. See ibid., pp. 31, 42.

7. Ibid., pp. 2, 4–14, 31–32, 36–37.

8. Ibid., pp. 5, 6–8, 10–11, 14, 15–25.

9. For a discussion of the legal position of the northern bonder see ibid., pp. 38–40, and Barrow, "Northern English Society," pp. 12–13.

10. Jolliffe, "Northumbrian Institutions," pp. 2, 40–42.

11. Ibid., pp. 24–29.

12. Barrow, "Northern English Society," p. 17.

13. R. B. Smith, *Blackburnshire*.

14. Jolliffe, "Northumbrian Institutions," pp. 20, 40–42.

15. Rees, "Ancient Celtic Custom," pp. 153–68; Barrow, "Northern English Society," pp. 9–17.

16. Jolliffe, "Northumbrian Institutions," pp. 40–41; Glanville R. J. Jones, "The Tribal System in Wales," pp. 111–32; Jones, "Settlement Distribution in Northern England," pp. 194–96.

17. For a discussion, see S. Applebaum, "Roman Britain," pp. 264–65. Barrow, *The Kingdom of the Scots*, p. 13.

18. William F. Skene, *Celtic Scotland*, 3:281. See his comment on thanage.

19. Jolliffe, "Northumbrian Institutions," pp. 30–31; Barrow, "Northern English Society," p. 18; Barrow, "Rural Settlement in Central and Eastern Scotland," pp. 124–25; Barrow, *The Kingdom of the Scots*, pp. 28–36. The services of the peasants at Fishwick and at Kelso were recorded in the late thirteenth century; see *The Priory of Coldingham*, ed.

James Raine, p. lxxxvii; *Liber S. Marie de Calchou, 1113–1567*, ed. Cosmo Innes, 2:461. The principal difference between these services and those found south of the Tweed is the apparent absence of grain renders and cornage at Fishwick and Kelso.

20. *RRS*, 1:46; Barrow, "Northern English Society," p. 18. See also Barrow, *The Kingdom of the Scots*, pp. 37–53, for an extended discussion of these points.

21. Barrow, "Northern English Society," pp. 18–22.

22. Ibid., p. 22.

23. Ibid., pp. 18, 20, 22–23; Barrow, *The Kingdom of the Scots*, pp. 11, 27–28, 58–64.

24. This is a curious subject because it is very hard to see why Barrow chose the cain of southwestern Scotland as representative of cain in general. In this area it was predominantly a livestock render (Barrow, "Northern English Society," pp. 18–19), but in eastern Scotland it was not. Throughout the oldest part of the kingdom the cain generally consisted of oats, malt, and cheese in addition to hides and tallow. See *RRS*, 1:57, 118, 195, 243, 245. Barrow may have been encouraged to generalize the cain of the Southwest by his identification of certain livestock renders that the king received in Lothian and the Merse with cain, but this identification is utterly conjectural. These renders are never connected with cain in the charters (*RRS*, 2:52). Archibald A. M. Duncan, *Scotland*, pp. 152–54, denies that cain and coneveth were separate renders.

25. See Jolliffe, "Northumbrian Institutions," pp. 10–11.

26. See *RRS*, 2:52; Skene, *Celtic Scotland*, 3:228–29.

27. Both Jolliffe, "Northumbrian Institutions," p. 11, and Barrow, "Northern English Society," p. 15, speak as if waiting were a common obligation in Northumbria, but their evidence for its existence is very limited. It is mentioned only four times in Boldon Book (*Boldon Book*, p. 327).

28. Rees, "Ancient Celtic Custom," pp. 157–58, 166 map.

29. For a discussion of this subject see Stenton, "The Danes in England," pp. 233–36. Cf. Glanville R. J. Jones, "Early Territorial Organization in Northern England and Its Bearing on the Scandinavian Settlement," pp. 67–70. For a recent appraisal of these effects, consult Gillian Fellows Jensen, "The Vikings in England."

30. *Documents Illustrative of the Social and Economic History of the Danelaw from Various Collections*, ed. F. M. Stenton, pp. cix–cx.

31. Stenton, "The Danes in England," pp. 217–18, 233.

32. Jolliffe, "Northumbrian Institutions," p. 42.

33. J. E. A. Jolliffe, "The Era of the Folk in English History," pp. 18–19.

34. In ibid., pp. 19–26, he argued that the Danes were not respon-

sible for the assessment of Yorkshire in ploughlands; this theory, which may well be correct, has attracted little notice.

35. P. H. Sawyer, "The Density of the Danish Settlement in England," pp. 1–17. See Jones, "Scandinavian Settlement," pp. 70–71; H. P. R. Finberg, "Anglo-Saxon England to 1042," p. 469; Gwyn Jones, *A History of the Vikings*, p. 218, n. See Jensen, "The Vikings in England," pp. 200–201, for a discussion of Sawyer's modifications of his theories on the formation of place names in response to more recent research.

36. *The Kalendar of Abbot Samson of Bury St. Edwards and Related Documents*, ed. R. H. C. Davis, pp. xl, xxx–xxxvii, xliv–xlvii.

37. Ibid., p. xlvi.

38. See Kenneth Cameron, "Scandinavian Settlement in the Territory of the Five Boroughs," pp. 147–64; Jensen, "The Vikings in England," pp. 197–201; Barrow, *The Kingdom of the Scots*, pp. 22–28, 56–64.

39. Jones, "Scandinavian Settlement," pp. 77–79; Jones, "Settlement Distribution in Northern England," pp. 196–200.

40. See Applebaum, "Roman Britain," pp. 48–55, 264–65.

41. Jones, "Scandinavian Settlement," pp. 76–84. Cf. Cameron, "Scandinavian Settlement," pp. 162–63; and Jensen, "The Vikings in England," p. 199.

42. Stenton, "The Danes in England," p. 210, n. 2.

43. Lusien Musset, *Les Invasions*, pp. 253–60.

44. *EYC*, 2:viii.

45. *Records of the Templars in England in the Twelfth Century*, ed. Beatrice E. Lee, pp. 117–18, 123–24, 126.

46. *YI*, 1:nos. LIV, LVI, CXXXI.

47. See Terence A. M. Bishop, "The Distribution of Manorial Demesne in the Vale of York," pp. 386–406.

48. Jolliffe, "Northumbrian Institutions," p. 31.

49. *YI*, 1:4, and no. LIV.

50. *The Survey of the County of York Taken by John de Kirkby, Commonly Called Kirkby's Inquest*, ed. Robert H. Skaife, pp. 411, 435–37.

51. Jolliffe, "Northumbrian Institutions," p. 31, n. 4; *Calendar of Inquisitions Post Mortem and Other Analogous Documents Preserved in the Public Record Office*, 3:472–73; *YI*, 3:no. LXXXV.

52. *EYC*, 3:no. 1276.

53. See Chapters 4 and 6.

54. *YI*, 1:no. CXXXI.

55. Ibid., no. CII.

56. Ibid., no. XLIII.

57. *EYC*, 2:nos. 883, 755, 712, 847.

58. Jolliffe, "Northumbrian Institutions," pp. 21–22, 25.

59. *YI*, 1:nos. LVI, LXXV; *EYC*, 2:no. 980.

60. See Chapter 6.

61. *Kirkby's Inquest*, p. 411; *Domesday Book*, ed. Henry Ellis, 1:fol. 303b.

62. *YI*, 1:no. XLV; *Domesday*, 1:fol. 315.

63. *Domesday*, 1:fol. 299; *YI*, 1:no. XLIII.

64. *EYC*, 2:no. 883; *Domesday*, 1:fol. 305.

65. *Kirkby's Inquest*, pp. 435–37; *Domesday*, 1:fol. 303b.

66. *Inquisitions Post Mortem*, 3:472–73; *Domesday*, 1:fols. 299b–300, 301b; *YI*, 3:no. LXXXV.

67. *Domesday*, 1:fol. 298. Barrow tries to forestall this objection by equating sokemen and drengs (*The Kingdom of the Scots*, pp. 14–15, 27); but this is incorrect.

68. *Domesday*, 1:fols. 269b–270.

69. Ibid., fols. 269b, 298b.

70. Ibid., fols. 300–301b. The figure of 328 manors was reached by counting the manors listed in the text. Sokeland was excluded from the count as was material from the summary which Farrer added to the text.

71. Ibid., fol. 269b.

72. Ibid., fols. 300–301b. The values are given for 149 of the 328 manors. In 132 cases (88.6 percent) the relationship between the value and the number of plowlands is expressed by one of the ratios mentioned in the text or by simple multiples and fractions of these ratios:

Value per plowland	Number of instances	Value	Number	Value	Number
3s.4d.	2	2s.6d.	1	11d.	1
6s.8d.	19	5s.	20	3s.	2
13s.4d.	6	10s.	37	6s.	5
2s.	2	15s.	6	12s.	1
4s.	4	20s.	20	2s.8d.	1
8s.	7	30s.	1	3s.2d.	1
16s.	2	40s.	2	5s.8d.	1
32s.	4			7s.6d.	2
				8s.4d.	1
				11s.5d.	1

73. William Farrer, "Introduction to the Yorkshire Domesday," p. 147. Presumably this is an example of the Normans failing to describe accurately a native tenure as a result of their own conception of mesne tenures.

74. Grain renders are recorded at Drax and at Buttercrambe (*YI*, 1:nos. CVII, CXXXI). *Cougeld* was paid in the fee of Bowes castle (ibid., no. CXXX).

75. Thomas of Burton, *Chronica Monasterii de Melsa, a Fundatione usque ad Annum 1396*, 2:236; *EYC*, 1:95, note.

76. Jolliffe, "Northumbrian Institutions," pp. 11–12.

77. See *Chronica de Melsa*, 1:lxx–lxxxi.

78. *EYC*, 1:141, note.

79. Ibid., nos. 97, 99, 166, 176; 2:no. 1196.

80. The Danes in Normandy seem to have maintained many of the old Carolingian fiscal exactions; see Musset, *Les Invasions*, pp. 253–54.

81. Jolliffe, "Northumbrian Institutions," p. 14; Rees, "Ancient Celtic Custom," pp. 160–62. The literature on cornage is extensive. In addition to the work of Jolliffe and Rees, the following discussions are relevant: Barrow, "Northern English Society," pp. 14–15, 18–20; Gaillard T. Lapsley, "Cornage and Drengage," pp. 670–95; Maitland, "Northumbrian Tenures," pp. 625–33; N. Neilson, "Customary Rents," pp. 120–24; R. R. Reid, "Barony and Thanage," pp. 185–87; J. H. Round, *The Commune of London and Other Studies*, pp. 278–89; James Wilson, "Introduction to the Cumberland Domesday, Early Pipe Rolls, and Testa de Nevill," pp. 312–26.

82. Barrow, "Northern English Society," pp. 14–15, 18–20, 22. Actually this identification is not new. Reid equated cain and cornage in 1920 ("Barony and Thanage," p. 185); and Wilson apparently thought something similar in 1901 ("Cumberland Domesday," pp. 315–16).

83. *Magnum Rotulum Scaccarii, vel Magnum Rotulum Pipae de Anno Tricesimo-Primo Regni Henrici Primi*, ed. Joseph Hunter, pp. 141, 143; Barrow, "Northern English Society," p. 15, n. 59.

84. Barrow, "Northern English Society," p. 15, n. 60; *Pipe Roll of 31 Henry I*, p. 131.

85. Barrow, "Northern English Society," p. 15; *YI*, 1:no. CXXX. *Coumale* and *betincou* were paid at Skerton (*Lancashire Inquests, Extents, and Feudal Aids*, ed. William Farrer, 1:no. CXLIII). For similar payments at Overton and Singleton, see ibid., no. LXXVII; 2:no. XCVI; 3:no. CCXXII.

86. Barrow, "Northern English Society," p. 18.

87. *RRA-N*, 2:no. 1491; *Pipe Roll of 31 Henry I*, pp. 131, 141, 143. Neilson suggested that cornage was a royal render coordinate with the geld or the Northumbrian equivalent of the geld ("Customary Rents," pp. 120–22); but this attractive hypothesis is probably not correct because cornage was found as a manorial payment in Lancashire, where the geld was paid in 1066.

88. *RRA-N*, 2:no. 1586, records Henry I granting the cornage of *Bortona* to the monks of Durham.

89. H. C. Darby and I. S. Maxwell, *The Domesday Geography of Northern England*, p. 501.

90. Farrer, "Yorkshire Domesday," pp. 145–46.

91. R. Welldon Finn, *Domesday Studies: The Norman Conquest and Its Effects on the Economy, 1066–86*, p. 93.

92. Jolliffe, "Northumbrian Institutions," pp. 2–3.

93. *Domesday*, 1:fols. 269b–270, 301b–302.

94. Jolliffe, "Northumbrian Institutions," pp. 3–4, 25–28.

95. Edmund Craster, "The Patrimony of St. Cuthbert," pp. 188–96.

96. *De Obsessione Dunelmi*, pp. 215–20.

97. Gaillard T. Lapsley, "Introduction to the Boldon Book," pp. 279–82. The clerks who wrote Boldon Book seem to have called the molmen "firmars." Molmen are mentioned once at Newton by Boldon. This entry comes near the beginning of the survey; thereafter firmars appear. They are burdened with the same type of services as the molmen and do not constitute a different peasant group (*Boldon Book*, p. 328).

98. Four villages, Newton by Boldon, Wardon, Morton, and Carlton, were inhabited exclusively by firmars (ibid., pp. 328–29, 338). In seven vills, South Sherburn, Sedgefield, Norton, Stockton, Cokerton, Blackwell, and Redworth, they were found alongside villeins and cottars (ibid., pp. 330–31, 337–38, 340).

99. The labor services of sokemen generally receive little emphasis, probably because they complicate the usual picture of sokemen as free peasants. Actually, a favored legal position and labor services were not necessarily incompatible, and the thirteenth-century inquisitions show that such obligations lay upon sokemen in Yorkshire. They are mentioned in general in the sokes of Snayth and Driffield (*YI*, 1:nos. XLV, LXXV) and are described in detail at Pocklington, where the sokemen paid 20d. rent a year for each bovate and owed suit to their lord's mill and court. These are Stenton's "honorable" dues. They also, however, plowed twice a year, harrowed two times, and hoed for one day. In autumn they did two boon days, cut the hay for two days, and made two cartings (ibid., no. XLVIII). These obligations have a remarkable parallel in the services of the firmars of Sedgefield in Durham: "Also there are . . . 20 firmars, every man of whom holds three bovates and renders 5 shillings and ploughs and harrows half an acre, and finds 2 men for mowing 2 days, and the same number for raking and piling hay, and 1 cart for 2 days for carrying corn and hay in the same manner. And all the firmars do 4 boon-days in autumn with their entire household except the housewife" (*Boldon Book*, p. 330). The services of these firmars were nearly the same as those of the sokemen at Pocklington, and this suggests that the major difference between the Northumbrian firmar (molman) and the sokeman was a matter of names.

100. Jolliffe, "Northumbrian Institutions," pp. 4–5.

101. There does seem to be a notable tendency for villages granted to Durham to be undivided; see *Historia de Sancto Cuthberto*, pp. 208–13.

102. *Boldon Book*, pp. 331–32, 339–40.

103. *Liber Feodorum*, ed. [H. C. Maxwell Lyte], 1:26–28. The correct

number is difficult to determine because although twenty-four villages are listed, neither Norham nor Fenwick is included.

104. *Historia de Sancto Cuthberto*, pp. 208, 211, 213. Barrow, *The Kingdom of the Scots*, pp. 28–32. The figures for Berwickshire and Coldinghamshire are based on Barrow's suggestion that Renton was part of Coldinghamshire.

105. Except for Howden, these figures are based on the text, not on the summary. They disagree with Farrer's figures in "Yorkshire Domesday," p. 147. He felt competent to adjudicate between the text and the summary, but this would seem to be a hazardous endeavor because the reasons why these two sections differed are unknown. Consequently, the figures are based on either the text or the summary, and the two are not combined except for Wakefield. In the case of villages divided between a berewick and sokeland, each property has been counted separately.

The figures for three of the sokes require comment. The text gives twenty-four places for Wakefield in the main entry describing the estate (*Domesday*, 1:fol. 299b); but if the eighteen other pieces of sokeland that are recorded only in the summary are combined with four properties whose status as sokeland or thaneland was uncertain and with two pieces of sokeland that were added after the conclusion of the main entry, then the total would be forty-eight (ibid., fols. 379b, 299b). Sherburn's berewicks are not named in either the text or the summary, but Farrer identified them as twenty-three places mentioned in later documents ("Translation of the Yorkshire Domesday," ed. and trans. William Farrer, p. 210, n. 4). Finally, Tanshelf is a problem. The main entry names only four places (*Domesday*, 1:fol. 316b); and the rest of the soke is described in isolated entries mixed with the rest of Ilbert's land. These would bring the total to twelve if two villages, *Notone* and *Cevet*, which seem to have been independent manors (each had a hall, the normal mark of manorial status in Yorkshire), are excluded (ibid., fol. 317).

106. *Domesday*, 1:fols. 309, 321. They had been held respectively by Earl Harold and Earl Edwin.

107. Jolliffe, "Northumbrian Institutions," pp. 10–11.

108. *The Kalendar of Abbot Samson*, ed. Davis, pp. xxx, xliii–xliv, xlvi–xlvii. See Barrow, *The Kingdom of the Scots*, p. 25, for a similar explanation.

109. Stenton, "The Danes in England," p. 216, n. 1.

110. *EYC*, 2:viii. Caro wapentake was called Burghshire. Bulmer was called Bulmershire, and Craven, Cravenshire. Furthermore, the honor of Richmond was made up of Gillingshire and Langershire.

111. Eric John, *Orbis Britanniae and Other Studies*, pp. 69–70, 104, 108, 114, 117.

112. Landholding had clearly become both fluid and complicated

by 1066. In particular, the claims mention the case of Asa. She had been married to Bernulf but had held the lands that she had brought with her into the marriage so completely that he could not give them away, sell them, or forfeit them. Moreover, when they separated, she kept her family lands. This example shows the reality of female inheritance in the North, and the prohibitions that limited Bernulf's control over her land suggest that alienation was not unlikely (*Domesday*, 1:fol. 373).

113. See Archbishop Oswald's survey of some of the lands of York, *EHD*, 1:521. At the end of the survey it is recorded that Archbishop Oscetel had obtained Helperby and its soke "in compensation for illicit cohabitation."

114. *Domesday*, 1:fol. 298. The general burdens that lay across Northumbrian society are very obscure. No pre-Conquest documents show whether the king's three burdens existed above the Tees, but a charter from 1137 suggests that a similar system had been in force. In that year, Edgar, son of Cospatric, confirmed a piece of land to Ralph de Merlay to be held in frank marriage freely except for army service, cornage, and castlework (*exceptis tribus serviciis, videlicet comunis excersitus in Comitatu, et cornagio, et comune opus castelli in Comitatu*, Lapsley, "Cornage and Dreng- age," p. 679). Furthermore, sometime between 1139 and 1152, Earl Henry freed Tynemouth Priory from work on the castle of Newcastle and from army and escort (?) service (*Quieti ab omni exercitu et equitatu*) (*RRS*, 1: no. 28; see also no. 43).

115. See Kenneth Jackson, *The Gaelic Notes in the Book of Deer*, pp. 88–96, 117–22.

116. Stenton, "The Northern Danelaw," pp. 11, 13–14, 50.

117. This survey is printed with a translation, notes, and bibliog- raphy in *Anglo-Saxon Charters*, ed. A. J. Robertson, no. LXXXIV, and pp. 413–16.

118. John F. McGovern, "The Meaning of 'Gesette land' in Anglo- Saxon Land Tenure," pp. 590–91.

119. Stenton, "The Northern Danelaw," p. 50.

120. *Domesday*, fol. 299.

Chapter 4

1. *Vita Ædwardi Regis qui apud Westmonasterium requiescit S. Bertini monacho ascripta*, ed. and trans. Frank Barlow, p. 53.

2. Dorothy Whitelock, "The Dealings of the Kings of England with Northumbria in the Tenth and Eleventh Centuries," pp. 77–83.

3. Ibid., pp. 83–84; Frank Barlow, *Edward the Confessor*, p. 194.

4. Edward A. Freeman, *The History of the Norman Conquest of England*, 2:375–77.

5. Barlow, *Edward the Confessor*, pp. 193–94.

6. Florence of Worcester, 1:223.

7. *ESSH*, 1:595–96, note; *Anglo-Saxon Writs*, ed. F. E. Harmer, pp. 418, 575; Freeman, *Norman Conquest*, 2:376–77. Tostig may also have been earl of Lincolnshire; this is suggested by the presence of a large number of his retainers in Lincoln in 1065 (*Vita Ædwardi*, p. 51).

8. Symeon of Durham, *HDE*, p. 97.

9. Ibid., pp. 94–95, 101.

10. *ASC, s.a.* 1056 D, p. 132; H. H. E. Craster, "The Red Book of Durham," p. 528.

11. Symeon of Durham, *HDE*, p. 92.

12. Ibid.

13. *Chronicle of the Kings of Scotland*, in *ESSH, s.a.* 1057–58 D, 1:600, 602–3.

14. *Vita Ædwardi*, p. 43; Gaimar, ll. 5085–86.

15. Ibid., ll. 5085–97; Symeon of Durham, *HR*, p. 174; *Vita Ædwardi*, p. 43. R. L. Graeme Ritchie, *The Normans in Scotland*, p. 16, assigns this meeting between Malcolm and Edward to ca. 1062, apparently on the authority of Gaimar, but this is incorrect. Gaimar actually places this meeting before Tostig's trip to Rome in 1061 (ll. 5087–99); Symeon of Durham says that it took place in 1058 (*HR*, p. 174). Finally, Archbishop Kynsige of York, who participated in these negotiations according to both Gaimar and Symeon, died in December of 1060 (*ASC, s.a.* 1060 D, p. 135). The date Malcolm gave hostages to the English was not recorded, but it was probably also in 1058 (*Vita Ædwardi*, p. 43).

16. Symeon of Durham, *HR*, pp. 174–75. *De Obsessione Dunelmi*, p. 220, mentions in general terms warfare and the devastation of certain Durham estates while Tostig was earl, probably a reference to Malcolm's invasion of 1061 because it is unlikely, although not impossible, that the Scottish raids before 1058 reached this far south.

17. Florence of Worcester, 1:223.

18. *Domesday Book*, ed. Henry Ellis, 1:fols. 301b–302.

19. William Farrer, "Introduction to the Lancashire Domesday," p. 271. Neither the *ASC, s.a.* 1065 CDE, pp. 137–38, nor Florence of Worcester, 1:223, mentions any devastation of Tostig's estates. The only source that reports such destruction is the *Vita Ædwardi*, p. 50, and it is highly biased in favor of Tostig and attempts to show the rebels in the worst possible light. Its evidence is, therefore, doubtful when unsupported by the other sources.

20. Hugh the Chantor, *The History of the Church of York, 1066–1127*, p. 32; Symeon of Durham, *HR*, pp. 191, 221–22.

21. Gaimar, ll. 5115–22, says that Tostig went to Scotland after his return from Rome. This would put his visit in 1062 except that Gaimar also says that the revolt of 1065 took place upon Tostig's return.

22. Symeon of Durham stands in the way of either suggestion. He had sources for northern history that were independent of the southern chronicles, and they would have mentioned any invasion of Scotland by Tostig. It is also asserted in the *HR*, p. 191, that Malcolm held Cumberland unjustly in 1070.

23. See Bertie Wilkinson, "Northumbrian Separatism in 1065–1066," p. 508, for such an approach.

24. Florence of Worcester, 1:223.

25. H. W. C. Davis, "Cumberland before the Norman Conquest," pp. 63–65. Barlow, *Edward the Confessor*, p. 235, n. 3, questions this identification, but his doubt is unjustified. The position of the house of Bamburgh was of sufficient importance for Cospatric, even in his old age, to be a threat to Tostig's government.

26. *Vita Ædwardi*, p. 50, n. 4; *Anglo-Saxon Writs*, ed. Harmer, pp. 423–24.

27. *Vita Ædwardi*, pp. 50–51.

28. Barlow, *Edward the Confessor*, pp. 298–99.

29. *Vita Ædwardi*, p. 53.

30. *ASC, s.a.* 1065 C, p. 138.

31. Florence of Worcester, 1:223.

32. *Domesday*, 1:fol. 269b.

33. Ibid.; William Farrer, "Introduction to the Yorkshire Domesday," pp. 139–41; F. M. Stenton, "Introduction [to the Domesday Survey of Lincolnshire]," p. x.

34. J. E. A. Jolliffe, "A Survey of Fiscal Tenements," pp. 161–62, 171 map.

35. This was Farrer's original opinion, in "Yorkshire Domesday," p. 139. Subsequently, he held that this low assessment was a post-Conquest attempt to ease the tax burden on the lands harried in 1069 (*EYC*, 1:x). This is an attractive hypothesis, but there seems to be no supporting evidence. No tax reduction is mentioned in the folios of the Yorkshire Domesday, nor would such a theory explain the general low assessment of all the North. Farrer himself eventually abandoned or became uncertain of this theory of Norman reassessment (Reginald Lennard, "The Origin of the Fiscal Carucate," p. 57). In fact, it seems likely that this low assessment was very old. As late as the twelfth century, Northumberland had not been assessed in carucates (Jolliffe, "Fiscal Tenements," pp. 161–62, 171); and in the tenth century the men of York are said to have urged Guthred to revolt against Athelstan because they had always had their own king and had never paid tribute to a southern king (*The Chronicle Attributed to John of Wallingford*, ed. Richard Vaughan, p. 45; see Whitelock, "Dealings with Northumbria," p. 71). If this story represents an accurate tradition, it is unlikely that the kings of Wessex would have found it politically expedient

to burden the North with heavy taxes once they took over the area. They would have been much more likely to allow the pre-Danish tax system to stand (F. M. Stenton, "Types of Manorial Structure in the Northern Danelaw," p. 90, n. 2). The territorial extent of this low assessment did, in fact, generally correspond with the limits of the Norwegian kingdom of York, and J. E. A. Jolliffe has argued that this fiscal system was a survival from the days of the old Northumbrian kingdom ("The Era of the Folk in English History," pp. 20–25). This idea is probably basically correct, but there is an additional possibility that Cnut regularized the system (Stenton, "The Northern Danelaw," pp. 86–90),

36. Symeon of Durham, *HDE*, pp. 87–89; II. II. E. Craster, *The Parish of Tynemouth*, pp. 41–42. The Durham version of this story is to be preferred.

37. *ASC*, *s.a.* 1065 CD, pp. 137–38; Florence of Worcester, 1:223.

38. *ASC*, *s.a.* 1065 D, p. 138.

39. Wilkinson, "Northumbrian Separatism," pp. 510–11.

40. *Vita Ædwardi*, p. 51; Barlow, *Edward the Confessor*, p. 236. If Tostig was, in fact, earl of Lincolnshire, the slaughter of his retainers there may represent a local revolt rather than an invasion of the northern rebels.

41. *ASC*, *s.a.* 1065 DE, p. 138.

42. Barlow, *Edward the Confessor*, pp. 237–39; *ASC*, *s.a.* 1065 D, p. 138.

43. Wilkinson, "Northumbrian Separatism," pp. 509–15.

44. Symeon of Durham, *HR*, p. 198; *De Primo Saxonum Adventu*, p. 383; Barlow, *Edward the Confessor*, p. 194, n. 3. Actually, the idea that Waltheof was earl of Northamptonshire is somewhat conjectural. He may have been subearl of Yorkshire.

45. William of Malmesbury, *The Vita Wulfstani of William of Malmesbury*, pp. 22–23; Michael Dolley, *The Norman Conquest and the English Coinage*, p. 37.

46. William of Malmesbury, *Vita Wulfstani*, pp. 22–23; *ASC*, *s.a.* 1066 CD, p. 140.

47. See Barlow, *Edward the Confessor*, pp. 243–44, for the alliance between the two families.

48. *ASC*, *s.a.* 1065 D, p. 138; *s.a.* 1066 D, p. 140.

49. Ibid., CDE, pp. 140–41; Florence of Worcester, 1:225.

50. *ASC*, *s.a.* 1055 CD, pp. 130–31; *s.a.* 1058 D, p. 134; *s.a.* 1066 CDE, p. 141; Florence of Worcester, 1:225; Gaimar, ll. 5159–93.

51. *ASC*, *s.a.* 1066 C, p. 142; F. M. Stenton, *Anglo-Saxon England*, p. 587.

52. *ASC*, *s.a.* 1066 CD, pp. 141–43; Florence of Worcester, 1:225–26.

53. Symeon of Durham, *HR*, p. 180.

54. *ASC, s.a.* 1066 C, p. 143. The text is ambiguous; it says that "Earl Edwin and Earl Morcar assembled from their earldom as large a force as they could muster." Several interpretations could be put on this passage, but perhaps the most likely one is that "their earldom" refers to Mercia, the traditional earldom of their family. Gaimar says that they had an army drawn from seven shires, which hardly suggests that they had as large a force as they could theoretically raise (l. 5214).

55. *ASC, s.a.* 1066 C, pp. 143–44; CE, pp. 141–43; Florence of Worcester, 1:226–27.

56. Gaimar, ll. 5252–55.

57. Guillaume de Poitiers, *Histoire de Guillaume le conquérant*, p. 236; Symeon of Durham, *HR*, p. 198.

58. *ASC, s.a.* 1066 C, p. 142.

59. *Vita Ædwardi*, pp. 52–53.

60. Symeon of Durham, *HR*, p. 198; *HDE*, pp. 97–98.

61. *ASC, s.a.* 1066 DE, pp. 142, 145; Symeon of Durham, *HR*, p. 198.

62. *ASC, s.a.* 1066 D, p. 145; E, p. 142; see pp. xiv–xvii, for a discussion of these versions of the text.

63. Symeon of Durham, *HR*, p. 199.

64. *ASC, s.a.* 1067 D, p. 146; Florence of Worcester, 2:2.

65. Orderic Vitalis, 2:214–18.

66. *ASC, s.a.* 1067 D, p. 148.

67. Orderic Vitalis, 2:216.The implication of Cospatric and Mærleswein in the revolt is shown by their flight to Scotland after its collapse (*ASC, s.a.* 1067 D, pp. 146–48; Florence of Worcester, 2:2).

68. This is presumably the meaning of Orderic Vitalis, 2:216.

69. Ibid., 2:218; Guillaume de Poitiers, *Histoire*, p. 265.

70. *ASC, s.a.* 1067 D, p. 148; Florence of Worcester, 2:2; Orderic Vitalis, 2:218.

71. Orderic Vitalis, 2:218.

72. Ibid., pp. 218, 222; Florence of Worcester, 2:2.

73. *ASC, s.a.* 1069 DE, pp. 149–50; Gaimar, ll. 5380–402; *Domesday*, 1:fols. 373–74.

74. Symeon of Durham, *HR*, pp. 186–87; *HDE*, pp. 98–99. *ASC, s.a.* 1068 DE, p. 149.

75. Orderic Vitalis, 2:222; *ASC, s.a.* 1068 DE, p. 149.

76. Orderic Vitalis, 2:222.

77. *Rursus Angli post regis discessum contra utrunque præsidium congregati sunt, sed Guillelmo comite cum suis uiriliter in quadam ualle dimicante non præualerunt, sed pluribus eorum captis seu trucidatis alii fuga mortem distulerunt* (ibid.). If this passage is accepted as it stands, one must suppose that the rebels reassembled with the intention of attacking the castles but that

William fitz Osbern defeated them before they reached the city. Alternatively, this sentence might mean that the rebels in fact reimposed the siege but that they were driven away and defeated after leaving the city. The former interpretation was adopted in the text. In her edition of Orderic, Chibnall suggests that *ualle* (valley) is a mistake for *uallo*, (fortification), "since the text implies fighting in the city" (ibid.), and she translates the passage in accordance with this emendation: "The English made one further attack on both castles after the king's departure, but they could not prevail against Earl William and his men who engaged them hotly in one of the baileys, killing and capturing many whilst the remainder prolonged their lives for awhile through flight" (ibid., p. 223).

78. Symeon of Durham, *HDE*, pp. 99–100. The date of this expedition is uncertain, but it probably occurred after William fitz Osbern's victory over the rebels.

79. Orderic Vitalis, 2:224–26.

80. Ibid., pp. 226–28; *ASC, s.a.* 1069 DE, pp. 149–50; Symeon of Durham, *HR*, pp. 187–88; Florence of Worcester, 2:3–4.

81. Symeon of Durham, *HR*, p. 188.

82. *ASC, s.a.* 1070 E, p. 151.

83. Orderic Vitalis, 2:228–30.

84. Ibid., p. 230. The suggestion made by Stenton, *Anglo-Saxon England*, p. 604, that William repeated the tactic that had won him London by devastating a path north and west of York is incorrect. It contradicts Orderic Vitalis, 2:230, and would not have worked, in any case, because the Danes controlled the Humber.

85. Florence of Worcester, 2:4.

86. Orderic Vitalis, 2:230–32; *ASC, s.a.* 1069 DE, p. 150; Florence of Worcester, 2:4.

87. Orderic Vitalis, 2:232–34; Symeon of Durham, *HR*, p. 189; *The Priory of Hexham*, ed. James Raine, 1:viii. Orderic Vitalis says that after Christmas William pursued a band of rebels who had hidden *in angulo quodam regionis latitare, mari uel paludibus undique munito. Vnicus aditus per solidum intromittit, latitudine tantum uiginti pedum patens* (2:232) ("in a narrow neck of land sheltered on all sides by sea or marshes. It could be reached only by one narrow causeway, no more than twenty feet wide." Ibid., p. 233).

The rebels' lair has been taken to be Tod Point at the mouth of the Tees (ibid., n. 3), but this identification is incorrect. As the king approached their base, the rebels fled; and he followed them to the Tees: *auia perrumpit, quorum asperitas interdum peditem eum ire compellit* (ibid.) ("forcing his way through trackless wastes, over ground so rough that he was frequently compelled to go on foot." Ibid., p. 233). This is not the description of a ride down the south bank of the Tees, but it would fit a march from the East

Riding across the North York Moors to the Tees very well. Probably the rebels had been established in Holderness. Chibnall translates *in angulo quodam regionis* as "in a narrow neck of land" (ibid., p. 233); and either her translation or the more literal "in a certain corner of the province" applies perfectly to Holderness, which was nearly an island in this period. It was cut off from the rest of the East Riding by the marshes along the river Hull and by the upper reaches of the river, which almost reached the sea in the neighborhood of Lisset and Gransmoor, and it was only accessible through the vicinity of Skipsea (Maurice Beresford, *New Towns of the Middle Ages*, p. 514).

88. *ASC, s.a.* 1070 D, p. 151; Florence of Worcester, 2:4; Symeon of Durham, *HR*, p. 188.

89. *Chronicon Abbatiae de Evesham ad Annum 1418*, ed. William D. Macray, pp. 90–91.

Chapter 5

1. *ASC, s.a.* 1069 D, p. 150. The chapter title is taken from Jean Scammell, "The Origin and Limitations of the Liberty of Durham," p. 453.

2. *Domesday Book*, ed. Henry Ellis, 1:fols. 299–301b.

3. Florence of Worcester, 2:6.

4. See Z. N. Brooke, *The English Church and the Papacy from the Conquest to the Reign of John*, pp. 112–26; R. W. Southern, "The Canterbury Forgeries," pp. 193–226.

5. Hugh the Chantor, *The History of the Church of York, 1066–1127*, p. 3.

6. *ASC, s.a.* 1075 DE, pp. 157–58; *s.a.* 1085 E, p. 161; quotation *s.a.* 1070 E, p. 151.

7. Orderic Vitalis, 2:232.

8. Symeon of Durham, *HR*, p. 188.

9. Ibid., p. 190. Symeon seems to say that Malcolm's raid occurred after the Danes had left the Humber. According to Florence of Worcester, 2:7, this happened around the time of the feast of St. John the Baptist (24 June).

10. See R. L. Graeme Ritchie, *The Normans in Scotland*, pp. 26–27; John H. Le Patourel, "The Norman Conquest of Yorkshire," p. 3. Later in this essay (p. 5), Le Patourel seems to reapproach Ritchie's interpretation. See also Archibald A. M. Duncan, *Scotland*, p. 114.

11. Symeon of Durham, *HR*, pp. 190–91.

12. Ibid. The interpretation I have given is the most likely explanation for what happened, and it closely follows the *HR*, although there is a slight possibility that events were not this simple, because the course of events in this passage is unclear. The compiler of the *HR* brings the Scots all the way to Wearmouth and a meeting between Malcolm and Edgar the

Atheling before he mentions Cospatric's raid: *Inter has Scottorum vastationes ac rapinas, Gospatricus comes . . . Cumbreland invadit* ("During the Scots' pillaging and wasting, Earl Cospatric went into Cumberland," p. 191).

Malcolm then learns of the raid as he watches the church of Wearmouth burn and orders retaliations. If taken at face value, this means that Cospatric raided Cumberland after Malcolm had crossed the Tees, but Cospatric's foray could have taken place earlier, for the meeting between Malcolm and Edgar may be fictitious. If so, then Malcolm probably invaded Durham to punish Cospatric, a fact that a writer from Durham would have suppressed because he was loath to admit that the Northumbrian earls had jurisdiction between the Tyne and the Tees.

13. Ibid., pp. 191–92.

14. Ibid., p. 195; *HDE*, pp. 105–6. *ASC, s.a.* 1069 D, p. 150.

15. Symeon of Durham, *HR*, pp. 190, 195; *HDE*, p. 105.

16. *ASC, s.a.* 1071 D, p. 154.

17. F. M. Stenton, *Anglo-Saxon England*, p. 606.

18. Ritchie, *Normans in Scotland*, pp. 32–33.

19. *ASC, s.a.* 1072 DE, pp. 154–55; Florence of Worcester, 2:9.

20. Ritchie, *Normans in Scotland*, pp. 29, 32, 33–34; Stenton, *Anglo-Saxon England*, p. 000, *ASC, s.a.* 1072 DE, p. 155; Florence of Worcester, 2:9; Alan O. Anderson, "Anglo-Scottish Relations from Constantine II to William," p. 11.

21. Symeon of Durham, *HR*, pp. 196, 199.

22. *Vita Oswini Regis*, ed. James Raine, pp. 20–21.

23. Symeon of Durham, *HR*, p. 199.

24. Stenton, *Anglo-Saxon England*, p. 610; Frank Barlow, *William I and the Norman Conquest*, p. 98.

25. Symeon of Durham, *HR*, pp. 199–200.

26. Symeon of Durham, *HDE*, p. 106. Cf. Bernard Meehan, "Outsiders, Insiders, and Property in Durham around 1100," pp. 50–51.

27. Symeon of Durham, *HR*, pp. 199–200.

28. *Vita Ædwardi Regis qui apud Westmonasterium requiescit S. Bertini monacho ascripta*, ed. and trans. Frank Barlow, p. 51.

29. *Capitula de Miraculis*, 1:243.

30. Certainly the account of Tostig and the robbers cannot be accepted as it stands in the *Vita Ædwardi*, pp. 50–51. The author of this work was a foreign clerk, who probably lacked enough knowledge of the North to put his information on northern brigandage into its proper context and who used what he did know about Tostig's efforts to establish peace in his earldom as the reason for the revolt of 1065. This, of course, was incorrect.

31. *Domesday*, 1:fols. 301b, 309, 310b, 332. In 1066, Earl Edwin held Gilling and Catterick, but they had probably been held by Tostig before the revolt of 1065.

32. *Vita Ædwardi*, p. 43.

33. See G. W. S. Barrow, "The Anglo-Scottish Border," pp. 21–42, for the best recent discussion of the northern border.

34. *RRS*, 1:38; P. A. Wilson, "On the Use of the Terms 'Strathclyde' and 'Cumbria,'" pp. 88, 90–91.

35. Jocelin of Furness, *Vita Kentegerni*, pp. 182–83; Wilson, "The Terms 'Strathclyde' and 'Cumbria,'" p. 83, tries to explain away the statements concerning the extent of Cumbria.

36. Wilson, "The Terms 'Strathclyde' and 'Cumbria,'" p. 85; *ESC*, no. 50.

37. Teviotdale had probably been subject to the bishop of the Cumbrians throughout the eleventh century and presumably earlier, although it is usually assumed to have remained subject to Durham until ca. 1101. The view that Durham had kept Teviotdale through the period of Danish invasions and the subsequent expansion of the Cumbrians and the Scots rests on exceedingly bad evidence. There is no contemporary evidence that shows that the connection had survived the tenth century, and the proposition rests on early twelfth-century evidence; see D. P. Kirby, "Strathclyde and Cumbria," p. 91; H. H. E. Craster, "A Contemporary Record of the Pontificate of Ranulf Flambard," p. 37. Its main support is a passage in the first continuation of Symeon's *HDE* that says Bishop Ranulf Flambard was unable to recover both Teviotdale and Carlisle, appendages of his bishopric that had been lost to other bishops because of Ranulf's problems with Henry I (ibid., p. 139). This statement is plausible but unlikely. The passage was not written until some forty years after the supposed loss of Teviotdale and Carlisle, and it is difficult to imagine to whom the former was lost, for there is no evidence that there was either a bishop of Glasgow or of St. Andrews at the time (ibid., p. xxiv; Norman F. Shead, "The Origins of the Medieval Diocese of Glasgow," p. 223). Neither the late date nor the imprecision of this passage inspires confidence, an impression that is strengthened by three writs from the 1090s which reveal that the inhabitants of Carlisle were loath to accept the jurisdiction of the bishop of Durham before Flambard's episcopate. These documents are, unfortunately, too general to disclose whether the difficulty stemmed from the preference of the Normans at Carlisle for the spiritual jurisdiction of York or from the repugnance of the natives to the jurisdiction of either York or Durham; in either case, these writs show that the statement of Symeon's continuator cannot be taken at face value. For the writs, see Craster, "A Record of Flambard," pp. 37–39. Beyond his testimony, two other documents are usually employed to show that Teviotdale was subject to Durham in this period. A confirmation of Durham's privileges made by Archbishop Thomas I (1070–1100) includes Teviotdale in Durham's diocese, but this document is a forgery (*The Historians of the Church of York and Its Archbishops*,

ed. James Raine, 3:17–20). A prohibition from Archbishop Thomas II (1109–14) forbids Algar the clerk from dispensing chrism and oil from Glasgow to the inhabitants of Teviotdale because their chrism and oil should have come from Durham, but this only establishes that Durham claimed Teviotdale, which is not in doubt, and that the claim was not accepted by the local priests (ibid., p. 37; Craster, "A Record of Flambard," pp. 38–39; Shead, "The Origins of Glasgow," pp. 221–23).

There is, then, no real basis for the idea that Teviotdale was subject to Durham as late as 1100 other than the common conviction that nothing had basically changed in the North since the days of Bede, and there are, in fact, two stronger pieces of evidence for the contrary proposition. In the 1070s, Aldwin and Turgot were prevented from refounding Melrose by Malcolm III because *jurare illi fidelitatem noluerunt* ("they were unwilling to swear fealty to the former," Symeon of Durham, *HDE*, p. 112); and Malcolm's readiness to defy Walcher's monks presumably means that this area, which was later included in Glasgow's diocese and stood at the gateway from the West into the lower Tweed and Teviot, was already thought to be ecclesiastically part of Cumbria. Of course, a close scanner of boundaries might object that this does not establish that Teviotdale was part of Cumbria, only that the upper Tweed was; but David's Cumbrian inquisition shows that the two areas went together. This inquest was initiated to determine what property had traditionally belonged to Glasgow (presumably this term stood for the old bishopric of the Cumbrians; see Shead, "The Origins of Glasgow," p. 9), and it was based upon the assumption that all of "Glasgow's" lands had lain within Cumbria (*ESC*, no. 50). The boundaries of this region are not given; but the names of the jurors indicate that it included a very wide area. In addition to Oggo and Leysing, *Cumbrenses judices*, who presumably came from the West, and Gille, son of Boet, the lord of the western end of the Tyne gap, they included two men with Northumbrian names, Echtred, son of Waltheof, and Halden, son of Eadulf, who presumably came from Teviotdale or perhaps Tynedale. This in itself is suspicious, but the really important point is established by the location of the lands that were said to have anciently belonged to Glasgow. The jurors swore that Glasgow had possessed lands not only in Clydesdale and Galloway, as might have been expected, but also a number of estates in Teviotdale (Morebattle, Ancrum, Ashkirk, and Lillesleaf) and others in Tweeddale (Traquair, Peebles, Stobo, and others) that linked the holdings in Teviotdale with the church's western lands (ibid.; *EHD*, 2:no. 54). Unless this inquisition is rejected, it puts the matter beyond doubt. In terms of these men's memories, Teviotdale was traditionally part of the Cumbrian bishopric, and this connection was probably the result of a political connection that had been formed during the years of Cumbrian power in the tenth century.

38. James Wilson, "Introduction to the Cumberland Domesday, Early Pipe Rolls, and Testa de Nevill," p. 310.

39. Barrow, in *RRS*, 1:111, has conjectured that the king of Scots had a claim on Tynedale, and he is probably correct. The idea that this valley was English is an anachronistic assumption. There is absolutely no evidence for English overlordship between 1000 and 1100. After the latter date, there is a slight possibility that Henry I may have pushed English power up the North Tyne, although the valley may have remained Scottish until the late 1150s, when Henry II opened the Tyne gap by taking over Gilsland and creating the barony of Langley (*Liber Feodorum*, ed. [H. C. Maxwell Lyte], 1:202; I. J. Sanders, *English Baronies*, p. 127). Even after this, the connection with England was nominal (*RRS*, 2:54).

40. Perhaps this Scottish salient explains why Galwegians in the Tyne valley who had been confounded by mists sent by Northumbrian saints easily found themselves back home by the time the mists lifted.

41. Symeon of Durham, *HR*, p. 198.

42. Symeon of Durham, *HDE*, p. 102.

43. Symeon of Durham, *HR*, p. 188.

44. Edward A. Freeman, *The History of the Norman Conquest of England*, 4:540.

45. *Cartularium Abbathiae de Whiteby*, ed. J. C. Atkinson, 1:xxxviii.

46. H. C. Darby and I. S. Maxwell, *The Domesday Geography of Northern England*, fig. 132, p. 449; Terence A. M. Bishop, "The Norman Settlement of Yorkshire," p. 2.

47. Long ago William Farrer expressed doubt that Lancashire above the Ribble, which was surveyed with the West Riding, was ever visited during the compilation of Domesday, and he drew a comparison between its description in Domesday and a geld book ("Introduction to the Lancashire Domesday," p. 273). More recently, W. E. Wightman has maintained that Domesday gives no information about the settlements in the Pennines (*The Lacy Family in England and Normandy, 1066–1194*, pp. 52–53); similar reservations concerning the validity of Domesday's description of Craven and northern Lancashire have been expressed by R. Welldon Finn, *Domesday Studies: The Norman Conquest and Its Effects on the Economy, 1066–86*, p. 210; and by D. E. Greenway in *Charters of the Honour of Mowbray, 1107–1191*, p. xxi. There can be no reasonable doubt, of course, that many of the Pennine settlements were waste, but the idea that the uplands and the West were covered by great, unbroken bands of empty vills depends upon an unwarranted interpretation of a specific Domesday formula that gives only the name of the vill, its geld assessment, and its owners in 1066 and 1086. These entries have been interpreted as showing that such vills were unpopulated in 1086 (Darby and Maxwell, *Domesday Geography*, p. 61; Bishop, "Norman Settlement," pp. 2, 6–7). But this is an

exceedingly questionable inference. The information that Domesday provides in these instances is more likely to be incomplete than a sign there was no population for it amounts to no more than what would have been available from a list of geld liabilities. Furthermore, some of these villages must have been inhabited because archaic examples of shire custom were found in some of them in the thirteenth century (J. E. A. Jolliffe, "Northumbrian Institutions," pp. 28–29, 31). The views of Farrer and Wightman, then, contain some truth. Large portions of Domesday's account of western Yorkshire and northern Lancashire need not have been compiled any closer to the Pennines than York castle.

48. William of Malmesbury, *Willelmi Malmesbiriensis Monachi de Gestis Pontificum Anglorum Libri Quinque*, p. 285.

49. Parts of the southern Pennines were omitted from Domesday altogether. See F. M. Stenton, "Introduction to the Derbyshire Domesday," pp. 303–4; C. F. Slade, "Introduction to the Staffordshire Domesday," p. 12.

50. *ASC, s.a.* 1074 D, p. 155.

51. Cospatric's return to Scotland is hard to date because of the *HR*'s vagueness. It notes Cospatric's flight to Flanders and then says that he returned *post aliquantum tempus* ("after some time," Symeon of Durham, *HR*, p. 199). Inexplicably, Ritchie, *Normans in Scotland*, p. 26, states that Cospatric got the earldom of Dunbar from Malcolm before he was reinstated as earl of Northumbria by William in 1070.

52. *ASC, s.a.* 1074 DE, pp. 155–56. See David C. Douglas, *William the Conqueror*, p. 230, for a different interpretation.

53. *ASC, s.a.* 1074 D, p. 156.

54. Stenton, *Anglo-Saxon England*, pp. 610–12; Douglas, *William the Conqueror*, pp. 231–33; Barlow, *William I*, pp. 157–60.

55. Specifically, the accounts of Florence of Worcester and Orderic Vitalis seem to have been influenced by Waltheof's miracles. Florence of Worcester says that Waltheof joined the conspiracy under pressure from the other two earls and that he afterward threw himself on William's mercy (2:10). Orderic takes this line of explanation a step further by asserting that Waltheof refused to join the conspiracy but promised not to divulge its existence (2:312–14). Neither of these accounts can be trusted on the question of Waltheof's involvement in the revolt. William of Malmesbury, who was undecided on this point, believed that the question of Waltheof's guilt was decided on nationalistic lines, the Anglo-Saxons being prepared to excuse his conduct (*Willelmi Malmesbiriensis Monachi de Gestis Regum Anglorum Libri Quinqui*, 2:312–13). The writers of the *Anglo-Saxon Chronicle*, which contains the oldest accounts of the revolt, betray no doubt concerning Waltheof's complicity (*s.a.* 1075 DE, p. 157).

56. Symeon of Durham, *HDE*, p. 107. The miracle cannot be dated

precisely. It is preceded by a short account of William's Scottish expedition of 1072 (p. 106), and it is followed by a long description of Aldwin's monastic revival in the North (p. 108). The latter came north sometime in 1073 or 1074 (David Knowles, *The Monastic Order in England*, p. 167). Ralph's visit probably occurred in one of these two years. Jean Scammell has suggested that the incident took place in 1096 ("Liberty of Durham," p. 450, n. 2), but this is unlikely.

57. Symeon of Durham, *HDE*, p. 107.

58. Symeon of Durham, *HR*, p. 200. This event is entered under 1073, but Symeon's narrative is a year behind the true date at this point. See *De Obsessione Dunelmi*, p. 219.

59. *ASC, s.a.* 1075 DE, p. 157. Florence of Worcester, 2:10. Waltheof was, of course, an Anglo-Dane, and if Alan O. Anderson's genealogy for Siward is correct, he was a cousin of the Danish king (*ESSH*, 1:598, n. 2).

60. Stenton, *Anglo-Saxon England*, pp. 611–12; Douglas, *William the Conqueror*, p. 232; John Beeler, *Warfare in England, 1066–1189*, pp. 48–49.

61. Stenton, *Anglo-Saxon England*, p. 611.

62. The E version of the *Anglo-Saxon Chronicle, s.a.* 1075, p. 157, does not mention the submission of Waltheof, but says only that the king arrested him upon his return to England. The D version, however, mentions Waltheof's journey to Normandy and his submission, but it places them out of clear chronological order. The sequence is as follows: (1) Norwich castle falls; (2) William returns to England and arrests Roger; (3) Waltheof goes to Normandy and confesses, but William does not arrest him until they are back in England.

63. Ibid., pp. 157–58.

64. See Douglas, *William the Conqueror*, pp. 233–35.

65. *ASC, s.a.* 1076 DE, p. 158.

66. Symeon of Durham, *HDE*, p. 114; *HR*, p. 199. Roger of Wendover, *Rogeri de Wendover Chronica sive Flores Historiarum*, 2:17.

67. Symeon of Durham, *HDE*, pp. 108, 113.

68. Ibid., pp. 105–6, 113–14.

69. See ibid., pp. 108–13.

70. Symeon of Durham, *HR*, p. 209; Florence of Worcester, 2: 13–14.

71. Symeon of Durham, *HDE*, p. 114; Ritchie, *Normans in Scotland*, p. 49; Stenton, *Anglo-Saxon England*, pp. 613–14; Douglas, *William the Conqueror*, p. 240.

72. *ASC, s.a.* 1077 D, p. 159; *s.a.* 1079 DE, p. 159; Florence of Worcester, 2:13.

73. Florence of Worcester, 2:14. Florence's account is repeated nearly verbatim in Symeon of Durham, *HR*, pp. 208–10. In the *HDE*, p. 114, however, Symeon of Durham does not mention this incident, and the

narrative of Walcher's murder is somewhat vague on the question of the Northumbrians' motive (pp. 116–17).

74. Florence of Worcester, 2:14.

75. Ibid., pp. 14–16; *ASC, s.a.* 1080 E, p. 160. *De Primo Saxonum Adventu*, p. 383, says that Eadulf Rus, son of Cospatric, killed Walcher. The sources attributed to Symeon of Durham provide somewhat different details. In the *HR*, pp. 197–98, Eadulf is named as the killer, but he is said to have been the grandson of Cospatric. In the *HDE*, p. 115, the killer is an unidentified Waltheof.

76. Ibid., pp. 117–18.

77. Ibid., p. 118.

78. The best description of Odo's expedition is in ibid. The statement that the Northumbrian nobility was severely reduced as a result of this expedition is based on the fate of Walcher's murderers, which, although mentioned in the paragraph preceding Odo's expedition, is clearly connected with the latter. The incident is also briefly described by Florence, who indicates that William led the army (2:16), and in Symeon of Durham, *HR*, p. 211.

79. Ritchie, *Normans in Scotland*, p. 50. Ritchie relies heavily on the account in the *Chronicon Monasterii de Abingdon*, ed. Joseph Stevenson, 2:9–10, for his interpretation. This description is, however, rhetorical and is probably more of a war story of the abbot who went with Robert to Scotland than a straightforward account of what took place.

80. Symeon of Durham, *HR*, p. 211.

81. Douglas, *William the Conqueror*, p. 241; Ritchie, *Normans in Scotland*, p. 51.

82. Symeon of Durham, *HR*, p. 199.

83. *Inde rex dedit illum honorem* [the earldom] *Albrico. Quo in rebus difficilibus parum valente, patriam que reverso* . . . , (ibid.). Stenton, *Anglo-Saxon England*, p. 614, identifies *Albricus* with Aubrey de Coucy.

84. R. R. Reid, "Barony and Thanage," p. 197; F. M. Stenton, *The First Century of English Feudalism, 1066–1166*, pp. 194–96; Beeler, *Warfare in England*, p. 286; Le Patourel, "The Conquest of Yorkshire," pp. 425–26.

85. J. C. Holt, *The Northerners*, pp. 197–98; Reid, "Barony and Thanage," pp. 191–92.

86. Beeler, *Warfare in England*, p. 287; Stenton, *English Feudalism*, p. 196.

87. Stenton, *English Feudalism*, p. 215; Beeler, *Warfare in England*, p. 38; F. M. Stenton, "Introduction to the Nottinghamshire Domesday," p. 228.

88. Gaimar, ll. 5682–92.

89. Wightman, *The Lacy Family*, pp. 21–27.

90. Symeon of Durham, *HR*, p. 188.

91. *Domesday*, 1:fols. 323b–325.

92. William Farrer, "Introduction to the Yorkshire Domesday," pp. 165–66; Stenton, "Nottinghamshire Domesday," p. 223.

93. Wightman, *The Lacy Family*, pp. 19–20.

94. Farrer, "Yorkshire Domesday," p. 156; Ritchie, *Normans in Scotland*, pp. 69–70.

95. *Domesday*, 1:fols. 269b–270, 276, 332; Stenton, "Derbyshire Domesday," pp. 303–4.

96. *ASC, s.a.* 1085 E, p. 161.

97. See Edward A. Freeman, *The Reign of William Rufus and the Accession of Henry the First*, 1:28–32, 89–119. Cf. H. S. Offler, "The Tractate 'De Iniusta Vexacione Willelmi Episcopi Primi,'" pp. 321–41.

98. No lands above the Ribble had been given to undertenants by 1086 (*Domesday*, 1:fols. 301b–302, 332). A few of the barons above the Tyne claimed in the thirteenth century that their tenures went back to the Conquest or made statements that northern antiquarians have interpreted as having the same meaning. There is, however, no contemporary support for most of these claims, and they are, with one possible exception, untrue. See Sanders, *English Baronies*, Bolam, p. 17; Morpeth, p. 65; Redesdale, p. 73; Alnwick, p. 103; Bothal, p. 107; Callerton, p. 109; Mitford, p. 131; *Liber Feodorum*, 1:200–203; W. Percy Hedley, *Northumberland Families*, 1:22, 24, 26–27, 145, 191–93, 196, 198–99, 208–9. See Chapter 7.

99. Ritchie, *Normans in Scotland*, p. 50.

100. Lynn H. Nelson, *The Normans in South Wales, 1070–1171*, pp. 79–89.

101. Holt, *Northerners*, p. 214. See William Farrer, *Records Relating to the Barony of Kendale*, 1:viii–x. Farrer theorized that the grant to Ivo Taillebois was made in 1091 or 1092 (p. ix), but it may have been made as early as 1087–88.

102. John C. Hodgson, *The Parish of Bywell St. Peter*, pp. 18–19; Sanders, *English Baronies*, p. 25; Ritchie, *Normans in Scotland*, p. 148, n. 2.

103. The Umfravilles said that they had held Redesdale *de antiquo feffamento* (*Liber Feodorum*, 1:201). This has been interpreted to mean that they were given this fee either by William I or Rufus (C. H. Hunter Blair, "The Early Castles of Northumberland," p. 135; Sanders, *English Baronies*, p. 73). In fact, this phrase merely means that the lordship existed before 1135; see Hedley, *Northumberland Families*, 1:208–9; and Chapter 7, n. 34.

104. Ritchie, *Normans in Scotland*, pp. 55–56; Freeman, *William Rufus*, 1:295–96; Anderson, "Anglo-Scottish Relations," p. 12; Nelson, *The Normans in Wales*, pp. 82–90.

105. Ritchie, *Normans in Scotland*, pp. 55–56.

106. Symeon of Durham, *HR*, pp. 221–22; Freeman, *William Rufus*, 1:296; Ritchie, *Normans in Scotland*, pp. 55–56; Frank Barlow, *The Feudal Kingdom of England, 1042–1216*, p. 155.

107. Although he is following the narrative of Florence of Worcester, 2:28, the compiler of the *HR* omits Florence's mention of the Scottish withdrawal and makes Rufus's invasion of Scotland follow Malcolm's invasion of the North with no break (Symeon of Durham, *HR*, p. 218).

108. *Capitula de Miraculis*, 2:338–39. The army of knights may have come from southern England (*ASC, s.a.* 1091 E, p. 169).

109. *Capitula de Miraculis*, 2:340–41.

110. Symeon of Durham, *HR*, p. 218.

111. *ASC, s.a.* 1091 E, p. 169; Florence of Worcester, 2:28; Symeon of Durham, *HR*, p. 218. Orderic Vitalis, 4:268–70, gives a very detailed account of the meeting of 1091 which Ritchie accepts (*Normans in Scotland*, pp. 56–57).

112. Ritchie, *Normans in Scotland*, p. 58.

113. *ASC, s.a.* 1092 E, p. 169; Florence of Worcester, 2:30.

114. Symeon of Durham, *HR*, p. 218; *ASC, s.a.* 1093 E, p. 170.

115. *ASC, s.a.* 1093 E, p. 170. Florence of Worcester indicates that there had been some negotiations prior to Malcolm's journey to Gloucester and that the object of the meeting was to reestablish peace (2:31). Duncan denies in the strongest terms the existence of any connection between the agreement in question and the status of Cumberland. He believes that the twelve vills Rufus had promised Malcolm in 1091 were a traditional endowment for the support of the Scottish kings when they visited the English kings and that, in 1093, Malcolm came south to demand their restoration (Duncan, *Scotland*, pp. 120–21). This is a plausible theory, but as Duncan admits, Malcolm III held no lands of the English king in 1086 although he had earlier. Nor is there any evidence for the existence of such an endowment in Anglo-Saxon times unless one accepts the circumstantial details of the thirteenth-century accounts of the cession of Lothian in 973. These details probably reflect later arrangements; see Marjorie O. Anderson, "Lothian and the Early Scottish Kings," pp. 106–10. Finally, such an explanation ignores the strategic importance of Cumberland. Malcolm would have had to have been blind to this importance to allow Rufus to unilaterally alter the configuration of the border without any opposition.

116. *ASC, s.a.* 1093 E, p. 170.

117. The idea that the Cumbrian Dolfin was Cospatric's son is commonly held by both English and Scottish historians: Freeman, *William Rufus*, 1:315; *Scottish Annals from English Chronicles, A.D. 500 to 1286*, ed. and trans. Alan O. Anderson, p. 96, n. 7; F. M. Stenton, "Pre-Conquest Westmorland," p. 221; Ritchie, *Normans in Scotland*, p. 58; Duncan, *Scotland*, pp. 120–21; *ASC*, p. 169, n. 6. Insofar as this identification is based on anything other than the similarity of the names, it is an inference drawn from the fact that Cospatric's son Waltheof held Allerdale in Cumberland under Henry I. But Henry gave Waltheof this lordship (he also

reestablished Cospatric's youngest son, Cospatric II, in Northumberland), and Waltheof's possession of Allerdale in no way suggests that his father and grandfather had held it. In his grandfather's time it had been held by Thorfinn and after that presumably by his son, another Dolfin. Moreover, Cospatric is known to have raided Cumberland in 1070. See *Liber Feodorum*, 1:198; John C. Hodgson, *The Parish of Edlingham*, pp. 26–30; Symeon of Durham, *HR*, p. 191.

118. See Chapter 2.

119. Symeon of Durham, *HR*, pp. 191, 221–22; *ASC*, *s.a.* 1079 E, p. 159; *s.a.* 1091 E, p. 169. Florence of Worcester, 2:13, 28. Unfortunately, the descriptions of these two invasions are so general that this point cannot be stressed. Duncan is also of the opinion that Dolfin ruled Cumberland independently (*Scotland*, pp. 120–21).

120. *ASC*, *s.a.* 1093 E, p. 170.

121. Florence of Worcester, 2:28; Anderson, "Anglo-Scottish Relations," p. 10.

122. *ASC*, *s.a.* 1093 E, p. 170.

123. Florence of Worcester, 2:31: [Rufus] *insuper etiam illum ut, secundum judicium tantum suorum baronum, in curia sua rectitudinem ei faceret, constringere voluit; sed id agere, nisi in regnorum suorum confiniis, ubi reges Scottorum erant soliti rectitudinem facere regibus Anglorum, et secundum judicium primatum utriusque regni, nullo modo Malcolmus voluit.* Cf. Anderson's translation in *Scottish Annals*, p. 110. He renders *rectitudinem* as "justice."

124. Orderic Vitalis, 4:270.

125. Symeon of Durham, *HR*, p. 222; *ASC*, *s.a.* 1093 E, p. 170.

126. *ASC*, *s.a.* 1093 E, p. 170; Archibald A. M. Duncan, "The Earliest Scottish Charters," p. 128.

127. *ASC*, *s.a.* 1093 E, p. 170; Florence of Worcester, 2:32; William of Malmesbury, *Gesta Regum*, 2:308.

128. William of Malmesbury, *Gesta Regum*, 2:476; Duncan, "Earliest Charters," p. 128.

129. *ASC*, *s.a.* 1093 E, p. 170; Florence of Worcester, 2:32; Duncan, "Earliest Charters," pp. 126–34.

130. The accepted chronology of these events is that Donald reigned for six months (mid-November 1093 to mid-May 1094) and that Duncan reigned for the next six months (to mid-November 1094). These dates first appear (at the latest) in the works of E. W. Robertson, *Scotland under Her Early Kings*, 1:158, cited by Freeman, *William Rufus*, 2:35–36. The difficulty with this chronology is that it flatly contradicts the *Anglo-Saxon Chronicle*, which asserts that Duncan became king before Christmas of 1093 (*s.a.* 1093 E, p. 170). Florence of Worcester agrees with the *Chronicle* (2:32). Robertson apparently based his dates on Fordun, who was wrong, but Freeman accepted them nonetheless because he did not believe there

was time for Duncan to come north, beat Donald, and be ambushed before Christmas of 1093 (*William Rufus*, 2:32–35). This timing, of course, is debatable, but the dates have persisted, nevertheless. Their only support other than repetition is the reign lengths given in the Scottish regnal lists; see Marjorie O. Anderson, *Kings and Kingship in Early Scotland*, pp. 43–77, 235–90. These are divided into two groups, the X and Y groups, and certain members of the X group, specifically F, I, and K, give Donald and Duncan successive six-month reigns (pp. 276, 284, 289). The Y group's main representative, E, however, does not agree, for it gives Duncan six months and Donald three years, seven months (p. 255). Anderson could not accept the annihilation of Donald's first reign (p. 75), but E is probably closer to the truth than the members of the X group. The archetypes for both groups were composed in the mid-twelfth century (p. 52). There is no reason to prefer their authority to the *Anglo-Saxon Chronicle* and Florence, both nearly contemporary documents with the events in question. Furthermore, the regnal lists are demonstrably wrong on the length of the reign of Duncan's father, Malcolm III (p. 49). Finally, it might be noted that *Brechan's Prophecy*, in *ESSH*, 2:91, has Malcolm succeeded by a king who reigns one month and four days, a regnal length that supports the chronology of the English sources.

131. *ASC*, s.a. 1093 E, p. 170; *s.a.* 1094 E, p. 172. Florence of Worcester, 2:32, 35.

132. The charter is printed in the *Feodarium Prioratus Dunelmensis*, ed. William Greenwell, pp. lxxxii–iii. H. W. C. Davis accepts it as genuine, *RRA-N*, 1:no. 345. Scammell, "Liberty of Durham," p. 453, also accepts it.

133. There is disagreement on this matter. See Beeler, *Warfare in England*, pp. 68, 338 n. 59, for the various opinions on the subject. He thinks that Robert took control of Newcastle at the beginning of the revolt and that Rufus's first move after arriving in the North was to retake it (p. 68). This is not impossible, but it must be emphasized that neither the *Anglo-Saxon Chronicle*, s.a. 1095 E, p. 172, nor Florence of Worcester, 2:38, mentions a siege of Newcastle and that the two charters, *RRA-N*, 1:nos. 366, 367, made *apud obsidionem Novi Castri* that Beeler regards as proof of the siege (*Warfare in England*, p. 338, n. 59) probably refer to the siege castle built at Bamburgh. *RRA-N*, 1:no. 363: *Hoc autem factum est eo anno quo Rex Willelmus . . . fecit novem castellum ante Bebbanburgh super Robertum*.

134. *ASC*, s.a. 1095 E, pp. 172–73; Florence of Worcester, 2:38; Orderic Vitalis, 4:278–81; Beeler, *Warfare in England*, pp. 66–67; Austin L. Poole, *From Domesday Book to Magna Carta, 1087–1216*, p. 109.

135. Orderic Vitalis, 4:278.

136. For the campaign see Beeler, *Warfare in England*, pp. 66–70.

137. According to Orderic's account, Robert had planned to ambush the king (4:280).

138. Symeon of Durham, *HR*, p. 199; *De Primo Saxonum Adventu*, p. 384; Duncan, *Scotland*, p. 124.

139. *ESC*, nos. XV, XVI. See Duncan, "Earliest Charters," pp. 103–18, 126–27, 136–37. The *Vita Oswini*, pp. 21–22, mentions an expedition that went into Scotland at some date between 1093 and 1097. See Ritchie, *Normans in Scotland*, p. 65.

140. *ASC*, *s.a.* 1097 E, p. 174. In this instance, Duncan's translation has been followed ("Earliest Charters," p. 133). See also Florence of Worcester, 2:41.

Chapter 6

1. Reginald Lennard, *Rural England, 1086–1135*, pp. 155–56; Henry R. Loyn, *Anglo-Saxon England and the Norman Conquest*, p. 328.

2. Frank Barlow, "The Effects of the Norman Conquest," p. 135. Cf. Loyn, *Anglo-Saxon England*, p. 328; David C. Douglas, *William the Conqueror*, p. 310; F. M. Stenton, *Anglo-Saxon England*, p. 480.

3. R. Welldon Finn, *Domesday Studies: The Norman Conquest and Its Effects on the Economy, 1066–86*, pp. 5–6.

4. See John H. Le Patourel, "The Norman Conquest of Yorkshire," pp. 17–19; Douglas, *William the Conqueror*, pp. 83–104; Lucien Musset, "Naissance de la Normandie," pp. 122–25.

5. F. M. Stenton, "Types of Manorial Structure in the Northern Danelaw," p. 52.

6. Terence A. M. Bishop, "The Distribution of Manorial Demesne in the Vale of York," pp. 405–6.

7. Ibid., p. 403.

8. Terence A. M. Bishop, "The Norman Settlement of Yorkshire," p. 13, n. 2.

9. J. E. A. Jolliffe, "Northumbrian Institutions," p. 25.

10. H. C. Darby and I. S. Maxwell, *The Domesday Geography of Northern England*, p. 445, fig. 130, p. 448.

11. Ibid., pp. 420, 448–501; see fig. 131, p. 447; fig. 132, p. 449.

12. Ibid., see fig. 9, p. 32; fig. 11, p. 38; fig. 28, p. 115; fig. 30, p. 121; fig. 47, p. 189; fig. 49, p. 196; fig. 63, p. 249; fig. 64, p. 252. H. C. Darby, *The Domesday Geography of Eastern England*, fig. 8, p. 49; fig. 10, p. 54.

13. This assertion served as the premise of W. E. Wightman's article, "The Significance of 'Waste' in the Yorkshire Domesday." He supported it with the proposition that rural communities quickly recover from natural disasters and the fact that many of the waste holdings in Shropshire had recovered by 1086 (p. 55). The harrying, however, cannot be compared with either an act of nature or the effects of plundering within a small area. It differed from either in that it struck directly at the peasants and at several elements in the rural economy at the same time and over a wide

area. Indeed, it was nothing less than an attempt to create an artificial famine on a regional scale; and no matter how successful the peasants were at eluding the Normans in the first instance, the survivors came home to find their huts, plows, and food destroyed and their oxen's fodder burned. Given the geographical extent of the wasting, these things could not be replaced. Both the chronicles and the low densities of population and teams in 1086 leave no doubt as to the result.

14. Bishop, "The Norman Settlement," pp. 1–14. In 1907, John Beddoe and Joseph H. Rowe suggested that the Normans must have brought peasants into Yorkshire from their estates outside the county ("The Ethnology of West Yorkshire," p. 58), but there is no evidence of this. Wightman based his investigation of this question on the proposition that there was little real waste in the lower parts of Yorkshire (except along the coast) in 1086 and went on to explain that "waste" merely meant that an estate was administratively worthless ("The Significance of 'Waste,'" pp. 55, 70–71). The term was reputedly applied to manors that the Normans had consolidated with other manors, to estates for which no paying tenant could be found, and to vills subject to such other conditions as afforestation, poor village siting, and disputed ownership (pp. 58–63, 68–70). In no instance can he actually demonstrate that one of his major definitions applied to a particular estate. His explanations are inferences, and they are not convincing in detail. This is unfortunate because some of his suggestions seem reasonable, especially his theory that the Normans combined holdings and that land values were low because it was difficult to find tenants. See also W. E. Wightman, *The Lacy Family in England and Normandy, 1066–1194*, pp. 43–54, especially his discussion of Leeds, p. 46.

15. Bishop, "The Norman Settlement," pp. 2–10. Bishop admitted that there were several exceptions to this rule, but he thought that they were the result of special circumstances. Hugh fitz Baldric's fief, for instance, was prosperous because Hugh had utilized his position as sheriff to rustle the king's cattle and peasants (p. 11). William de Warrene's estate of Conisborough was in good condition because it had not been devastated (p. 9); and the fiefs of Geoffrey de la Wirce and Roger de Busli in southern Yorkshire owed their prosperity to colonization from their owners' estates in Lincolnshire and Nottinghamshire (pp. 9–10).

16. Darby and Maxwell, *Domesday Geography*, pp. 67–71, 145–50, 217–21, 450–54.

17. Finn, *The Norman Conquest and the Economy*, pp. 27–28, apparently still accepts Bishop's theory.

18. *Ipse vero in saltuosa quædam et difficillime accessibilia loca contendit, et abditos illic hostes persequi summopere studuit* (Orderic Vitalis, 2:230. "He himself continued to comb forests and remote mountainous places, stopping at nothing to hunt out the enemy hidden there." Ibid., p. 231).

19. See Chapter 5, n. 47 and the accompanying text.

20. Darby and Maxwell, *Domesday Geography*, pp. 71, 453–54.

21. See Chapter 5.

22. See Bishop, "The Norman Settlement," pp. 3–5.

23. See Darby and Maxwell, *Domesday Geography*, pp. 40–44, 122–25, 197–200. Cf. Finn, *The Norman Conquest and the Economy*, pp. 6–18.

24. Bishop, "The Norman Settlement," p. 4. Wightman explained the overstocked manors as the result of the expansion of a village's arable or the consolidation of two or more manors with one of them described as waste and its plows attributed to the other ("The Significance of 'Waste,'" pp. 59–60, 69–70).

25. The opinions of both Darby and Farrer are against this argument, but their pious assertions that all the churches in Yorkshire were not enumerated in Domesday are without positive foundation beyond their own unwillingness to admit the low position of the church in the shire in 1086. See Darby and Maxwell, *Domesday Geography*, p. 425; William Farrer, "Introduction to the Yorkshire Domesday," pp. 186, 190. In fact, the small number of churches recorded in Domesday is not suspicious. Many must have gone out of existence in 1069–70, and they had probably not been as numerous before this date as in southern England. Indeed, an account from Abingdon concerning the acquisition of a relic of St. Wilfrid in Yorkshire during the reign of Edward the Confessor says this explicitly ("where owing to the devastation hardly a church was to be found." Frank Barlow, *The English Church, 1000–1066*, see p. 176); *Chronicon Monasterii de Abingdon*, ed. Joseph Stevenson, 2:47.

26. In the compilation of these figures, the following method was followed. First, overstocked linked entries have been counted on the basis of their parts. It might be thought that this procedure would yield too high a result, but this is not a serious problem. Few linked entries were overstocked, and any error introduced by this method should not affect the relative standings of the areas too seriously. Second, Domesday makes three types of statements concerning churches in Yorkshire. Usually it says that there is a church and a priest in a village. At other times, however, it mentions only a church or a priest. These statements have been taken at face value in preparing the total for functioning churches in Yorkshire. The first and the third statements have been combined, but the second, the mention of a church with no specific reference to a priest, has been omitted from the calculations.

27. Symeon of Durham, *HR*, p. 190; *ASC*, *s.a.* 1085 E, p. 161. The chronicle does not say explicitly that Holderness was wasted, but given the courses of the last Scandinavian invasions, it is the single most likely area.

28. See Darby and Maxwell, *Domesday Geography*, fig. 130, p. 445; fig. 131, p. 447; and fig. 132, p. 449. These maps seem to be open to the interpretation given above.

29. Orderic Vitalis, 2:230–32. See Chapter 4, n. 87.

30. Darby and Maxwell, *Domesday Geography*, fig. 130, p. 445.

31. Symeon of Durham, *HR*, pp. 190–92. Wightman initially confronted the question of the redevelopment of Yorkshire as it concerned the castlery of Pontefract, which lay in an area that was unusual because it had not been methodically harried. By 1086, waste, although it existed, was not of great proportions in Pontefract outside the Pennines, and the area contained the greatest concentration of overstocked manors in the shire. Faced with these conditions, it is small wonder that Wightman came to doubt that the term could be taken at face value (*The Lacy Family*, pp. 43–54)

32. Symeon of Durham, *HR*, pp. 190–92.

33. Darby and Maxwell, *Domesday Geography*, p. 501; *Domesday Book*, ed. Henry Ellis, 1:fol. 299.

34. Darby and Maxwell, *Domesday Geography*, p. 501.

35. Ibid.

36. *Domesday*, 1:fols. 327–28.

37. *Anglo-Saxon Charters*, ed. A. J. Robertson, no. LXXXIV; *Domesday*, fol. 303b.

38. *Anglo-Saxon Charters*, ed. Robertson, no. LXXXIV.

39. *Domesday*, 1:fol. 303b.

40. Ibid., fol. 302b. These berewicks are not named. *Anglo-Saxon Charters*, ed. Robertson, no. LXXXIV.

41. *Domesday*, 1:fol. 302b.

42. *YI*, 1:nos. XLV, CXXXI.

43. *Domesday*, 1:fol. 327b. Carlton and East Hardwick were not separately surveyed in Domesday, but they were presumably included in the description of Tanshelf, which was overstocked (fol. 316b). Their omission may account for the fact that Tanshelf appeared to have more plows than it had actual land for; see Wightman, *The Lacy Family*, p. 48.

44. Bishop, "The Norman Settlement," pp. 13–14.

45. See Bishop, "Manorial Demesne," pp. 403–6.

46. See Chapter 4 after n. 86.

47. Gaillard T. Lapsley, "Introduction to the Boldon Book," pp. 269–70.

48. Jolliffe, "Northumbrian Institutions," pp. 10, 25.

49. M. M. Postan, "The Chronology of Labour Services" [a revised version], pp. 95–96.

50. *Boldon Book*, p. 331.

51. The bondage vills similar to Butterwick listed in *Boldon Book* were Binchester, p. 331; Herrington, p. 337; Hutton, p. 337; Oxenhall, p. 338; Sheraton, p. 337; Urpath, p. 331; and West Aukland, p. 333. The bondage vills that apparently lacked drengs in *Boldon Book* were Braffer-

ton, p. 331; Iveston, p. 335; Little Burdon, p. 328; Lutrington, p. 333; Mainsforth, p. 330; and Tursdale, p. 330.

52. *Boldon Book* includes five clear examples of villages inhabited by molmen: Carlton, pp. 337–38; Morton, p. 329; Newton by Boldon, p. 328; Redworth, p. 340; and Wardon, p. 329.

53. The main representatives of this type of village in *Boldon Book* were Craucrook, p. 336; Great Usworth, pp. 336–37; the Heighington-shire villages, pp. 339–40; Langchester, pp. 334–35; and Witton, p. 335. Stanhope, p. 334, perhaps also should be classed with this group.

54. Ibid., p. 327.

55. Ibid.

56. The Boldon villages were Cleadon and Whiteburn, ibid., p. 328; Easington and Thorpe, pp. 329–30; Hertburn, p. 337; Middleham and Cornford, p. 330; North Sherburn, Shadeford, and Cassop, pp. 329–30; Norton, p. 330; Preston, p. 337; Ryhope and Burdon, p. 328; Sedgefield, p. 330; Shotton, p. 329; Stockton, p. 337; and Wearmouth and Turnstall, p. 328. Whickham, pp. 335–36, may have been a Boldon vill.

57. The non-Boldon manors in which the villeins did week work were Haughton, ibid., p. 339; New Ricknall, p. 338; and Whessoe, p. 339. Three of the Auklandshire villages, North Aukland, Escombe, and New-ton, pp. 340–41, also belonged to this group, but their descriptions are defective.

58. Houghton, ibid., p. 329; Little Coundon, p. 333; and Newbottle, pp. 328–29.

59. Lapsley, "Introduction to Boldon Book," pp. 269–70.

60. Postan, "Labour Services," p. 95.

61. *Boldon Book*, pp. 327–28.

62. Ibid., pp. 339–40; Jolliffe, "Northumbrian Institutions," pp. 8–9.

63. Jolliffe, "Northumbrian Institutions," p. 11; *Boldon Book*, pp. 327–28.

64. Orderic Vitalis, 2:233. See Chapter 4, n. 87.

65. Symeon of Durham, *HR*, p. 189.

66. General accounts of the Conquest frequently ignore the harry-ing of Durham. See Douglas, *William the Conqueror*, p. 220; Stenton, *Anglo-Saxon England*, p. 604; R. Allen Brown, *The Normans and the Norman Conquest*, p. 196. But there can be no doubt that William penetrated at least to the Tyne (Symeon of Durham, *HR*, p. 189), if not into southern North-umberland (*The Priory of Hexham*, ed. James Raine, 1:viii); and a bungled passage in Orderic Vitalis must be interpreted in this light: *Mense ianuario rex Guillelmus Haugustaldam* [Hexham] *reuertebatur a Tesia, uia quæ hactenus exercitui erat intemptata, qua crebo acutissima iuga et uallium humillimæ sedes, cum uicinia serenitate uerna gaudet, niuibus compluuntur* (2:234) ("In January

King William left the Tees and returned to Hexham, following a route no army had hitherto attempted, where towering peaks and precipitous valleys between them would be deep in snow even when the countryside around blossomed with the spring." Ibid., p. 235). The passage as it stands is nonsense because it is preceded by an account of William's march to the Tees and is followed by his arrival in York. Presumably Orderic originally said that William returned to the Tees from Hexham, and a later copyist reversed *Tesiam* and *Haugustalda* and regularized their endings. This interpretation seems to lie behind the accounts of two historians who have gone to the trouble to familiarize themselves with the northern sources, Frank Barlow, *William I and the Norman Conquest*, p. 93; John Beeler, *Warfare in England, 1066–1189*, p. 42. Cf. Orderic Vitalis, 2:234, n. 1.

67. Symeon of Durham, *HR*, p. 189.

68. Ibid., p. 188.

69. H. H. E. Craster, *The Parish of Tynemouth*, pp. 222–24, 319, 330, 404; *Boldon Book*, p. 332.

70. John C. Hodgson, *The Parish of Warkworth; The Parish of Shilbottle*, p. 363.

71. Ibid., p. 19; Craster, *The Parish of Tynemouth*, pp. 41–47.

Chapter 7

1. J. C. Holt, *The Northerners*, p. 202.

2. *ASC*, s.a. 1097 E, p. 175; Florence of Worcester, 2:41; *Tigernach Annals, Continuation*, in *ESSH*, s.a. 1099, 1:119.

3. *Annals of Winchester*, in *Scottish Annals from English Chronicles, A.D. 500 to 1286*, ed. Alan O. Anderson, s.a. 1099, p. 119.

4. See the witnesses to Edgar's charters, *ESC*, nos. XV, XX. R. L. Graeme Ritchie bases his interpretation of the reigns of Edgar, Alexander, and David upon the assumption that they were viewed as usurpers, but he has no proof (*The Normans in Scotland*, p. 106). See n. 19.

5. *RRA-N*, 1:nos. 367, 463, 478.

6. *Liber Feodorum*, ed. [H. C. Maxwell Lyte], pt. 1, pp. 197–203. The baronies in question are Bolam, Callerton (DeLaval), Dilston, Mitford, Morpeth, and Morwick. The holders of Bothal and Redesdale said that their families had held *de antiquo feffamento* (pp. 201–2). This phrase has been taken to imply an origin during the reign of William the Conqueror, but it surely indicates merely an origin prior to 1135; see J. H. Round, *Feudal England*, pp. 236–46; W. Percy Hedley, *Northumberland Families*, 1:22, 24, 26–27, 143, 145, 196.

7. Between 1107 and 1116, Henry I confirmed to Tynemouth the tithes of several villages that had been given to the priory by Earl Robert and his men. Among them were the tithes of two villages, Black Callerton and Dissington, that later were included in the barony of Callerton (*RRA-*

N, 2:no. 1170; H. H. E. Craster, *The Parish of Tynemouth*, p. 49, n. 2). This fact alone proves nothing, but in a notification of a similar date, Henry specifically confirmed the tithes that had been given by Herbert de la Val. His confirmation included the tithes of Black Callerton and Dissington and creates the presumption that Herbert had been a follower of Earl Robert and had held these villages prior to 1095 (*RRA-N*, 2:no. 1172; Hedley, *Northumberland Families*, 1:145).

8. *RRA-N*, 2:nos. 363–68.

9. Gaimar, ll. 6129–75. Gaimar's account of this revolt is hard to reconcile with the earlier descriptions. He seems to say that Rufus came north, built an unidentified new castle, and besieged Morpeth before moving up to Bamburgh (ll. 6149–57). Both the *Anglo-Saxon Chronicle, s.a.* 1095 E, p. 172, and Florence of Worcester, 2:38, record that Rufus initially besieged Tynemouth and that while this siege was in progress, he captured an unnamed small castle. This might have been Morpeth, but Gaimar's failure to mention the siege of Tynemouth makes his assertions suspect. William de Merlay is also mentioned in *De Injusta Vexatione Willelmi Episcopi I*, pp. 190–91. See Hedley, *Northumberland Families*, 1:196.

10. *Liber Feodorum*, 1:201. Guy might be mentioned in *RRA-N*, 1:no. 412, although the erasure of all but the first letter of the name makes it impossible to be certain. See Hedley, *Northumberland Families*, 1:203.

11. In 1080, one hundred of Walcher's men were killed (*ASC, s.a.* 1080 E, p. 160; *De Injusta Vexatione*, p. 186).

12. *RRA-N*, 2:nos. 541, 589–90, 642, 643.

13. Archibald A. M. Duncan, "The Earliest Scottish Charters," pp. 104–5, 118.

14. Donald Nicholl, *Thurstan Archbishop of York (1114–1140)*, p. 16.

15. Ritchie was of the opinion that Normans had been in Scotland as early as the reign of Malcolm Canmore (*Normans in Scotland*, pp. 68–83). But see G. W. S. Barrow, "The Beginnings of Feudalism in Scotland," pp. 1–2, and *The Kingdom of the Scots*, pp. 279–81.

16. *ASC, s.a.* 1101 E, p. 177; Ritchie, *Normans in Scotland*, p. 145.

17. Ritchie, *Normans in Scotland*, pp. 101–6; Edward A. Freeman, *The Reign of William Rufus and the Accession of Henry the First*, 2:383, 390–91; Austin L. Poole, *From Domesday Book to Magna Carta, 1087–1216*, pp. 1–2; Frank Barlow, *The Feudal Kingdom of England, 1042–1216*, p. 174. Duncan interprets the marriage as illustrating the reality of Scottish vassalage ("Earliest Charters," p. 134).

18. Orderic Vitalis, 4:118–20, 149, 256–58.

19. Ritchie says that Edgar and Alexander needed Henry's support because they were usurpers (*Normans in Scotland*, p. 106), but this is only an assertion and there is no evidence of antidynastic feeling in Scotland till 1130. Neither Edgar nor Alexander faced any revolts. The one that

is usually placed in Alexander's reign (1107–24) is first recorded in Wyntoun and deserves no serious respect (Andrew of Wyntoun, *The Orygynale Chronykil of Scotland*, 2:174). Bower, Fordun's continuator, also notes the story, but this is no better evidence. See William F. Skene, *Celtic Scotland*, 1:452.

20. *ASC*, *s.a.* 1107 E, p. 181.

21. William of Malmesbury, *Willelmi Malmesbiriensis Monachi de Gestis Regum Anglorum Libri Quinque*, 2:476; *The Brut y Tywyssogion*, in *ESSH*, *s.a.* 1111 (=1114), 2:144.

22. Orderic Vitalis, *Orderici Vitalis Angligenæ Coenobii Uticensis Monachi Historiæ Ecclesiasticæ Libri Tredecim*, 4:164–67. See R. W. Southern, "The Place of Henry I in English History," pp. 132–55.

23. Southern, "Henry I," pp. 133–34; Barlow, *Feudal Kingdom of England*, p. 182; Round, *Feudal England*, p. 472; C. Warren Hollister, "Magnates and *Curiales* in Early Norman England," pp. 80–81.

24. *RRA-N*, 2:no. 631; *EYC*, 3:nos. 1418–21; W. E. Wightman, *The Lacy Family in England and Normandy, 1066–1194*, pp. 36–37.

25. *EYC*, 2:432; Holt, *The Northerners*, p. 214. Cf. Wightman, *The Lacy Family*, p. 20.

26. *EYC*, 2:v, 11–12.

27. *Charters of the Honour of Mowbray, 1107–1191*, ed. D. E. Greenway, pp. xvii–xix, xxiii–iv.

28. I. J. Sanders, *English Baronies*, pp. 56, 150.

29. *EYC*, 3:143, 148; Wightman, *The Lacy Family*, pp. 66, 68, 72.

30. *EYC*, 3:2–3, n.

31. Ibid., 1:385–86; 2:326. Holt, *The Northerners*, p. 215; Ritchie, *Normans in Scotland*, pp. 145–47.

32. *EYC*, 1:466; 2:133–37, 176, 432, 462; 3:457.

33. G. V. Scammell, *Hugh Du Puiset Bishop of Durham*, p. 187; Holt, *The Northerners*, p. 214; Hedley, *Northumberland Families*, 1:26, 191–93, 203. In addition to the Bertrams of Mitford and the Balliols, several other Northumbrian baronies (Whalton, Bolam, and Bothal, probably also Gosford) contained estates in southern Durham (Hedley, *Northumberland Families*, 1:22, 24, 26, 54–55, 203, 205, 233).

34. For Styford see *Liber Feodorum*, 1:201; Sanders, *English Baronies*, pp. 84–85; Ritchie, *Normans in Scotland*, pp. 142–43; Hedley, *Northumberland Families*, 1:22–25. On Prudhoe, see Ritchie, *Normans in Scotland*, p. 73; *Liber Feodorum*, 1:201. Redesdale represents a problem. The *Liber Feodorum*, 1:201, says that the Umfravilles had held it *de antiquo feffamento*. Northumbrian antiquarians have taken this to mean that William the Conqueror gave Redesdale to Robert de Umfraville; see Madeleine Hope Dodds, *The Parishes of Ovingham, Stamfordham, and Ponteland*, pp. 80–81. To sustain this view, they have had to invent a mythical Robert de Umfra-

ville "I" to help fill the time gap until Robert de Umfraville "II" appears in charters ca. 1120 (ibid., p. 81). In fact, of course, this "second" Robert de Umfraville was the founder of the Northumbrian Umfravilles. In 1207, Richard de Umfraville, the descendant of Robert, was of the opinion that there had been but one Robert, and the phrase that is used as the foundation for an origin before 1087 actually means that the barony was created before 1135. Finally, it is unlikely that Robert de Umfraville would have accepted Redesdale, which was probably valueless, unless it was combined with the grant of Prudhoe, which he is known to have received from Henry I. Cf. Hedley, *Northumberland Families*, 1:208–9.

35. The lords of Mitford claimed that their ancestors had held since the Conquest (*Liber Feodorum*, 1:201). The first known holder of this barony, however, was William, who appears during the reign of Henry I (C. H. Hunter Blair, "Mitford Castle," p. 74). The Bertrams of Bothal claimed an origin before 1135 (*Liber Feodorum*, 1:202; Sanders, *English Baronies*, p. 107). Hedley has suggested that Bothal came to the Bertrams as a result of William Bertram's marriage to a daughter of Guy de Balliol (*Northumberland Families*, 1:26–27, 191–93).

36. Arthur M. Oliver, "Early History of the Family of Morwick," pp. 264–65; *Liber Feodorum*, 1:203; Sanders, *English Baronies*, p. 119; *Pipe Roll of 31 Henry I*, pp. 132–33; Hedley, *Northumberland Families*, 1:96.

37. *Liber Feodorum*, 1:200, 203; Sanders, *English Baronies*, p. 41. Many sources say that Eustace received Alnwick from Ivo de Vesci, who had obtained it from William Tyson, its supposed lord in 1066 (ibid., p. 103), but this is groundless. See Freeman, *William Rufus*, 2:596. Hedley believes that Ivo did hold Alnwick before Eustace (*Northumberland Families*, 1:34, 198–99).

38. *Liber Feodorum*, 1:200; Sanders, *English Baronies*, pp. 100, 149; Ritchie, *Normans in Scotland*, pp. 146–47; Hedley, *Northumberland Families*, 1:37, 224; *RRA-N*, 2:nos. 993, 1001. The conclusions of Arthur M. Oliver on the origins of Wooler should be taken with caution ("The Family of Muschamp, Barons of Wooler ," pp. 243–44).

39. James Wilson, "Introduction to the Cumberland Domesday, Early Pipe Rolls, and Testa de Nevill," pp. 303–4; Ritchie, *Normans in Scotland*, p. 150; Holt, *The Northerners*, p. 214.

40. Wilson, "Cumberland Domesday," p. 310; Sanders, *English Baronies*, p. 124.

41. Sanders, *English Baronies*, p. 115.

42. William Farrer, *Records Relating to the Barony of Kendale*, p. x; *Charters of Mowbray*, ed. Greenway, pp. xxii, xxiv n.

43. Sanders, *English Baronies*, p. 142.

44. The date Lancashire came into the possession of Stephen has not been definitely established; see R. H. C. Davis, *King Stephen, 1135–1154*, p. 6. William Farrer seems to have thought that he received it

ca. 1118 ("Feudal Baronage," pp. 292–93). The idea that Ranulf Meschin held Lancashire before Stephen depends upon a charter of Ranulf's son, Ranulf Gernons, in which Ranulf confirms the tenure of some land near Penwortham held by Evesham. The monks were to hold it as they had *tempore comitis Rogeri Pictavensis et tempore Rannulfi comitis patris mei* (*Lancashire Pipe Rolls*, p. 319). If this evidence can be believed, Ranulf Meschin had held Lancashire. Farrer was reluctant to accept this idea ("Feudal Baronage," p. 292), as was James Tait (*Mediæval Manchester and the Beginnings of Lancashire*, pp. 164–65).

45. *RRA-N*, 2:no. 640.

46. C. H. Hunter Blair, "The Sheriffs of Northumberland, Part I, 1076–1602," pp. 25–26.

47. Ibid. Hedley has maintained that Odard was not Ligulf's son, but was French (*Northumberland Families*, 1:142).

48. *Pipe Roll of 31 Henry I*, pp. 140–42; Wilson, "Cumberland Domesday," p. 313, n. 2.

49. *The Register and Records of Holm Cultram*, ed. Francis Grainger and W. G. Collingwood, p. 119; Nicholl, *Thurstan*, pp. 134, 148.

50. *EYC*, 2:505 n.

51. *Register of Holm Cultram*, ed. Grainger and Collingwood, p. 119.

52. *RRA-N*, 2:xvi; *EYC*, 2:505 n.

53. *EYC*, 2:505 n.; *RRA-N*, 2:nos. 1279, 1639.

54. *EYC*, 3:317 n.; *ESC*, p. 375 n.

55. Wilson, "Cumberland Domesday," p. 313, n. 2; *RRA-N*, 2:nos. 1203, 1560, 1563; Sanders, *English Baronies*, p. 42; H. H. E. Craster, *The Parish of Corbridge*, p. 41. If Hedley's genealogy of William son of Siward is correct, Henry also confirmed or granted Gosforth with Middleton in Teesdale to a native family (*Northumberland Families*, 1:54–55).

56. *Liber Feodorum*, 1:198–99, 203, 205; Sanders, *English Baronies*, p. 122.

57. John C. Hodgson, *The Parish of Edlingham*, pp. 28–30. Hodgson's remarks on Allerdale below Derwent are somewhat confused because he assumed that the Dolfin expelled by Rufus in 1092 was Cospatric's son (pp. 24–27). See Chapter 5, n. 117.

58. See Ritchie, *Normans in Scotland*, pp. 118–20, 297–300.

59. G. W. S. Barrow, *The Kingdom of the Scots*, p. 321.

60. Ibid., pp. 165–87; William of Malmesbury, *Gesta Regum*, 2:476–77; Orderic Vitalis, 4:274.

61. Barrow, *The Kingdom of the Scots*, p. 321; Ritchie, *Normans in Scotland*, pp. 142ff.; Skene, *Celtic Scotland*, 1:454–60.

62. Barrow, *The Kingdom of the Scots*, p. 173.

63. Ibid.; Ritchie, *Normans in Scotland*, pp. 407–10; Aelred of Rievaulx, *Relatio de Standardo*, p. 193.

64. Ritchie, *Normans in Scotland*, p. 137.

65. There are three clear accounts of the loss of Lothian and a fourth curious reference. Orderic Vitalis asserts that Edward the Confessor gave it to Malcolm Canmore when the latter married Margaret (4:268–70). In *De Obsessione Dunelmi*, pp. 218–19, it is said that Eadulf Cudel gave it to the Scots ca. 1016 rather than fight them, and in *De Primo Saxonum Adventu*, p. 382, King Edgar is said to have given it to King Kenneth after the latter had performed homage. Finally, in its description of Rufus's invasion of Scotland in 1091, the *Anglo-Saxon Chronicle*, *s.a.* 1091 E, p. 169, asserts in passing that Lothian lay in England. The truth of these statements is not at issue here, but any one of them could be used as a basis for the revival of an English claim to the province. This characteristic of the stories is suspicious because all three of them were written down between ca. 1100 and ca. 1140 (Marjorie O. Anderson, "Lothian and the Early Scottish Kings," pp. 104, 111).

66. Barrow, *The Kingdom of the Scots*, p. 321; Ritchie, *Normans in Scotland*, pp. 142ff.

67. Ritchie, *Normans in Scotland*, pp. 274, 284. Barrow says that the first phase of Norman immigration into Scotland ended in the 1140s (*The Kingdom of the Scots*, pp. 320–21).

68. D. F. Renn, *Norman Castles in Britain*, p. 100; Reginald of Durham, *Reginaldi Monachi Dunelmensis Libellus De Admirandis Beati Guthberti Virtutibus*, p. 92.

69. C. H. Hunter Blair, "The Early Castles of Northumberland," pp. 132–33, 135, 142, 153–54, 162, 164. Blair dates Elsdon too early upon the assumption that William the Conqueror gave Redesdale to Robert de Umfraville.

70. Ibid., pp. 161, 165–66; Hodgson, *The Parish of Edlingham*, p. 31.

71. Blair, "Castles of Northumberland," pp. 138–39, 156; Symeon of Durham, *HDE*, p. 140.

72. Renn, *Norman Castles*, pp. 54–55, 90–92, 113, 118, 124.

73. G. W. S. Barrow, *Robert Bruce and the Community of the Realm of Scotland*, p. 28.

74. *ESC*, no. L.

75. Barrow, *Robert Bruce*, pp. 28–29.

76. *Wigtownshire Charters*, ed. R. C. Reid, pp. xiv–xv.

77. Barrow, *Robert Bruce*, pp. 28–29.

78. Tynemouth received the land and service of Graffard ca. 1110 (*RRA-N*, 2:no. 995). Guy is mentioned in nos. 575, 709. The second of these forbids the laity of Northumbria to hunt in St. Cuthbert's forests, but Guy de Balliol is the only Norman mentioned. No. 918 (A.D. 1109) is the record of a settlement between the bishop of Durham and the Northumbrians concerning forest rights. It mentions no Normans at all. See Florence of Worcester, 2:64.

79. *RRA-N*, 2:nos. 832–33 and 1015a; 993, 1001; 1180 and 1241; 1062 and 1241; 1154 or 1166 and 1233; Florence of Worcester, 2:64. Rarely is it possible to know with certainty when a Norman settler first got lands in Scotland. That a grant has been made usually only appears when the recipient later gives part of it to the church. David's charter giving Annandale to Robert de Brus is an exception to this rule, and it seems to have been made around 1124 (*ESC*, no. LIV). Even this charter recognized an already existing situation, for Robert already had a castle in Annandale. On military grounds it is unlikely that Annandale stood alone, and the presence of Ranulf de Soules and Hugh de Moreville, the sometime lords of Liddesdale and Cunningham, as witnesses to David's charter probably means that they received their western lands in this period. Walter fitz Alan (Renfrew) and Robert Avenel (Eskdale) do not appear as witnesses until 1136 and ca. 1141, respectively (Ritchie, *Normans in Scotland*, p. 277, n. 6; Barrow, *The Kingdom of the Scots*, p. 338). This has been taken as proof that their enfiefment was after these dates (Duncan, *Scotland*, p. 136); but these dates constitute only the terminus ad quem for their arrival in Scotland. Indeed, given the haphazard survival of David's charters, it is probable that they were in Scotland earlier.

80. In 1119, Eustace witnessed his first act concerning Northumberland (*RRA-N*, no. 2:1217); and by 1121, he had land above the Tyne (no. 1279). Walter Espec and Forne are first addressed in writs referring to Northumberland in 1121 (no. 1264). This is the first mention of either. See Dodds, *The Parishes*, pp. 80–81; Ritchie, *Normans in Scotland*, p. 142.

81. Symeon of Durham, *HDE*, p. 140; *Scottish Annals*, p. 129, n. 1; George S. Pryde, *The Burghs of Scotland*, p. 3.

82. *RRA-N*, 2:xxx; Orderic Vitalis, 4:435.

83. Symeon of Durham, *HDE*, pp. 130–32. For a discussion and paraphrase of this passage, see Ritchie, *Normans in Scotland*, pp. 88–91.

84. Barrow, *Robert Bruce*, pp. 28–29; Barrow, *The Kingdom of the Scots*, pp. 323–25; Ritchie, *Normans in Scotland*, pp. 154, 277–78, 280.

85. Barrow, *The Kingdom of the Scots*, p. 321.

86. Ritchie, *Normans in Scotland*, pp. 157–58, 188, 222, 276; Barrow, *The Kingdom of the Scots*, p. 324.

87. Ritchie, *Normans in Scotland*, pp. 155–56, 188, 277–79, 289.

88. Ibid., pp. 154–55, 188; Barrow, *The Kingdom of the Scots*, p. 324. Barrow does not accept the idea that the Ridels originally came from Guienne.

89. Ritchie, *Normans in Scotland*, pp. 144, 274, 277, 281–82; George F. Black, *The Surnames of Scotland*, pp. 191, 588.

90. Ritchie, *Normans in Scotland*, pp. 148, 214, 276. There is disagreement concerning the origin of the early Scottish Balliols. Ritchie identifies them with the Balliols established in Northumberland (p. 148). This family

came from Bailleul-en-Vimeu in Picardy (Lewis C. Loyd, *The Origins of Some Anglo-Norman Families*, p. 11). Barrow, however, says the Scottish Balliols came from Bailleul-Neuville in Normandy (*The Kingdom of the Scots*, p. 328).

91. *Liber Feodorum*, 1:200, 202–3; Sanders, *English Baronies*, pp. 68, 127, 150; Hedley, *Northumberland Families*, 1:160–61, 231.

92. *Liber Feodorum*, 1:203; Sanders, *English Baronies*, pp. 17, 42, 65, 100, 106–7, 119, 131.

93. Sanders, *English Baronies*, pp. 41 n. 3, 68, 73; Loyd, *Anglo-Norman Families*, pp. 17, 47, 108.

94. Oliver, "The Family of Morwick," pp. 264–65; *RRA-N*, 2:xi; Sanders, *English Baronies*, p. 53; G. E. C[okayne], *The Complete Peerage of England, Scotland, Ireland, Great Britain and the United Kingdom*, 12:268–74. Walter Espec cannot be definitely traced to Lower Normandy. But Especs held land there, and Walter's three sisters all married men from this part of Normandy. Walter's father held land in Bedfordshire (Ritchie, *Normans in Scotland*, pp. 146–47).

95. Loyd, *Anglo-Norman Families*, p. 53. Cf. Hedley, *Northumberland Families*, 1:145.

96. *Liber Feodorum*, 1:197–99.

97. On Ranulf Meschin, his brother William, and Hugh de Morville, see Ritchie, *Normans in Scotland*, pp. 150, 154; Sanders, *English Baronies*, p. 115; Barrow, *The Kingdom of the Scots*, pp. 323–24. Adam son of Alan (Ravenwic) was apparently a Breton. Robert de Trevers (Trivers), who held Burgh by Sands before Hugh de Morville, was probably from Trevieres, northwest of Bayeux. He married Ranulf's sister (Sanders, *English Baronies*, p. 23). Richard de Boiville (Kirklinton) was apparently from Biville west of Cherbourg (*Calendar of Documents Preserved in France*, ed. J. H. Round, p. 556; Sanders, *English Baronies*, p. 58). Philip de Valonies (Thorpennou) was presumably from Valoignes in Manche (*Calendar of Documents, France*, p. 663).

98. G. W. S. Barrow, "The Anglo-Scottish Border," p. 27.

99. Farrer, *Kendale*, p. x; Loyd, *Anglo-Norman Families*, p. 100. The Taillebois came from around Cristot, west of Caen. Aubigny is in Manche. It is sometimes said that Robert de Stuteville held Kendale between Ivo and Nigel, but the only evidence for this is a claim made by William de Stuteville in 1200–1201 (*Charters of Mowbray*, ed. Greenway, p. xxii). If this were true, which is doubtful, it would represent an exception to the general pattern for Stuteville is Etoutteville-sur-mer in Upper Normandy (Loyd, *Anglo-Norman Families*, p. 40).

100. Loyd, *Anglo-Norman Families*, p. 87; Sanders, *English Baronies*, p. 142.

101. Farrer, "Feudal Baronage," map between pp. 290 and 291. On Gilbert, see pp. 358–59. There was also another small fee, Butler of

Amounderness, above the Ribble. Its first lord was Hervey Walter, who was a Breton, according to Farrer, p. 350. The Montebegon lands in northern Lancashire (Hornby) were acquired by marriage with a descendant of Adam son of Swane (Tait, *Mediæval Manchester*, p. 190). For Michael le Fleming, see ibid.; *Lancashire Pipe Rolls*, pp. 301–2. This charter also refers to two other men, Roger Bristwald (*Bristoldum*) and Warin the Little, who had held land in Furness before the foundation of the monastery.

102. Ritchie, *Normans in Scotland*, pp. 374–75; Barrow, *The Kingdom of the Scots*, pp. 289–91.

103. John H. Le Patourel, "The Norman Conquest of Yorkshire," p. 11.

104. *Johnson's Dictionary*, ed. E. L. McAdam and George Milne, p. 268.

105. Arthur Young, *A Six Months Tour through the North of England*.

106. Ibid., vols. 1 and 2; 3:16–103, 110.

107. Ibid., 1:136–37, 153, 3:117–220.

108. Ibid., 3:221–312; Celia Fiennes, *The Journeys of Celia Fiennes*, pp. 204–5.

109. J. Bailey and G. Culley, *General View of the Agriculture of the County of Northumberland*, pp. 79–82, 85; A. Pringle, *General View of the Agriculture of the County of Cumberland*, pp. 220, 310–13, 337–38; John Holt, *General View of the Agriculture of the County of Lancaster*, pp. 56–57; Joseph Nicholson and Richard Burn, *The History and Antiquities of the Counties of Westmorland and Cumberland*, 1:11.

110. Fiennes, *Journeys*, pp. 188, 190–91. See pp. 193–94, on the making of clapbread. Joan Thirsk, "The Farming Regions of England," p. 19.

111. F. J. Singleton, "The Influence of Geographical Factors on the Development of the Common Fields of Lancashire and Cheshire," pp. 33–34.

112. *Yorkshire Lay Subsidy*, ed. William Brown, pp. 16–113; A. H. Inman, *Domesday and Feudal Statistics*, pp. 149–50.

113. *Pipe Roll of 26 Henry III*, p. 118; *Pipe Roll of 12 John*, p. 149; *Pipe Roll of 13 John*, p. 44.

114. *Pipe Roll of 13 John*, p. 40; *Boldon Book*, p. 328, and passim.

115. *Pipe Roll of 18 Henry II*, pp. 55, 66, 69.

116. L. Dudley Stamp and Stanley H. Beaver, *The British Isles*, pp. 187–88.

117. Ibid., fig. 55, p. 71; fig. 61, p. 78.

118. Ibid., pp. 187–88; see especially fig. 98, p. 186, which shows the distribution of wheat cultivation in 1931, the year with the lowest acreage ever recorded.

119. Ibid., pp. 189–93; Charles Parain, "The Evolution of Agricultural Technique," pp. 161–63.

120. *EYC*, 1:95–96 n., no. 166. See Chapter 3 at n. 75.

121. Gaillard T. Lapsley, "Introduction to the Boldon Book," p. 302; *Boldon Book*, pp. 331, 339–41, and passim; Craster, *The Parish of Tynemouth*, pp. 223, 225; John C. Hodgson, *The Parish of Warkworth*, pp. 197, 363.

122. *Records of the Templars in England in the Twelfth Century*, ed. Beatrice E. Lee, pp. 117–18, 123–24; *YI*, 1:nos. XLVIII, LIV.

123. In the records of the late twelfth and thirteenth centuries, two distinct traditions of boon plowing are apparent in Northumbria. Peasants in unmanorialized bondage vills usually plowed once a year. J. E. A. Jolliffe apparently thought that this tradition was dominant ("Northumbrian Institutions," pp. 7–9); and examples of this type of requirement are common. For example, peasants plowed once a year at Fishwick in the Merse, at Thornton in Norhamshire, and at Elwick, Shorston, and Sunderland near Bamburgh (*The Priory of Coldingham*, ed. James Raine, p. lxxxvii; *Boldon Book*, p. 332; Edward Bateson, *The Parish of Bamburgh with the Chapelry of Belford*, pp. 408–9; *Calendar of Inquisitions Miscellaneous (Chancery) Preserved in the Public Record Office*, 1:9). One boonere was also required in several of Tynemouth's villages (West Chirton, Flatworth, Whitley, and Monkseaton), and apparently the inhabitants of St. Cuthbert's bondage vills plowed once a year, although in several this obligation must have consisted of two days' work (Craster, *The Parish of Tynemouth*, pp. 337–38, 389–90; *Boldon Book*, pp. 329, 331, 335–37). These examples represent the original demands of Northumbrian custom, but there was a second tradition. In villages that had been manorialized by the Normans, that is, the Boldon villages in Durham and several of Tynemouth's villages, peasants plowed twice a year (*Boldon Book*, pp. 331, 336–37; Craster, *The Parish of Tynemouth*, p. 223).

124. Edward A. Freeman, *The History of the Norman Conquest of England*, 4:542.

125. Georges Duby, *Rural Economy and Country Life in the Medieval West*, p. 9.

126. Ibid., p. 90.

127. *EHD*, 2:515–16; *Lancashire Pipe Rolls*, pp. 254–55; *Pipe Roll of 19 Henry II*, p. 113.

128. *EHD*, 2:422–27; quotations on pp. 422 and 423.

129. Giraldus Cambrensis, *The First Version of the Topography of Ireland*, pp. 14–15.

130. Freeman, *Norman Conquest*, 4:542–43; Sanders, *English Baronies*, p. 24.

131. *Domesday Book*, ed. Henry Ellis, 1:fols. 315–18.

132. H. C. Darby and I. S. Maxwell, *The Domesday Geography of Northern England*, fig. 17, p. 66; fig. 35, p. 146; fig. 36, p. 149. In later times the cultivation of wheat was sometimes extended up the river valleys because of the necessity of maintaining a proper standard of living. The monks of Bolton doggedly planted wheat every year at their home farm far up the Wharfe in the early fourteenth century even though the crop was always precarious and the peasants in Craven were content to plant oats. See Ian Kershaw's fascinating *Bolton Priory*, pp. 21, 38–41, 64.

133. *Domesday*, 1:fols. 274–76, 309–12, 321b–322.

134. Stamp and Beaver, *The British Isles*, fig. 61, p. 78.

135. Farrer makes this statement in his introduction to *Lancashire Pipe Rolls*, p. xiv.

136. *Domesday*, 1:fols. 269b–270. Farrer sets the number around twenty (*Lancashire Pipe Rolls*, p. xiv).

137. This hypothesis would explain why it is impossible except in a few cases to establish a convincing connection between the tenurial structure of Lancashire at the time of Domesday and the tenurial structure of this area in the twelfth century. See William Farrer, "Introduction to the Lancashire Domesday," pp. 279–81.

138. *Domesday*, 1:fols. 269b–270.

139. See the witness list of Roger's charter to Seez, *Lancashire Pipe Rolls*, pp. 289–90; *Liber Feodorum*, 1:208–21; Jolliffe, "Northumbrian Institutions," p. 25.

140. See Chapter 6.

141. *Boldon Book*, pp. 329, 331, 335–37.

142. Stamp and Beaver, *The British Isles*, pp. 187–88. The Normans who settled in eastern Scotland carried the cultivation of wheat with them. It appears as a render in the king's farm in the second half of the twelfth century, and William the Lion is known to have been accustomed to eating like a French noble. See Duncan, *Scotland*, pp. 152–54; *RRS*, 1:nos. 131, 243; *RRS*, 2:nos. 16, 107, 139, 407; Roger of Hoveden, *Chronica Magistri Rogeri de Houedene*, 3:244–45. From the twelfth century onward, however, the supply of wheat in Scotland was occasionally inadequate, and supplies had to be imported from abroad. See I. F. Grant, *The Social and Economic Development of Scotland before 1603*, p. 113; Duncan, *Scotland*, pp. 323–24, 504–5. This was accompanied by wide fluctuations in the price of wheat. At Berwick on Tweed, for example, a quarter of wheat cost 2s. in 1248, 16s. in 1253, 1s. 6d. in 1287, and 30s. in 1301 (Thomas B. Franklin, *A New History of Scottish Farming*, p. 103).

143. *Vita Oswini Regis*, ed. James Raine, pp. 20–22; Richard of Hexham, *The Chronicle of Richard, Prior of Hexham*, p. 155. Cf. Duncan, *Scotland*, pp. 464–70, where he argues that Crail, Perth, and Edinburgh date from before David's reign.

144. *ESC*, nos. XX, XXIV; *ASC*, s.a. 1054 D, p. 129; s.a. 1072 DE, p. 154; s.a. 1091 E, p. 169; *Vita Oswini*, pp. 22–23; Florence of Worcester, 2:28.

145. *ESC*, no. L; Joceline of Furness, *Vita Kentegerni*, pp. viii–ix; Reginald of Durham, *Libellus de Vita S. Godrici*, pp. 176–79; Barrow, *Robert Bruce*, p. 6; Aelred of Rievaulx, *De Standardo*, pp. 185–87, 196; Ralph de Diceto, *Ymagines Historiarum*, 1:376. The cain of Galloway consisted entirely of animals and their by-products (*ESC*, nos. XXV, CXXV, CXCIV). See G. W. S. Barrow, "The Pattern of Lordship and Feudal Settlement in Cumbria," pp. 125–30.

146. The Galwegian atrocity stories stemming from the invasions of Stephen's reign were widely reported. Southern writers tended to attribute them to the Scots in general as did later northern writers. See Henry of Huntingdon, *Henrici Archidiaconti Huntendunensis Historia Anglorum*, pp. 260–61; Symeon of Durham, *HR*, p. 191; *HR, Continuata per Joannem Hagulstaldensem*, pp. 290–91. The oldest accounts are probably those of Richard of Hexham, *Chronicle*, pp. 151–53, 156–57, 170–71; and Aelred of Rievaulx, *De Standardo*, pp. 187–88, and *The Saints of the Church of Hexham*, p. 183. These writers from Hexham made a distinction between the Scots proper and the Galwegians, who are portrayed as responsible for the worst excesses.

147. J. H. Round, *Studies in Peerage and Family History*, pp. 124–25; Barrow, *Kingdom of the Scots*, p. 321.

148. *Calendar of Documents, France*, 1:nos. 724, 727, 776, 780–81, 797, 836, 838, 912, 926–27, 980; "Extracts from the Cartulary of Mont-Saint-Michel," nos. 7, 14, 19, 31–32, 36, 38, 48.

149. John H. Le Patourel, "Geoffrey of Montbray, Bishop of Coutances, 1049–93," pp. 155–56.

150. Norman J. G. Pounds, *An Historical Geography of Europe, 450 B.C.–A.D. 1330*, p. 286; J.-P. Bardet et al., "Laborieux par nécessité," pp. 302–3.

151. Bardet, "Laborieux," pp. 302–3. C. T. Smith, *An Historical Geography of Western Europe before 1800*, pp. 216, 218–19; N. Neilson, *The Medieval Agrarian Economy*, p. 23.

152. Orderic Vitalis, 4:32; William of Malmesbury, *Gesta Regum*, 2:478.

153. Guillaume de Poitiers, *Histoire de Guillaume le conquérant*, pp. 108, 110, 112.

154. Henri Touchard, "Le Moyen age breton (XIIe–XVIe siècles)," pp. 166–67; François L. Ganshof and Adriaan Verhulst, "Medieval Agrarian Society in Its Prime," pp. 304–6; David C. Douglas, *William the Conqueror*, p. 18; Smith, *Historical Geography*, pp. 216, 218–19.

155. See Harald Uhlig, "Old Hamlets with Infield and Outfield Systems in Western and Central Europe," pp. 288–95 and passim.

156. Pounds, *Historical Geography*, p. 286.

Chapter 8

1. After the initial failure of the revolt of Angus, the earl of Moray, and Malcolm Macheth in 1130, the latter apparently fled to the Southwest and continued his revolt. Usually it is assumed that this second part of the revolt took place in Moray or Ross (R. L. Graeme Ritchie, *The Normans in Scotland*, pp. 230–32); but this is apparently incorrect. King David was unable to put down the revolt until 1134, and he was successful in that year because he obtained Norman aid. Walter Espec summoned the northern barons to Carlisle and gathered a fleet, and these preparations induced the rebels to surrender (Aelred of Rievaulx, *Relatio de Standardo*, p. 193). How a Norman expeditionary force in Carlisle could so intimidate rebels in Moray or Ross that they would capitulate without a battle defies the imagination, but the difficulty vanishes if one assumes that the rebels were in the Southwest.

2. After the battle of the Standard, Robert de Brus the elder "imprisoned" his son Robert in Annandale for siding with the Scots, and the latter is known to have complained because wheat could not be grown in the area; see Ritchie, *Normans in Scotland*, p. 278.

3. See J. C. Holt, *The Northerners*, pp. 208–10.

4. Lucien Musset, *Les Invasions*, pp. 257–60.

SELECTED

BIBLIOGRAPHY

Chronicles

Aelred of Rievaulx. *Relatio de Standardo*. In *Chronicles of the Reigns of Stephen, Henry II, and Richard*, edited by Richard Howlett, 3:181–99. Rolls Series, vol. 82. London, 1886.

      The Saints of the Church of Hexham. In *The Priory of Hexham: Its Chroniclers, Endowments, and Annals*, edited by James Raine, 1:173–203. Surtees Society, vol. 44. Durham, 1864.

Andrew of Wyntoun. *The Orygynale Cronykil of Scotland*. Edited by David Laing. 2 vols. The Historians of Scotland, vols. 2 and 3. Edinburgh, 1872.

The Anglo-Saxon Chronicle, according to the Several Original Authorities. Edited and translated by Benjamin Thorpe. 2 vols. Rolls Series, vol. 23. London, 1861.

The Anglo-Saxon Chronicle: A Revised Translation. Edited and translated by Dorothy Whitelock, David C. Douglas, and Susie I. Tucker. New Brunswick, 1961.

Annales Lindisfarnenses et Dunelmenses. Edited by Georgius H. Pertz. In *Monumenta Germania Historica, Scriptores*, 19:502–8. Hanover, 1866.

Capitula de Miraculis et Translationibus. In *Symeonis Monachi Opera Omnia*, edited by Thomas Arnold, 1:229–61; 2:333–63. Rolls Series, vol. 75. London, 1882–85.

The Chronicle Attributed to John of Wallingford. Edited by Richard Vaughan. Camden Miscellany, vol. 21. London, 1958.

The Chronicle of Melrose from the Cottonian Manuscript, Faustina B. ix in the British Museum. Edited by Alan O. Anderson and Marjorie O. Anderson. Studies in Economics and Political Science, no. 100. London, 1936.

Chronicles of the Picts, Chronicles of the Scots, and Other Early Memorials of Scottish History. Edited and translated by William F. Skene. Edinburgh, 1867.

Chronicon Abbatiae de Evesham, ad Annum 1418. Edited by William D. Macray. Rolls Series, vol. 29. London, 1863.

Chronicon Monasterii de Abingdon. Edited by Joseph Stevenson. Vol. 2. Rolls Series, vol. 2. London, 1858.

De Injusta Vexatione Willelmi Episcopi. In *Symeonis Monachi Opera Omnia*, edited by Thomas Arnold, 1:170–95. Rolls Series, vol. 75. London, 1882.

De Obsessione Dunelmi. In *Symeonis Monachi Opera Omnia*, edited by Thomas Arnold, 1:215–20. Rolls Series, vol. 75. London, 1882.

De Primo Saxonum Adventu. In *Symeonis Monachi Opera Omnia*, edited by Thomas Arnold, 2:365–84. Rolls Series, vol. 75. London, 1885.

Eadmer. *Eadmeri Historia Novorum in Anglia*. Edited by Martin Rule. Rolls Series, vol. 81. London, 1884.

Early Sources of Scottish History, A.D. 500 to 1286. Edited and translated by Alan O. Anderson. 2 vols. Edinburgh, 1922.

Encomium Emmae Reginae. Edited by Alistair Campbell. Camden Society, 3d ser., vol. 72. London, 1949.

Florence of Worcester. *Florentii Wigorniensis Monachi Chronicon ex Chronicis*. Edited by Benjamin Thorpe. 2 vols. London, 1848–49.

Gaimar, Geoffrey. *L'Estorie des Engles*. Edited and translated by T. D. Hardy and C. T. Martin. 2 vols. Rolls Series, vol. 91. London, 1888.

Giraldus Cambrensis. *The First Version of the Topography of Ireland*. Translated by John J. O'Meara. Dundalk, 1951.

Guillaume de Poitiers. *Histoire de Guillaume le conquérant*. Edited and translated by Raymonde Foreville. Les classiques de l'histoire de France au moyen age, vol. 23. Paris, 1952.

Henry of Huntingdon. *Henrici Archidiaconti Huntendunensis Historia Anglorum*. Edited by Thomas Arnold. Rolls Series, vol. 74. London, 1879.

Historia de Sancto Cuthberto. In *Symeonis Monachi Opera Omnia*, edited by Thomas Arnold, 1:196–214. Rolls Series, vol. 75. London, 1882.

The Historians of the Church of York and Its Archbishops. Edited by James Raine. 3 vols. Rolls Series, vol. 71. London, 1879–94.

Hugh the Chantor. *The History of the Church of York, 1066–1127*. Translated by Charles Johnson. London, 1961.

Joceline of Furness. *Vita Kentegerni*. In *Lives of S. Ninian and S. Kentigern Compiled in the Twelfth Century*, edited by Alexander P. Forbes, pp. 159–242. The Historians of Scotland, vol. 5. Edinburgh, 1874.

John of Fordun. *Chronica Gentis Scotorum*. Edited by William F. Skene. The Historians of Scotland, vols. 1 and 4. Edinburgh, 1871–72.

John of Hexham. *Historia Regum, continuata per Joannem Hagulstadensem* [sic]. In *Symeonis Monachi Opera Omnia*, edited by Thomas Arnold, 2:284–332. Rolls Series, vol. 75. London, 1885.

Jordan Fantosme. *The Metrical Chronicle of Jordan Fantosme*. In *Chronicles of the Reigns of Stephen, Henry II, and Richard*, edited by Richard Howlett, 3:202–377. Rolls Series, vol. 82. London, 1886.

Lawrence of Durham. *Dialogi Laurentii Dunelmensis Monachi ac Prioris*. Edited by James Raine. Surtees Society, vol. 70. Durham, 1880.

Orderic Vitalis. *The Ecclesiastical History of Orderic Vitalis*. Edited and translated by Marjorie Chibnall. Vols. 2–5. Oxford, 1969–75. In progress.

————. *Orderici Vitalis Angligenæ Coenobii Uticensis Monachi Historiæ Ecclesiasticæ Libri Tredecim*. Edited by Augustus le Prevost. 5 vols. Société de l'Histoire de France, nos. 13, 22, 39, 69, 79. Paris, 1838–55.

The Priory of Hexham: Its Chroniclers, Endowments, and Annals. Edited by James Raine. Vol. 1. Surtees Society, vol. 44. Durham, 1864.

Ralph de Diceto. *Ymagines Historiarum*. In *Radulfi de Diceto Decani Lundoniensis Opera Historica*, edited by William Stubbs. 2 vols. Rolls Series, vol. 68. London, 1876.

Reginald of Durham. *Libellus de Vita et Miraculis S. Godrici, Heremitae de Finchale*. Edited by J. Stevenson. Surtees Society, vol. 20. London, 1847.

————. *Reginaldi Monachi Dunelmensis Libellus de Admirandis Beati Guthberti Virtutibus*. Edited by [James Raine]. Surtees Society, vol. 1. N. p., 1835.

Richard of Hexham. *The Chronicle of Richard, Prior of Hexham*. In *Chronicles of the Reigns of Stephen, Henry II, and Richard*, edited by Richard Howlett, 3:139–80. Rolls Series, vol. 82. London, 1886.

Robert of Torigny. *The Chronicle of Robert of Torigni, Abbot of the Monastery of St. Michael-in-Peril-of-the-Sea*. Vol. 4 of *Chronicles of the Reigns of Stephen, Henry II, and Richard*, edited by Richard Howlett. Rolls Series, vol. 82. London, 1889.

Roger of Hoveden. *Chronica Magistri Rogeri de Houedene*. Edited by William Stubbs. 4 vols. Rolls Series, vol. 51. London, 1868–71.

Roger of Wendover. *Rogeri de Wendover Chronica sive Flores Historiarum*. Edited by H. O. Coxe, vol. 2. London, 1841.

Scottish Annals from English Chronicles, A.D. 500 to 1286. Edited and translated by Alan O. Anderson. London, 1908.

Symeon of Durham. *Historia Ecclesiae Dunhelmensis*. Vol. 1 of *Symeonis Monachi Opera Omnia*, edited by Thomas Arnold. Rolls Series, vol. 75. London, 1882.

————. *Historia Regum*. Vol. 2 of *Symeonis Monachi Opera Omnia*, edited by Thomas Arnold. Rolls Series, vol. 75. London, 1885.

Thomas of Burton. *Chronica Monasterii de Melsa, a Fundatione usque ad Annum 1396*. Edited by Edward A. Bond. 3 vols. Rolls Series, vol. 43. London, 1866–68.

Vita Ædwardi Regis qui apud Westmonasterium requiescit S. Bertini monacho ascripta. Edited and translated by Frank Barlow. London, 1962.

Vita Oswini Regis. In *Miscellanea Biographica*, edited by James Raine. Surtees Society, 8:1–59. London, 1838.

William of Malmesbury. *Willelmi Malmesbiriensis Monachi de Gestis Pontificum Anglorum Libri Quinque.* Edited by N. E. S. A. Hamilton. Rolls Series, vol. 52. London, 1870.

_____. *Willelmi Malmesbiriensis Monachi de Gestis Regum Anglorum Libri Quinque.* Edited by William Stubbs. 2 vols. Rolls Series, vol. 90. London, 1887–89.

_____. *The Vita Wulfstani of William of Malmesbury.* Edited by Reginald R. Darlington. Royal Historical Society, vol. 40. London, 1928.

William of Newburgh. *Historia Rerum Anglicarum of William of Newburgh.* Vol. 1 of *Chronicles of the Reigns of Stephen, Henry II, and Richard*, edited by Richard Howlett. Rolls Series, vol. 82. London, 1884.

Documents

Anglo-Saxon Charters. Edited by A. J. Robertson. 2d ed. Cambridge, 1956.

Anglo-Saxon Charters: An Annotated List and Bibliography. Edited by P. H. Sawyer. London, 1968.

Anglo-Saxon Writs. Edited by F. E. Harmer. Manchester, 1952.

Boldon Buke: A Survey of the Possessions of the See of Durham Made by the Order of Bishop Hugh Pudsey. Edited and translated by William Greenwell. Surtees Society, vol. 25. Durham, 1852.

Calendar of Documents Preserved in France Illustrative of the History of Great Britain and Ireland. Vol. 1, *A.D. 918–1206*, edited by J. H. Round. Public Record Office. London, 1899.

Calendar of Documents Relating to Scotland. Vol. 1, *1108–1272*, edited by Joseph Bain. Public Record Office. Edinburgh, 1881.

Calendar of Inquisitions Miscellaneous (Chancery) Preserved in the Public Record Office. Vols. 1–2. London, 1916.

Calendar of Inquisitions Post Mortem and Other Analogous Documents Preserved in the Public Record Office. Vols. 1–5. London, 1904–12.

Cartulaire de l'abbaye de Redon en Bretagne. Edited by M. Aurélien de Courson. Collection de documents inédits sur l'histoire de France, première série, histoire politique, no. 17. Paris, 1863.

Cartularium Abbathiae de Rievalle. Edited by J. C. Atkinson. Surtees Society, vol. 83. Durham, 1889.

Cartularium Abbathiae de Whiteby. Edited by J. C. Atkinson, vol. 1. Surtees Society, vol. 69. Durham, 1879.

Cartularium Prioratus de Gyseburne. Edited by William Brown, vol. 1. Surtees Society, vol. 86. Durham, 1889.

Cartularium Saxonicum: A Collection of Charters Relating to Anglo-Saxon History. Vol. 3, *A.D. 948–975*, edited by Walter de Gray Birch. London, 1893.

Charters of the Honour of Mowbray, 1107–1191. Edited by G. E. Greenway. Records of Social and Economic History, n.s., vol. 1. London, 1972.

Chartularium Abbathiae de Novo Monasterio. Edited by J. T. Fowler. Surtees Society, vol. 66. Durham, 1878.

The Chartulary of Brinkburn Priory. Edited by William Page. Surtees Society, vol. 90. Durham, 1893.

Codex Diplomaticus Aevi Saxonici. Edited by John M. Kemble. 6 vols. London, 1839–48.

Craster, H. H. E. "A Contemporary Record of the Pontificate of Ranulf Flambard." *Archaeologia Aeliana*, 4th ser. 7 (1930): 33–56.

————. "The Red Book of Durham." *English Historical Review* 40 (1925): 504–35.

Documents Illustrative of the Social and Economic History of the Danelaw from Various Collections. Edited by F. M. Stenton. Records of the Social and Economic History of England and Wales, vol. 5. London, 1920.

Domesday-Book: Seu liber censualis Willelmi Primi. Edited by Henry Ellis. 2 vols. Record Commission. London, 1816.

Durham Episcopal Charters, 1071–1152. Edited by H. S. Offler. Surtees Society, vol. 179. Durham, 1968.

Early Scottish Charters prior to A.D. 1153. Edited by Archibald C. Lawrie. Glasgow, 1905.

Early Yorkshire Charters. Edited by William Farrer and C. T. Clay. 12 vols. Yorkshire Archaeological Society Record Series, extra ser. Edinburgh, 1913–65. In progress.

English Historical Documents. Vol. 1, *c. 500–1042*, edited by Dorothy Whitelock. London, 1955. Vol. 2, *1042–1189*, edited by David C. Douglas and George W. Greenway. London, 1953.

"Extracts from the Cartulary of Mont-Saint-Michel." In *Chronicles of the Reigns of Stephen, Henry II, and Richard I*, edited by Richard Howlett, 4:331–60. Rolls Series, vol. 82. London, 1889.

Farrer, William. *Records Relating to the Barony of Kendale.* Edited by John F. Curwen, vol. 1. Cumberland and Westmorland Antiquarian and Archaeological Society, Record Series, vol. 4. Kendal, 1923.

Feodarium Prioratus Dunelmensis. Edited by William Greenwell. Surtees Society, vol. 58. Durham, 1872.

The Great Roll of the Pipe for the Twenty-Sixth Year of King Henry the Third, A.D. 1241–1242. Edited by Henry L. Cannon. New Haven, 1918.

The Great Rolls of the Pipe of the Reigns of Henry II, Richard, and John. Multivolume. Pipe Roll Society. London, 1884–1955.

The Kalendar of Abbot Samson of Bury St. Edmunds and Related Documents. Edited by R. H. C. Davis. Camden Society, 3d. ser., vol. 84. London, 1954.

Lancashire Inquests, Extents, and Feudal Aids. Edited by William Farrer. 3 vols.

The Record Society of Lancashire and Cheshire, vols. 48, 54, 70. Liverpool, 1903–14.

The Lancashire Pipe Rolls and Early Lancashire Charters. Edited by William Farrer. Liverpool, 1902.

The Laws of the Kings of England from Edmund to Henry I. Edited by A. J. Robertson. Cambridge, 1925.

Liber Feodorum: The Book of Fees Commonly Called Testa de Nevill. Pt. 1, *A.D. 1198–1242*, edited by [H. C. Maxwell Lyte]. Public Record Office. London, 1920.

Liber S. Marie de Calchou, 1113–1567. Edited by Cosmo Innes. 2 vols. Bannatyne Club. Edinburgh, 1846.

Magnum Rotulum Scaccarii, vel Magnum Rotulum Pipae de Anno Tricesimo-Primo Regni Henrici Primi. Edited by Joseph Hunter. Record Commission. N.p., 1833.

Memorials of the Abbey of St. Mary of Fountains. Edited by John R. Walbran. Surtees Society, vol. 42. Durham, 1863.

The Priory of Coldingham. Edited by James Raine. Surtees Society, vol. 12. London, 1841.

The Priory of Hexham: Its Title Deeds, Black Book, etc. Edited by James Raine, vol. 2. Surtees Society, vol. 46. Durham, 1865.

Records of the Templars in England in the Twelfth Century: The Inquest of 1185 with Illustrative Charters and Documents. Edited by Beatrice E. Lee. Records of the Social and Economic History of England and Wales, vol. 9. London, 1935.

The Red Book of the Exchequer. Edited by Hubert Hall. 3 vols. Rolls Series, vol. 99. London, 1896.

Regesta Regum Anglo-Normannorum, 1066–1154. Vol. 1, *Regesta Willelmi Conquestoris et Willelmi Rufi, 1066–1100*, edited by H. W. C. Davis. Oxford, 1913. Vol. 2, *Regesta Henrici Primi*, edited by Charles Johnson and H. A. Cronne. Oxford, 1956.

Regesta Regum Scottorum. Vol. 1, *The Acts of Malcolm IV, King of Scots, 1153–1165*, edited by G. W. S. Barrow. Edinburgh, 1960. Vol. 2, *The Acts of William I, King of Scots, 1165–1214*, edited by G. W. S. Barrow and W. W. Scott. Edinburgh, 1971.

The Register and Records of Holm Cultram. Edited by Francis Grainger and W. G. Collingwood. Cumberland and Westmorland Antiquarian and Archaeological Society, Record Series, vol. 7. Kendal, 1929.

The Register of the Priory of St. Bees. Edited by James Wilson. Cumberland and Westmorland Antiquarian and Archaeological Society, Chartulary Series, vol. 3. Kendal, 1915.

The Sheriff Court Book of Fife, 1515–1522. Edited by William C. Dickinson. Publications of the Scottish Historical Society, 3d ser., vol. 12. Edinburgh, 1928.

The Survey of the County of York Taken by John de Kirkby, Commonly Called Kirkby's Inquest. Edited by Robert H. Skaife. Surtees Society, vol. 49. Durham, 1867.

"Text to the Boldon Book." Edited and translated by Gaillard T. Lapsley. In *The Victoria History of the County of Durham*, edited by William Page, 1:327–42. London, 1905.

Three Lancashire Documents of the Fourteenth and Fifteenth Centuries. Edited by John Harland. Chetham Society, vol. 74. Manchester, 1868.

"Translation of the Yorkshire Domesday." Edited and translated by William Farrer. In *The Victoria History of the County of York*, edited by William Page, 2:191–327. London, 1912.

Two "Compoti" of the Lancashire and Cheshire Manors of Henry de Lacy, Earl of Lincoln. Edited and translated by P. A. Lyons. Chetham Society, vol. 112. Manchester, 1884.

Wigtownshire Charters. Edited by R. C. Reid. Publications of the Scottish History Society, 3d ser., vol. 51. Edinburgh, 1960.

Yorkshire Inquisitions of the Reigns of Henry III and Edward I. Edited by William Brown. 3 vols. Yorkshire Archaeological and Topographical Association, record ser., vols. 12, 23, 31. Leeds, 1892–1902.

Yorkshire Lay Subsidy: Being a Ninth Collected in 25 Edward I (1297). Edited by William Brown. Yorkshire Archaeological Society, Record Series, vol. 16. London, 1894.

Books

Anderson, Marjorie O. *Kings and Kingship in Early Scotland*. Edinburgh, 1973.

Armstrong, A. M., et al. *The Place-Names of Cumberland*. Pt. 3. English Place-Name Society, vol. 22. Cambridge, 1952.

Bailey, J., and Culley, G. *General View of the Agriculture of the County of Northumberland*. 3d ed. London, 1805.

Barlow, Frank. *Edward the Confessor*. Berkeley, 1970.

———. *The English Church, 1000–1066: A Constitutional History*. London, 1963.

———. *The Feudal Kingdom of England, 1042–1216*. 3d ed. London, 1972.

———. *William I and the Norman Conquest*. London, 1965.

Barrow, G. W. S. *Feudal Britain: The Completion of the Medieval Kingdoms, 1066–1314*. London, 1956.

———. *The Kingdom of the Scots: Government, Church and Society from the Eleventh to the Fourteenth Century*. London, 1973.

———. *Robert Bruce and the Community of the Realm of Scotland*. Berkeley, 1965.

Bateson, Edward. *The Parish of Bamburgh with the Chapelry of Belford*. Vol. 1 of *A History of Northumberland*. Newcastle-upon-Tyne, 1893.

Beeler, John. *Warfare in England, 1066–1189*. Ithaca, 1966.

Beresford, Maurice. *New Towns of the Middle Ages: Town Plantation in England, Wales, and Gascony*. New York, 1967.

Black, George F. *The Surnames of Scotland: Their Origin, Meaning, and History*. New York, 1962.

Blair, Peter Hunter. *An Introduction to Anglo-Saxon England*. 2d ed. Cambridge, 1977.

_____. *Northumbria in the Days of Bede*. New York, 1976.

Bloch, Marc. *French Rural History*. Translated by Janet Sondheimer. London, 1966.

Brooke, Christopher. *The Saxon and Norman Kings*. London, 1963.

Brooke, Z. N. *The English Church and the Papacy from the Conquest to the Reign of John*. Cambridge, 1952.

Brown, P. Hume. *History of Scotland*. Vol. 1, *To the Accession of Mary Stewart*. Cambridge, 1899.

Brown, R. Allen. *The Normans and the Norman Conquest*. New York, 1968.

_____; Colvin, H. M.; and Taylor, A. J. *The History of the King's Works*. Vol. 1, *The Middle Ages*. London, 1963.

C[okayne], G. E. *The Complete Peerage of England, Scotland, Ireland, Great Britain and the United Kingdom*. Revised and enlarged by Geoffrey White with R. S. Lea. 13 vols. in 14. London, 1910–59.

Cooper, Janet M. *The Last Four Anglo-Saxon Archbishops of York*. Borthwick Papers, no. 38. York, 1970.

Craster, H. H. E. *The Parish of Corbridge*. Vol. 10 of *A History of Northumberland*. Newcastle-upon-Tyne, 1914.

_____. *The Parish of Tynemouth*. Vol. 8 of *A History of Northumberland*. Newcastle-upon-Tyne, 1907.

Curtis, Edmund. *A History of Medieval Ireland from 1086 to 1513*. 2d ed. London, 1938.

Darby, H. C. *The Domesday Geography of Eastern England*. 3d ed. Cambridge, 1971.

_____, ed. *A New Historical Geography of England*. Cambridge, 1973.

_____, and Maxwell, I. S. *The Domesday Geography of Northern England*. Cambridge, 1962.

Davis, H. W. C. *England under the Normans and Angevins, 1066–1272*. 11th ed. Vol. 2 of *A History of England in Eight Volumes*, edited by Charles Oman. London, 1937.

Davis, R. H. C. *King Stephen, 1135–1154*. London, 1967.

Denton, John. *An Account of the Most Considerable Estates and Families in the County of Cumberland*. Edited by R. S. Ferguson. Cumberland and Westmorland Antiquarian and Archaeological Society, Local Tract Series, no. 2. Kendal, 1887.

Dickinson, William C. *Scotland from the Earliest Times to 1603*. Vol. 1 of *A New History of Scotland*. 2d ed. rev. London, 1965.

Dodds, Madeleine Hope. *The Parishes of Heddon-on-the-Wall, Newburn, Long Benton, and Wallsend*. Vol. 13 of *A History of Northumberland*. Newcastle-upon-Tyne, 1930.

———. *The Parishes of Ovingham, Stamfordham, and Ponteland*. Vol. 12 of *A History of Northumberland*. Newcastle-upon-Tyne, 1926.

Dolley, Michael. *The Norman Conquest and the English Coinage*. London, 1966.

———. *Viking Coins of the Danelaw and of Dublin*. London, 1965.

Douglas, David C. *The Norman Achievement, 1050–1100*. Berkeley, 1969.

———. *William the Conqueror: The Norman Impact upon England*. Berkeley, 1964.

Duby, Georges. *Rural Economy and Country Life in the Medieval West*. Translated by Cynthia Postan. [London], 1968.

Duncan, Archibald A. M. *Scotland: The Making of the Kingdom*. Vol. 1 of *The Edinburgh History of Scotland*. New York, 1975.

Fiennes, Celia. *The Journeys of Celia Fiennes*. Edited by Christopher Morris. London, 1947.

Finn, R. Welldon. *The Domesday Inquest and the Making of Domesday Book*. London, 1961.

———. *Domesday Studies: The Norman Conquest and Its Effects on the Economy, 1066–86*. N.p., 1971.

———. *The Making and Limitations of the Yorkshire Domesday*. Borthwick Papers, no. 41. York, 1972.

Franklin, Thomas B. *A History of Scottish Farming*. London, 1952.

Freeman, Edward A. *The History of the Norman Conquest of England*. 6 vols. Rev. Am. ed. Oxford, 1873–79.

———. *The Reign of William Rufus and the Accession of Henry the First*. 2 vols. Oxford, 1882.

Freeman, T. W.; Rodgers, H. B.; and Kinvig, R. H. *Lancashire, Cheshire and the Isle of Man*. London, 1966.

Fussell, G. E. *Farming Technique from Prehistoric to Modern Times*. Oxford, 1965.

Galbraith, V. H. *The Making of Domesday Book*. Oxford, 1961.

Grant, I. F. *The Social and Economic Development of Scotland before 1603*. Edinburgh, 1930.

Gray, Howard L. *English Field Systems*. Cambridge, Mass., 1915.

Hedley, W. Percy. *Northumberland Families*. Vol. 1. [Newcastle-upon-Tyne], 1968.

Hinde, John Hodgson. *A History of Northumberland in Three Parts: Part 1 Containing the General History of the County*. Newcastle-upon-Tyne, 1858.

Hodgson, John C. *The Parish of Bywell St. Peter; The Parish of Bywell St. Andrew with Blanchland*. Vol. 6 of *A History of Northumberland*. Newcastle-upon-Tyne, 1902.

_____. *The Parish of Edlingham; The Parish of Felton; The Parish of Brinkburn*. Vol. 7 of *A History of Northumberland*. Newcastle-upon-Tyne, 1904.

_____. *The Parish of Warkworth; The Parish of Shilbottle*. Vol. 5 of *A History of Northumberland*. Newcastle-upon-Tyne, 1899.

Hollister, C. Warren. *Anglo-Saxon Military Institutions on the Eve of the Norman Conquest*. Oxford, 1962.

Holt, J. C. *The Northerners: A Study in the Reign of King John*. Oxford, 1961.

Holt, John. *General View of the Agriculture of the County of Lancaster*. London, 1795.

Inman, A. H. *Domesday and Feudal Statistics: With a Chapter on Agricultural Statistics*. London, 1900.

Jackson, Kenneth. *The Gaelic Notes in the Book of Deer*. Cambridge, 1972.

John, Eric. *Land Tenure in Early England: A Discussion of Some Problems*. Vol. 1 of *Studies in Early English History*, edited by H. P. R. Finberg. [Leicester], 1960.

_____. *Orbis Britanniae and Other Studies*. Vol. 4 of *Studies in Early English History*, edited by H. P. R. Finberg. [Leicester], 1966.

Johnson, Samuel. *Johnson's Dictionary: A Modern Selection*. Edited by E. L. McAdam and George Milne. New York, 1963.

Jones, Gwyn. *A History of the Vikings*. London, 1968.

Kendrick, T. D. *A History of the Vikings*. New York, 1930.

Kermack, W. R. *The Scottish Highlands: A Short History (c. 300–1746)*. Edinburgh, 1957.

Kershaw, Ian. *Bolton Priory: The Economy of a Northern Monastery, 1286–1325*. Oxford, 1973.

Kirby, D. P. *The Making of Early England*. London, 1967.

Knowles, David. *The Monastic Order in England*. 2d ed. Cambridge, 1963.

Körner, Sten. *The Battle of Hastings, England, and Europe, 1035–1066*. Vol. 14 of *Bibliotheca Historica Lundensis*, edited by Jerker Rosén. Lund, 1964.

Kosminsky, E. A. *Studies in the Agrarian History of England in the Thirteenth Century*. Edited by R. H. Hilton. Translated by Ruth Kisch. Vol. 8 of *Studies in Mediaeval History*, edited by Geoffrey Barraclough. Oxford, 1956.

Lamb, H. H. *The Changing Climate: Selected Papers*. London, 1966.

Lang, Andrew. *A History of Scotland from the Roman Occupation in Two Volumes*, vol. 1. Edinburgh, 1900.

Lapsley, Gaillard T. *The County Palatine of Durham: A Study in Constitutional History*. New York, 1900.

Lennard, Reginald. *Rural England, 1086–1135: A Study in Social and Agrarian Conditions*. Oxford, 1959.

Lewis, Archibald R. *The Northern Seas: Shipping and Commerce in Northern Europe, A.D. 300–1100.* Princeton, 1958.

Loyd, Lewis C. *The Origins of Some Anglo-Norman Families.* Edited by Charles T. Clay and David C. Douglas. Harleian Society, vol. 103. Leeds, 1951.

Loyn, Henry R. *Anglo-Saxon England and the Norman Conquest.* London, 1962.

———. *The Norman Conquest.* 2d ed. London, 1967.

Mackenzie, Agnes M. *The Foundations of Scotland.* Edinburgh, 1938.

Mackenzie, William M. *The Scottish Burghs.* Edinburgh, 1949.

Mackie, R. L. *A Short History of Scotland.* Edited by Gordon Donaldson. 2d ed. Edinburgh, 1962.

Mackinder, H. J. *Britain and the British Seas.* 2d ed. Oxford, 1907.

Maitland, F. W. *Domesday Book and Beyond: Three Essays in the Early History of England.* Cambridge, 1897.

Margary, Ivan D. *Roman Roads in Britain.* Vol. 2, *North of the Foss Way–Bristol Channel.* London, 1957.

Matthew, D. J. A. *The Norman Conquest.* New York, 1966.

Maxwell, Hubert E. *A History of Dumfries and Galloway.* Edinburgh, 1896.

Monkhouse, F. J. *The Geography of Northwestern Europe.* New York, 1966.

Musset, Lucien. *Les Invasions: Le Second assaut contre l'Europe chrétienne (VIIe–XIe siècles).* "Nouvelle Clio": L'histoire et ses problèmes, no. 12bis. Paris, 1965.

Neilson, N. *The Medieval Agrarian Economy.* New York, 1936.

Nelson, Lynn H. *The Normans in South Wales, 1070–1171.* Austin, 1966.

Nicholl, Donald. *Thurstan Archbishop of York (1114–1140).* York, 1964.

Nicolson, Joseph, and Burn, Richard. *The History and Antiquities of the Counties of Westmorland and Cumberland,* vol. 1. London, 1777.

O'Dell, A. C., and Walton, K. *The Highlands and Islands of Scotland.* London, 1962.

Orwin, C. S., and Orwin, C. S. *The Open Fields.* 3d ed. Oxford, 1967.

Poole, Austin L. *From Domesday Book to Magna Carta, 1087–1216.* 2d ed. Vol. 3 of *The Oxford History of England,* edited by G. N. Clark. Oxford, 1966.

Pounds, Norman J. G. *An Historical Geography of Europe, 450 B.C.–A.D. 1330.* Cambridge, 1973.

Pringle, A. *General View of the Agriculture of the County of Cumberland.* London, 1805.

Pryde, George S. *The Burghs of Scotland: A Critical List.* London, 1965.

Renn, D. F. *Norman Castles in Britain.* London, 1968.

Ritchie, R. L. Graeme. *The Normans in Scotland.* Edinburgh University Publications: History, Philosophy, and Economics, no. 4. Edinburgh, 1954.

Rollinson, William. *A History of the Lake District.* London, 1967.

Round, J. H. *The Commune of London and Other Studies*. Westminster, 1899.
———. *Feudal England: Historical Studies on the XIth and XIIth Centuries*. London, 1895.
———. *Studies in Peerage and Family History*. New York, 1901.
Sanders, I. J. *English Baronies: A Study of Their Origin and Descent, 1086–1327*. Oxford, 1960.
Sawyer, P. H. *The Age of the Vikings*. 2d ed. London, 1971.
Scammell, G. V. *Hugh Du Puiset, Bishop of Durham*. Cambridge, 1956.
Seebohm, Frederic. *The English Village Community*. 4th ed. Cambridge, 1890.
Skene, William F. *Celtic Scotland: A History of Ancient Alban*. 3 vols. 2d ed. Edinburgh, 1886–90.
Smailes, Arthur E. *North England*. London, 1961.
Smith, C. T. *An Historical Geography of Western Europe before 1800*. London, 1967.
Smith, R. B. *Blackburnshire: A Study in Early Lancashire History*. Leicester University, Department of English Local History: Occasional Papers, no. 15. [Leicester], 1961.
Smyth, Alfred P. *Scandinavian Kings in the British Isles, 850–880*. Oxford, 1977.
———. *Scandinavian York and Dublin: The History and Archaeology of Two Related Viking Kingdoms*, vol. 1. Dublin, 1975.
Stamp, L. Dudley, and Beaver, Stanley H. *The British Isles: A Geographic and Economic Survey*. 5th ed. London, 1963.
Stenton, F. M. *Anglo-Saxon England*. 3d ed. Vol. 2 of *The Oxford History of England*, edited by G. N. Clark. Oxford, 1971.
———. *The First Century of English Feudalism, 1066–1166*. 2d ed. Oxford, 1961.
———. *Preparatory to Anglo-Saxon England: Being the Collected Papers of Frank Merry Stenton*. Edited by Doris M. Stenton. Oxford, 1970.
Steward, Ian H. *The Scottish Coinage*. London, 1955.
Symon, J. A. *Scottish Farming Past and Present*. Edinburgh, 1959.
Tait, James. *Mediæval Manchester and the Beginnings of Lancashire*. Manchester, 1904.
Tuke, John. *General View of the Agriculture of the North Riding of Yorkshire*. London, 1800.
Vinogradoff, Paul. *English Society in the Eleventh Century: Essays in English Medieval History*. Oxford, 1908.
Wainwright, F. T. *Scandinavian England: Collected Papers by F. T. Wainwright*. Edited by H. P. R. Finberg. Chichester, 1975.
Waites, Bryan. *Moorland and Vale-Land Farming in North-East Yorkshire: The Monastic Contribution of the Thirteenth and Fourteenth Centuries*. Borthwick Papers, no. 32. York, 1967.

Wightman, W. E. *The Lacy Family in England and Normandy, 1066–1194*. Oxford, 1966.

Young, Arthur. *A Six Months Tour through the North of England*. 4 vols. London, 1770.

Articles

Anderson, Alan O. "Anglo-Scottish Relations from Constantine II to William." *Scottish Historical Review* 42 (1963): 1–20.

Anderson, Marjorie O. "Lothian and the Early Scottish Kings." *Scottish Historical Review* 39 (1960): 98–112.

Applebaum, S. "Roman Britain." In *The Agrarian History of England and Wales*, vol. 1.2, *A.D. 43–1042*, edited by H. P. R. Finberg, pp. 3–277. Cambridge, 1972.

Armitage, Ella A., and Montgomerie, Duncan H. "Ancient Earthworks." In *The Victoria History of the County of York*, edited by William Page, 2: 1–72. London, 1912.

Baker, Derek. "Scissors and Paste: Corpus Christi, Cambridge, MS 139 Again." *Studies in Church History* 11 (1975): 83–124.

Baker, L. G. D. "The Desert in the North." *Northern History* 5 (1970): 1–11.

Bardet, J.-P., et al. "Laborieux par nécessité. L'Economie normande du XVIe au XVIIIe siècle." In *Histoire de la Normandie*, edited by Michel Boüard, pp. 287–318. Toulouse, 1970.

Barlow, Frank. "The Effects of the Norman Conquest." In *The Norman Conquest: Its Setting and Impact*, by Dorothy Whitelock et al., pp. 123–61. London, 1966.

Barrow, G. W. S. "The Anglo-Scottish Border." *Northern History* 1 (1966): 21–42.

———. "The Beginnings of Feudalism in Scotland." *Bulletin of the Institute of Historical Research* 29 (1956): 1–31.

———. "Northern English Society in the Early Middle Ages." *Northern History* 4 (1969): 1–28.

———. "The Pattern of Lordship and Feudal Settlement in Cumbria." *Journal of Medieval Studies* 1 (1975): 117–38.

———. "Rural Settlement in Central and Eastern Scotland: The Medieval Evidence." *Scottish Studies* 6 (1962): 123–44.

Beddoe, John, and Rowe, Joseph H. "The Ethnology of West Yorkshire." *Yorkshire Archaeological Journal* 19 (1907): 31–60.

Bishop, Terence A. M. "Assarting and the Growth of the Open Fields." *Economic History Review* 6 (1935): 13–29.

———. "The Distribution of Manorial Demesne in the Vale of York." *English Historical Review* 49 (1934): 386–407.

———. "The Norman Settlement of Yorkshire." In *Studies in Medieval History Presented to Frederick Maurice Powicke*, edited by R. W. Hunt, W. A. Pantin, and R. W. Southern, pp. 1–14. Oxford, 1948.

Blair, C. H. Hunter. "Baronys and Knights of Northumberland, A.D. 1166–1266." *Archaeologia Aeliana*, 4th ser. 30 (1952): 1–56.

――――. "The Early Castles of Northumberland." *Archaeologia Aeliana*, 4th ser. 22 (1944): 116–70.

――――. "Mitford Castle." *Archaeologia Aeliana*, 4th ser. 14 (1937): 74–94.

――――. "The Sheriffs of Northumberland, Part I, 1076–1602." *Archaeologia Aeliana*, 4th ser. 20 (1942): 11–89.

Blair, Peter Hunter. "Some Observations on the 'Historia Regum' Attributed to Symeon of Durham." In *Celt and Saxon*, edited by Nora K. Chadwick, pp. 63–118. Cambridge, 1963.

Boüard, Michel de. "La Normandie ducale: Economies et civilisations." In *Histoire de la Normandie*, edited by Michel de Boüard, pp. 159–93. Toulouse, 1970.

Brown, R. Allen. "The Norman Conquest." *Transactions of the Royal Historical Society*, 5th ser. 17 (1967): 83–108.

Butlin, R. A. "Northumberland Field Systems." *Agricultural History Review* 12 (1964): 99–120.

Cameron, Kenneth. "Scandinavian Settlement in the Territory of the Five Boroughs: The Place-name Evidence Part III, the Grimston-hybrids." In *England before the Conquest: Studies in Primary Sources Presented to Dorothy Whitelock*, edited by Peter Clemoes and Kathleen Hughes, pp. 147–64. Cambridge, 1971.

Corbett, William J. "The Development of the Duchy of Normandy and the Norman Conquest of England." In *The Cambridge Medieval History*, edited by J. R. Tanner et al., 5:481–520. Cambridge, 1926.

――――. "England, 1087–1154." In *The Cambridge Medieval History*, edited by J. R. Tanner et al., 5:521–53. Cambridge, 1926.

Craster, Edmund. "The Patrimony of St. Cuthbert." *English Historical Review* 69 (1954): 177–99.

Davis, H. W. C. "Cumberland before the Norman Conquest." *English Historical Review* 20 (1905): 61–65.

Davis, R. H. C. "East Anglia and the Danelaw." *Transactions of the Royal Historical Society*, 5th ser. 5 (1955): 23–40.

Demarest, E. B. "The Firma Unius Noctis." *English Historical Review* 35 (1920): 78–89.

Dodds, Madeleine Hope. "The Bishops' Boroughs." *Archaeologia Aeliana*, 3d ser. 12 (1915): 81–185.

Duncan, Archibald A. M. "The Battle of Carham, 1018." *Scottish Historical Review* 55 (1976): 20–28.

――――. "The Earliest Scottish Charters." *Scottish Historical Review* 37 (1958): 103–35.

Farrer, William. "Feudal Baronage." In *The Victoria History of the County of Lancaster*, edited by William Farrer and J. Brownbill, 1:291–375. London, 1906.

————. "Introduction to the Lancashire Domesday." In *The Victoria History of the County of Lancaster*, edited by William Farrer and J. Brownbill, 1:269–83. London, 1906.

————. "Introduction to the Yorkshire Domesday." In *The Victoria History of the County of York*, edited by William Page, 2:133–90. London, 1912.

————. "The Sheriffs of Lincolnshire and Yorkshire, 1066–1130." *English Historical Review* 30 (1915): 277–85.

Finberg, H. P. R. "Anglo-Saxon England to 1042." In *The Agrarian History of England and Wales*, vol. 1.2, *A.D. 43–1042*, edited by H. P. R. Finberg, pp. 385–525. Cambridge, 1972.

Ganshof, François L., and Verhulst, Adriaan. "Medieval Agrarian Society in Its Prime." In *The Agrarian Life of the Middle Ages*, edited by M. M. Postan, pp. 291–339. Vol. 1 of *The Cambridge Economic History of Europe*. 2d ed. Cambridge, 1966.

Glover, Richard. "English Warfare in 1066." *English Historical Review* 67 (1952): 1–18.

Hockey, S. F. "The Transport of Isle of Wight Corn to Feed Edward I's Army in Scotland." *English Historical Review* 77 (1962): 703–5.

Hollister, C. Warren. "Magnates and *Curiales* in Early Norman England." *Viator* 8 (1977): 63–81.

Jackson, Kenneth. "Angles and Britons in Northumbria and Cumbria." In *Angles and Britons: O'Donnell Lectures*, edited by Henry Lewis, pp. 60–85. Cardiff, 1963.

Jensen, Gillian Fellows. "Place-Name Research and Northern History: A Survey." *Northern History* 8 (1973): 1–23.

————. "The Vikings in England: A Review." *Anglo-Saxon England* 4 (1975): 181–206.

Jolliffe, J. E. A. "The Era of the Folk in English History." In *Oxford Essays in Medieval History Presented to Herbert Edward Salter*, edited F. M. Powicke, pp. 1–32. Oxford, 1934.

————. "Northumbrian Institutions." *English Historical Review* 41 (1926): 1–42.

————. "A Survey of Fiscal Tenements." *Economic History Review* 6 (1936): 157–71.

Jones, Glanville R. J. "Basic Patterns of Settlement Distribution in Northern England." *Advancement of Science* 18 (1961): 192–200.

————. "Early Territorial Organization in Northern England and Its Bearing on the Scandinavian Settlement." In *The Fourth Viking Congress, York, August 1961*, edited by Alan Small, pp. 67–84. Aberdeen University Studies, no. 149. Edinburgh, 1965.

————. "Post-Roman Wales." In *The Agrarian History of England and Wales*, vol. 1.2, *A.D. 43–1042*, edited by H. P. R. Finberg, pp. 281–382. Cambridge, 1972.

————. "The Tribal System in Wales: A Re-assessment in the Light of Settlement Studies." *Welsh History Review* 1 (1961): 111–32.

Kirby, D. P. "Strathclyde and Cumbria: A Survey of Historical Development to 1092." *Transactions of the Cumberland and Westmorland Antiquarian and Archaeological Society*, n.s. 62 (1962): 77–94.

Kristensen, Anne K. G. "Danelaw Institutions and Danish Society in the Viking Age: *Sochemanni, Liberi Homines,* and *Königsfreie.*" *Mediaeval Scandinavia* 8 (1975): 27–85.

Lapsley, Gaillard T. "Cornage and Drengage." *American Historical Review* 9 (1904): 670–95.

————. "Introduction to the Boldon Book." In *The Victoria History of the County of Durham*, edited by William Page, 1:259–326. London, 1905.

Lennard, Reginald. "The Origin of the Fiscal Carucate." *Economic History Review* 14 (1944): 51–63.

Le Patourel, John H. "Geoffrey of Montbray, Bishop of Coutances, 1049–93." *English Historical Review* 59 (1944): 129–61.

————. "The Norman Colonization of Britain." In *I Normanni e la loro espansione in Europa nell'alto medioevo*, pp. 409–38. Settimane di studio del centro Italiano di studi sull'alto medioevo, vol. 16. Spoleto, 1969.

————. "The Norman Conquest of Yorkshire." *Northern History* 6 (1971): 1–21.

Lund, Niels. "King Edgar and the Danelaw." *Mediaeval Scandinavia* 9 (1976): 181–95.

McGovern, John F. "The Meaning of 'Gesette land' in Anglo-Saxon Land Tenure." *Speculum* 46 (1971): 589–96.

Maitland, F. W. "Northumbrian Tenures." *English Historical Review* 5 (1890): 625–33.

Meehan, Bernard. "Outsiders, Insiders, and Property in Durham around 1100." *Studies in Church History* 12 (1975): 45–58.

————. "The Siege of Durham, the Battle of Carham and the Cession of Lothian." *Scottish Historical Review* 55 (1976): 1–19.

Megaw, Basil R. S., and Megaw, Eleanor M. "The Norse Heritage in the Isle of Man." In *The Early Cultures of North-West Europe (H. M. Chadwick Memorial Studies)*, edited by Cyril Fox and Bruce Dickins, pp. 141–70. Cambridge, 1950.

Moore, J. S. "The Domesday Teamland: A Reconsideration." *Transactions of the Royal Historical Society*, 5th ser. 14 (1964): 109–30.

Musset, Lucien. "Naissance de la Normandie." In *Histoire de la Normandie*, edited by Michel de Boüard, pp. 75–130. Toulouse, 1970.

Neilson, N. "Customary Rents." In *Oxford Studies in Social and Legal History*, edited by Paul Vinogradoff, 2:5–206. Oxford, 1910.

Offler, H. S. "The Tractate 'De Iniusta Vexacione Willelmi Episcopi Primi.'" *English Historical Review* 66 (1951): 321–41.

Oliver, Arthur M. "The Baronies of Bolbec." *Archaeologia Aeliana*, 3d ser. 21 (1924): 142–54.

———. "Early History of the Family of Morwick." *Archaeologia Aeliana*, 4th ser. 12 (1935): 263–76.

———. "The Family of Muschamp, Barons of Wooler." *Archaeologia Aeliana*, 4th ser. 14 (1937): 243–57.

Page, William. "Some Remarks on the Northumbrian Palatinates and Regalities." *Archaeologia* 51 (1888): 143–55.

Parain, Charles. "The Evolution of Agricultural Technique." In *The Agrarian Life of the Middle Ages*, edited by M. M. Postan, pp. 125–79. Vol. 1 of *The Cambridge Economic History of Europe*. 2d ed. Cambridge, 1966.

Postan, M. M. "The Chronology of Labour Services." *Transactions of the Royal Historical Society* 20 (1937): 169–93. Reprinted with revisions in M. M. Postan, *Essays on Medieval Agriculture and General Problems of the Medieval Economy*, pp. 89–106. Cambridge, 1973.

Rees, William. "Survivals of Ancient Celtic Custom in Medieval England." In *Angles and Britons: O'Donnell Lectures*, edited by Henry Lewis, pp. 148–68. Cardiff, 1963.

Reid, R. R. "Barony and Thanage." *English Historical Review* 35 (1920): 161–99.

Sawyer, P. H. "The Charters of Burton Abbey and the Unification of England." *Northern History* 10 (1975): 28–39.

———. "The Density of the Danish Settlement in England." *University of Birmingham Historical Journal* 6 (1958): 1–17.

———. "The Wealth of England in the Eleventh Century." *Transactions of the Royal Historical Society*, 5th ser. 15 (1965): 145–64.

Scammell, Jean. "The Origin and Limitations of the Liberty of Durham." *English Historical Review* 81 (1966): 449–73.

Schofield, R. "Roger of Poitou." *Transactions of the Historic Society of Lancashire and Cheshire* 117 (1965): 185–90.

Scott, Forrest. "Earl Waltheof of Northumbria." *Archaeologia Aeliana*, 4th ser. 30 (1952): 149–215.

Shead, Norman F. "The Origins of the Medieval Diocese of Glasgow." *Scottish Historical Review* 48 (1969): 220–25.

Singleton, F. J. "The Influence of Geographical Factors on the Development of the Common Fields of Lancashire." *Transactions of the Historic Society of Lancashire and Cheshire* 115 (1963): 31–40.

Slade, C. F. "Introduction to the Staffordshire Domesday." In *The Victoria History of the County of Stafford*, edited by L. Margaret Midgley, 4:1–36. London, 1959.

Southern, R. W. "The Canterbury Forgeries." *English Historical Review* 73 (1958): 193–226.

———. "The Place of Henry I in English History." *Proceedings of the British Academy* 48 (1962): 127–69.

Stenton, F. M. "The Danes in England." *Proceedings of the British Academy* 13 (1927): 203–46. Reprinted in *Preparatory to Anglo-Saxon England*, edited by Doris M. Stenton, pp. 136–65. Oxford, 1970.

―――. "Introduction [to the Domesday Survey of Lincolnshire]." In *The Lincolnshire Domesday and the Lindsey Survey*, edited and translated by C. W. Foster and Thomas Longley, pp. ix–xlvi. Lincoln Record Society, vol. 19. Horncastle, 1924.

―――. "Introduction to the Derbyshire Domesday." In *The Victoria History of the County of Derby*, edited by William Page, 1:293–326. London, 1905.

―――. "Introduction to the Nottinghamshire Domesday." In *The Victoria History of the County of Nottingham*, edited by William Page, 1:207–46. London, 1906.

―――. "Pre-Conquest Westmorland." In *Preparatory to Anglo-Saxon England*, edited by Doris M. Stenton, pp. 214–23. Oxford, 1970.

―――. "The Scandinavian Colonies in England and Normandy." *Transactions of the Royal Historical Society*, 4th ser. 27 (1945): 1–12. Reprinted in *Preparatory to Anglo-Saxon England*, edited by Doris M. Stenton, pp. 335–45. Oxford, 1970.

―――. "Types of Manorial Structure in the Northern Danelaw." In *Oxford Studies in Social and Legal History*, edited by Paul Vinogradoff, 2:3–93. Oxford, 1910.

Stevenson, W. H. "Yorkshire Surveys and Other Eleventh-Century Documents." *English Historical Review* 27 (1912): 1–25.

Thirsk, Joan. "The Farming Regions of England." In *The Agrarian History of England and Wales*. Vol. 4, *1500–1640*, edited by Joan Thirsk, pp. 1–113. Cambridge, 1967.

Touchard, Henri. "Le Moyen age breton (XIIe–XVIe siècles)." In *Histoire de la Bretagne*, edited by Jean Delumeau, pp. 153–216. Toulouse, 1969.

Uhlig, Harald. "Old Hamlets with Infield and Outfield Systems in Western and Central Europe." *Geografiska Annaler* 43 (1961): 285–312.

Wainwright, F. T. "Æthelflæd Lady of the Mercians." In *The Anglo-Saxons: Studies in Some Aspects of Their History and Culture Presented to Bruce Dickins*, edited by Peter Clemoes, pp. 53–69. London, 1959.

Watts, V. E. "Place Names." In *Durham County and City with Teeside*, edited by John C. Dewdney, pp. 251–65. Durham, 1970.

Whitelock, Dorothy. "The Dealings of the Kings of England with Northumbria in the Tenth and Eleventh Centuries." In *The Anglo-Saxons: Studies in Some Aspects of Their History and Culture Presented to Bruce Dickins*, edited by Peter Clemoes, pp. 70–88. London, 1959.

Wightman, W. E. "The Significance of 'Waste' in the Yorkshire Domesday." *Northern History* 10 (1975): 55–71.

Wilkinson, Bertie. "Northumbrian Separatism in 1065–1066." *Bulletin of the John Rylands Library* 23 (1939): 504–26.

Wilson, David M. "Scandinavian Settlement in the North and West of the British Isles—An Archaeological Point-of-View." *Transactions of the Royal Historical Society*, 5th ser. 26 (1976): 95–113.

Wilson, James. "Introduction to the Cumberland Domesday, Early Pipe Rolls, and Testa de Nevill." In *The Victoria History of the County of Cumberland*, edited by James Wilson, 1:295–335. Westminster, 1901.

Wilson, P. A. "On the Use of the Terms 'Strathclyde' and 'Cumbria.'" *Transactions of the Cumberland and Westmorland Antiquarian and Archaeological Society*, n.s. 66 (1966): 57–92.

INDEX